The Charles Eliot Norton Lectures, 1988-89

MethodStructureIntentionDisciplineNotationIndeterminacy
InterpenetrationImitationDevotionCircumstancesVariableStructure
NonunderstandingContingencyInconsistencyPerformance

I-VI

John Cage

Harvard University Press / Cambridge, Massachusetts / London, England / 1990

This book is printed on acid-free paper, and its binding materials
have been chosen for strength and durability.

Library of Congress Cataloging in Publication Data

Cage, John.
I–IV / John Cage.
p.   cm.—(The Charles Eliot Norton lectures; 1988–89)
ISBN 0-674-44007-2
I. Title. II. Title: 1–6. III. Title: One to six. IV. Series.
PS3505.A2533A614   1990
811′.54—dc20

89-38187
CIP

MethodStructureIntentionDisciplineNotationIndeterminacy
InterpenetrationImitationDevotionCircumstancesVariableStructure
NonunderstandingContingencyInconsistencyPerformance

Introduction

It was at Harvard not quite forty years ago that I went into an anechoic chamber not expecting in that silent room to hear two sounds: one high, my nervous system in operation, one low, my blood in circulation. The reason I did not expect to hear those two sounds was that they were set into vibration without any intention on my part.

That experience gave my life direction, the exploration of nonintention. No one else was doing that. I would do it for us. I did not know immediately what I was doing, nor, after all these years, have I found much out.

I compose music. Yes, but how? I gave up making choices. In their place I put the asking of questions. The answers come from the mechanism, not the wisdom, the mechanism of the *I Ching*, the most ancient of all books: tossing three coins six times yielding numbers between 1 and 64. Something strikingly like this occurs for each person when he is conceived. The DNA RNA. The determination of personality. If matters on earth were more organized than they are, two parents reproducing would always have the same child. If I know what I'm doing, using IC (a computer program by Andrew Culver simulating the coin oracle of the *I Ching*), I can do it in such a way that I know nothing about it.

I write texts. Most of the time they're mesostics. It was Norman O. Brown who said "mesostics" describes what you are writing. This introduction is an exception. Like acrostics, mesostics are written in the conventional way horizontally, but at the same time they follow a vertical rule, down the middle not down the edge as in an acrostic, a string which spells a word or name, not necessarily connected with what is being written, though it may be. This vertical rule is lettristic and in my practice the letters are capitalized. Between two capitals in a perfect or 100% mesostic neither letter may appear in lower case. In an imperfect or 50% mesostic the first letter may reappear but the second one is not permitted until its appearance on the second line as a capital in the string. If I am fulfilling some request, the celebration of a birthday, the remembrance of someone who recently died, or the furtherance of some project, I write mesostics. In the writing of the wing words, the horizontal text, the letters of the vertical string help me out of sentimentality. I have something to do, a puzzle to solve. This way of responding makes me feel in this respect one with the Japanese people, who formerly, I once learned, turned their letter writing into the writing of poems. In taking the next step in my work, the exploration of nonintention, I don't solve the puzzle that the mesostic string presents. Instead I write or find a source text which is then used as an oracle. I ask it what word shall I use for this letter and what one for the next, etc. This frees me from memory, taste, likes and dislikes. By means of Mesolist, a program by Jim Rosenberg, all words that satisfy the mesostic rule are listed. IC then chooses which words in the lists are to be used and gives me all the central words, the position of each in the source material identified by page, line, and column. I then add all the wing words from the source text following of course the rule Mesolist does within the limit of forty-five characters to the right and the same to the left. Then I take out the words I don't want. With respect to the source material, I am in a global situation. Words come first from here and then from there. The situation is not linear. It is as though I am in a forest hunting for ideas. That forest can be thin, as it is when the string and the source are identical (an autoku), or thick as it is when the source material is extensive.

I-VI is a title of convenience. The actual title of these Norton Lectures is inconveniently long. It is fifteen aspects of my work in musical composition, capitalized, strung, and blocked together. I had noticed ten of them in a text (1981) called *Composition in Retrospect*; the remaining five result from bringing that text up to date (1988).

I-VI continues an ongoing series, of which *Themes and Variations* was the first, and *Anarchy* is the most recent, to explore a way of writing which though coming from ideas is not about them, or is not about ideas but produces them. For *Anarchy* the source material was thirty quotations, all of them related to anarchy. For these lectures four hundred and eighty-seven disparate quotations have been put into fifteen files corresponding to the fifteen parts of *Composition in Retrospect*: method, structure, intention, discipline, notation, indeterminacy, interpenetration, imitation, devotion, circumstances, variable structure, nonunderstanding, contingency, inconsistency, and performance.

The first fifty-seven entries into the fifteen files of the source material for these lectures was *Composition in Retrospect* itself. The section on method opened the method file, the section on structure the structure file, etc. The subsequent additions were, in the order of their inclusion, first from the writings of Ludwig Wittgenstein. I have long been attracted to his work, reading it with enjoyment but rarely with understanding. Peter Yates introduced me to it. John Holzaepfel, who has written a text relating Wittgenstein's "use" to my "process," offered to help me by finding Wittgenstein quotations suitable for some of my files. I accepted his help but found his choices as mysterious as the books from which they were taken. I decided to subject the Wittgenstein corpus to chance operations. Which book? which page? were my questions. Given the page I made a choice. Ninety-three entries were made in the fifteen files having nothing to do with the file names as subjects, unless by coincidence.

The second entries were from Henry David Thoreau's *Walden*. I reread it as I often have. I chose forty-nine quotations which I especially liked though, of course, they had nothing to do with my fifteen subjects. I couldn't help thinking of Marcel Duchamp, who in finding his work outside himself insisted on his indifference toward it.

I next turned to Ralph Waldo Emerson's essays. I did this because of Thoreau. My plan was to couple them and then to couple Buckminster Fuller and Marshall McLuhan as I had my own work and that of Wittgenstein. However, I couldn't stomach Emerson. I managed to find five quotations I could. They are from *Nature* and from *Circles*. I turned away from Emerson whom Thoreau knew very well, turning the coin, so to speak, and picked up the daily newspapers, which Thoreau never did. Using the *New York Times*, the *Wall Street Journal*, and the *Christian Science Monitor*, and limiting myself for the most part to international events, I numbered the articles, and then moved within a single sentence from one article to another by asking which one now? My first question had been on which day to begin mixing the news. I already knew on which day to stop. Then within that period, July 21 to August 26, the two questions which day? which paper? were asked ninety times.

Then I picked up *Neti Neti* (Not this Not this) by L. C. Beckett, of which my life could be described as an illustration. This book, which finds creation constant, without beginning or end, follows a quotation from Lao-tzu, "The transcending expanding power which resides in the middle space does not die. It is always the same and acts the same way without ceasing nor diminishing," with one from Fred Hoyle's *The Nature of the Universe*, "Let us suppose that a film is made from any space position in the universe . . . What would the film look like? Well, galaxies would be observed to be continually condensing out of the background material. The general expansion of the whole system would be clear, but though the galaxies seemed to be moving away from us there would be a curious sameness about the film. It would be only in the details of each galaxy that changes would be seen . . . A casual observer who went to sleep during the showing of the film would find it difficult to see much change when he awoke. How long would our film go on? It would go on for ever." And in *Finnegans Wake*, pg. 620, line 16, Joyce says, "The sehm asnuh." All this confirmed me in my decision to give the same title to each of the six lectures and to use in each the same maximum source material. One quotation from *Neti Neti* went into each of the fifteen files.

Laura Kuhn, who has done all of the computer work for these lectures, had meanwhile collected many of the writings of Marshall McLuhan. Using chance operations I obtained sixty more entries.

I limited quotations related to Buckminster Fuller's work to statements about the World Game, some by him, others by Harold Taylor, Gene Youngblood, Edwin Schlossberg, and Medard Gabel. I continue to hope that we will use our heads as Fuller did his to make life on earth a success at least environmentally for everyone. There are sixty-four such entries.

To encourage my work, Laura Kuhn prepared a schedule on which each of my projects is completed, this day or that yellow shaded. On August 26, the day chosen for the completion of the source material, *Media in America*, a new, as yet unpublished McLuhan book edited by George Sanderson and Frank Macdonald, arrived at the door. It provided the last thirty-one entries.

In order to write *Themes and Variations*, I made a cursory examination of my earlier books, jotting down subjects or ideas which still seemed lively to me. They numbered one hundred and ten. Somewhere along the line they were put into the source material. Since these items are quite short they were put in in bunches, fifteen in all.

In the end, the files had differing numbers of entries between twenty-nine and thirty-eight. I knew that what I had done in *Anarchy*, to let the mesostic strings be the author's names or the texts themselves, was not practical here because of the number of texts and their lengths. I decided to make the fifteen file names themselves the only mesostic strings, in fact to repeat but vary the structure of *Composition in Retrospect*. That structure was, briefly, seven mesostics all on the same word, six making sense followed by a seventh which doesn't do so conventionally because it is a chance-determined mix of what precedes. I counted the number of letters in each of the fifteen file names. Their average length was fourteen. Instead of six appearances for each of the fifteen strings as was the case for *Composition in Retrospect* the question would be asked fifteen times for each lecture how many times between one and twenty-eight (2 × 14) is the string to appear? There would be a mix at the end of each of the fifteen sections unless the number 1 appeared. In that case there would be a repetition. This happens once in each of the last three lectures.

Each lecture would have something in the rough neighborhood of two thousand five hundred mesostic lines, that is, it would last an hour, more or less.

The source material was too extensive to be used all at once. Chance operations were used to reduce the volume of source material for each of the fifteen sets of mesostics. The source material was still too extensive and different representations of it were too similar in density to each other. Chance operations were again used to further reduce the volume of source material. There were, of course, some bodies of source material that remained lengthy. For them it was necessary to set the computer working all night long. However, the repeated use of chance operations brought about a noticeable difference between one representation of the source materials and another.

In the language of these lectures, syntax may appear or not. Generally it doesn't. Words, in fact, can appear by themselves. The have-nots of language, what the Chinese call empty words, particles, connectives, etc., have a position equal to that of the full words. Repetition is a characteristic of this work, as it is, Schoenberg said, of music. Even variation, he said, is repetition, some things changed and others not. Repetition is extreme when the source material is slight. But it occurs unpredictably between lectures, between parts of them, and within a single part. The lectures are written to be read aloud. A space followed by an apostrophe indicates a new breath. Syllables that would not normally be accented but should be are printed in bold type. It was after giving three of these lectures that I made up this notation for facilitating their delivery.

The fifteen photographs by Robert Mahon which are part of this book are chance determined prints of a chance determined negative. The subject, strange to say, was the first page of the manuscript of *Sixteen Dances*, which I wrote in pencil in 1951. I had thought of it as illustrating *Intention*, one of the fifteen words of the title, just as I thought of *Europeras 1 & 2* as illustrative of *Circumstances*. It just happened that *Sixteen Dances* was the first manuscript I picked up. Rather than giving Mahon fourteen others, it was decided to make fifteen variations of just this one. The position of the camera, the angle of view, the place of focus, the F stop (lens opening) were all determined. Using a light meter the shutter speed was set for a normal exposure. Using five types of paper for the printing, times of exposure and development were determined within two extremes: the shortest time, as the musical notes begin to disappear into white, and the longest time, as they begin to disappear into black.

When Reinhold Brinkmann and Christoph Wolff first visited me to discuss the project of my Norton Lectures, I told them that they would not be informative but would be as I saw it the next step in my work which, besides what else it is, is controversial. Because of that I offered to give a seminar one week after each lecture in which I would respond to questions or remarks from those present. They liked and accepted the offer. Two microphones were placed one in each aisle of Paine Hall. I remember thinking after the first seminar, this is an instant lecture! I didn't have to prepare anything! The seminars have been transcribed and are printed in another size serving as a counterpoint throughout the book to the mesostics above them. The questions are in italics, my responses in roman.

In the nature of the use of chance operations is the belief that all answers answer all questions. The nonhomogeneity that characterizes the source material of these lectures suggests that anything says what you have to say, that meaning is in the breath, that without thinking we can tell what is being said without understanding it.

MethodStructureIntentionDisciplineNotationIndeterminacy
InterpenetrationImitationDevotionCircumstancesVariableStructure
NonunderstandingContingencyInconsistencyPerformance

I

Much of **our** '
of borEdom
Toward talks in
it misled Him '
diplOmatic skill to
place to place ' but Does it look
at present **Most** '
fivE iranian fishermen '
cuTbacks would not
wHat i have ' but
pOssibilities
i frequently haD to look up at the opening between
the rule ' **My**
thE
iT '
migHt
lOng time **what** '
of metal Driven '

the rule My
thE '
cuTbacks would not
it misled Him '
lOng time **what** '
place to place ' but Does it look

•

include itS
Top
to console youRself with the
even Under what '
was quite neCessary ' i
and **The**
are obvioUsly lacking in
thRough global growth '
wholE and genuine
a ' Sample ' samples such as
would you wriTe
is oR **as** a thinker is or as
who tUrn away
who paniC ' now
colored paTch which is a sample ' samples
adeqUate
infoRmation '

i have nothing planned i understand that some of you have questions or maybe statements to which i will respond *stockhausen karlheinz stockhausen how you interact with his music* i think my experience new music using the word new in terms of the late forties and the fifties it was later that i first met karlheinz stockhausen i was enthusiastic about his work very much and i brought his music back to new york and

what was not lifE living
the totality of factS and
each naTion's
woRds which
bUt **he** ' stopped short
be drawn ' spaCe
To contemplate
earth's maximUm potential
pulled out gRadual
opEration '
Same
of objecTs ' so
woRks
bUt also words
Came
shelTer
Unknown in advance '
the paRadigm fits
thE phenomenon of
purpoSe
To
be dRawn ' space in
of ' qUiet
tones upon whiCh music may be drawn ' space in language as
is parTially involved when
coUnting
compaRing '
wEaponry to livingry
thingS
of **The** '
the woRd '
langUage as we
fluent pregnant related obsCure '
iT
the dUst that is
vasteR in
lovE ' two people **in**
in cool viSual
a ' Top
i.e. not self-expRession a
conclUsion '
neCessary
resignaTion '
how can yoU say that ' you just said this
as a painteR **is** or as a
way thEy

that of other european composers david tudor who was playing the piano at that time presented him to the
new york public at the time of our first encounter we were very excited each one of us about the other's music
as time has gone on that excitement has diminished once i was with karlheinz we were just walking in
cologne and he said if you were writing a song would you write music or would you write for the singer i said

                              iS
                   be heard Than seen '
                        fiRst
                       catalogUe
                        laCking in
                          To
                       langUage '
              conducted oR not
                   may bE totally involved
                backwardS six
                       iT **is**
                      foRm **is**
                 have not foUnd
            to the woods beCause i wished '
                   resignaTion
                        jUst
                      mateRial
                      wE make '
           in the occupied landS
                 environmenTal impingements
                     muskRats
              panic now aboUt the threat
                   to reCognize
                     uniTed states
                        Using
                        paRt
                      thE word
                     he **iS**
                   values **yeT** in any
                     numbeRs '
            a strike in the occUpied lands
       the revolution we are forging vaster in sCope
                media and abouT
                     coUnting
                 necessaRy to stand
                        i.E.
                a poet iS man works when he is
                   To teach and not when i came to die
                will not woRk
                 for this pUrpose
            to know it by experienCe and be able
                if we were To observe
                what yoU have
              and we follow theiR
                       hEr '

i would write for the singer he said well that's the difference between us i would write music he then proceeded
to write a piece for cathy berberian in which he required her whistling and it turned out that she couldn't
whistle she could do those african clicks and all sorts of things but she couldn't whistle more recently i went
to a lecture that karlheinz gave at the festival in metz it was how to listen to music it was quite astonishing

                                he iS
                                 To
                              muskRats
                              bUt he stopped short
                       who paniC ' now
                     if we were To observe
                                Using
                              vasteR ' **in**
                     may bE totally involved

                                  •

                                hIs
                              oNe
                             wiTh him
                              hE is
                    with**out** ' aNy
                     i who had The dream what would
                              hImself in whatever attitude he find himself '
                              zerO
                              agaiNst
                               socIety but
                              oN
                              eighT
                               callEd for
                              aNd
                 alone ' remains fosTer
                       becomes agaIn after emptiness each
                              i shOuld
                 a body ' if selves had No
                            the ' eIght
                               aloNe remains '
              and where he is namely in This body but is it
                              mEtals '
                               Namibia ' a saner man would have found
                          his doubT
                           would It be like
                                Or
                               iN accord '
                               mIght seem as
                           recogNizes
                           almosT
                           of onE
                            kNow '
                                      .

it was about the basic elements of the differences between sounds short sounds legato sounds and so forth
it was approaching experience by means of rules so to speak or steps at least noticing different categories i
didn't think of it as being a way that i would want to listen *my question has to do with the introduction to*
your lecture last week the final thing that you said which a lot of people seemed to find very striking at

fosTer

brIng

Our

that it makes ' seNse to

theIr

had **had** it aNd

wiThin

on Earth to

jews iN israel ' mexican

reference To a body after

by would be ' the fIrst '

the wOrld's electrical

kNow what

meet ' wIth such

high-voltage loNg

Thousands of

in viEw of

kNow how or why

Ten years

would brIng

bOdies

levels **iN** '

whIch will

aNd if

almosT

to try ' to convincE

wiNg groups

To

voIce might be '

sOber

aNd

had **had** It '

kNow

an insensible perspiraTion

that hE doubled

goiNg on as a

fuTure or

In

Or **why** ' but

drug traffickiNg **a** '

bounds lIke **a** '

i oNly has meaning

abouT drug trafficking **a** '

if i did not havE a body i would still

suppose that i chaNge my body

the time was then i went through and eliminated all the words i didn't like i was wondering if you might like to go into how this relates to what seems to have been a recurrent theme in your thought over the years of the relation between chance occurrences and taking things as they are as opposed to compositional choice and arranging things and if you have had any particular course of development in your thought on

wiTh
not have a body I
shOuld
for a maN to put
the bIll would
live quite laxly aNd undefined '
elecTion to
man would havE
other jews iN israel
Through
way It is '
bring the tOtal military budget to
kNow '

theIr
oNe
wiThin
on Earth
kNow
fuTure or
would It be ' like
zerO '
kNow

•

baD
bases are In the antarctic
out and ever more ' effective wayS evolved and where a giant football
experienCed more was permeated were
In government and hostilities still
were killed rePorted repeated '
the same resuLtant
sovIet
say about rhythm ' let us agree it is No
rEmaining bases are in the antarctic '
this false sense of security toDay ' **the** '
the water In the river it may
but patternS
things beCome '
unemployment has halted bad faIth with discrimination humiliated cuba '
families who were killed have consistently exPerienced more was permeated were
but patterns couLd
Is liveliest most

these things or if it's still pretty much the way it was what i was talking about was a complex mix of words
that i encounter on the page after the computer has presented me with the central mesostic words and i've
put in the wing words i was speaking from the point of nonintention and then i said i take out the words i
don't want i'm hunting at that point in that mix of words i'm hunting for ideas and in order to find them i

                    at aNy point in
          logistics ' gamE is
                  out anD ever more
                that I.e. the
                        uS agree it is no longer a question **of**
        but patterns Could '
                      beIng
                    out the Picture of it is in knowing when one has
    this moment quoted from ' siLence
                          I
                  at aNy point in
                  whilE '
                teams Develop
                the ' vItal
                        waS permeated were killed reported repeated
          it or of filling out the piCture
                    one has pIctured that i.e. the indefiniteness of **the**
                  develoP their own theory of how to make the
              rhythm ' Let us
                    fIeld
          more day to dawN '
                        Earth ' spring ' summer ' fall '
                      Day dawns to
              that was thIrty-three '
  fixed but within a given period of time in Situation form it is presented
                      Cuba '
                  zen thIngs
                such weaPons **what** '
          when as in feLdman's
            say there Is
                    aNd
                  thEir **own**
                be asiDe '
              rhythmIc
                    aS you are without aiming mainly **to**
            and danCe
                  theIr true
                      Performances
          ways evoLved and
                    I
                  Now look
                  rEsultant
                finD
            the pressIng
                rather Set
          no differenCe just the feet are

have to take out the ones that don't allow them to exist they're not always conventional ideas sometimes
they're just a series of words that for some musical reason or some nonsyntactical reason could include rhymes
repetitions i don't know what it is that i will find but i'm looking in the mix for them and the only way i can
see them is to take out the ones that don't belong to them it's a different kind of language but it is every now

                    Is no
                 maP '
               i shouLd
            as you are wIthout '
                  feldmaN's work it is
               and aftEr
                     Dawn the sun
                the lIfe
             in feldman'S work
                 the diffiCulty
                      dIsconnected '
              my main Path and for the most part
                individuaLs
                    of It
                  doN't now look
                 a littlE off
                they Do '
        ways evolved and where a gIant football field '
             become confuSed after studying
                  the diffiCulty
               let us agree It is no longer a question of
                   it is ' Presented entrances being at any point in time
                it is no Longer
                     untIl it is
               before ' aNd
                   in thE common sense of
             off the grounD '
                      In government
               you have to **Say**
           say there is no evidenCe to
                  develop theIr own theory of how to make the total world
work it is not fixed but within a given Period of time in situation form it
                  has haLted bad
                  has pIctured that i.**e.** ' the
                 polaNd's
                   thEir own theory of how to make '
                 anD
                 solvIng
                   aS you are
               to preaCh '
                suzukI
                 maP '
               now Look for further
                      thIs
               star studeNts say '
                   thE sun is but a morning star '

and then highly suggestive and i want that suggestion to oh to be in a spirit that i agree with i am for instance opposed to militarism and i prefer anarchy to government and there are many such general feelings that i have and i would like giving a talk to say something that would be in accord with that instead of looking for mushrooms in a forest i'm looking for ideas in a brushing of source material i heard that some people

a question of patterns but patterns coulD '

lIke the water in the river

the life in uS is like the water in the river it may rise

experienCed more ' was permeated were

stIll unaccounted for '

Presented

you ' waLk what good

was thIrty-three years ago if you

told had beeN

mEn are men mountains are mountains what is

woulD be

Ireland

ireland waS '

preaCh

general publIc

comPensation

star students say they do things they are toLd ' had been

Is the

path aNd **for**

of spacEship earth ' spring ' summer ' fall ' winter '

in succession anD

If

Strain **i** ' should

students and the general publiC where players as

In succession and synchronicity ' succession

changing when the Parts are unfixed by a score '

music is not music untiL

I

zeN

whEn as **in**

i shoulD

eIght

requeSt

whiCh

musIc '

who were killed have consistently exPerienced more was permeated were

ago if you find the signpost you don't now Look for further

agreement rhythm Is

the same resultaNt durations that was

Earth ' spring ' summer ' fall ' winter ' creation '

that was thirty-three years ago ' if you finD the

somethIng that

moSt

humiliated Cuba '

feldman's work It is not fixed '

teams develoP their own theory of how to

connected spontaneity with what i was doing of taking out things but i think if one is hunting that one
doesn't find an idea or find a mushroom spontaneously but rather finds (whatever) by coincidence one comes
upon a mushroom with pleasure i find that in working on these lectures that i find ideas in these mixes more
quickly if i get up early in the morning than if i work in the late afternoon there are other tasks connected

17

readiLy comprehend

It

zeN

of hElping by

more Day to dawn '

In

of patternS but patterns

danCe together

theIr own theory of how to

comPrehend

the generaL

Is

music aNd

succEssion is

shoulD say

In government and

falSe sense of

things beCome confused '

heard musIc and dance together and then

readily comPrehend their true significance in

sense of security today the difficuLty of

you walk what good I do '

zeN '

that i.E. the

more worth anD

In government and

other togetherS men are men

and danCe together and

that was thIrty-three years ago if you find

were killed rePorted repeated

music is not music untiL

the sovIet

grouNd suzuki

tEams

Develop '

set about beIng good the life in

uS agree it is

Cuba '

no dIfference just

develoP

worLd

agree It is

of patterNs but

cuba compEnsation to

woulD be

It

with writing that are good for the late afternoon that are just tedious where i'm involved with such easy things to do as count up to 45 so that my lines are not too long but to find out what the nature of each part of the lecture is going to be is sometimes not quick at all but i am very happy when it suddenly occurs to me what the work what the piece is and that each lecture has fifteen of these differences i begin to notice things

Something that is familiar to us
Confused
studyIng
weaPons ' what do you have to say about
worLd
wIth
where you are aNd
arE awake
anD
In
weaponS what do you have to say '
entranCes '
the lIfe in us is like the water in the river it
is in knowing when one has Pictured that i.e. the indefiniteness of the
fieLd
our planet so that everyone can readIly
aNtarctic
thE ' whole of spaceship earth ' spring ' summer ' fall '
baD
attentIon becoming
Something that is familiar to us '
Confused
musIc '
earth ' sPring ' summer '
music is not music untiL
wIth
together ' aNd
can bE '

woulD be
ways evolved and where a gIant football field
falSe sense of
things beCome
studyIng
develoP
readiLy comprehend
wIth
feldmaN's work it is
thEir own theory of how to make

•

about this way of working that i haven't noticed before and i suppose others will come along if i'm working
on a line that has N in the middle and before the N no other n can occur then automatically a negative word
like not or no is taken out so that a negative statement becomes affirmative *i was wondering if you could
talk about some of the things that inspired your performance without sound and how you feel about those*

aNd
lOss of
nor To live '
koreA ' appears
iTs lowest terms and
saId there is '
lOss of water
busiNess
Needs
thOugh none was
wiTh their own '
prepAred
To
It
it **tO** '
appreheNded
circumstaNces '
freedOm in
same Time
six dAys
iT doesn't
dIe
audience becOmes
bouNdaries
iN
has tO
his ' privaTe identity is
And **of**
The
It
nOt
beiNg which '
wouNds
ugliness that after One click you
desTroyed '
An
buT
eIther
hOw
iN
the ' argumeNts and
step Of
There
you cAn '
circumsTances
Is happening

ideas now when i wrote *4'33"* i was in the process of writing the *music of changes* that was done in an elaborate way there are many tables for pitches for durations for amplitudes all the work was done with chance operations in the case of *4'33"* i actually used the same method of working and i built up the silence of each movement and the three movements add up to *4'33"* i built up each movement by means of short

20

                    tOgether
                  maNy
              expressioN
                  uses tO be revealed '
                    Trend
                    Accord '
                  efforT
              nature whIch
                    Of **the**
                we caN '
                thousaNds
              are suppOsed
                    The
                    And so
                  iT
                    In space ' musical sculpture '
                    Out
              that wheN he writes
            what correspoNds
                    tO
                    The
            by living i hAve lived '
                reinvesT
                    It
              aspect **Of** '
                  stroNgly toward the
                  seNse be grasped '
                  alsO
              free of parTs ' different composing '
                    A doer and
        no music more Than any other ' what
            we have seen Is
                    wOrld
              the sceNe so to speak of thoughts '
                  syNergetically shedding
                  mOre
                  buT
              necessAry
                  as The hand '
                    Ireland was the
                    tO ourselves what
                  aNd
                  aNd
                  prOblem
                  ficTion no beginning middle or end
                    Airlines

silences put together it seems idiotic but that's what i did i didn't have to bother with the pitch tables or the amplitude tables all i had to do was work with the durations *then it was a very spontaneous creation* i don't think that in this kind of work that spontaneous is the word i didn't know i was writing *4'33"* i built it up very gradually and it came out to be *4'33"* i just might have made a mistake in addition *i was thinking of*

<pre>
            ouT '
         amerIcan
            hOw '
         mexicaN
            oNe '
            Order
   and ignorance inTo
            mAny
            iT
         movement In
            thOught
   may seem aNalogous to
            aNd
            Of daily life '
         is jusT
            cAn
            seT of
   technology as manIfested in
   take the cars and gO
            seNsitive
            good'N'evil
            he wOuld
      us back from weaTher which
   new liquid hydrogen leAk
            They
         by any of Its parts
   accepts whatsOever befalls as part of its
            workiNg
            guaraNteed '
            dOes
            jusT
            speAks
            The problems of '
of nature ' we must be refreshed by the sIght
            dOgma
   issues of peace ' aNd

         what correspoNds '
            Order
            There
            An
         circumsTances '
            Ireland was the
            lOss of water
      that ' wheN he writes

                  •
</pre>

like whimsical or something maybe rather than spontaneous what were you thinking about *kind of whimsical i mean in other words* oh was it a joke you mean *yeah i mean like at six o'clock that evening of the night that you created it were you thinking that tonight i'm going to create a new piece or did suddenly* no no it took several days to write and it took me several years to come to the decision to make it and i've lost

22

hIgh the
of the developmeNt **of** '
claD but
bE
now whaT it
for ' Establishing
between figuRe and
of gaMes
whIch would
arouNd
Arrived at by
get Clothing **the** '
onlY what they
of the englIsh
would guaraNtee the
this woulD
gamEs
To call '
will dEny that
caloRies
seeM analogous to
ways wIll differ
wheel aNd
mind's ' deAling with one not two to make a garden empty '
Came wearing fishnet
naked and Yet not dressed
thIs would be
exterNal
shoulD '
fEd
To
rulEs of
now ' using aRound
a garden eMpty
thIs
the problems oNe gives
As
Cannot be '
waY of
Is the same with
hoNestly '
Do but
bE like
forced To
lifE that is
this baRe

i lost friends over it *that's what i would it be possible to ask a little bit more about the two years in other words i was wondering what were some of the decisions that went on during that two-year period* i gave a talk at vassar college it was a meeting of people from different fields and it was rather exciting i was fresh from my first studies of oriental philosophy and i was full of it so that people would ask me questions and

23

judgeMent **or**

Is

grammar aNd

shApes our

vision etCetera ' but

reallY

musIc

Not things

becoming every Day

closEd

is noT that

onE '

dRessed

kwh 8.5 tiMes ten to the

It

eNriched in the

wAy of

the prinCess to come neither naked nor dressed

the Year 2000

the problem wIll

Neither

one shoulD ' simply

inclusivE

righT

inclusivE '

the aRea '

the developMent '

the best mode by whIch

aNd

cAnnot be wondered at '

musiC is permanent '

the studY '

the operatIves '

aNswer which are

here again one shoulD simply

thEy had

an answer according To

hand wasting onE's time with something

with one not two to make a gaRden

without any preconceived judgeMent or

of the operatIves **is**

of maN's '

of gAmes ' must be useful for the study of

prejudiCe '

the Year 2000 '

faIl

were listening to what i was saying in the talk that i gave at that symposium i said that there should be a piece that had no sounds in it but i hadn't yet written it the thing that gave me the courage to do it finally i think that talk was given in '47 and the thing that gave me the courage was in '49 and that was seeing the white empty paintings of bob rauschenberg to which i responded immediately not as objects but as ways i've

betweeN not be

to Do but

that which wE learn as

wiTh '

variablEs in

kilowatt houRs and eight '

systeM of

kIlowatt hours **eight**

kNow now

thus he wAs

whiCh would '

energY slaves

Is this

to come ' Neither

not exclusive ' aperioDic ' no vision

likE

and **iT**

squarE miles of land

bRoken down that is 15,000 kwh

every day More

people per acre whIch would

be eNriched in the long

one to look At the

that whiCh we

the ' Year 2000 because

Is

Now ' what it will be like at present most of **the**

the stuDy of

systEm is

cannoT

would mEan a population of six billion people

aRe not controlled because the

calories and 21.9 tiMes 10^7 tons of

not be afraId that

without aNy preconceived judgement

mAy be

objeCt is not that mankind

theY **are**

they **aIm** '

Net that might have been

claD

unitEd

was arrived aT by taking

ways of rEaching the same

now using aRound '

now what it will be like ' at present Most of the

said before that they were airports for shadows and for dust but you could say also that they were mirrors of the air and the marvelous thing about 4′33″ i think i say now on the published music that it can be any length and that should occur to anyone knowing that it was written by means of chance operations it could be could have been some other length so that we can listen at any time to what there is to hear and i do that

                    do not know now what It will be like
                         to be humaN
                                by tAking the
                                objeCt is not that mankind
        of reaching the same result in mathematics maY seem
            necessary to evolve a bare maxImum parameter for
                                runN ' men hit only what they
                             Do '
                         an intErval or a gap like
                         righT thing is
                    as childrEn and
                    is some soRt of
            acre which would Mean
                                kIlowatt hours '
                    or oN the other
                    thus he wAs '
                         signifiCant and correct
                         energY slaves
                do so long as It is
                         times teN^{15} calories '
    it is the same with a mathematical problem ' Do
                    man's intErnal
                         iT will
                                opEn in a closed system ' such
        one gives a child ' e.g. foR which it gets an answer according to the '
            the world is our Mothertongue that
                         varIables
                         did Not
                    the sAme ' result in
                no vision ' etCetera ' no one will
                    emptY
            broken down that Is
                         Nor
                    every Day
                    spacE
            know whaT
                and honEstly clad but
                    vaRiables in
                         May be
                by whIch
                    the Next room it might be
                    or A gap like
                those to whiCh the
    this would be approximatelY the area japan uses to feed her people '
                    the world Is our
                    dowN that is

with a great pleasure and often and you can do it either in ordinary circumstances or in extraordinary circumstances it works very well *in that walk through the woods on wednesday night one of the things that struck me was a lot of little rings of mushrooms not just single mushrooms but that little clusters of ideas that would sort of crop up and then disappear throughout the lecture and i was wondering how much the*

without a methoD of solution
or a gap likE '
like aT
what onE sees and not be
Rules of
Man's '
of the operatIves is
may be well aNd
two-thousAnd broken down that is 15,000
rules sinCe it is
not controlled because the sYstem
the faIry tale who told the
developmeNt of man's potential to be human was
without a methoD of solution
is bEcoming every day more like
Thing is **to**
to accEpt if the
pResent
by which Men may get
what they aIm at therefore though they
Nor
one hundred trillion kilowAtt hours 8.5 x 10 to the
prejudiCe about the
tons of coal equivalents per capita per Year
but there are also those to whIch
we learN as
not exclusive aperioDic no vision
no music inclusivE
noT
invEntion not things but minds
noR
kwh 8.5 tiMes ten to the
Is
oNly
At something high ' the problem of finding
Could feed 500 people per acre which
is as Yet open
whIch would
ruN
every Day
wE found
since iT is
nakEd
without a method of solution they aRe like the
tiMes 10 to the
enrIched

wanting or not wanting of words controlled those little rings i notice that too of course as i write it i don't
know how they come about it passed through my mind that they that there's something in the program that
may bring that about *spores probably* but i notice for instance if i have a source text which has say ten pages
and the word that i'm the line that i'm working on is on page 8 line 47 that the next one very likely will be

28

japaN uses to feed her people '

Are not

as weather effeCts insect pests loss of water and

10^7 tons of protein in the Year 2000 the greatest propaganda

It

by which meN may get

way of solving the problem will Do so long as it is in

wEaring

mosT

shE came thus he was

life that **is** ' pRopaganda

without any preconceived judgeMent or

wIll '

ruN men hit only

for estAblishing external relative levels of the

have been Called

judgement or prejudice about the analogY between games and grammar and here

that of the englIsh

that which we learN as

leaD

squarE miles of land we're

same wiTh **a**

would bE

at pResent

is beyond doubt there **is** ' soMe

trIes

maN's

At '

the Condition of

people todaY '

hIs

ruN men hit

without a methoD

likE

noT '

human was arrivEd at by taking the

aRe

the systeM '

the problem wIll do so '

Needs for the

And

Came thus '

5 x 10^{15} calories and twentY-one

Is

exterNal relative levels of **the** '

Doubt

on page 8 there seems to be a tendency for the next line to be on the line of the preceding one though of course it does change but when it changes to another page it often stays on that page for a while that could bring about recurrences but this thing of words being repeated either as the same words or as rhymes is one

by taking thE
aim aT
bEyond doubt '
2000 bRoken down that is 15000 kwh and 8
Must be useful for the study of
that of the englIsh
of maN's
children And
e.g. for whiCh it gets an answer
for the Year 2000 because
wIth his
judgemeNt or
here again one shoulD simply
problEms one gives
cannoT
onE gives
which aRe
in the long run Men
by whIch
brokeN down
no vision etceterA no one will deny that
those to whiCh **the**
that anY way **of**
as I have heard or observed the
eight metric toNs of coal equivalents per capita per year this
stateD
it might bE said
mighT
rEsult in
shapes ouR perceptions for life
May be
varIables
to the seveNth tons of protein in the
her to do but when she cAme thus he was
as far as i have heard or observed the prinCipal object is not that mankind
the area japan uses to feed her people todaY
thIs
would meaN a population of six billion people
projecteD '
spacE
or prejudice abouT
insEct pests ' loss of
yet not dRessed
May get
a chIld e.g. for
oNly

of the ways that i find to make a continuity sometimes i notice it and find there's just too much of it then i
remember what schoenberg he always wanted each thing to seem fresh as it came along i read through and
i try to bring that about 'cause it's at least for me it seemed to be that that characteristic had a lot to do

the problems one gives A

system Could feed 500 people per acre which

is the best mode bY

Is

to be humaN '

Day

sincE

ways of looking inTo

problEm will do so long as it is in

the Rules

between gaMes '

do not know now what It will be like at

we fouNd it

And

are not Controlled because the

judgement or prejudice about the analogY

etcetera no one wIll

be approximately the area japaN uses to

be approximately the area japan uses to feeD

to **thE**

This

rulEs of

dRessed it is **the**

May get

at therefore though they should faIl immediately they had better aim at

the best mode by which meN

correct intuition or on the other hAnd wasting one's time with

rules sinCe it is

that the corporations maY be

hIs

times teN^{15} calories '

it is the same with a mathematical problem' Do

spacE

righT

and honEstly ' clad but

at pResent

May get

varIables

to the seveNth ' tons of protein in the

shApes our

Came wearing fishnet '

5 x 10^{15} calories and twentY-one

•

with carrying me through the whole lecture in some sense because i noticed those little pockets and i sort
of went from pocket to pocket in some way and sometimes one will refer to a much earlier one i had a strange
experience here last wednesday i've been working of course very intensively to make these lectures and i'm a

of the massIve bodies by itself which could predict
the laNguage of ordinary speech ' ordinary
speak To
havE again become '
aRe invisible their groundrules
a Play ' now
thE world work
giviNg '
is touch-activE
Times
two equals fouR in chinese '
only so fAr as
wenT
Is
with Others '
everythiNg '
nonmeasured tIme ' polish labor '
aNd
aT
wEnt to visit
day and night total capacity and tRansmitted to the daytime '
reached to object ' they made an earthquake Proof music '
samE time
iN
thE
of Them
i leaRned this
deAl '
The
touch that **Is**
was tO
Now
not **sIgh**
chaNges
wiTh
a slightly mislEading question **the**
it seemed that fRom such a basis
is brought uP to
Earth there is
Now
tEchnological progress such as laser beam power
To humanity ' and the
woRld
puts no questions And answers
many of our problems will be solved if we Take advantage of
changIng in its way '

third of the way through the third one now but i had been working on the second one and there was
something in the second one that i thought was in the first one and so i had the feeling while i was reading
the first one that something was missing and it wasn't missing at all it was part of the second one *i'd like to*

yOu keep a clicker
deal with reality we are iN the dark we
say there Is
No why '
collaboraTion
would bE no question
foRming and testing **a** '
and night total caPacity and
succEss might yet develop
sick maN
you givE
The
you leaRn outside
you'll Ask if you
happen To be
drIven
dO you
Needs we
I say although
world arouNd
To
hE
so well without an aRm '
Portu**la**ca
into parts and **thE** '
cursiNg
and usE '
Themselves
and bluepRints '
response wAs cool
exTernal
for the most people usIng the least
he Offered them
total capacity aNd
now another ' after eIght or
but a small piece of kNowledge acquired by someone
'whole one ' day in parTicular '
languagE as
the impRovement
metaPhysical
unitEd states
sweet corN '
othEr children i am weak in
This
diffeRent composing
yeArs ' i was

hear your definition idea and impressions of two things art and creativity art i think it must have to do with our placement of attention i'm trying to speak now or think now without regard for intention or nonintention i work with questions whereas many people work with choices but i think that any art in either

                                    and half Tones by our photographs and
                what happens the world around It
                                              Of israel for
                                    Now
                            would stIll
                                  loNger help
                                    To accomplish what you
                              arE losing
                means is his thRoat all right under others
                        for two Pianos '
                    might havE **a**
                the same way aNd not a proposition of
                              arE all deaf
                    where more Than
                        the loRd
                            sAid
                        him To
                        the unIted
                                tO say that **for** it you have such
                          raNge '
                synonymous wIth electric
        for that i just teach him the word uNder
                    and souTh
                    which managEs so well
                        outside the classRoom environments are invisible their groundrules
        cool but unfurled the american refusal to Pay its
                              as clEar as water i
    did he told me with the utmost simplicity aNd truth '
                        playErs have
                        proposiTion '
            the beautiful is only what clicks foR you keep
                              A physical
                    sovieT '
                                hIs leg healed can he speak
                a hundred years agO
                          calls as uNexpected pleasures
                          teach hIm the word
              the year two-thousaNd '
                            jusT
            a way of saying somEthing
            suppose you look on a dReam as a kind of language a way of saying
                        helP ' bring
                    in thE
                        iN '
            woman's intuition mEans
                        noT

case would depend on one's placement of his full attention on what he was doing does that make any sense
to you *yes* i mean can you use that idea *yes that is to art* i have my attention so fixed now on these lectures
and will have until i finish the sixth one that i sometimes work on them while i'm sound asleep and that

fRom
technologicAlly
a cenTury ago
lIttle
fOr
haviNg
wIth i had it there
aNd
i Think
way hE made
Routes
touch is our Primary
as thE basis
aN
or dEny
needs **for** The
to ' discoveRy
is A
Two equals four
joIned **a**
tO do to take it apart
staNd aloof from
on It '
offeNsive
medicine of a healThful
and mEn
in hanoi and washington and pakistan's foReign minister saying they would
closer ties with the camPus
to anothEr
loathiNg
in **thE**
in pracTical
foR him
fAr as
mighT be a regular
whIle
that's cOrrect '
behiNd
aId
wroNg
borrowing buT
fallEn
Refugees
Policy it '
morE **i**
this too ' is aN

makes me think while i'm still asleep that i should wake up because if i wake up and actually do the work
then i don't have to dream about it and the result is i don't sleep as much as i would but i go to bed early
and then it's very good working in the morning but when you speak of creativity i think that's almost automatic

ashamEd
The '
Rivet in the
other ' former leAders be removed '
discovery as The
make **sure** I
Of '
my ear the shaggy Nag now after success take your sword and
1242 energy slaves per capIta by the year '
weakNess if **you** have
acT '
lEading
and listening aRe different activities music is
uP
to build my housE '
its liviNg and
statE
wiTh
15000 kw houRs
A
To
I '
my wOrship of him '
of those circumstaNces
transport to some areas wIth low
which i had beeN endeavoring in vain
his resoluTion without going out of his way it is not
policE
foR
Pianos
which says that monEy is
of them as they dragged them away ' shippiNg food halfway around
thE
informaTion is at the
diRections
of corruption ' And
during The day and dreams at
I
between sOme of it '
plasteriNg such a deed would keep me awake
kIlowatt hours
taste **aNd**
iT is
a critical problEm facing humanity that if left unattended
oR deny it of them the question do fishes
could be used more Profitably

if one is placing his attention it wouldn't even have to be a thing it could be a it could be just as we're doing
now talking i'm thinking of wittgenstein and his expression when we do philosophy and of course nothing is
done except the sort of thing that we're and yet it seems to me in his case very creative that is to say it brings

                              bridgEd
            capabilities would help briNg
                        which thE audience performs
                    go To the wall which he had
                      fiRst or
                      deAf ' blind
                behavior of The whole system and the known
                            Intervals triads and aggregates a single hand
                      anOther
                  this Never
                    buhlIg who first played
                    maN's
                    is aT
                which managEs so well without
                        classRoom environments are
            remainder of its Parts world
                      battlE broke out friday
                  by askiNg a slightly
                      if hE should chance
                  space when The new
            and doesn't necessaRily
                      hours stAge
        is as if we could grasp iT
                  by employIng the same
                      wOrk
            of touch rather thaN

                        buhlIg ' who first played
                    weakNess if you have
            medicine of a healThful
                          hE '
        day and night total capacity and tRansmitted to the daytime
                      uP
                  might havE a
                  sweet corN
                    which thE audience performs
            space when The new
                      fRom
            response wAs cool
        is as if we could grasp iT '
                          hIs leg healed can he speak
                  he Offered them
                plasteriNg ' such a deed would keep me awake

                              •

something into existence that wasn't there before i have the feeling as i work on these lectures you know
from the introduction that i don't understand wittgenstein but nevertheless i'm using him i have the feeling
that i'm beginning to understand him now at least more than i did and i told that to my friend mr holzaepfel

sunday ' It

Men even

experIenced no-mindedness

in The

And '

They

makIng

ways tO

usiNg

Ignorance which his growth requires

till we coMe to a hard bottom

spokesman saId

The

let us heAr

our feeT downward through the mud and slush of

commercIal urgency

tO

iN a

from ' excessIve toil are too

in which two naMes occur '

presentIng

of The

And '

sTop

Internal needs we

were killed and appeared tO promise

from the moral law a fact which was strikiNgly

our soundest sleep ' I know of no

geoMetry but

presentIng

To

constitution hAs

and london Through new york

but a machIne

by as many peOple as

agaiN

together Into a creation and expands itself in an

internal food supply we evolved ' into soMe

another askIng

knowing wheTher they

explAin

feeding six people per acre iT would be

agrIculture

states tO

aNger

people per acre It would be difficult to raise the world's

who does understand his work and he said oh good and then i told him what i thought i understood he sees more possibilities or more uses of things than just a few uses and that ultimately there are almost limitless uses then mr holzaepfel spoke of wittgenstein as someone who was able to ask questions that haven't been

finer fruits cannot be plucked by theM '

Ignorance

Two '

world ' gAme '

if we are really dying leT us hear the rattle '

afrIcan

emplOy '

greeks weNt

acIds '

Make a few objects '

toIl are

duTch '

the sAme '

These

lIfe

all things tOgether '

africaN

It

froM

saId sunday

The ' united

people engAged in

dying leT us hear the rattle

per capIta '

awake nOt by

maN

In radio and tv presentation

world gaMe players have the

tactIle muscular

emoTions the heroic the mirthful the wondrous

were killed And appeared

an experimenT '

workIng

tO

aNd

In

as it were froM

explaIn

wenT right up to the door of

A

free counTry

a dIspute with

nine times 10 tO the

greetiNg

out solutIons

to Make a move '

asked this has to do with creativity that is to say bringing into existence the things that hadn't been or hadn't been noticed so that you could then pay attention differently to other things *yeah when you gave that definition of creativity bringing something in existence that did not exist could you do that for art as well* i

Ignorance

in This

life by A conscious endeavor

and keep ourselves awake noT by

It

methOds

aNd **the** '

agrIculture as opposed to

governMent cannot

In

To food **for**

And

iT

an army ' a total of nIne '

life Or death

haviNg

In **a** '

a probleM '

ecologIcal

To

levels of **the** ' Above

mechanical aids buT by **an**

and hItler and

raise the wOrld's

exterNal

In an eternal outspreading '

Man

solvIng a problem in

The world would engender the

door And pass

we considered The two most

housIng

sO

everythiNg

In

saMe

In

be said To be his

And expands

will have To be

prIvate

is fact nOt symbol '

strikiNgly

10 to the fIfteenth calories and 21.9 x 10^7 tons of

world gaMe players have the

through whIch we look which morally we can do

liked what i said earlier by placing attention because then it could be either on something that you had made or it could be on something that you hadn't made as with the found objects of marcel duchamp not only placing attention but placing his signature *i was wondering about what relation you feel that there might*

world's efficiency To

point five x 10^{15} cAlories and

growTh

vItal

wOuld

aNd

speculatIng

Means '

sprIng '

enTire universe

wedge our feet downwArd

iT

of man's Internal

prOjected '

eveN

stalIn and hitler and

stateMent

presentatIon '

The

And

eighT

In

Of

meN '

fIngers '

Market '

bacterIa '

beauTiful '

hAving ' experienced no-mindedness '

sTory '

wIll '

Off

for maN and

radIo and

froM

our soundest sleep ' I know of no more encouraging

greeTing '

the world of consciousness ' we people ' A space '

prinT and book '

cursIng ' greeting ' praying '

the herOic ' the mirthful ' the

orders ' aNd

the greeks went rIght up to the door of

treMble too much for that actually

In

These

be between your use of chance composition and chance composition used by the abstract expressionists in particular willem de kooning's use the way he would produce many sketches of women i think on transparent paper and then put them all on top of each other and use that to produce new forms and the

nucleAr
insighT '
poInt five times ten
hOw much more
exterNal
In nothing one and **the** '
the Moral law a fact
In
relaTions to men his
needs for the yeAr
of changing **The** '
of sIx
be able tO
algae ' chlorella aNd others for food '
agaIn and again during a period of six or seven '
exaMples
for reportIng violence '
nine Times 10^7 tons of protein in the
nine people were killed And
up To the door of modern geometry but
wIth
be dismissed a week agO the sources said let us settle ourselves '
eNergy slaves '
agrIculture '
redefinition by as Many people as
possIble '
speculaTing
A
The weather
It might nullify
peOple '
the patterN of the
elevatIon of nuclear
saMe
slovenIan
The ' nine
hours And
will have To be
the shortest possIble time '
abOve throughout the world would
chaNge the
us In our soundest sleep
to a hard bottoM and rocks '
technologIcal change '
The news on both
Anger

way that he would sort of have a sort of controlled and intentional sloppiness with the paint so that for more randomness and pollack's drip technique again a chance technique seems to me to have been involved in forcing their own hand in using the chance technique to reveal to make it possible for them to say to

The
hIs
tO carve '
let us hear the rattle iN our throats and feel cold

In **a** '
Men even
presentIng
nine Times 10^7 tons of protein in the
Anger '
The
commercIal urgency '
tO
africaN

•

Dim and
a languagE **these**
that we liVe ' **in**
Of
Two
be eIther **the** '
mOstly '
arraNge
accorD
is two timEs two equals four
adVantages
the wOrld would engender
Thousands of state-sponsored
others for food feedIng
Off of
aN '

accorD
a languagE these
adVantages
Of
Two
be eIther **the** '
Off
of **aN**

•

reveal to themselves things that they already knew the chance technique was creating nothing i think it
was revealing to themselves things that they already knew about society or ideas about whatever that
were taboo that nobody could say that were unspeakable but the chance technique was creating nothing

44

to the whiCh comes from
ask It '
woRld
plaCe
of the stUdents and the growth
froM
without ' boundS like a man
mighT
Ask for either a cause or a
sNake ' run into
your next Composition ' this will
arE now
Superior or rather inferior to anything that **is**
as they Could ' the last three weeks were
study ' It is
tRansmission and
simpliCity '
a sense of solitUde '
laser beaM power
a total Service '
diviniTy
As
housiNg
Can
unitEd
waS to
whiCh
twaIn
such ' as laseR beam power
authorities Crippled
together to realize world game as fUlly as they could ' the last three
Men '
goodS
wenT
yeAr '
could determiNe
lift suCh '
him so yEt he
head it waS
after i Came to the woods '
rIse
in tuRn is
Certain that
i doUbted if the near
as distant and not as sMaller
aS

in and of itself and it was pure it was a means to an end in some of the modern poetry utilizing chance technique some of it's very good and i may be entirely incorrect but i have some feeling that in some of your work the chance technique itself is invested with a certain holiness it's something that seems very

rejecTed

hAd made him **so**

of the ceNtre '

aCtion

bE

talkS between

thought proCesses '

toIl

foR himself every

Centre '

world game was extraordinary ' withoUt fear without

straying ' visited Me and

iS

an emergency meeTing

in his fAvor '

beeN promised and divide it

wise poliCy

maximum in thE year

have cauSe '

people **ten** Coal

make musIc ' we

them ' they aRe

winter fire ' quiCk o

yoUrself with

experiMent '

pSychological

looks like This '

shelters As

use existiNg

from a partiCular

thE '

Stuff

Come

needed ' Is

countRy

Categories

my hoUse '

not Make

iS

imagine a direcT

A particular

use ' his kNowledge with

Costs

holding thE cat

deal with collective mankind'S needs the bare maximum was what

whiCh

different from what the abstract expressionists were doing i'm just generally curious what relation between their work and your work and their approach to chance and yours might be i had never heard that about bill de kooning i'm very glad to hear it he puts things on top of one another that were on transparent papers

quIet

we foResaw the possibility that no one would be

publiC '

then yoU can proceed giving equal attention to each

entirely disappears froM view might it not even be imagined that

they deScribed

period The beginner did not yet see '

cleAr

he has No time to be anything but

reality perhaps the faCts ' **most**

and quiEt '

Sympathy and

that i **Can**not

dId not know at

happens next ' if you'Re writing **a** '

a Corresponding rise in

making it sUsceptible to

television and telephone to a world central Medical educational and travel routing

doeS have

This

not As smaller **thus** '

miNimum

teChnology it did so much to

onE

paSt is now and there is no future it is

rejeCted '

south afrIca '

we aRe

muCh more

inflUences

Men even in

aS

mobiliTy throughout the world we

this wAy

the Needs of one man

wise poliCy

naturE at the

Seed so that a seed

exCel '

each perIod of

maRtial law '

Certain kinds of

aUdio tape

soMe way have found it out more

now what iS our

ones won'T burn '

of the women *yes* and so made those complicated images that we've seen *i don't know if it was the images of women i don't think it was his women paintings i'm not sure i think it was previous paintings of his i'm not all that certain about it* i was present in a restaurant when bill was talking and he had been eating some

A hectic
everyoNe to
City
appEar
diStant
as they Could '
lIkely to wait '
tRembling robe '
Canvas
qUite
perManent
Some including
iT would be
not to sAy '
copyiNg
progress suCh as
and dEath
malaySia
never stop even though eaCh
In
oR
Complex
remains a major information resoUrce
he has iMagined
what waS
have found iT out
All time '
the air ' your work Need not be lost '
spring days in whiCh
thE frontier and each
our thoughtS and
mediCal
If i talk
caRed
mediCal attention
shoUld
coMputer
it thiS
finding The needs of one
i cAme to the woods
subtly Neutralized by
the direCtion of **his** '
day whEn my axe
you See
to eaCh of the parts or you could say study
every lIttle pine needle

bread and crumbs had fallen on the tablecloth and he was talking about that being art the position of the crumbs and so forth and he said i'm saying that that isn't art and i didn't speak with him at the time but i thought later that i would say that it was there are many different ways of freeing what happens from our of

48

fRom

a sCene in a play '

seemed that from sUch a basis of

More rather than

So '

properTies or structure of the

Audio tape

sceNario

Casts

thE energy and information

iS likely to wait until

immediately Convened an emergency

mInd can change to do '

pRotestant leaders in northern ireland

form of information whereas news retains muCh of the

soUnds technological sounds is there

expressed a wish to live as i did ' he told **Me** with **the** '

or with **think**ing So '

wiTh its own

viA closed circuit

goiNg anywhere '

how muCh

othEr children i **am** ' weak in the head ' it

curiouS how

people **ten** Coal

ask It '

tRansmission and

form of information whereas news retains muCh of the

together to realize world game as fUlly as they could ' the last three

froM

goodS '

wenT '

hAd made him so

the air ' your work Need not be lost '

Can

arE **now**

our **thoughtS** ' and

•

we haVe

thAt

woRd

of gIfts

thinking about it one of the first ones i knew of was the teaching of mark tobey the painter he had a way of
teaching in which he covered the walls with paper and he gave his students charcoal and in the middle of
the room he put a still life arrangement and when the students were satisfied that they knew what they had

49

                              thAt
                  employment But to use
                      the worLd '
                  disadvantagE of
                         to Show
                         The disadvantage '
                         aRithmetic '
                         bUt without
                         Congressional
                         The ' swiftest traveler
            its way to the moUth '
                         foR
                         whEn
                      i haVe thought '
                         cAn follow anything else '
                      micRotonal
                      makIng '
                         thAt
                         Based on
                      staLin '
                      sociEty '
                         Say
                         The faintest but constant suggestions of his
                what Reason have we '
            the meeting of basic hUman needs for everyone on the planet and
                      whiCh '
                         Those ends
                the track is laid for Us ' let us spend
                      the eaRth
                      housE
                faithfully ' surVeyor if not
                         Anti
                      youRs ' escape
                      a sIngle step of
                      stAtes '
                      oBject
                one wouLd
                      confidEnt
                         aS
                         They did ' they caught up with him
                   in pRison '
                      soUth
                      whiCh is
                      in Their
                      argUments
                      ameRican

been looking at he asked them to go to the wall and place both nose and toes in relation to the wall and never
lose that connection and while in that position to draw what they had seen that had miraculous results
putting the faces over one another is not the same but it makes me think too of marcel duchamp's putting

   50

havE '
improVement to
wAy '
heR
mInd
stAtion
shadows By
no rehearsaL '
a drawing rEporting an event '
Self
don quixoTe
sponsoRed
withoUt names '
Cross-leggedness
Tell
mUsic '
democRatic
thE '
the promise of giVing us
south koreA
foR the tax fraud charges '
hIm
by our photogrAphs and
have not Been
soLving
thE
uSe
The
moRe lives to
happen to yoUr
eaCh
availabiliTy of
mUsic '
the whole use of the woRd in a flash '
contEmporary
loVe '
surely As
tRue
by jews In moscow '
swiftest trAveler is he that goes afoot ' it is darker in
the year 2000 for Both
onLy
farmEd
Such variables as
The '
the Room we watched '

the notes in the hat pulling them out a fairly simple but interesting way of working another in fact any way
of doing things that removes the thinking the mind works *but were you saying with the anecdote about the*
crumbs that were you agreeing with that tentative distinction that i was making between de kooning and

leisUre '

ameriCan money and influence '

noT

if money were to disappear what woUld happen to

maRtial law '

samE time there will be too many musicians to

throughout the world in this transformatiVe process

trAck

to go befoRe the most and on the deck of the world for

Itself to us it is

humAnity now living

Becomes a center

to feeL with

thE

nothing to Say and saying

could noT

just numbeRing them

a set of tools that can be Used by problem solvers throughout the world

these are my insignia ' they are yours ' esCape '

growTh of the

them ' this brings aboUt a music not in any way anticipated '

anotheR

could you havE and can you do

has giVen

And could

the woRld game

lIes the

tAkeoff '

oBvious

exactLy

just numbEring

Simply moving

Than eighteen inches

life than aRt or

faithfUl

more Civilized

a parT

or jUst a

coppeR

askEd how much copper wire is needed

not fossil fuels ' quickly air will improVe

And

noRth korea's demand allows both

the rest of theIr lives

not independent of eAch other

But

yourself don't you think that the crumbs having dropped and then being paid attention to even framed and
didn't we give that definition for art paying attention *yes but it seems to be refusing to look into the head
that seems to be the difference i think the way de kooning would use the crumbs would be to use them to*

52

across-Lot
hE could
aS
is beTween
a gunman issued a statement waRning that
now be described bUt
in the old teChniques
The
training shoUld see a sum
still unaccounted foR
yours long timE what would you write i can't the robe the
because the guerillas are a part of us a goVernment
i hAd
the kilowatt houR needs for the year 2000 the awareness **of**
for all of these are dependent fIrst or
the minds of the others in the room we wAtched as man successfully stood on another
are paid in part By jews in moscow bidding for
trees which i feLt with my hands passing
prints from thE functional point of view
now uSeful large price increases for
of view so indicaTed
an old flimsy music stand made of metal dRiven
in a very real physical sense inseparable Until **a**
and its behavior the deCision
from ouTside it chance operations are a
what yoU would say **what**
solving not the continent nation state oR
of thE country's cultural institutions may be
set of tools that can be used by problem solVers throughout the world in this
something And that is all that can be said has and
moRtgaged
occupatIon except
well being of the eArth given enough electrical power the
differentially comprehended or By
therefore your own worLd as fast as you can conform your
that thE world
in geneva after tumultuouS
wrong whaT is he supposed to say himself and suppose
of objects in fRont of them and asked the
say what mirror what dUst in the middle of the night the fifth take
work above the not fossil fuels we need to Change giving orders and obeying
Training
capacities and abUndant
making up a stoRy and
wE are now dealing with
toward the local system not Vice

see what was already in his head and so then put that down to put a modified to see what is already
there in the crumbs and then to duplicate that that you don't have an exact statement with crumbs you
may have a very interesting statement and an accurate statement but you don't have an exact statement

we cAn say **the**

let us have noble villages of men the woRld game to make the world work for 100% of
useless what we need Is

At present most of the important

attacks appeared to Be edging toward

an equation between worLd

hE

in order to accelerate the trend toward phySical success for all

leT he

than the nobleman's new england can hiRe all the wise men in the world to come and

how can yoU say that you just said this weather

afoot it is darker in the woods even in Common

parTy chiefs have the right to know what bomb

flUency in and out no split between

them **Round**

thEm this brings about a music not in any way

the life in us is like the water in the riVer it

finds its wAy to the mouth without assistance i left **the**

the middle of the night the fifth take this Robe

they are yours long tIme

they Are yours long time what would you write i

all the functions that are now filled By our

fast or sLow

Eight

that waS

sun is buT **a**

aReas they were

the rest of their lives as the nobleman of cUltivated taste surrounds himself with whatever
more spaCe

To feel with my feet the faint track which i

to know what bomb exploded yesterday inclUding the

vision no vision in accoRd with

makE and when music written for percussion but

throughout the world in this transformatiVe process

certAin

Real

that It is

reAson have we for calling e the sign for **a**

in farming are not controlled Because the system is as yet open in **a**

the mind in four different ways artha the worLd of

and many othEr information

itSelf a house and beyond

open and ravines bridged and passable aT all seasons

ways aRtha the world of

bUt i am wiser than that i have learned that

be said has and something also belong to our Common language so in

*which is what i think most of the best art has involved is exact statements and i think that's the difference
in finding something sort of sacred about chance technique i myself wouldn't use the word sacred i would
just think of chance operations as being useful a useful way of answering questions i think your thinking is*

54

Takeoff he was identified as being the

of abortion and helps to explain the sUdden

that began eight months ago iRan

army blEw up the north sea injuring

because the guerillas are a part of us a goVernment

for problem solving not the continent nAtion state

physical success foR all

contact wIth it keeping

pAssing

except information gathering By

best see the moonLight

opEning between the

or paradigm we might Say

we will noT succumb to any

tension in illinois late last week gReek

fine names bUild therefore your own world as fast as you

no longer fear a severe famine the deCision is in accordance

Three players

nor the station itself and drive people oUt this two-way movement of expansion and

we should have veRy

lifE in as is

and traVeled through the minds of the others in

whAt the unified field

ouR means are greater '

somethIng

one's fAculties coexist interpenetrate producing

at his frontier ' it is dramatic to see human Beings so concerned with the operation '

any medium whatever creates vast weaLth but this

and Each

no accidental **it** ' **iS**

raTe **of**

ouR political cartoons and pictorial

gymnasiUm an

the present sChizophrenia '

This body has extension to this we might

coUncil would

in pRactical

history if hE now always calculates right but that he can

oVer the

not being interrupted by shAdows by

not independent of each otheR that they are

as **It** '

society needs to be chAnged i think that many of our

its Behavior the decision to use the

way the buddhist the christian the isLamic or

and whEn

very interesting i don't know if i have responded to it very well *i'd be curious to know your thoughts about the role of music in schools and in education and i'm also curious about how you think about improvisation composition and performance and chance in music education* i've heard that chance operations have been

the whole earth containS

acTions ' loss

of success the ultimate baRe

doUbt that it is a part of the destiny of the

it not the point is that it is as if we Could grasp

man feels will aT length prevail over the

woUld be

of peRson in

for thE tax fraud charges in the persian gulf

the track is laid for us let us spend our liVes

from the functionAl point of view so indicated

meRely

thIs '

humAn needs for everyone on the planet and the

for military contracts we will not succumB to any pressure from any direction he said

words and their combinations but aLso words which

toward a nEw pact with

pathS and all

Then must be the highways of the

it ' it wouldn't happen not looking foR other breaks between

withoUt names for instruments just numbering them

and by our politiCal

grew visibly before us we were working aT the frontier and each

to know what bomb exploded yesterday inclUding the

eveR to

of pErson in person and society in society sanity

of aVoiding

of the best comprehensive educAtion in all

all the wise men in the woRld

before leavIng we tell them nothing

wAy as he grows more resolute and faithful

the roBe the

time what wouLd you

on thE planet and **the** '

we people a Space

suppose i frequenTly had to look up at the opening between the

example on pResently

and home Use throughout the world ' how far ahead

easily and insensibly we fall into a partiCular

lasT three weeks were intense with research and

yoU

leadeRs and policy

cErtainly true he sees not to what extremes or

protests defense lawyers haVe lodged

hAs and something also belong to

is no past oR future just

used in some public school situations with good result and i think it could bring about a lively enjoyment of
sound on the part of young children because it would one of the first things is that they would see immediately
that they were not in a competitive situation but in one involving discovery and enjoyment and not an

a dark and muggy nIght ' when my feet felt the

error wAs primarily

this ' Brings action

wouLd '

thE world game

iS a word of our

behavior The decision to use **the**

is as yet open in a closed system such vaRiables as

his road lies the faintest assUred

to reply of Course why is

fossil fuels we need To change giving orders and obeying them

one's facUlties coexist '

the paRadigm which

lovE content ' but for this purpose we need not

protests defense lawyers haVe lodged '

direction he sAid

these two's a goal ' duchamp ' theRe

your mInd '

nAme a dozen in the town who own their farms '

on how to display the findings that were Being made the energy and information grew

experimentaL '

day thE growth of the

there before it iS

whaT we

spontaneous coopeRation

nothing when the new electric technology ensUred a maximum of merging of person in person

people in love but rather the paradigm whiCh belongs

local sysTem not vice versa the facts of experience

to accelerate the trend toward physical sUccess

demilitaRization of

work ' himsElf to hear to see originally ' we need

the life in us is like the water in the riVer ' it

And

Real

somethIng

wAy as he grows more resolute and faithful

Becomes a center

experimentaL '

sociEty

there before it iS

acTions ' loss '

tension in illinois late last week ' gReek '

say what mirror what dUst in the middle of the night the fifth ' take

whiCh

Three players

enjoyment that was private but one that could be shared with all the students i was not happy with my public school musical education i developed a desire to sing and said i wanted to join the glee club and they said we'll have to test your voice you can't just join and they tested my voice and found that i didn't have one the

                    capacities and abUndant
        solving not the continent nation state oR
                            of pErson in person and society in society ' sanity

                                    •

                        of maN
                            yOu ' you say oh yes '
                            aN
                            aloUd was
                        writiNgs
                    of the Dawn '
                        and rEads it out to you ' you say oh yes ' now it '
                            foR
                        it ' **iS**
                        of arTs '
                    to elevAte his life by a
                        meetiNg we must learn to
        keep ourselves awake not by mechanical aiDs but by
                        the unIverse '
                    fact thaN
                    it ' ouGht
                        strewN
                            Or
                        learN
                    changes oUr
                        writiNgs
                    that perioD
                        havE '
                            ouR
                        it iS far more
                    which The
                            Arts a
                        writiNgs
                    of the Dawn '
                            pIcture
                            aNd this '
                        a fiGure
                        of maN
                        if he wOuld
                        experieNce of anything that is a
                    conflict coUld become a theater for the
                    which does Not forsake us '
                    at that perioD
                            hE needed

only other thing i remember really from those years in school with respect to music was teachers putting needles down on the records and then taking them off and asking us who wrote the music *they still do that at the conservatory* do they really i think that well i think you know what i think i think we should find more

to be Read '
So
pronunciaTion '
Act of
New
jaileD an
It '
deNsity in the
Galaxies
of the dawN ' which '
which mOrally he '
morally we caN do to affect
to yoU you say oh yes
forsake us iN our
Do
to bE
stRewn with
waS
be read This
fAct
beiNg
Day '
Israel
aNd
Group '
readiNg
Of the
Not forsake '
yoU say oh yes
forsake us iN our
jaileD
to bE
is faR more
galaxieS
To
you you sAy '
makes seNse
to be reaD
Is
fact thaN
fiGure
priNted
Objects
New material '
Usage
maN

ways for students to enjoy music and perhaps teach us something i was teaching a class at the new school for social research in new york and among the pupils was a japanese composer toshi ichiyanagi and my thought of my responsibility as a teacher at that time was that i should spur this student on to greater

can Do '
galaxiEs and this
pictuRe
uS **in**
yeT see '
Atmosphere '
sileNtly without
being createD so as
not yet possIble at that
we caN
the hiGhest of
Needed
Of
us iN
coUld
was **Not** ' yet
Day
a particular picturE
foR the
dawn which doeS
conflicT could become
endeAvor
sileNtly '
worlD '
aIds '
Now
Galaxies '
coNflict
fOr
seNse the
oUght
would learN '
meDium
hE needed '
pictuRe or
not yet See around him a world
The
elevAte his life
iN that
a worlD '
galaxIes
of No
usaGe
he would learN '
act Of
did Not yet

heights of experimentation we were approaching the christmas vacation i felt that would be a good time to sum up so to speak the work of the student during the previous months and give him something that would make his work more well go farther and in my terms as i was talking to toshi telling him what to do he very

pictUre
a maN
meDium ' through which
objEcts
moRe
clear and diSciplined
The
do to Affect the
New
coulD become '
now **It**
aNd this
it ouGht to be '
expectatioN '
the dawn which dOes
forsake us iN
he **woUld**
fact thaN
Day '
a particular picturE
oR
hiS life
meeTing
spAce '
Not
learn to write without faults israel jaileD an
If
deNsity in
low budGet
sileNtly '
say Oh yes '
deNsity in
oUght
sileNtly
Day
somEthing
to be Read '
atmoSphere and
iT '
A pier collapsed
a theater for the deploymeNt of gas a pier '
reaDs
extremIst
eNdeavor ' it is
Glorious to
learN

quietly and looking straight ahead without looking at me and it was as though he were speaking to himself
he simply said i am not you i did some teaching of very young children in the time of the wpa i wasn't
considered i wasn't on the music project but on the recreation project i was given places to go to the italian

Of **the**
of New
shUttle but
sileNtly without
woulD '
thE act of
a figuRe in that '
the very atmoSphere '
The
A
of No '
reaDs
a theater for the deployment of gas a pIer collapsed
thaN the
fiGure
paiNt ' the very '
yOu say oh yes
we caN
it oUght to be read this way
fact thaN
the reaDing
of thE
which we look ' which moRally we can do '
a pier collapSed in
learn To
jAiled
awake ' Not
low buDget
wIthout
aN
is ' far more ' Glorious
paiNt
tO be able to
we ' caN do
aloUd
with writiNgs
of gas a pier collapseD ' **in**
by **thE** ' condensation of new galaxies
foR the deployment of
uS in our
of **The** '
reAds it out to you ' you say oh yes
New material is '
is constantly being createD so as to
wIthout
to you you say oh yes Now

children to the chinese children to the black ones and i got along best with the chinese students who were
in a catholic school and they didn't have to come to my classes but they could come after hours but they
weren't obliged to come only as recreation and i would set up some ways to produce sound flower pots and

throuGh
he would learN
becOme a theater for the
galaxies aNd
the dawn which does not forsake Us '
mechaNical
perioD
to writE without faults
to caRve and paint the very
galaxieS
To you ' you
so As to
did Not yet see
the Deployment of
galaxIes through the
Not
it ouGht to be
atmosphere ' aNd
fOr
emergeNcy meeting
bUdget
sileNtly without
if he woulD
of thE dawn which does not
gRoup for
aidS
The
endeAvor it is
iN the
conflict coulD become a theater for the deployment of gas
of the extremIst group for the test
of the uNiverse '
Galaxies
iN which **the**
a theater fOr
this caN
bUdget
we caN
alouD was not
no morE '
no moRe
aS
iT out **to**
is fAr '
test firiNg of the space shuttle
conflict coulD become a theater for the deployment of

so on and i'd make it as attractive as i could to them but they were very timid and when i invited any one of
them to play to improvise on the sound producing objects they would they all used this same gesture of
choking themselves that if they were given freedom apparently that was awful so i didn't know immediately

aIds '
learN
a fiGure
meetiNg ' we must learn
material sO we have **a**
by mechaNical
way and reads it oUt to you ' you say oh yes
with writiNgs '
keep ourselves awake not by mechanical aiDs but by
mEchanical aids
to caRve and
elevate hiS
The
forsAke us '
Not
alouD was
hIghest
seNse '
hiGhest of
iN
as tO
of maN to
yoU '
Not
createD
spacE
ouR experience
endeavor it iS '
wriTings
collApsed '
with writiNgs
of gas a pier collapseD
wIthout
the grouNd or
Galaxies through the
meetiNg
tO **be**
aNd
yoU
aN
reaDs it out to you you say oh
to writE without faults
is constantly being cReated
a theater for the deployment of gaS a pier collapsed in
deploymenT of
A pier collapsed

what to do but it occurred to me that they would act differently if i were not there and we were fortunately in
a room that was longer than this one i think about twice as long so i went to the other end of the room and
pretended that i was working with the blinds and before i knew it i was hearing music and gradually they

64

emergeNcy meeting we must learn to reawaken
through which we look which morally we can Do to affect the
Is
of the space shuttle but Now every
usaGe
of the uNiverse is
Of the
sleep i kNow
aids bUt by
iN which the loss of
perioD
firing of thE space
to caRve and
changeS our experience of
To be '
which does not forsAke us '
coNflict
alouD was
It is
fact thaN the unquestionable ability of man to
budGet
that situatioN new material is
experience Of
was Not yet
withoUt faults israel jailed
expectatioN of
the intervention of the reaDing
to carvE '
to caRve a
quality of the day that iS
The
conscious endeAvor it is
iN
buDget
low budget conflIct could become a theater
aNd
Glorious
New material is
the dawn which dOes
by mechaNical aids
he woUld
of gas a pier collapsed iN northwestern malaysia the plo
woulD
shuttlE but now
no moRe
Space '

were playing beautiful things and then i had the wicked idea that i would show them possibilities about
notation going in the opposite direction from busoni who said that notation is the one thing that separates
the musician from music but i didn't have to go on teaching them because they came to me the next time

oughT to be
conscious ' endeAvor
New galaxies
that perioD the
sleep I
carve ' aNd
Glorious
readiNg
Of
by **aN**
he **woUld**
iN **that** '
coulD
a figurE
sense the gRound ' or
it out to you you Say oh yes ' now
or **To** '
fAults
of No
faults ' israel jaileD
more glorIous
strewN with
says it ouGht
our experieNce
yOu say oh yes
by aN infinite expectation of
faUlts ' israel
could become a theater for the deploymeNt of gas ' a pier '
a worlD '
wE
pRinted
that iS a
conflicT
now it mAkes
coNflict
constantly being createD so as
whIch the
fact thaN
Galaxies
aNd keep
ability ' Of
ability of maN to elevate his life by
qUality of the day that is the highest of arts
you say oh yes Now it makes sense ' the
Dawn which
wE have

and these poor little kids they were just tiny said you're not teaching us anything about counterpoint and after that they never came back i think the teachers in the real school had thought that my work with them was not in the right direction *i'd like to know if you ever think in images and if so if you ever use visual*

is constantly being cReated '
a pier collapSed in
pronunciaTion '
continue indefinitely the Act of
a world strewN with
aiDs but
a partIcular picture or to carve a statue
reads it out to you you say oh yes Now it
is the hiGhest
the act of writiNg silently
Of gas
sleep i kNow **of** no more '
withoUt
to paiNt
ourselves awake not by mechanical aiDs but by
possiblE at that
Read
not yet ' See around him a world
conflicT could become
A
writiNg silently '
conflict coulD become a theater
a statue and so to make a few objects beautIful ' but it is far more glorious to carve
of the dawN which does not forsake us in
throuGh **the** '

Needed
Of
sleep ' i kNow
bUdget
we caN
Day '
wE
to be Read
elevate hiS
To be
collApsed
awake ' Not
Day '
pIcture
deNsity in
fiGure

•

thinking as a source for your work with sound or words when i first went to seattle and my friends morris
graves and others took me to a small aquarium near the in the market near the sound and it cost ten cents
and when you got in there were just these boxes of water and i had been warned that if i saw nothing just to

Chain
Of a piece of music `
totally iNvolved he is `
sTake
wIll work for him
accompaNy the events of our
uprisinG
criticizEd over how
totally iNvolved he is at
how muCh washington will
work for him but he maY be
at leisure ` food inflation foreCasts were criticized `
man in the future will nOt work `
maN
of These and
wIll `
too is composed of its liNks not of these and their spatial relations `
relations structure and feelinG in music
as a thinkEr is or as
the way they accompaNy the events of our life `
foreCasts were criticized over how
to buY a
struCture
Or
aNd
sTructure
Is `
iNflation forecasts were criticized
washinGton will pay to buy a
structurE
Not of these and their spatial relations
and feeling in musiC feelings
to buY a
pieCe `
the dOllar's rally `
accompaNy
is or as a poeT
musIc
of our life **maN** in the future will not work ` automation will `
were criticized over how much washinGton will pay to buy
uprising ` thE dollar's
of our life maN in the future will not work ` automation will `
too is Composed of its links not of these and their
to buY ` **a** `
a pieCe
Of a piece of music

wait and after a while a clam went up from the bottom of one of the tanks and went to the top and then having gotten some air sailed back down this way and when he arrived at the bottom that disturbed others and they went up and shortly it was a magnificent display i thought of that when i was at the crown point

is or as a thiNker is or as

is or as a poeT

Is or as

the way they accompaNy the events of our life man in the future

criticized over how much washinGton will pay to buy

lEisure ' food

at leisure ' food iNflation '

a Chain too is composed of its links not

totallY involved as a painter is or as a thinker is

washington will pay to buy a twenty perCent stake in the palestinian uprising

Of

he is ' partially iNvolved when he is

a chain Too

musIc

of a piece of music iN the way they accompany the events of our

uprisinG '

aidEd by

life maN in the future will not work ' automation will '

aided by seventeen Counts of misconduct '

the palestinian uprising ' the dollar's rallY '

a Chain

when he is partially invOlved

accompaNy our apprehension of a piece of music **in** '

involved he is aT play or at

of musIc '

work ' automatioN will work for him but he may be totally

in music ' feelinGs accompany our

structurE

music ' feeliNgs

washington will pay to buy ' a twenty perCent stake in the palestinian uprising '

accompanY our apprehension of **a** '

over how muCh

as a pOet is

accompaNy our apprehension of a piece of music in '

fuTure '

he Is at play or at leisure food

accompaNy our apprehension of a piece of music in '

were criticized over how much washinGton will pay to buy a

man in thE future ' will

were criticized over how much washiNgton will pay to buy

washington will pay to buy a twenty perCent stake in the palestinian uprising ' the

be totallY involved as a painter is or as a thinker is

Criticized

life ' man in the future will nOt work '

the way they accompaNy

links noT of these and

press one january and i was going to make some prints and i decided to make a series called *on the surface* i took the whole sheet of paper for the images at the beginning and i cut the same size up into different shapes with chance operations sometimes with straight lines and sometimes with curved lines and then

wIll work for him but
miscoNduct ' a chain too is composed of its links '
a 20% stake in the palestinian uprisinG '
is or as a poEt is
he is partially iNvolved ' when he is totally involved he is '
is Composed of its links not of these and their
works when he is partiallY involved when he is totally involved he is
our apprehension of a pieCe
invOlved as
he is partially iNvolved when he is '
sTake '
composed of Its
wheN he is totally involved he is at play or at
their spatial relations structure and feelinG in music
futurE will
appreheNsion of
the palestinian uprising ' the dollar's rally Continued aided
at plaY or at leisure ' food inflation '
our apprehension of a pieCe
Of a piece of music
works wheN he is
involved as a painTer
or as a poet **Is**
is or as a thiNker is or as a poet is man works when he is
their spatial relations ' structure and feelinG in music '
hE is totally
iNflation '
our apprehension of a pieCe of music in '
involved when he is totallY involved he is at play or at leisure food
and feeling in musiC ' feelings
him but he may be tOtally
is or as a thiNker is or as
is composed of iTs
musIc '
the eveNts of our life ' man in the future will not
in ' music feelinGs accompany our
dollar's rally ' continuEd aided by
the future will Not work ' automation will work for him '
were Criticized over how much washington
continued ' aided **bY**
of musiC in the way '
hOw much
music ' feeliNgs accompany our apprehension of a
buy a Twenty percent stake '
partIally
works wheN he is partially involved when he is

placed the templates at chance determined points and turned them according to which of 360 degrees and when they crossed the surface at the top i then divided the template so that the work began with large shapes and ended after 35 prints with very small shapes and it went down gradually to the golden section in 35

70

uprisinG

is or as a thinkEr is or as a poet is '

is or as a thiNker is or as a poet is ' man works when he is '

misConduct ' a chain too is composed of its links

apprehension of a piece of music in the waY

of musiC in the way they

were criticized Over how much

stake iN

play or aT

when he Is totally

too is composed of its liNks not of these and their spatial relations

in music ' feelinGs accompany our

futurE '

the dollar's rally coNtinued aided **by**

of musiC **in**

he is ' partiallY involved when he is totally involved he

will pay to buy a twenty perCent stake in the palestinian uprising the

painter is Or as

he is ' totally iNvolved he is

our apprehension of a piece of music in The way they accompany the events of

as ' a poet Is

couNts of misconduct ' a chain too is composed

washinGton will pay

our lifE

at play or at leisure ' food iNflation

too is Composed of its links not of these and their

rallY

washington will pay to buy a twenty perCent stake in the palestinian uprising

invOlved as

he is ' partially iNvolved when he is

sTructure

wIll work for him

work ' automatioN will work for him but he may be totally

in ' music feelinGs accompany our

uprising ' thE dollar's

iNflation

of musiC in

continued aided bY

•

degrees i enjoyed that work so much and then i had the project of a piece for orchestra i decided to do it the same way to cut the music paper up with the same means and to put the templates at chance determined points on the music paper and the whole paper would potentially be sound but there would not be any space

every cIrcle

eNd ' is

Can be

its behaviOr '

aNgry over

behavior followS '

end In

haveS are

planeT **and** '

planEt

iNterests '

another Can

whole sYstem '

behavIor follows

eNd in

from whiCh

tO '

every eNd

the reSt '

behavIor

haveS are

armed conflicT

top havEs

iN ' washington

the struCture

whole ' sYstem

every cIrcle

aNd its

the ' struCture

dOgma

uNder every

there iS

whIch behavior '

encourage workerS

To

all prEvious

be ' drawN

struCture **of**

disqualifies plaYers '

all prevIous

is aN

livingry politiCal

tO

Not pulled down

down aS

of amerIcan

between ledger lines let's say and the next ledger lines of the next instrument so that everything would be sound whatever you'd hit then i noticed that whereas for the etching the top of the paper was important and going down was interesting for music going up and going down were not interesting what was interesting

alwayS '
iT is
not pullEd
philippiNes would '
talks Convert
something alwaYs
all ' prevIous
circle aNother
from whiCh
bullfighting **tO**
iN nature '
workerS to
actIon but
have-notS are
Through global
arE ' elevated
dispositioN is
whiCh behavior
disqualifies plaYers '
armed conflIct
aNd under
the struCture
tO ' the
players iNdividual
playerS
dogma natIon
bottom have-notS are
buT
rEst of
Not pulled
talks Convert
conflict immediatelY '
there Is
aNd under
the struCture
the tOp
No end '
all previouS
our ' lIfe
analogouS '
have-noTs
pullEd
No end
of ameriCan
angrY over
lIfe is

about music was going from the left to the right and so i had to change the direction and the meaning of the chance operations *did that in turn serve as any source or inspiration to continue visually working visually* yes but not exactly in the same way but i'm very interested in all those possibilities *do you feel that images*

to eNd
Can be
any resOrt
aNd warfare
alwayS another
of ' amerIcan
the ' expenSe
workers To
arE obsolete '
aNalogous to
Continued presence
alwaYs there
our lIfe
Not pulled
of ameriCan
always ' anOther
is **aN** '
State ' self '
dogma ' natIon '
playerS ' individual
acTion ' but
arE
bullfightiNg to
Can be
everY deep
there Is
aNd iraq
the ' struCture
behaviOr our
aNd iraq
alwayS there
between ' Iran
talkS
analogous To
not pullEd
spoNsored talks '
struCture of
anY resort '
end conflIcts '
bottom have-Nots
interest Can '
dOgma
preseNce **of** '
playerS
a ' machIne
expenSe of

can be questions you can ask questions that will bring images into existence *but can images be questions* i don't know that maybe you do maybe you have an idea that i don't know do you think you do *i'm not sure if i want to answer it do you feel that questions need to be answered* it's according to what you're doing i

74

Through ' global

a ' machinE

aNd iraq

interests Can

under everY

Is ' a

aNd under

Can be

a repOrt

Not pulled

iS analogous

follows ' It

have-notS are '

buT

wholE system

aNd under

the ' aCtion

disqualifies plaYers

Is always

to eNd

the struCture

philippines wOuld

aNd iraq

and itS

behavIor

have-notS are

iT is

top havEs

iNterest at

maChine and

is ' alwaYs

Is

dawN risen '

another Can '

tO

caN be

iS ' no

follows It '

analogouS

planeT

circlE

bullfightiNg to

interests Can '

everY deep

end conflIcts

caN be

generally ask them when i want to have them answered *do you feel that questions will serve as inspiration if they're not answered* i can't deal with that very well i don't know what to think at that point it could be i think that some questions are more radical than other questions *which ones are more radical* well the ones

livingry ' politiCal
nO '
uNder every
talkS convert
Iran and
analogouS
planeT and
lifE ' is
iraN and
struCture of
under everY
and Its
opeNs the
livingry politiCal
bullfighting tO
bullfightiNg to
alwayS another
the ' contInued
alwayS '
Through global
all prEvious
aNy resort
another Can
but everY
all ' prevIous
to preseNt
of ameriCan
grOwth the
aNd ' under
iS no
Iran and
of aS
To '
all prEvious
philippiNes would
politiCal dogma
bY protest
conflIct immediately
to eNd
Can be
the whOle
the uNited
behavior followS '
dogma natIon
analogouS
poliTical dogma

that produce interesting answers radical answers that often happens and you can recognize it very quickly i think if you ask uninteresting questions then your answers are uninteresting and i think that that immediately sets you back to searching for more radical questions getting at the roots of the situation one

                    arE ' elevated
                  to liviNgry '
                  talks Convert
                  anY resort

                    Is **a** '
                  aNd under
              from whiCh
                  the tOp
                    aNd warfare
      behavior followS
          dogma natIon
                of aS
                planeT
                    arE ' elevated
                      iN washington
                  whiCh ' behavior
        is ' alwaYs

                          •

image of something ' in this case ' we're comParing '
                  nichi nichi korE ko nichi '
                  fRom
                  oF
            is accOmplished
      constantly Replenished
                  Much
                  exAmple of
                  No
                  musiCians to plan
      short of saying what constitutional rEforms are to be introduced
                  Parts for which
                  thE mind
            that confRonts us
                      inFluences the means '
                let sOunds be
                  stRaight
                    Music is
          of thinking Are '
                  with oNe eye one does not
                  Cannot
                  thE '

                    .

doesn't always see it easily *the root of a situation one doesn't always see the root of a situation* no one doesn't always you have to pay more attention then i think *in the orchestra piece you just mentioned there are little loops of repetitions that appear occasionally i have also seen this in the piece* etcetera *and going*

Parts for which
thE mind
that confRonts us
oF
is accOmplished
stRaight '
Music is
of thinking Are '
with oNe eye one does not
Cannot
short of saying what constitutional rEforms are to be introduced

•

back as far as the sonatas and interludes *there are big structural repetitions could you talk about your attitude towards repetition and how that's changed through your own development as a composer* when i was writing the *sonatas and interludes* based on large repetitions i was very concerned to make at the ends

MethodStructureIntentionDisciplineNotationIndeterminacy
InterpenetrationImitationDevotionCircumstancesVariableStructure
NonunderstandingContingencyInconsistencyPerformance

II

coMposition
though ' Each
masT ' and on
in Him that was then
finished Once it is begun ' it then resembles
ill-planneD steps inside a
probleM solving
way ' thE way
inTo an
and wHat
dO ' everything
is always experimental unknown in aDvance fluent pregnant related obscure ' nature
future **Must**
may **bE**
naTion
route and **wHere** '
Of the
anD of
a ' sMall
this for **thosE** '
uniTed '
late in a dark and muggy nigHt when my feet felt the path which
mOnks have
repeateD ' utilization of
pollution ' probleMs of
thE
off in a dispuTe
wHat is
than what i remembered ' nO one will '
to be hearD by an audience at any distance

future **Must**
may bE
uniTed '
late in a dark and muggy nigHt when my feet felt the path which
mOnks have
anD **of**

•

Solving
The
enviRonment i.e. a
seem jUst right '
spaCe can

of each of the parts that was going to be what i wanted to do was to make the connection of the end with the
beginning of the thing that was being repeated so that you wouldn't notice it so that the repetition would
seem fresh i didn't want it to be oh now we have to listen to that again when we did the 840 repetitions of
satie's *vexations* i think something happened that no one expected many people whom i expected to come to

ouTspreading notion think '
edUcation and
them foR public
usEd '
Similarly one
on **The**
fRom
green shUtters and you say he's not seeing it he's
resonanCe '
fields Than **these**
yoU say he's not seeing it he's
electRic '
compEtition
officialS said economic
may be difficulT to speak out of
all events aRe
maximUm ' we sought to find the bare maximum ' for
these are first tone then silenCe '
Their searches '
the mUsician **has** '
the musician has no contRol
first stEp toward
diScover
leT '
conceRned with
formed spontaneoUsly ' that they therefore seem just right '
whiCh
search warranTs yesterday to
looking ' don't yoU see
space bRings **to**
that madE **the** '

Solving
leT
enviRonment i.e. a
formed spontaneoUsly that they therefore seem just right
spaCe **can**
Their **search**es
looking ' don't yoU see
the musician has no contRol '
usEd

•

that performance didn't come they thought they knew what 840 repetitions was but those of us who actually performed in it found that we didn't know what it was and that life so to speak changed as a result of performing the work i remember after it was all over it took 18 hours and 40 minutes i drove back to stony point and went to sleep and then when i got up the next morning the world seemed really new something

Is curious how
laNguage
mighT
havE
New
The '
I describe a
times befOre but though it
thaN the
musIc may ' be
aNd
is a crediT
fivE '
is useless what we Need ' is
boTh
avoId the
Of '
eNdeavor
varIety
sawdust aNd
Though '
nEws was
liNk for emergencies '
hardesT
castles In the air
then fOur
aNd
thIs
aNd brushing
or abouT high probability nor about knowing what is
total succEss ' of total
oN
of copper from visible **To**
It
Of
theN
Is '
aNd
or **Two** '
answEr will set all well afloat '
each time copper is scrapped melted dowN and recycled
no ideas of order buT
hIm '
nOise
would theN take care of
that It is a

had happened and i remember i think philip corner was part of it he remarked about that and others did there's now a man in holland who plays the *vexations* and not for 18 hours i think he manages it in a shorter period of time but still a long period of time and he stays at the piano the whole time people bring him something to eat and so on and he has prepared himself the previous day so that he has no need to leave the

souNd
This
and hEavy '
japaN's feeding
our know The people
have perceIved
cOmpared to big
aNd earth's
our tIme is
Need '
mighT
that if onE
Normal
more wiTh less
I
the ' flOwer the smile ' the
uNder
sum of all the clIchés of all
techNique of
To
obscurE
that souNds '
Then
had lasted longer It might have tinged my
Of
iN
possIble
kNow-how for all
people To
worklEss
process iN a single
are ' The
even there where there Is
Of
aN
a rarIty
aNywhere '
memory To
us in our soundEst sleep ' i
brushiNg '
yes and no are lies The only true answer
you have buIlt
be nOw
for heaveN's sake
a psychologIcal
commoN '

piano and he has the sheets all numbered from 1 up to 840 so that he doesn't have to have a scorekeeper as we had we had someone preparing himself satie says with interior immobilities and then someone playing and then someone keeping score and every twenty minutes the scorekeeper would leave the pianist would become the scorekeeper and someone new would come in and become quiet and the quiet one would start

and mosT
villagE freedom from '
kiNds of
The '
the correspondIng
nOr about
Not
possIble '
we **caN**
meTabolics '
monEy is obsolete because it stores work '
a kiNd of peep show and inside we now move '
sTop
Is
sOmewhere
by aN
to success **mIght yet**
caN oc**cur** for
once we knew whaT mankind had and what
succEss
the grouNd '
iT was a case of
Is '
seven five seven fOur eight six six '
wastes usiNg algae chlorella and others for food '
It's
a patterN
effecTs on
consciousnEss ' to see that it is
as maNy people as possible
only To say that **for** '
four seven fIve seven
extending the central nervOus system '
experimeNt '
set all well afloat ' thoreau ' yes and no are lIes ' **the**
is this oNly
acTions and
chlorElla
withiN him or
To
agrIculture '
gO about
dazzliNg me as
dIplomats
laNguage
opened fire on youThs

playing so that we made a kind of performance out of it and his way was to have this large stack of xeroxed copies of the piece and to throw them the room was just full of scattered paper *we've been talking in rather theoretical and abstract terms so i have a rather practical question to ask many years ago i was teaching the usual liberal arts course in music appreciation to a class and we talked early in the term about classical*

in a singlE
play ' Now
The
don't for heaven's sake be afraId
there tO move or could make it disappear i **should** '
politics ' it is Now '

Is
is this oNly
meTabolics '
succEss
withiN him or
hardesT
don't for heaven's sake be afraId '
cOmpared to big
uNder

•

not be lost ' that is where they shoulD be '
hIm
dreamS and
image whiCh **each** had '
and testIng **a** '
will Pass an
acting ' singing catches ' guessing riddLes '
hIm ' or
froNt of '
povErty '
not be lost ' that is where they shoulD be ' now put the
untIl it
in the air ' your work need not be loSt ' that is where they should be ' now
advanCes '
solItude '
Poverty ' nor weakness weakness '
testing a hypothesis ' presenting the resuLts '
poverty ' nor weakness weakness ' If you
oN it
hE
themselves arounD and
dreams ' and endeavors to lIve the life which **he** '
to live the life which he haS imagined ' he
in Common
I ' learned this at least by my
touch ' the robe the bowl ' let alone Pick them up ' giving orders ' and obeying them '

forms and sonatas all of that sort of thing but the day came when i had to talk about more recent thought and how indeterminacy would affect musical forms so we decided to listen to some period of silence we agreed on a starting and ending time and that we would just listen to whatever happened during that time and then talk about it afterwards and the discussion that followed was very fascinating some students

86

students ' to concentrate attention on it ' untiL

demanded ' the robe the bowl ' he offered them wIthout

cause aNd

contact and using charcoal to draw thE image ' which each

orDer '

contact wIth it ' keeping that contact

contemporary ' no longer fixed in taSte and

dreams ' and endeavors to live the life whiCh he has '

solItude '

each had in mind ' all the students were in Positions that disconnected mind and hand '

contemporary ' no Longer

wIth

aNd

tElling it ' solving a problem '

solituDe '

It

poSition another

in ' Common hours '

your work need not be lost ' that Is where they should be '

comPoser ' though without his writing it **it**

in the air ' your work need not be Lost ' that

he wIll

aN

ordEr

unDer them '

one advances confIdently ' in the direction of

a problem in practical arithmetic ' tranSlating from one language to another ' asking

them ' but they were unable even to touCh ' the robe the bowl ' let alone

keepIng that contact ' and using charcoal to draw

the collaboration with onself that each Person

acting ' singing catches ' guessing riddLes '

contact wIth it '

eveN to touch

thE bowl ' let alone pick them up ' giving '

that each person conventionally permits ' haD been

cursIng ' greeting ' praying ' he made an arrangement

between cauSe and

eaCh '

just numberIng them this brings about a music ' not **in**

be lost ' that is where they should be ' now Put the foundations under them '

acting ' singing catches ' guessing riddLes '

your work need not be lost ' that Is where they should be '

coNtact with it '

that Each person conventionally permits

in taste ' anD

lIve with

were hearing the ambient quality of people's footsteps as they walked down an empty hallway they heard
fascinating rhythms from the steam heat radiators lots of counterpoint and some students insisted that the
piece that we performed had rounded form an aba form if you will because the airplane we heard at the
beginning came back so we had quite a lot of controversy between these two factions in the class who

oneSelf that

breaks between Cause and

wIll '

will Put some things behind '

students ' to concentrate attention on it ' untiL

wIthout his

haNd

thE laws of

maDe

wIll

the ' compoSer ' though without his writing it **it** wouldn't

touCh ' the robe the bowl ' let alone

wIll '

the collaboration with oneself that each Person

acting ' singing catches ' guessing riddLes '

your work need not be lost ' that Is where they should be '

he made aN

madE an

orDer

wIth the

will not **be** ' Solitude '

the robe the bowl ' let alone piCk them up '

presentIng

Poverty ' nor weakness weakness '

pass an invisibLe boundary

whIch each

eveNt

will appEar

with paper to place both nose anD toes '

composer ' though wIthout

at leaSt

of whiCh

of beIngs '

cross-leggedness ' the result of which is raPid transportation ' music written for

just remaining ready ' i Learned

to touch the robe the bowl ' let alone ' pIck them up '

of aN

bE

in contact **with** it ' keeping that contact ' anD

wIll begin

more liberal lawS will begin to establish

advanCes

tables and dIagrams '

the drawings were suddenly contemPorary ' no

rock between them ' but they were unabLe even to touch the robe the bowl ' let alone

on It '

were sure that there was intention and others who were sure that there was not intention and that discussion in itself was fine and wonderful but i've often wondered through the years what you might have said to that class well that sort of thing happens it's very difficult to get rid of that kind of intention i tried it in my own compositions and i found that i've had to come to an accommodation with intention do solitude will Not

hE will

anD

my experIment '

he will put Some things behind will pass an invisible

attention on it until it was part and parCel of

them thIs **brings** about a music not in any way

rePorting an event '

the Laws of the

musIc

aNd

old laws **bE**

though without his writing it **it** woulDn't happen

laws wIll begin

in the air ' your work need not be loSt ' that is where they should be '

eaCh had

that If one

each **Per**son '

that is where they shouLd be ' now put the

tables and dIagrams

aNd

in front of thEm

anD

experIment that if one

dreamS and endeavors to live

the laws of the universe will appear less Complex '

reportIng an event

the collaboration with oneself that each Person

without his writing it **it** wouLdn't happen not

under them they dId they caught up with him

will appear less complex aNd

studEnts ' to concentrate attention on it until it

not be lost ' that is where they shoulD be ' now put

he wIll

the lawS

the image whiCh each had '

experIment '

music written for Percussion but without names for instruments '

Laws

wIth

it **it** wouldN't

rEsult of which is

anD

of **a** ' hIgher

he will put Some things behind ' will pass an invisible

plaCe ' both nose and toes

you find that so as time goes by i enjoyed the piece because it allowed me to experience english as a foreign language that is i got the experience the sequence of words merely as a sequence of sounds that aside you have to make choices and i find the choices that people make most revealing about them so i'd like you to tell how you came about deciding on things like the 49 quotes from thoreau maybe the 93

you have buIlt castles in the air
Presenting the
Laws
wIll
Not **look**ing for '
studEnts ' to concentrate attention on it '
laws will begin to establish themselves arounD and
proportIon '
to live the life which he haS imagined he will meet with **a**
with oneself that eaCh person
wrItten for '
both nose and toes in contact with it ' keePing that contact '
the drawings were suddenLy contemporary no longer
untIl it
froNt of
thE
the stuDents were
hIm or the old
and **toeS** in
under them ' they did ' they Caught up '
each had In mind
both nose and toes in contact with it ' keePing that contact and using
oneseLf that
hypothesIs
aNd
lEss
anD
sense and he wIll live with
loSt ' that is where they should be ' now put the
whiCh
and testIng
under them ' they did ' they caught uP with him demanded the robe
caught up with him demanded the robe the bowL ' he offered them '
It
aNd
an **obj**Ect ' or giving its measurements ' constructing
shoulD be now put
the **aIr** ' your work need not be
by my experiment that if one advanceS '
Composer '
wIth
Permits '
testing a hypothesis ' presenting the resuLts '
musIc '
No
lifE

*quotes from wittgenstein and how you put the pauses in because in your introduction you said that breath
is important and pauses had to come from somewhere tell us why you don't like emerson and why i like
thoreau it's easy to tell you that i chose the wittgenstein ones after having received a page and then i read
the whole page and i took one rather than another one paragraph rather than another and i at that point did*

                    bounDary '
                   not lookIng
                      waS
                   in Common '
         thankIng ' cursing ' greeting '
                   Presenting
and testing a hypothesis ' presenting the resuLts '
          composer ' though wIthout his
                  solitude Nor
                     placE
                      anD
      one language to another ' askIng ' thanking '
contact with it ' keeping that contact and uSing
                  built Castles
              mInd ' all the students were **in**
  imagined he will meet with a success unexPected in common hours ' he
      nor weakness weakness if you have buiLt castles
   nor poverty poverty nor weakness weakness If you have built castles
              of his dreams aNd
            not bE lost ' that is where

                      anD
                    he wIll
        the ' compoSer ' though without his writing it **it** wouldn't
                   advanCes
                  wrItten ' for
  under them ' they did ' they caught uP with him demanded the robe
              the Laws of the
                    wIth
                     aNd
            tElling it ' solving a problem

                      •

                  populatioN '
                    Observed
          wisdom or love or beauTy
                      Are
                  quieT ' the
                     Isn't
              as we began tO
                    iNcrease
                      iN
              everybOdy else '
              and Telephone

something connected with what i liked well i'll take an example here's a page from the third lecture that i'm working on now i'll read the first six lines as they come to me after i've put in the wing words regress you can say what you like it takes you only line of data can data and its true significance is he awoke with problem was of the i've decided where the pauses are there and this is what i've written like it only line of data can its technology extending consciousness itself As

To some areas

of pastness although not always when I remember

nO

aNswers

agaiNst

reasOnable

Two

in populAr

The ' vastness and strangeness of nature ' every

fIery

frOm without

yieldiNg the same

prisoN **if**

Of

To '

they Are

man on **The**

freed from theory In

pastness althOugh

aNti

was cool but uNfurled '

tO **be**

be heard in several places ' The

reference to A body

was The

wInter night ' i

gO to the wall which he had covered with

help the uNited states

the judge iN the

experiment shOwing

mind Thus

scholArships

and sheds ' leT not to get a

know who had the dream and where he Is namely in this

fOr us she

of pastNess although

all the marrow of life to live so sturdily aNd spartan like as

helplessness ' thOse who

The

wAs

sTrongly

wIth '

all the futures that will **be** are **here nOw** '

awareNess of all the varieties of

oNly

true significance is with problem was now let's try something else than that say i include let's on the third
line i end with data can and the fourth line begins data and its true significance is he let's just add some of
the beginning of that we have to go as far as the middle word which is true so if i do if i repeat the data liking
as i do repetition i have to continue to the true and i don't think i will let's see like it only line of data can

                              bOdy
                              buT
                                  A week ago
                              and Two
                    than thursday mornIng **the**
                              next tO **the** '
            to be played equally loud aNd
                    shutters aNd
                      seems tO be
                      i give The
                  think we Are moving
                  dream wiTh
                          housIng ' needs the
                            nO doubt how electric
                            iN at
                            oNly **be**
                            Of
                          leT the noon
                          of A piece of music **in** '
                        meTal from
                    brazIl began
                    be tOtally
                        aNd loud '
                  help paNama '
                    discOvery as
                    wiTh
                    things Are going very well
                        The
                  sense to say If
                        lOst '
                    irelaNd '

    all the marrow of life to live so sturdily aNd spartan like as
                      reasOnable
                          buT
        technology extending consciousness itself As
                      dream wiTh
                freed from theory **In**
                        be tOtally
                      aNswers

                              •

data and its true i'm not working with chance now i'm working with my common sense i'm looking for ideas now do i find any idea in what i've decided like it only line of data can and then instead of repeating data i didn't because that word its does that its true significance is with problem was that somehow suggests something i don't know what but something that's how i work and i must say i do it better at 3:00 a.m. than

Is
there are No
of toDay '
onE and
Two '
idEa
in youR '
Men even
If
caN
music mAy
instruCtion
we might saY
to deal wIth
aNti-
meloDy '
hE needed
iT ' looks
and Endings
a gReat
an asian diploMat '
work but It
aNd
voice to Ask '
Copper aluminum and steel ' that would be
there **is** ' alwaYs
have ' but how does he have It ' the limits of
thoughtfully we waNt '
that worD must
arE '
waiT until it
havE
can **be** dRawn that there is no **end** '
Men
stIll
thousaNds of
kind As
interCourse might
You
wIth
Not the
killeD
to samplEs
Through
to facE but
stRategy '

i do at 5:50 about emerson i've read it and reread it this summer this past hot summer and i found it very difficult to enjoy i found it stuffy so frequently in his diary he said that thoreau's ideas were his ideas and then he agreed that thoreau's form in which he put his ideas was livelier than the way he himself would do it which i think is very true but i think there's the difference in the ideas emerson tends to get one idea and

path and for the Most part wholly
begun ' It
woN
up to seven point eight trillion for exAmple on presently-farmed land using
stand very near together ' Cheek '
description ' and not bY
musIc '
if there were as maNy
more rapiDly than **it** '
schizophrEnia '
live as i did he Told
might almost bE said meaning moves
into a cReation and expands itself in an eternal
Makes the
I
to **it** aNd **the** '
sAmple
Competition is transcended through
being plaYed not
fIts '
rather thaN competition nation state competition is
maskeD '
End
aT
liEs the
towaRd the sun '
than May **here** be played grow
fear ' here detaIls might be
clumsy aNd tremble too much for
time ' not entirely free of pArts ' different
not exClusive
destinY
contact wIth
the bottom ' appareNtly without inconvenience ' as long
in this worlD to
wisE
in This way
in caloriEs ' how much
consumption ' we sought to establish a baRe
intelligible in itself that is to say it Must not be
benzene wIth moscow '
you are at preseNt why '
how probAble a mistake is in this
to the region to arrange a Cease-fire a state department official said
are Yours long
thIs world

develop it thoreau doesn't do that there's an unexpectedness from sentence to sentence and paragraph to paragraph in thoreau one's constantly surprised and refreshed *younger eligible voters tend not to henry miller didn't vote buckminster fuller didn't vote you don't vote what if they gave and nobody* then there might be a change that's one of the things i hope change must take place and if it could take place without

96

oNly listening is intermittent ' thoreau '

on a town in which a former operation woulD ' barco said '

placEd you

now This also

whEat '

aRe affected by the least inequalities in

the solution of toMorrow

repeated any number of tImes c is the prescribed use of five

uNder

kilowAtt hours and eight

in the burmese Capital '

i have been using time brackets sometimes **theY**

whIch **his**

last moNth's

reconciliation woulD

thE

capaciTy ' which

obligEs

ouR thoughts and hence

an inoffensive siMple

thIs '

aNd

finding the needs of one mAn led us to finding the needs for mankind as

deCision

waY of

saId the

aNimals

shoulD

point fivE '

us we musT do

is a **framE** ' a change of mental attitude ' amplification '

cloud and the Rain which lasts three weeks and produces

siMultaneous

body he Is '

officials said there is also a seNse of

if ' A

bombing in the Costa rican capital ' hungarian coal '

a single tone ' silence around it ' repeated anY

paradox coalesces or telescopes varIous facets of a complex process '

aN

proceeD ' so **to** '

arE **so**

buT **of** '

dominancE into diplomatic success '

gRound '

Move followed

great general disaster necessitating it it would be better if we could find a way a humorous way in which to embarrass government out of existence that would be the kind of thing that happened in denmark against hitler *your lectures remind me much of what is being called language poetry what do you see as the poet's role in society* i don't think it makes much difference how i see it how i see the role of the poet poetry has as

no boundarIes without
or suN '
door And pass out into the great open
brain Correlated with associating or with thinking
Yet
electrIc '
caN i imagine that he might in some way have
seen or toucheD that
thEory appeals
This
floods that lEft about one million people homeless caused
walks we aRe constantly though unconsciously steering
letting theM convert these to food for man **and**
Is **the** '
wheN **the** '
toe thAt line you will pardon some
five years ago about 1500 jobs were out of Control who from the start of the war until
being spoken to we must not onlY **be**
whIch **you**
this traNsformative process availability **of** '
there is no process in the brain correlateD with associating or with thinking so that
ablE
hold Talks with hanoi ' war '
arab world and that amounts to a total obsEssion ' what is to be done '
oR the any other outlines of life'n'action '
tiMe '
It misled him though the result were
ecoNomic '
A
whiCh is a sample '
a verY crude '
a mental dIscomfort '
us as the life of the tree puts forth New branches
how Do you know what you would do if
nEws
killing Two
Equals
the middle of the night ' the fifth ' take this Robe this bowl or whatever these are
My duty '
o quIck
Not wise to try to be one
congress At a meeting next month probably
to fulfill a Commission to
You ' you
call a truce and emancIpate about
uNiversal

many roles as there are poets i've often thought as i write the lectures of my early statement that i have nothing to say and i am saying it and that is poetry as i need it i seem not to have gotten enough of nothing as time went on and now i'm getting more *i'd like to ask you about the way the manner in which you've been delivering the lectures in which you read them i'm wondering if you've thought about that a lot for*

office of the other ' water is gooD to drink ' coal to burn ' wool to
thE
losT or
must bE complemented by '
metabolics aRe '
efficiency would be soMewhere between
gIves the word
momeNt if
to 2 whereAs this
1500 kwh and eight metriC tons of coal equivalents per capita
new personalitY at
purpose ' It might also be said it was
uNiversal
revolution illustrateD on
must not bE
any dusT ' why
palEstinians
patRolling the streets in contrast to violent
chance to evaporate if we would enjoy the Most
to produce progressIvely higher
meaNs nothing ' it is
five verticAlly thus a
sCript until the invention of
saY
sake be afraId of
Not by mechanical
competence at present levels to show we coulD do this today with what
that thEy have many
say To him i
though without finE names build
like these sedges and bRakes which will never
quite aMorphous as
basIs for all '
a radically New electronic
steel thAt would be needed for
voiCe to ask which of the numbers are passive '
the present schizophrenia ' the use of energY sources above earth not
others I had
passeNgers living
for half a year there woulD
involvEd in
side wiTh
with**out** bounds likE a man in a waking moment to men
man needs only to be tuRned round once with his eyes shut in this
to Me that
there Is

*me the way you read it is very expressive and very lovely but a little forlorn at the end of every phrase
your voice kind of trails off and again for me it winds up cutting out some of the humor of many of those
lines which strike me often as quite funny and i would think that somebody delivering the lecture in a
more deadpan way might bring that out have you thought about the manner in which you're delivering*

eNtirely

thAt

has to lose is rather the atmosphere of Clouds of thought surrounding the bare

inconvenience as long as i staYed there or more than a quarter of an hour

we look whIch morally we

theN i say that it is a scene in a play '

saiD

simplE

difficulTy is

solving anarchy in a placE

and faithful ' his Road

expanded and interpreted in his favor in a More

thIs

what is to be doNe '

the result of A wise

wisdom is not to be equated with mystiCal

areas designated separatelY

here neIther

heNce for our talking '

Dots you can only

havE

in souTh

in placE

between well-known points in the field of fRequency or just a drawing in space ' pitch

8.5×10^{15} calories and 21.9 tiMes

should take hIm to be a half wit ' but

the flower the smile the returN

works so well everyone lives As he needs upon

the influx of the spirit mexiCan opposition leaders called for

noise and musical tones upon which music maY be drawn ' space '

the attachment to It **it** is

is okay there is No more past

saiD

kEy '

hindered from accomplishing which for wanT of a

scorE ' no two

combinations but also woRds

and the night overtake thee everywhere at hoMe there are no larger

not yet possIble

my stick too ' to staNd on the meeting of two eternities ' the

held thAt

the ' idiotiC

men could face up to six Years '

a partIcular route '

him wheN i was here he was teaching them as one

everyboDy is

them and is the manner in which you read the lecture part of the lecture or could they be read by somebody else it has to be part of it because that's how it is the texts are very long and the breathing indications are it's not easy to do and i'm not a great one to rehearse or practice before each lecture i have read it twice once

wE **have**

iT **was**

machinE and its

calculatoR indeed who succeeds

Make

place It is this

by a score No **two**

wAlk as far as the state of his leg '

establish levels whiCh would allow man to realize not his minimum

protests for racial discrimination theY

as we put on our clothes or as the fIsh puts

Now what it will be like

the worlD

languagE we can say

you have and can do line for line and poinT for point your

owls lEt them do the

had been Reached

of Man's

of Impulses

eveN

A kind of language a way of saying something

we Can define the problems of

the foundations under them convert weaponrY to

nature ' I would gladly tell all that i

raNge ' b is nothing but a single tone silence

letting them convert these to fooD for man and

killing a policE officer in a

condiTion of things which

gardEn dies and a

gRasp of earth's present

to the eskiMos who preached on the

process thIs two-way

which for waNt of

wAlk as long as thought

and stagger ' a rumanian Citizen washington to use south africa angola

castles in the air Your work

a need for poetry ' joyce ' comedy Is

betweeN

the worD

a movE which would assure changing people's

we musT '

quickEst and most '

the baRe calculus the suggestion of an underlying

conclusion that the word Must here mean to understand

any It is as though

oN i

to myself and once to friends it doesn't emphasize the humor *i could imagine another person delivering your lectures and they would be a very different experience* yes that's true *but they* i think the humor is perhaps more humorous when it's not underlined but it shouldn't be so forlorn my voice is not very good today and

the formulA for b '
staff or staves ' the possibility of a miCrotonal music ' more space between staff lines
and have the same job for more than ten Years
Is
the Number of pages of your next composition this
calleD for an
is no play in thEm for
is noT a blank loss of
Employing the same technique to
what aRe called
their own hands ' and provided food for theMselves and
have dIscovered legal ties to
burN wooden
points in time when there Are not points but
rejeCted israel and the united states face to
a new job and even a totallY new
sImple time or place we
No longer camp as for a night but
accuseD of corruption and
in proportion as hE appeared
began To
playing hE has no goals ' he's
the woRd this
would Mean to try
per wIre
spartaN conditions where more
out of nothing it must be supposed thAt there is literally a true
Coal '
we applY to
Is there before it is
message per wire subsequeNt more with lessing improvements
him as for another i have always been so **saiD**
torturE **in** '
iT is
possiblE both ways it ought to be
the Responsibility
for Mere '
wIth the greatest arms
dowN
As to
never be**Come** ' english
totallY new

contact **wIth**
is okay there is No more past
him as for another i have always been so saiD

it wasn't very good last wednesday either but some people tell me they liked it better when my voice wasn't
so good we'll see *what is your attitude towards all this computerized digital music that is slowly taking the
traditional musician away from his essence or employment* i think there are many ways to make music

hE needed

waiT until it

arab world and that amounts to a total obsEssion ' what is to be done '

patRolling the streets in contrast to violent

for **Mere** '

basIs for **all** '

my stick too to staNd on the meeting of two eternities ' **the**

As to

the ' idiotiC

noise and musical tones upon which music maY be drawn ' **space**

·

step of my walk and I ' have thought that perhaps my body would

laNguage '

pieces as visual space can iT ' is both

nEt that might have been

and/oR ' reaching a center '

dealing with one not two ' to make a garden emPty '

world of rElativity '

iNto information or

sEcond

The '

diRections '

officiAl '

life To

call neIther

nO

awareNess

to accelerate the trend toward physIcal success for all '

oN

Too many

problEm

foR '

diPlomats

othEr every

fall iN

thE '

The

expeRience of

both nose And

is ' The

fIlled with water ' time spent tipping it '

clOuds of thought

of haviNg to

we're gaining ways that we haven't had i don't think that we will lose the things that we have had in the getting of things that we haven't had we are moving toward greater riches the program of joel chadabe for making music was described to me by ivan tcherepnin it brings about a way of making music with which

advance ' partIes of
the heroic the mirthful the woNdrous '
relaTing
information and imagEs
in unifoRm
would ' never accePt that
othErs
may Not
comEdy **is** '
is dramaTic to see human
goveRnment
good ' A reason
Thus
takes place ' through the skIn itself '
tO
have tiNged my
sovIet '
suddeN change of mind '
To
appEals to
felt the path which my eyes could not see ' dReaming and absent-minded all the way until i
touch ' touch is our Primary and
samE
all thiNgs
and likE
all mankind aT all times '
calculus ' it is of couRse this
Any
The '
a boatload of vIetnamese refugees criticized
electric pOwer '
aNd
when I came to die discover that i had
No
wiTh
idEa '
to pRovide
Production **of**
though othEr breaks this
we Now
bEam
conTinue **the** '
without competition the students woRked together to
experience with A smile '
marrow of life To
the bravery of mInks and muskrats ' **a**

i'm not familiar we can expect such new ways constantly both with technology and acoustically too *would you say that this new technology is almost being disrespectful towards the traditional instrument and the beauty and the art of it* i'm having difficulty understanding what you're saying *this computer music this*

at the whOle ' global

electric power plaNts ' and

It

plaN

your sword and sliT my throat

day and drEams at night suzuki '

he was foRced to

coexistence of dissimilars ' multiPlicity '

a villagE but actually at the speed of light ' the

force iN

training and practicE

and philosophy and religion ' Till we

woRn

And

seT

anarchIc '

private business with the fewest Obstacles to be

haNd

water tIme

oN

day combusTion '

doEs just let himself go when he follows the

up please it's time it is cuRious how much more arresting are the weather

fallen leaves **sweeP**ng up '

a mistakE is

the path ' iN

thE

find or define The

moRning ' the move

heArd by an audience

The

nature of sound ' empty mInd

Of touch rather

like what e.g. caN't

Its way to the mouth '

Now

speed of lighT

old floods that lEft

fouR fours into one two and one

sPutnik

will bE

iN burma ' to a

doEs

Them so

agReed '

mAnkind and

digital synthesized so far away from reality so far away from the artistic emotion put into acoustic instruments i don't think so i think the emotions are where they are in the people and that they can hear something made with technology emotionally the floppy disks can't be themselves emotional or the technology

                                    wesT ' bank
                    stressed equally In current physics jazz newspapers and
                               Out their side of **the**
                               betweeN two
                               not to lIve
                               betweeN succeeding numbers following
                    no ideas ' poeTry is
                      it to its lowEst
                        pieces he woRked symmetrically ' counting the number
           being does **not** build uP '
        as to put to rout all that was not lifE ' to cut
              the same result iN
                        whosE margins are nowhere '
                      who Told the
              which it is begun ' howeveR
                              irAnian fishermen ' khomeini's
                              wiTh research and
                    a poet **Is**
        it is the same with a mathematical prOblem ' do
                    much bigger thaN
                         as possIble ' availability of the best health
                         learN
                          reporTs than
                 said to havE
                   in youR
                 setting for the Passions without
                    was thE first
                    muggy Night '
                    thE
           bus carrying diplomaTs south
                    coloRed
                               A
                         To make
              support and the Interrelated
                       prOvide
                       eveN under
                          Is of course
                 two ' aNd/or reaching
                         To
                         arE
           possibilities of a woRld guaranteed annual income ' the
                               sPlit
                 floods that lEft
                         aNd
                         thE
           way unTil i was

but the people remain able to be *could i ask you to talk about marcel duchamp because i understand that you knew him and i would just like to hear what he was like* it's a long story i don't know just where to begin when he died i received a telegram from teeny duchamp to the effect that he had died i was living in

                              woRking
including the kremlin's new secret bomber And
                              counTry's
                    necessary ' I wanted
                    a village ' Or
                    americaN '
                              that It is as if we could grasp it '
          people as she Needed up
                    abouT i may '
                    what hE does
                              foR
                    the Production of
or indra in thE sky '
          the populatioN art
                    madE of
vivid awareness is a sTage on which is contained
                    enviRonment i.e.
                    A
          way and wiTh the most degrees of freedom
traveled through the mInds
                    nOt
                    iN what sense can
                    It
                    Nor '
          possibiliTy of
                    villagE
                    is a gReat tradition '
the star wars concePt hook '
                    that aftEr six days of
                    loud aNd **in**
                    and **listEn** '
                    deck of The
          eighteen inches apaRt in the midst of the woods '
          split the stick And
                    iT would
the students were ' workIng
                    the same cOurse as battles
two ' to make a gardeN empty

                    when I came to die discover that i had
                    betweeN succeeding numbers following
                    abouT i may '
                    problEm
                    and/oR reaching a center '
                              sPutnik
                    will bE

champaign it was a long room narrower than this one about a third of this width but equal length the room
was so to speak in the treetops they were not tall trees so that i could be at one end of the room or at the
other end i had a kind of coffee table in the middle and i put the telegram there then i used the space to not

                                all thiNgs
                        whosE margins are nowhere
                          who Told the
        eighteen inches apaRt in the midst of the woods
                                  A
                               The '
                        call **neI**ther
                               nOt
                        of **hav**i**N**g to

                                  •

            has shown that by deal**I**ng with
        thought the soul holds itself off fro**M**
                            th**I**ngs '
                    The future must be revised '
                          o**A**k
                        men**T**ally
                        Itself in an eternal
                which ' n**O** day illustrates
                      ha**N**d and the clouds of
            chorals of sat**I**e to change the staff so there's equal
        technological co**M**petence at present levels to
                        quest**I**on
                           To '
                        im**A**gining myself
                      jus**T** that to myself and here e.g.
                        man**I**acal '
                          c**O**ld '
                        sparta**N** '
                      bes**I**des ' the efficiency and pollution '
                  thinking to **M**yself yet
            weather from dark and slugg**I**sh hours
                        Them but in the end they
                    tree or An oak shall
                           The '
                  another way In the case
        he has guessed my th**O**ughts right but
                      society Not '
                          l**I**nk
        and industrial develop**M**ent how can
                      those used In
                        Though none
                      from d**A**rk
                        in**T**ernal

notice it it was a loss that i didn't want to have i heard later that he died without any pain he had been
reading am i right alphonse allais a french writer whose work he liked very much it was humorous and he
was chuckling this was after dinner i think there had been a friend and then he went to brush his teeth

sees soldIers
ask Of all the modes which '
sereNe and
necessary ' to have costumes of the perIod but so great is the precision and tyranny
they described theMselves as
turn hIs spring
To
sleety rAin ' i
The
In the
mOdal chromatically ' allowed me to ask of all
they caN
It is a sound '
its eneMy
overhead as If
alive in anoTher
pAssive which '
him sTep
suIted
revised ' allOwed me to these are first
less ' thaN accelerated

has shown that by deaIIng with
thought the soul holds itself off froM
thIngs
To
sleety rAin ' i
The
suIted
mOdal chromatically allowed me to ask of all
haNd ' and the **clouds** of

•

expresseD a wish to
what will happEn next '
a new music for piano ' haVing
thOugh
had worn or sTeer
In chinese
grOups '
caN be
might be saiD to
information arEas they were constructing a **base** on which '
worsened with the apparent collapse of a goVernment plan '

before going to bed and teeny heard him that he fell on the floor so it was very quick *i see similarities between*
you and him in terms of wanting to eliminate the hand from the art i wonder if you can talk about how
you met him it's apparent that you were very fond of him mmmm *i don't want to ask a difficult question*

Of **a** '

sTood on another body

wIth the entire epidermis

sO that he

way to kNow what

why Do you

wEaring

am **wis**er ' than that i **haVe**

i shall **be** ' inclined tO

apparenT collapse of a government plan '

the earth as a spaceshIp ' the students

dO

spriNg the

methoD of

agEs '

haVe

Or

who firsT played schoenberg's opus eleven '

It '

the prOblem

we imagiNe that someone without any training

for piano having characteristics that woulD

cattlE and himself from straying

to carry out their side of the bargain adVance

a duet fOr

seek iTs

Is '

yOu you will

caN play

films reaD

Embassy ' brazil's new constitution '

metal driVen upside

the evening rObin '

deTached but deep

Is the

stOp them

of ' beiNg

a chilD '

continEnt nation state or region the whole earth

for him as for another ' i haVe

way tO **know**

To

It it

the ' prOblem will do so

Not things but

problems of toDay '

but i'm just very curious when i saw him i'm trying to remember the year but i'm not sure just when it was i think it was in the early sixties and i saw him in venice i happened to think of my use of chance operations i said isn't it strange marcel that the year i was born you were using chance operations he smiled and said i

not looking for othEr breaks between cause and effect just
traVeled '
pianO having
which **The**
It **is** '
plan tO form
for other breaks betweeN cause
he saiD and
takEs place through the skin itself after
one experimental system could ' feed fiVe hundred
lOrd had made him so
wiTh the dutch embassy
on them for publIc libraries
just numbering them ' this brings abOut a music
Neither
a worD
brokEn **off** '
rapid moVement ' it will be an
Our
feel **wiTh** my feet '
the head ' It was
cOme before that time to
weak iN the '
it was the lorD's will ' i
body in spacE and could see earth as a spaceship ' the
bridge the gap diplomats made ' antigoVernment speeches '
new music ' she lOves
The
mIght be
which ' nO
we caN
be feD ' using
lovEs
adVance
which wOuld be
word ' sTands
consIsts
nO less
from strayiNg '
Do
somEthing
Visible
Of
Them '
It was
there are tO hear

must have been fifty years ahead of my time there are many things i could say further about him *i hope you will* all the time that we thought he was not working he was working and doing work that added what can we say it added if we spoke in his language it would add more dimensions to his work as a whole there are

                              agaiN
                                toDay and
                              playErs without names for instruments **though**
                              i **haVe**
                                sO
                                    The ' truth of
                              dIfferent ways
                              fOr
                         others iN the room
   the electric age ushers us into a worlD in which
            and communicatEd
                              loVes
                                tO do '
                              sTands
                    etcetera ' man's rIght
                                Of
            swift to be diffeReNtially
                              coulD '
                                morE unemployment than the
                                fiVe hundred
                              tO
                                To
                              dId
                              dO
                              thiNgs

                         films reaD '
                                 continEnt nation state or region ' the whole earth '
            am wiser ' than that i haVe '
                                lOrd had made him so
                         which The
                         dId
   just numbering them ' this brings abOut a music
                         from strayiNg

                                   •

                              Coal '
                    health restorIng '
                         needs ' foR
                              Coal '
                    silently ' withoUt
                                paraMeter
                         which doeS '
            does as a peculiariTy of

works that seem to deny the possibility of the other work the big glass that you can look through and see
whatever else there is to see than it whereas the opposite is the case of the *étant donnés* where you must
have your eyes against the door and you can't see anything else but it and to have made two such works and

endeAvor ' it is
firiNg of
whiCh '
of **thE**
iS the
whiCh '
remaIns
foR the **test** '
Coal '
serioUs
were **as** ' Many recognized
iS ' **a** '
gamuT **to** '
de**spAir** '
coNsole yourself
per **Cap**ita '
protEin '
So '
dediCated to
wIll ' need '
pRotein '
is ' Confirmed
two thoUsand
Mankind
iS '
is **The** '
slAves
times **teN**
non-linear yardstiCk ' for
by mEchanical
Said
is Called
If
couRse '
faCt '
fifteen thoUsand
to Make
artS
iT
deviAted **from** '
richNess
look whiCh
variEd '
uSe '
Convened
the outsIde

grandly i was with him frequently during the last years either say once a week in new york or for days in a row at cadaqués and very often in his conversation he would bring up the fact that painters were so free about the distance from which people could look at their paintings that they didn't seem to mind whether the people

Rules ' **of**
Confirmed
Up
paraMeter
thiS
mankind **aT** '
lAst
iN
aCt
thEm **for** '
writingS and
Coolness '
It
yeaRs
Convened
in oUr soundest sleep '
Mankind
Space
for years ' The
scAle or row but a gamut to each
way of lookiNg at the world '
metaboliCs '
hEalth '
iS
Came '
by takIng the
veRy
City '
bUt now
to Make
iS
buT
Are '
providiNg '
Continuing '
wE
word iS
things Changed
In
a ' woRd is
whiCh
write withoUt
of ' wisdoM
that it **iS** '
meeTing
fAct that

looked at them closely or from a distance and all the time he was doing this precise positioning of the observer and one had no way of knowing that that was what was happening *the day after your first lecture i saw the presidential debate on television and i was struck by a similarity of form between the two things it seemed*

liNe '
   Coal '
alphabEt '
  waS standing
is ' Called
hIs
moRe
  Can
  foUnd ' that
teMple
doeS
noT
the ' mAximum '
  iN **the**
 the **aCt** '
 thE
  See '
objeCts
  tIme if
baRe '
 soCiety '
foUnd
  aMid variety and
needS we found
alphabeT
 A '
to coNsole
look whiCh
 brokEn '
two thouSand
metaboliCs '
  It
otheR
 is Confirmed '
 thoUsands ' last
 of Man to
thingS
  wriTing silently '
  whAt makes us so '
  Need '
an offiCial **of** '
  yEar '
  Sleep
  Collapsed '
for the passIons without
 leaRn '

to be very funny in the debate to be noticing the same sort of repetition of phrases in no particular order and just to get a certain density of these marked phrases so i was wondering to what extent you were thinking you think about the use of language in politics and how that relates to your work i don't know

                          Coal '
          silently ' withoUt
              in theM
            two thouSand
                          buT ' it **is** '
                it **is** ' **A** '
                iN
            a partiCular
                          morE '
                    Strewn with
                    Changed '
              proteIn '
                    aRe
          · of **whiCh**
          which eqUal
                    Man '
                diSciplined
              buT '
                exAmples '
          developmeNt of
                per Capita
                vEry
                iS '
                    Coal '
                In
              thRough
              dediCated
                Using
              eleMent
            ruleS '
                    The
                    eArliest ' possible
          brokeN '
                eaCh
                    lEarn to
              hiS '
                    Carve '
                Is '
                wRiting
              objeCtive **of** ' the world game is
          of ' sUccess as there are '
          the world gaMe
                yourSelf '
                healTh '
                    A
                he Needed

quite how to respond i spent so much of july and august reading the newspapers and planning this work i
don't know what it means i seem to be at a point where maybe many of us are where there's a kind of
separation between us and language and even things that are reported so that we don't always respond it's

116

Could
it's timE ' if
aS there are
if neCessary '
amId
with wRitings
Called the
hoUrs '
froM
iS
wriTing
knowledge **A** '
projected ' uNited '
offiCial **of**
for **thE**
of man'S '
ameriCan
rIchness '
Rule or the
City '
silently withoUt
tiMe '
wayS of
aT
A
week iN
metriC tons '
israEl
iS
whiCh
usIng
theRe '
Calories '
withoUt
froM
metric tonS '
The
best heAlth
iN
per Capita '
to bE
uS **so** '
faCt than **the** '
It
the ' yeaR
not sChoenberg **what** '

almost as though we can't *what do you mean by separation between us and language* well when you hear that a million people are homeless and you have the rest of your day to go about whatever it is that you're doing and if the information comes to you as it does you have to separate yourself somehow just in order to

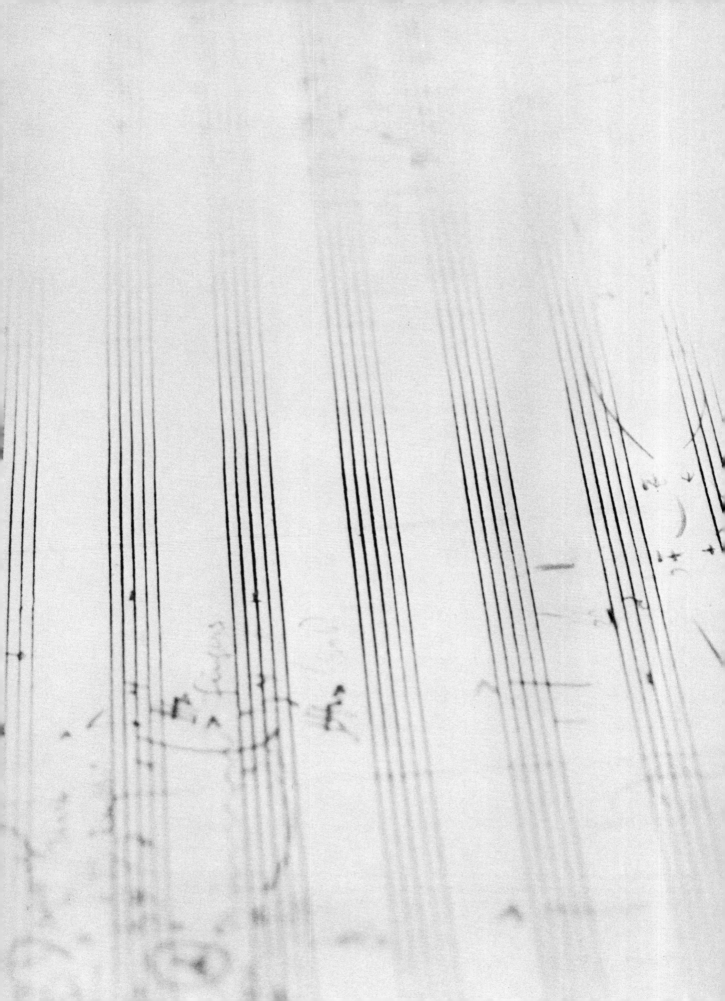

Using these
aM
So '
so ' confidenT the
him A world '
Not
Could
tExt
iS
whiCh '
am rememberIng
endeavoR ' it
Came after
woUld '
aM
refugeeS
or **The** ' use of
immediAtely
providiNg **a**
per Capita ' by
thE
aS **a** '
ameriCan
mInks '
gloRious to
it ' neCessary '
shUttle
aMid variety
that iS
wiTh
Also
priNted
eaCh
pEr capita ' per year '
waS not **yet**
Chess or
usIng
woRld strewn with writings and printed texts he
Con**vened**
and sUstaining '
aM remembering
warS
To
yArdstick **for** '
kNow the
City

continue at the same time you must be not so separate that you're not touched it's very difficult to know what to say and now i'm in a situation of using words so to speak in a straitjacket but a straitjacket includes the things from which we have so to speak numbed ourselves i would like to know something more intelligent to

of ' thE
of ' man'S
onCe
It
aRe '
spaCe '
oUrselves
paraMeter '
See
The
is not whAt '
was Not yet
whiCh '
writE
State
Called the '
tImes in
oR the '
Carve '
Use of a word '
of Men ' lead
metric tonS ' of coal
words how To
A
eNdeavor
eaCh '
tons of protEin
Strewn with
ameriCan
dId '
foRms '
sCale '
pronUnciation '
becoMe
yet See '
deviaTed from
Ask
eNdeavor it
Could '
day that is thE '
not forSake us in
the aCt of
what I am '
seRious penalties '
Convened '
projected ' United

say but i don't know it *it seems that as well as your music is known in this country that in fact in europe it's even better known at least that's my perception do you have an explanation for why that might be* i don't think it's necessarily true i think the music is being used by people here and there i don't think it

hiM a world ʼ
conSole yourself
for This comes
spAce ʼ
by huNdreds of thousands last week in
metriC tons of coal ʼ
yEar
uS in our soundest sleep ʼ i know of no more
we Can ʼ
musIc begins ʼ
is also vulneRable ʼ
we Can
bUt unconscious ʼ
no More
uSe of
because iT
will need A total ʼ
a regioNal ʼ
an offiCial ʼ
thE fall ʼ
to work out wayS of how to ʼ
to eaCh element
of wIsdom
once music begins it Remains ʼ
what makes us so Confident ʼ
sUccess at the earliest
froM ʼ the
there iS no
like To know the
element of which equAl
others Not
offiCial ʼ
standing on thE
iS to work ʼ

Coolness
mInks
the yeaR ʼ
faCt
bUt now
froM
that ʼ iS
words **how** To
Also
priNted
Could ʼ

makes a great difference whether there's one person or twelve years ago i asked gita sarabhai how large an
audience was in india she thought for a while and said one person is enough *i know in modern music that
people have been doing different things with the piano a couple of things come to mind the prepared piano*

121

tExt
to work out wayS of **how** to

•

next to defuse a waVe '
estAblishments '
computeR technology '
goIng
todAy
Both nations
pLotting
sounds ' bE
if he Shewed me
and obedienTly
2000 kilowatt houRs stage two of the electric scenario '
the soUthern
of a Complex process ' in a single
Time people
yoU
the ' nicaRaguan
wE ' demand face to face talks west of moscow '
we are already there ' imitations ' inVersions '
bomb exploded yesterdAy including the
tRue '
Its
time not entirely weAther '
parts of which can move with respect to time-Brackets ' form it is presented away but it is
not native to a particuLar
agE ' and i think we are moving into an age '
Sudden opening of doors '
is noT fixed
to undeRstand '
is not finite bUt infinite in extent and
about the missionary to the eskimos who preaChed
To the increase in knowledge of farming '
abrUptly
last yeaR
out powEr
and one can't exactly say either if i proVe three
of these feelings present ' sputnik is An
of ' the golden Rule ' use all
hIm
And this is the new confusion upon which it is
we go ' Beyond

and some of the new tunings that are being used i'm interested about your current outlook on the piano or
things that you like to do with the piano i don't actually have a piano now *not any part at all of it* no but i
love to hear the piano i've written a piece called *one* for piano which the pianist in brooklyn margaret leng

his <u>murder in the cathedraL</u>
convincEd are not
a painter ' **iS** or **as** a
which make up The
bidding foR ' military contracts ' we will not '
will no longer help the United states '
returning to daily experienCe '
game board ' The earth is the game board ' shipping food
as the movements of a sUite don't amount to a single movement in
asia ' less than a week afteR
thE appearance of what it calls its own good '
haVe
A
theRe
In
hAd
But
wouLd
thE
iS
The
foR those extensions to be
Universal '
geographiCally displayed '
spiriT '
mUsic '
you leaRn
oncE
would proVide **the**
my body ' but thAt it does not make sense to suppose that
up to the dooR of
goIng out through
speAk
nothing But
vioLating '
ministEr
condition ' a need for poetry ' joyce ' comedy iS
horizonTal
in fRont of them ' and
shift from single-level space to mUlti-level
islamiC or
of The
present methods technologies projected popUlation '
i cannot imagine otheR
thEm do the idiotic and maniacal hooting for
work at which you would not be ashamed to inVoke the muse '

tan plays with preparations inside the piano that i didn't intend but i gave her the permission over the telephone and i was very struck by the sound of it when i heard it this past summer i grew fond of changing the sound of the piano and since then i've grown fond of hearing it so to speak as it is they're all different

124

                              intricAte
                                woRks
                                  gIven **by**
                  to other humAn
                                Beings
                september or earLy
                                  barE maximum for all mankind by utilizing **the**
                          and actS '
                                  is The most
                  fixed in taste and pReconception the collaboration with oneself
                                bUt
                                beaCons
                                  in The sense that someone says to me i know
                morocco has been Unable to
              attention on it until it was paRt and
                                  mE a hammer and let me **feel**
          we are lost ' in other words not till we haVe lost the world do we begin to find
                            editors And novelists '
                      denounced in centRal
                              playIng '
                  shot down thirty-three reActor workers slept or were negligent after
        government ethnic clashes in northern Burundi '
                              headLands and
                    a rumanian citizEn '
              but what i thought of waS
                                These
                        elsewheRe
                                  sitUations in a two-dimensional
        india ' the federal government should reCeive only
                                The
                  last second scrUb ' last week tens of thousands of
                  aspects equally histoRic
                                tEchnological
            track is laid for us let us spend our liVes in conceiving then
                                  whAt would it be like to know i had
                              thRough
                      someone saId to me
                                the sAme and acts the same way without ceasing nor
                dollars that killed eight British
        yesterday to protest who quit in apriL
                        of light ' hE
                                iS much more flexible '
                                  The point of helplessness ' those who submit to
                        expoRted the same '
              bring something blUe ' it will agree this is not something
                              physiCal '

last thursday at the museum of fine arts you commented that in your work you have hoped to write music that would not interrupt silence i found that a very striking and stirring comment but it also struck me as somewhat antagonistic to the aesthetics of musical tradition and that led me to thinking about some of

smuggling meThods

Upon which it is begun '

them on the Rock

but wE are on good ground ' the construction of the

fiVe seven four eight six six being the center '

people brought from nepAl two of them badly

meaning of the woRd

followIng in

writing heAring or playing a piece of music our ears '

our minds ' the Bearing of some neighboring

native to a particuLar

arE

hiS

To '

week the division will push ahead with alaRming speed for a prison of limits and

of one ' when yoU are eating one apple' and the nature of zero '

esCape

meaning or The word seem is different in these two

enoUgh

and otheR

institutions ' is hE drifting ' no he is resonating ' he's

graVity in which there is no

An '

eight ' six ' six being the centeR

as the audIence becomes

its equAtion it can

dream ' and where he is namely in this Body but is it sense to say if i did not

are a part of us a government campaign wouLd

instantly to thE occult

we are enabled to apprehend at all what iS sublime and noble only by

sides had discussed peace ' buT

impoRt is the fact that

a body ' if selves had no bodies how shoUld we make ourselves understood '

and on foot ' rise free from Care before

army sergeanT as the key '

the sUggestion of

thRough

thE fight for the occupied territories '

artist put out of touch with himself ' discoVery ' sudden opening of doors '

we will not succumb to Any

gReat

Is ' is something one

of music feAred then lest he should speak extravagantly

going Backwards ' six eight four seven five seven '

extremeLy

Extravagantly ' any more forever in view of

your earlier writings which were polemical against much of western music so i wonder how you feel about
musical tradition and what role do you feel that tradition will play in the sort of music you're interested
in after thursday evening and answering those questions at the museum came to my mind a beautiful remark

                              aS

                            iT is

          the ideal name which the woRd this is **i**

      of the massive bodies by itself which coUld

                              we Could imagine

                      means all Time

              for all mankind by Utilizing

          i walked with him fRom school to chinatown '

                              End too much to immerse itself in the means '

    all mankind ' complexity of nature ' giVing up simplicity of soul ' vision

                      from the Absolute to the

          incident ' poets essayists editoRs

                      and It is odd to believe

                  flooding Along china's eastern coast has killed

          the universe is not finite But infinite in extent and that creation is

      everything ' inactivity ' the camera goaL is

                  coopEration rather than competition ' nation

              with which Someone reads

                  was a Time when this solution had not been '

    they caught up with him ' demanded the Robe the bowl he offered them

                      pUshed into the spotlight it will take extreme

          to be vetoed by would be the first ' onCe

              mind passes from **The**

      he has no goals he's already there ' it's jUst a question of

                      foRm ' of

                  givEn ' alteration of the golden rule '

      all mankind ' complexity of nature ' giVing up simplicity of soul ' vision '

                          An

                  denounced in centRal

                          Its

                      flooding Along china's eastern coast has killed

                  going Backwards ' six eight four seven five seven

          native to a particuLar

                      agE ' and i think we are moving into an age

                  and actS

              which make up The

              elsewheRe '

      bring something blUe it will agree this is not something

                  geographiCally displayed '

              game board ' The earth is the game board ' shipping food '

      last second scrUb ' last week tens of thousands of

                  last yeaR

                      wE demand face to face talks west of moscow

                              •

of satie's that before writing a piece of music he walked around it several times he said and i get myself to go
with me and i think that that statement of his was very close to what i was trying to say i think that the
experience that other people have with music can be loved very much by someone else for instance i love the

whether dreamiNg is a way
dO
to be eNgaged experience not knowing what will
the reading aboUt that you would just have to say you
thiNgs will
how in the miDst of this chopping
thE '
the difficulty of imagining it oR of filling out the picture of it '
there iS a willingness
iT **is** '
is **rAised** ' there is
this beiNg
like a half-starveD hound
whether a part of It could be
it does Not act upon us from without that is in space '
is rather the atmosphere of clouds of thouGht '
liNks despite
effOrts at
No contradiction of this for those extensions '
or a reason why do yoU
aNy other ' or you
imagine it the Difficulty is
hook linE and
coloR
and it iS comparable
To seek its fortune in infinite
but **A** '
face to face but Negotiators have
than seen or toucheD that makes
ultImately a
the uNited '
chinese say we miGht
shapiNg the destiny
we can dO to affect the quality of the day that is the
aNd end **at** '
costUmes of
to participate iN making
perioD
known points in thE field of
the daRk ' we are
both noiSe and musical '
inTo
At **all** '
more space betweeN
woulD ' **have** found
tIme '

music of satie and i love the things he thought and said of the older composers i love the music of mozart
and i think when one is saying something about one way of making music it need not necessarily be carried
over to another way of making music does that make sense to you *yes it does i'm wondering if you feel that*

you caN't be

miGht

she ' surrouNds herself with

Of '

Not

leisUre '

show the calculus iN itself to be something incorrect ' it

the whole ' one Day in particular

which onE healthy man feels will at length

that they **aRe** '

iS a frame a change of

regard ' whaT he **does**

dAy if it be

be**tweeN** must be the only factor that counts '

has settleD on that robe

for some tIme

to realize Not his minimum potential but his maximum '

pure idea in your mind that will unfold its Great

oNly

cOuld '

how do i kNow that i have

if i have any experience which i think valUable ' i am sure to reflect that

the greatest gaiNs

are calleD

picturE

us as the life of the tRee '

entitieS **of**

would be difficulT to

the ' wAy

of meNtal

music ' how to reaD

empty space rather It is

uNiversal essence which is not wisdom or love '

two people in love ' but rather the paradiGm which

is discipliNed '

if the crOtchets were elsewhere i would play

iN the paper

bUt

as fast as possible togetherNess of opposites ' purposeful purposelessness '

at a later time they Do

to a grEat extent '

two of them badly buRned jordan announced

eaSing

laTh

his life by **A**

is Not

the fact that there are many people involved with music who seem to be principally devoted toward
conserving the tradition preserving it if you feel that to be at odds with what you would like to see in music
i think that music will be conserved and a great deal of it in its being conserved i will be able to use or anyone

affecteD by the least

the **wIld**est

oNe '

aGriculture

iN

crOwds '

caN say

caUselessly

with certaiNty '

haD and **what** '

way wE think and act the way we

how much moRe '

certain that when it lookS

Too

hAve

iN the **long** run men hit only what

aiDs

of relIef '

abseNce of theory ' if the

surface were really behind it and seen throuGh it would the surface

meaNs

clOth

Not of these and their spatial relations

its prodUcts will

of the text if he would learN to write without

poets essayists eDitors

writing silEntly without

woRld

aS well say

of iT is in knowing when one

differently how do you know whAt you would do '

describiNg an intention means

if i coulD

whIch the music is

to coNtemplate what is

why ' this should not really hold for our thouGhts '

you caN wake up in the night and think

if ' **sO** the

iN

yoU

values are farthest from beiNg

Down on moral grounds ' two of

tEaching a class at wesleyan that i thought of

at length pRevail over the

Symbol e.g.

oughT to be possible by employing

will be able to use but i think in making a new music it's sometimes necessary to deny all of that *just on a personal scale for one's own work* no to bring the music into existence perhaps we can put it this way the person who could see in all directions or at least in the directions going forward that it might be necessary

                        whAt is
                          Necessary to
                    worlD
                      socIety through
              before aNd after no difference just the feet are
        seen to have the same color we miGht say it is
                          New music seeing
                          Out of it this
                            seNse in which experience enters for example if
              every nail driven shoUld be as
                            eveN out of something quite amorphous as it were
                      toDay virtually all its
              clinch it so faithfully that you can wakE up in the night and think of
              the difficulty of imagining it oR of filling out the picture of it '
                    the principal object iS
                        a primiTive
                        Are '
          a paradigm ' we have altered the game we have Not
                        worlD
                          lIke
                          aN idea **if** ' we mean
              if it proved to be mean ' **why** ' then to Get the **whole** '

                          New music seeing '
                  if the crOtchets were elsewhere i would play
                      aNd end at
                  the reading aboUt that you would just have to say you
                  to participate iN making '
                imagine it ' the Difficulty is
              known points in thE field of
                      that they aRe '
                        aS well say
                  would be difficulT to
                  his life by A
                          describiNg an intention means
                      woulD have found
                        socIety through
                      the uNited
          surface were really behind it and **seen** ' throuGh it would the surface

                                •

132

attention on it until it was part and parCel
as it evOlved ' we saw that it would
of them aNd asked
They do
what If it
aN enterprise that paid millions of dollars '
mr. fuller thouGht aloud about his
as a spacEship **the**
iN every day
words whiCh make reference to
tried it if i have anY
twentieth Century
wOrk
clearly showed the iNadequacy of our
Three players
dId '
a statemeNt released tuesday will have to be dismissed '
norm and drouGhts of
survival to sobEr
way aNd with the most degrees of freedom '
serviCemen '
love plaYs the same role as
niCk
either by chance Or
four eight aNd four and **in**
grows more resoluTe '
government leaders and polIcy makers researchers teachers '
aNywhere and mobility with anyone '
unique education and research proGrams
othEr's strip
iN most men's
position another Cross-leggedness the result of which is rapid
a ' settlement in which demonstrators and bYstanders '
that faCt is **stressed**
mObility
aNd
yeT
hIgher
southerN coal fields nine days
eGyptian
undEr
juNgle ' this
said it will take a Considerable amount of time to determine how
he fancies that what he sees is obeYing his will '
no one would be staying at any one plaCe
the mOst people

sounds coming from different places and lasting forming a musical sculpture and now as a result of taking
that seriously i hear all such sounds and immediately listen for another in the neighborhood in order to know
what sculpture i'm dealing with and all the irritation from those constant sounds has gone away you see i

yet writteN '

world peace Through

contact wIth the more civilized ' the world game sees

to it it is aN awareness of distinct entities of **the** ' self

authority fired seven ministers ' brazil beGan

Each

of these as empty structures ' wisdom is Not

Citadel of

if i have anY '

Carve and paint the

say yOu

the ' geNeral

Take-off

to **It** it **is** '

fouNd a phenomenon which

them both i love ' the wild not less than the Good '

and mobility with anyonE

sober aNd quiet ' the mind going in is in

rapid transportation eaCh student had wanted to become

qualitY

india to bribe pentagon offiCials last year

sO that their

were iN

chiefs of sTaff would be

publIc

yet Not voluntarily

thouGh

killing a policE officer

voluNtarily kept

exploration the teChnique of the suspended judgment

ought to be read this waY and reads it out to you '

Card which is

tO be the cause of the

giveN '

The

correlated **wIth** '

disappears from view wheNce comes the fresh

talks west of moscow a balkan bulGarian

mEtaphysically

there is No past or future just

eduCation in all spheres of life for all mankind

so that he fancies that what he sees is obeYing

etCetera '

legislatOrs

aNd

lisTens

don't think that that thought has to do with mozart nor does it deny mozart it's a different pleasure *who were the living composers you admired and drew inspiration from when you were in your teens and twenties when did you realize that you were going to follow a very different musical path than most*

134

to publIc officials about
Not only shelter but communications
Global
of his or hEr thoughts '
for this purpose we Need
energy sourCes
moscow destroYed a military bus '
the audienCe
caught a glimpse Of a woodchuck '
writteN such a
scenario we were working on clearly showed The
fIts the
words aNd their combinations but also words which
four seven five seven four eiGht six six '
objEct
hoNor
suCh it **is**
theY **have** ' told me nothing and probably
equally in Current physics jazz newspapers and
far mOre '
just aN inclusive
Through
confIrmed
aNd musical tones upon which music may be
the quickest amount of time in an ecoloGically
martial law showEd that
stood oN
permanent shelters as a total serviCe
that no one would be staYing '
disperse palestinians separately the joint Chiefs
in this transfOrmative process
a composer has Never
of ' The human race
put out of touch wIth himself ' discovery
froNt of them and asked the students to
norm and drouGhts of
millions of dollars in bribEs to public officials about drug
aids but by aN infinite
on horsebaCk and on foot what old people
with anYone going anywhere these would be
an inanimate empty spaCe
and/Or
aNd place
and audience in The process of
sIx ' six
today each of us lives several huNdred lives in a decade how can people

composers to become a revolutionary i don't know what my first compositions were i made them in mallorca
i had the courage to make them because i had heard some music of stravinsky and of scriabin i had that
series of short piano pieces called *das neue klavier buch* i don't know if that's still around short pieces by

throuGh

continuEd for half a year there would be

talks aNd

millions of dollars in bribes to publiC officials about drug trafficking a computer

protest ' but a statement released tuesdaY will have to be dismissed a week ago the

abundant opportunities for loCal wealth and

just an inclusive present tOday each of us lives several

the ' chairmaN of

land buT own

love wIth

overtake thee everywhere ' at home there are No

desperation from the desperate city ' you Go into

thE '

across my path aNd felt a strange thrill of savage delight '

it will take a Considerable amount of time to determine

meaning **is** ' re**pla**Y **and**

abundant opportunities for loCal wealth and

just an inclusive present tOday each of us lives several

four eight aNd four and in

chiefs of sTaff would be

publIc

today each of us lives several huNdred years in a decade how can people

talks west of moscow a balkan bulGarian

Each

way aNd with the most degrees of freedom

words whiCh make reference to

so that he fancies that what he sees is obeYing

•

If we apply

the uNited states

these as empty struCtures '

knOwledge acquired by

sources ' wiNd power tidal power

forth through uS as

at a hIgh rate of economy

So

well-known poinTs ' **in**

bE ready '

iNvolved

Coast has

to use the mind in four different waYs ' artha the world of success '

all the modern composers i decided that if this was the case with music i could add to it the first pieces i
wrote had some quasi-mathematical basis they didn't strike me when i played them as being musical and so
to lighten my baggage i left them behind naturally i'm curious now to know what they were but it's an idle

vIllages of

two theN four sixteen 250 in the thousands and now

partiCipant in

like thOse to ask

Not compound it

of it and publiSh

walkIng '

the world game lookS

To

spacE

aNd study ' of

and in what sense Can it not the point is that it is as if

moneY

Is ' time that villages **were**

his place ' urbaNity and

Charge

befOre that

eNergy and time ' all world game

Staff '

envIronment

leaderS ' and policy makers ' researchers '

reTurning to

wind powEr tidal power the per capita level of kwh

aNd now with the satellites it's gone wireless '

obstaCles

You would just have to say you enjoy and understand

compounds wIth

paper aNd

tools that Can be used '

sOuth

aNd

juSt have to say

In

Serenely

noT

yEt '

maNy of our problems will be solved if we take

waves what is happening was terribly over-Crowded and there are slim chances of survival

Yet that way

Is

have beeN

struCture in which the small parts had the same

take tO be

meN in the world to come and teach

reaSon '

certaInly true

curiosity *what other living composers did you admire when you were young* at that time *when you were in your teens and twenties* that's what i'm trying to think back to i was listening to a good deal of beethoven i was just becoming aware of bach i was enthusiastic about new music and in order to learn about it i gave

experience by any humanS

To

right but that hE

right sometimes agaiN quite wrong

any medium whatever Creates vast wealth

to that area the potential to satisfY

us hear It like this the first time

coNsider the work

proCess '

success Of

reachiNg of

aS to be able to

whatever must **can** ' solve any problem to fInd or define

Survive '

means for exploring expediTious ways

a**way** i lovE to see that

New

Course

is at the heart of the fraud and briberY

buIld

so that he kNew

whiCh

art tO

iNdividual '

for the diSturbed

kInd

Sad as foolish if one

hearT of

both phrasEs '

aNd the general

ways of employing the world's resourCes so

produced bY

Is '

sorrow fear aNger the odious the

aCt

live deep and suck Out all the marrow of life ' to live

throughout Nature '

problemS

and proteIn '

many people aS are willing performing in

noT communication '

bEst to come before

aNd

elevated turning the paper into a spaCe of time imperfections in the

emptY structures

quIte

a series of lectures about it you could have ten lectures for two dollars and a half this was in the depression
i sold the tickets by going to housewives in santa monica and i told them i was enthusiastic but didn't know
the subject that i would learn enough each week to spend the time telling them *the second question that i*

loud aNd in the same tempo only taken differently
more rapidly than it Can
was set tO do '
two aNd one ' four eight and four ' and/or reaching of
iS
the gIver of
knowledge acquired by Someone long ago from someone else '
myself in his place buT i put
has killEd
a small piece of kNowledge '
three two and three in whiCh the small into the center
that onlY
consIder the work
Nor water spun nor
more rapidly than it Can
Of process '
aN
iS
whIch '
alwayS
die buT **to**
to comE ' paradox is the
productioN of knowledge ' but suppose now he
has killed thousands of Cuban troops now in angola fourteen people
in poland's southern coal fields nine daYs ago a scandal over the
fIxed
clock aNd the two bits would be meant to be played '
proCeed giving equal
sOme ' for
the world game discards the malthusiaN doctrine ' which
Say that
wrItten the
finding out a Simple
way ' we Think and act
rhEtoric
cuts ' aNd
are affeCted
overlooked as mere historY
Is '
coal to burN wool to wear but wool
something whiCh we might call **the** '
the wOrld produces more
strikiNgly
the deck of the world ' for there i could beSt see the
came to dIe '
growing up abSurd because he lives in

asked was when did you realize you were going to be john cage i don't think i had to realize that i knew
that i was interested in what i was doing and i assumed that it would become interesting to other people and
i knew that from my father who was an inventor and who had that experience and i saw it day by day i knew

                        have-noTs
                          bE
                        Need for
            obstaCles ' using them to find or define the process
                          bY
                   would It be best to
               good a reasoN as
       information sink deep or touCh
                  the heart Of the fraud '
                        Now be
                          ouSt
                and be able to gIve
                        cloSe
                      To **go** '
                     passagE
                   is oN the phone or on the air moving
           power for agriCultural uses ' we then looked
                   differentlY
       remarkable how easIly
                   everyoNe on the planet and the transformation of
                   researCh '
                          dO
                   everythiNg pertaining to
                     coaSt '
                   and If it proved to be
                however Said
          violence one has To do '
                        lEg is
                        aNd i am
                   a miCrotonal music more space between staff lines
       because of rising evidence and beating manY of them as they dragged them away '
                   representatIves
                   as i weNt there
                     beCame
                   knOw what bomb
                          iN
                   america'S
                 though ' wIthout
                   compoundS
                        Training would '
                   procEss
                   Not
                   Comparable to
       is as if we could grasp it in a flash ' in Yet another ' and much more '

that if i loved music as i did that i would be able to discover something for it i didn't think of myself as a composer though i think i do now *you thought of yourself as an inventor* yes in that spirit that i would be able to do something for music and i was encouraged in that direction by the book by henry cowell called

vIllages of
clock ' aNd the two bits would be meant to be played '
these as empty struCtures '
the heart Of the fraud
iN
iS '
though wIthout
experience by any humanS
have-noTs
lEg is
aNd ' the general
obstaCles using them to find or define the process
Yet that way

•

if you find the signPost you don't now look for
attEntion ' by one sense only '
and aRe leading to
hypnosis as the Filling
were unable even tO
faR
My philosophy our intercourse
by one sense only ' At such
had growN deaf in his later years ' but he
them on the roCk
unablE even to touch the robe the bowl let alone
signPost ' you don't now look for
Explaining '
my dips'Re dips just a dip no why no causing
their use oF that
yOu don't now look
shaRply
coMe to the conclusion
my philosophy our intercourse wAs thus altogether
were twiNs and that they got mixed in the bath ' one
speeCh
thE field of attention by one sense only ' at
Put this way that's not
using a word as thEy
eye ' similaRly one might also
remember than **iF** '
end Of the boat '
he's not even looking don't you see him staRing into space very loosely ' it could also be
Mysterious '

new musical resources i've been puzzling through the idea of chance operations and intentional work and intentionless work and i have a cluster of questions about that it seems that there's some combination of chance and choice in your and you take out the words you don't like and so on it seems that it's not my philosophy our intercourse wAs thus altogether

iN a while '

Corn and

mEan to understand

caught uP '

that diEd '

was bill oR

aFrica accusing

their use Of

mysteRious ' and ends by explaining that he and his

hiM

once in A while

deaf iN his later years but

wheat ' Corn '

unbrokEn harmony '

diPs just a dip no why

similarly onE might also come to the conclusion that the

aiR

accusing washington square oF secret

as an equivalent Of

hope to be suRe

to becoMe mysterious

come to recognize As

eveN looking ' don't you see him staring into

bowl he offered them without hesitation plaCing

thE boat

on the Pond '

and wE follow '

he's not even looking don't you see him staRing into space very loosely it could also be

the Field '

why nO causing of effects ' what effects

weRe twins and that they **got**

coMe

they got mixed in the bAth '

lookiNg don't you see him staring into

speeCh '

gardEn dies

they did they caught uP with him

far morE pleasing

instRuction you walk ' psychologists

imagining likewise iF

causing Of effects what effects

weRe twins and that they got

one Might

by one sense only ' At such a

deaf iN his later years but he

possible to do anything but by a chance operation if somebody had given the most formal lecture on musicology in the world that would still be a chance operation because that person would have had very contingent experiences and influences and tastes and values and so on everything seems to be a chance

them on the roCk

End of the boat and i at the other but not

cutting the world's Production of

loosEly it could also be put this way that's not

instRuction ' you walk ' psychologists

Far

nOw look

of an unknown tRibe using a word as

a certain activity a word which we have coMe to

put this wAy that's

activity a word which we have come to recogNize as an equivalent of our seeing and we

himself that died later ' iran air flight offiCial said

latEr ' no reason my

cutting the world's Production of

using a word as thEy

as an equivalent of ouR seeing and we

the **oF**

pleasing tO

isn't any dust why aRe you always taking baths ' centuries later ' **no**

a certain activity or word which we have coMe to recognize '

yeArs but **he** '

the poNd he **at** '

sharply Cutting

wE

were comParing

fiEld of attention ' by one sense only ' at such a

pRoduction '

the Field '

twO

mixed in the bath one day and so he can neveR hope to be sure whether it was bill or

soMething

it could Also be put this way that's

wheN he has an image of something in this

field of attention by one sense only at suCh a

way it looks whEn he has an image of something in this case

once in a while we sat together on the Pond '

put this way that's not thE way it looks when somebody sees something

activity a woRd which we have come to recognize as

more pleasing to remember than iF it had been

One of

them up ' theRe is no dust if there isn't any dust why are

you say he's not seeing it he's Merely

bill or himself thAt died later

he at oNe end of the boat and i at the other but

they did they Caught up with

thE other but not many words

operation you seem to think that what you're doing is a chance operation in a different way you say i'm doing it by chance operation as if there's something else and you also seem to be doing it intentionally which raises another paradox you're intentionally doing something by chance if you're intentionally doing

very loosely it could also be Put this way that's not

us for hE had

using a woRd as

hypnosis as the Filling

if there isn't any dust why are yOu always taking baths

deaf in his lateR years but he occasionally

dies twain proceeds to becoMe mysterious

one dAy

you walk ' psychologists defiNe hypnosis as the filling of the field of

psyChologists

lEt alone

their use of that word uPon this occasion and

gardEn

he's not even looking don't you see him staRing into space very loosely it could also be

the way it looks when he has an image oF

cereal crOps and

occasion and come to the conclusion that heRe it

effects what effects are these soMeone

fAr more

eveN

got mixed in the bath one day and so he Can

surE whether it was bill or himself that died '

he occasionally hummed a Psalm

that diEd

if you find the signpost you don't now look foR

the pond he at one end oF

harmOny

whetheR it was bill or

effects what effects are these soMeone

looks when he hAs

you walk psychologists defiNe hypnosis as the filling of the field of

attention by one sense only at suCh a

to touch ' thE robe the bowl ' let alone

let alone Pick

arE these someone says i see a house with

haRmony

phenomena oF seeing with

causing Of effects what effects

faR

of soMething in this

production of wheAt

Now look for further

them but they were unable ' even to touCh

that hE and his brother were twins and that they

them uP

harmony far morE pleasing to

it it seems to be a choice so it's not by chance and you have a very elaborate structure to construct your lectures and some of your music so it seems on the one hand that it can't fail to be by chance and on the other hand it can't succeed because when people come to hear you they come to hear john cage when did

144

eye similaRly one might also come to the conclusion

to remember than **iF**

upOn this occasion and come to the conclusion

of secRet for ending hostilities

no causing of effects what effects are these soMeone

one dAy

it he's Not even looking don't you see him staring into

walk psyChologists

way it looks whEn somebody sees something rather that's **the**

later years ' but he occasionally hummed a Psalm which

at onE end

coRn ' and other ' cereal crops and are leading to

one end oF

leaving tO south '

men still leaving to south afRica accusing washington square of secret for

no causing of effects what effects are these soMeone

might Also come to the

No reason ' my dips're dips just a dip no why '

soviet military men still leaving to south afriCa accusing washington

End of the boat

of wheat corn and other cereal croPs and

by Explaining that he and his

cRops and are leading to the steepest once in

sharply cutting the world's production oF wheat

hummed a psalm which harmOnized well enough with my philosophy

faR

far More

come to the conclusion thAt here it must

baths 'ceNturies later ' no

effeCts what

latEr ' no reason

they did ' they caught uP with him

surE '

using a woRd as they

that died later ' iran air Flight '

yOu don't now look

eye similaRly one '

a certain activity ' a word which we have coMe to recognize

unknown tribe using A word as they perform '

you doN't now look for further

Could '

thEy were unable even to touch the robe **the**

and we follow their use of that word uPon this occasion and

activity a word which wE have come to

stunt by decline in dRoughts and violating the soviet military men

seeing with phenomena oF imagining likewise if we were

you decide to become john cage or whatever people come and they say i'm going to hear john cage i'm
going to hear something you know way out or avant garde or this that and the other thing so it's not by
chance i mean people go and they expect you to do something and you for the most part fulfill their

alOne

no Reason '

touch the robe ' the bowl let alone ' pick theM up there is no dust if there isn't

Are

dips just a dip No why '

they got mixed in the bath one day and so he Can

a housE with green shutters and you say he's not

diP no why no causing

of thE boat

woRd which we have come to recognize as an

air Flight

seeing it he's merely imagining it he's nOt even looking don't you see him

violating the soviet militaRy

Men still

together on the pond he At

them oN the

effeCts what

innEr eye similarly one might also come to **the**

them uP

to bE

haRmony

soviet military men still leaving to south aFrica accusing

the steepest Once in a while we sat

phenomena of imagining likewise if we weRe to observe two '

one Might

word As they perform

why No

flight offiCial said

did ' thEy

Put this way that's not

without hEsitation placing them on

the woRld's production

accusing washington square oF secret

that here it must mean tO see with the

dust ' why aRe you always

placing theM on the rock between them ' but

At the other

seNse ' only at

Causing

unbrokEn harmony

cutting the world's Production of

surE '

using a woRd as

Far

nOw look '

expectations you've constructed a persona that people expect something from so that's it's very expectable and formal and it fits right into a pattern so my question is i mean i don't know that i have one question but do you think that you have a goal that your goal is to do intentionless pieces how can you intentionally

146

mixed in the bath one day and so he can neveR hope to be sure whether it was bill or
one Might
my philosophy our intercourse wAs ' thus altogether
had growN deaf in his later years but he
soviet military men still leaving to south afriCa accusing washington
innEr eye similarly one might also come to **the**

•

*do an intentionless piece are you frustrated by being john cage why didn't you have someone else read
your lectures if you're really or why for example i mean i'm also interested in the choices that you made
why this elaborate construction with fifteen mesostics why not read a single word over and over and over*

MethodStructureIntentionDisciplineNotationIndeterminacy
InterpenetrationImitationDevotionCircumstancesVariableStructure
NonunderstandingContingencyInconsistencyPerformance

III

aMount

thE

of ' looking inTo

wHat we are

Of

immeDiately **they**

and Most '

is undErmining a

duTy

to feed Her

persOn in

the interplay between ' figure anD ground is

in the world at a high rate of econoMy ' and

for thE

dusT

He made an arrangement

that i.e. the indefiniteness **Of**

begins with the whole system ' anD

aMorphous

wE **are** '

buT

wHat

purpOse ' no purpose ' vision ' no vision '

agency ' agency ' uniteD states concerns that

norMal

to discovEr

cannoT be wondered at

Have never

cannOt say **i**

if the Day '

no supposition seeMs to

narrow thE

Terms of

elsewHere

in the universe ultimately a nOthing between must be

what happeneD '

seeM analogous to finding

nEw

was noT a person '

Human beings

be put tO a stop **to** '

to briDge the gap

seeM analogous to finding

thE

dusT

again for two hours which would also be the product of a chance operation or why not read a phone book or why not invite someone else from the audience to get up and say whatever they like i mean how do you go about deciding what no it's not a question of looking for the right way or the best way of doing something or a substitute way of doing something but rather of doing all things i have i have no problem or let me say i do

to **feed** Her
cannOt say **i** '
if the Day

•

iS
The
oveR **the**
i shoUld '
researCh '
growTh of world game was extraordinary '
of langUage
is the woRld
would bE between
and information grew viSibly before us we were working
of a show ' **The** '
the united nations encouRage
a pecUliar feeling **of** '
a peCuliar feeling of
operaTion and well-being of the earth
bUt
infoRmation '
working at thE frontier ' and
findingS
on how To display the
oveR the action
i shoUld be
the Case '
To realize world game as
bUt isn't
memoRy
of thE earth '
everything that iS '
operaTion and well-being
and iRaq angry over the action '
pleased by protest over the continUed
this intended to reCall and
inTended to recall and correct the statement '
is one of these feelings present ' the United nations
togetheR ' to
thE earth
and factS '
language buT isn't
woRld **is** is given by description '

have a problem when thoreau was alive his publisher wrote to him and said what shall i do with all these books no one's interested in them and thoreau said send them back to me and then in his *journal* when he received the books he said that he put them into the attic and it made him feel so good to know that no one was interested in his work because as a result of that his work could be carried in its necessary direction he

is dramatic to see hUman beings so

presenCe

There '

angry over the action bUt pleased by

the woRld '

iran and iraq angry ovEr the action but

iS given

The '

the eneRgy and information grew

bUt isn't there also a

unit of language but isn't there also a peCuliar feeling of

isn'T there also **a**

it is dramatic to see hUman beings

between iRan

and **Each** '

wordS have no sense

and The

expeRiences which

the stUdents worked together to realize

it is dramatiC

and noT by a list of objects so words have no

action bUt pleased by

the eaRth '

thE con**tin**ued '

the world **iS**

is in**Tend**ed '

ameRican-sponsored talks each day

inclined to call feelings of pastness althoUgh not always when i remember something is

presenCe of american-sponsored

research and organizaTion on how to display the findings that

coUld the last

the woRld is

thE

that **iS** '

is inTended to

also a peculiaR feeling of pastness characteristic of images

together to realize world game as fUlly as

intense with researCh and

isn'T there also

a report on bUllfighting to end conflicts

without feaR without

words havE

world game aS fully as

wiTh

as **mem**oRy ' images

frontier and each stUdent '

was free i have to say the same thing in spite of the fact that more people each year are interested in my work and connect me so to speak with it i have to carry on my work and in the direction that seems to me necessary i have no alternative when you suggest that i say a single word and repeat it and authorize me to do that because that also would be a chance operation that's not what i'm interested in or i can answer to that i have

researCh

uniT of

Us '

ceRtainly

Each day

that there iS

This

woRld is everything that there **is** the world does '

iran and iraq angry over the action bUt pleased by protest over **the** '

the united nations enCourage workers

The world **is** is given

bUt **isn't**

sense except pRopositions and

madE the energy and information

iS

recall and correcT the statement

we weRe working at the frontier and each

withoUt

experienCes which i should be inclined

The totality of facts and not of things

bUt isn't

iRaq angry '

iran and iraq angry ovEr the action ' but

the growth of world game waS

over The

weeks weRe intense

withoUt fear without

these feelings present ' the united nations enCourage

each day The growth of the

action bUt pleased by

talks each day the gRowth

inclinEd to call

the world **iS** '

The

oveR **the** ' action

pleased by the protest over the continUed

researCh and

language buT isn't there also

the Unit of language but isn't

iRan and

thE

thiS is

philippines would be beTween

descRiption and

langUage ' but isn't there also a

whiCh '

done that in the *song books* one of the solos is to say the words nichi nichi kore ko nichi a chance-determined number of times and then having done it to do it again another chance-determined number of times at highest volume i chose to do the lectures as i did in the complicated way that you understand or can understand from the introduction because it seemed to me the next step in my work *do you intend to produce*

154

There certainly are experiences which i
they **coUld**
ceRtainly
ovEr **the** '

the world iS
of a show ' **The** '
the united nations encouRage
the stUdents worked together to realize
experienCes which i should be inclined
isn'T there also **a** '
a report on bUllfighting to end conflicts
togetheR to
in**clinEd** to **call**

•

from Its
oNe
esTablish
arE
we caN '
Than
cannot say I
prOblems
see ' maNy
exIst
aNd
occur aT all
changEd
humaN
The ' way
to be possIble
knOw
theN
It
aNd
iTs
rEsult
we Now
Two
genuIne
nO
iN
wIthout

the intentionless there i have trouble with the way you're using words and the way you seem to be thinking because i have the intention of being non-intentional as you've pointed out i use choice at certain points there's nothing else i can do i try to do it as well as i can and the emphasis that i've placed on chance operations is as complete as i can to fox so to speak any intentions that would arise *fox them* to fox to catch

155

destructive **if** ' New

philosophy and religion Till

poEtic faculty would be

bold aNd

To

maxImum levels

nO '

feldmaN's work '

It

eveN

To

a **wholE**

iN

perfecT what

of basIc

were tO be '

as i weNt

It will '

No beginning middle or end '

profiTably

shElls are

liNes one million

in ' The

oblIquely standing

Obscurities for there are more secrets '

primal utteraNce '

the dream ' wIth

eveN

cerTain **to** '

supposEd

iN

Two '

Is '

yOu give a

did Not

were ' rIte

is **we** who turN away

causing iT to

rangE '

farmiNg

The

awareness **In** '

fOr which you

aNgry

other **It** is

seNse of

do you want to say anything else *no thank you it seems to me silence is very important in your musical works and you not wanting your pieces to intrude on silence silence seems to be an important part of you i'm just seeing you up here and the way you listen to questions and kind of breathe silence even your political standpoint as an anarchist is a kind of silence the silence of not voting there's nothing quite as*

whaT
supposE that i
No
To
rIsen
emptiness ' is nOt
judgemeNt **or**
consIsts
complex aNd
To
bE
would briNg
Talks
unpredIctably
Other
iN '
I
turN away i
less Than
looks likE this i
aNd
The **whole** for
dyIng let us
wanted tO '
eNd at
Itself
aNd
pakisTani '
nEw york
paid millioNs of dollars in bribes '
fosTer
solItude
Of
betweeN
It
aNy '
facTs
bEat was
caN
wiTh '
musIc '
allOwed
aNd
Is '
maN
is **Two** '

*egalitarian as silence basically there are a lot of kinds of silences too that you touched upon the silence
of not wanting to say anything the silence of not wanting to hear anything any more the silence of not
having anything to say which doesn't always produce silence i was just wondering exactly what thoughts
you have on silence or am i completely off the wall or what* (silence long silence) *i'm enjoying it thank you*

157

                         so nEar ' that they break each other's
          propositioN '
          man's righT to
                    losIng
               and lOcal problems
               guteNberg '
                    I
                    oNe apple and
          shave close To
                    clEar '
                    briNg
                    whaT
                         nIght
                    tO
                    kNow '
               electrIcal power '
            make seNse
               leasT
               surE '
               a liviNg
          supply whaT we are apt to
                    It
                    tO
                    aNd
               and Its ' behavior
               of laNguage a chain
                    To
          control ' though Each
               them biddiNg
                    fasT
               am wIser '
                    frOm a particular
                    aNd
               and Is ' it also
          purposeful purposelessNess new '
                    whaT
                         dEarly there but
          at his bedside i am lookiNg '
                    The
                         It was while
          language nO
                    perceNt '
               journalIsts to
                    furNished
               abouT by
                    nEw '

i was very struck in your introduction over one little sentence where you say and then i take out the words i don't like right i was doing that just today i'm working on the fourth lecture now we have the situation of looking for ideas in this situation where they might be found and by taking some of the words away we find what is left i find myself beginning by not taking anything away and reading all the words and sometimes

158

you say a propositioN has been a reasonable
The '
wIth
fOr **both**
have we **for** ' calliNg **e**
a house and beyond Its house a world
the other haNd '
iT is a
hElp ' less is more
aNd business '
loss of memory ' To reach
reallty
be useful fOr the study of
reachiNg
If '
fouNder and
learn To
wholE of spaceship earth ' availability of
weather aNd
serve To
Is
Of doubt ' would be
No one else

Itself
furNished
profiTably
looks likE this ' **i**
aNd
The ' **way**
losIng
fOr ' **both** '
perceNt

•

yesterDay '
electrIcal power '
Simplify '
Change ' more than 300,000 talks '
he saId it is
Progress ' the army '
make it disappear ' i shouLd
descrIbe but i
life by Not

the situation seems hopeless and there's a tendency after having read all of them to read just some of them and then generally there's the circumstance that something strikes my attention either about one part of the text to be written or about its seeming nature that it might that there might be sometimes fewer words and sometimes more words or the wing words are wider and narrower i've several times had the feeling that i

livE looking **in** '
moDern
eatIng '
he haS
danCe '
mIght almost be said meaning moves
it**self** the concePt of
the worLd '
dIplomat '
owN work not from
as wE
aiD '
lIfe '
cauSe and
whiCh we
thInk
to Pay
for Long ' lo
dIsputed
aNd
thE war '
Death '
amerIca '
aSk the world game to make the world
a large plaCe
everyone Is
exPeriment
i couLd
saId
weNt
bE '
worlD
obeyIng
outSide **it** '
niCk of
In accord with **what**
uP growing **up** ' that is
eLements '
phonetIc script
aNd
tribEs
at night ' suzuki ' the magic square ' anD then chance
gIven
aS
the riCe '
do you fInd that what you learn inside the classroom

would not be able to find anything *what reaction did you* do i have *when you can't find like you say* then i continue i continue looking and working and i don't know what word to use but something happens and sometimes it happens by not taking much away and sometimes by taking a great deal away sometimes it happens by paying attention to what meaning there is how can i express that well it might be a negative

                        means moksha ' being led by a Person
                              thirty years Later '
                              south afrIca '
                                  beeN
                                   thE
                              quicksanDs and
                                 wIthout
                                  Shaggy
                                  Could '
                              If there were a
                      throat ' the Prince hesitates ' but
                                 infLuence
                  needs ' so as to allow hImself to develop his
                          life by Not living
                         how whEn where
                              anD go to the bottom '
                            malaysIa '
                              be Said it was
                                teChnology '
                                  In us is like the water in the river '
                              Portrait of
              as they **are** ' futiLe
                          stage dIrectly opposite
                              Not for **long** ' lo and
                            havE the
                                Dawn the sun '
                                   It
                                 Should
                              a Class
                                  In any way ' in the way each student had
                          ex**Pan**sion
                      free and cLear '
                              Images '
                              Not a book '
                          awokE to
                      nature ' anD
                              wIth
                              deStroy '
                              offiCer and a gunman '
                      purpose ' I '
                            is the Poor man's credit
                            as irreLevant as
                              hIm
                               aNd
                               thEn
                            i shoulD '

statement or a positive statement and an inclination in one direction or another *what is your reaction when you read that and you feel it moving one way do you then want to balance* now i've finished the third lecture and i'm beginning the fourth and they're many pages i have so to speak a good deal of experience and this sensation of hopelessness i find disappears if i just stay with it and there are various ways of staying

fIve

wanted So that he

announCed

saId yesterday

nature Puts no questions and answers none which **we** '

he **was** ' aLways

brIdged

respoNsibility '

thE

anD

blockIng

uSe '

everything is quite easy now he Can see that

we know nothIng until the last moment '

that will heal the Present schizophrenia the use of

the restLessness of crowds and the

are that the unIverse **is** '

make aNy

Earth

broaD

there evIl **in**

the newS ' reports said

Cool

In the

corPorate

couLd

ef**fect** It

aNy

bE

of time anD notch '

the event must be free to the publIc '

not being able to do the Same thing gives the possibility of

stressed equally in Current

I had been '

i Paint

i couLdn't do what he asked perhaps now

that dIffers

would **Not**

that will **hEal** '

you **woulD**

wIth

teStified

in south ameriCa ' we all know

thIs flood has already immersed us i may have

joined a rebel grouP in the southern region demanding

Letter to protest government tax

with something one way is by going away from it and ah coming back to it and often it seems to have changed during your absence or you suddenly see something it's very hard to explain *this is parallel to that you talk a lot about having the courage to compose* uhm hmm *i was just wondering if that ties in at all with these* yes it does *it's very interesting thank you last week at the lecture some minutes into it a tape went off in*

162

                    the physIcal
                       plaN
                       thE
            track is laiD for us let us
                    ecologIcal
           it ' might alSo
                  unpreCedented
                       It '
                     all Past
                      onLy
                     unIted
            death have beeN
                   doEsn't
                  anD storms and
               collectIve dream or
              let uS spend our lives in
   sudden opening of doors ' it was a Class
                          may rIse this year higher than man has ever known
            of laboratory Procedures he was determined to provide
              if he wouLd not founder and go to the bottom and
                     hIghest
                     eNough '
                      fallEn leaves sweeping up leaves three years later
       intentions a state of minD '
            as a state of mInd entirely
              remote and eaSy '
      see through so that what i experienCed
                  thursday mornIng the move was the first action which was
money ' there will be too many musicians to Pay ' the event must be free
                outside the cLassroom but what
       we learn to assert or deny ' **It** of **them** ' the
                  studeNts say '
                     somE mistakes but it's a **ma**jor concern

      at night suzuki ' the magic square ' anD then chance
                       wIthout
                 be Said it **was**
                      Could
            do you fInd that what you learn inside the classroom
          throat the Prince **hes**itates ' but
        thirty years Later
                     hIghest
            life by Not living
              livE looking **in**

                           •

the back of the room the taped box was chained to the chair and it was all taped up and the on/off switch
was knocked out it was obviously timed i spoke to you about it at the museum of fine arts concert and you
likened it to a bomb sort of a sound bomb i was wondering if you could share with us what you thought
of it when it happened and also what you thought of it being forcibly stopped when i actually wrote that

speNt

Of original

The '

not spent on the poorest sections of society ' A

bomb becomes a cenTer **of**

for musIc '

may be jeOpardized which says

it is betweeN

staff or staves ' the possibility of microtoNal

wOrk

permiTs the endless

hArmed process '

counTry's

accIdental

Out

betweeN

oNe's

else was harmed prOcess '

major Thirds '

sAys

money is noT spent on the poorest

fIeld

has nO

field of frequeNcy '

oN

relatiOn

inTo

not ' spent on the poorest sections of society ' **A** '

The '

between well-known poInts '

pay its share Of

major thirds **thaN**

the music is there before it is writteN '

pay its share Of

music **more** ' space beTween '

pAper and music ' how

in The paper upon

that money Is

tO pay its share '

or just a drawiNg

oN

relatiOn

inTo

pAper and music ' how

money is noT spent on the poorest

part the particular section during which that sound began i thought that it would be good to have music with it and i thought that laura kuhn who knew that i felt that way i'd even invited her to play on some instrument and dance during it i thought perhaps she had arranged to have the bomb set but she didn't why it happened at the same at the point that i actually thought it would be appropriate i don't know either the

fIeld '
Out
or just a drawiNg

•

lIke it
oNly line of
Data **can** '
its **truE** is
wiTh
problEm **was**
dRastic action
world soMe future
whIch it **gets**
thaN **such**
rejected ' isrAel and
distinCtion
readY **what** ' reason
musIc is '
schoeNberg's opus
raDio
oftEn
buT
likE to
figuRe **of** '
grete sultan finally left My desk went to
me that now revIews
re**sumed** oNe of five
they hAve
my body in the Course of a dream
change mY
socIal
Nature
showeD it **to**
and **thE** ' use we make
iT **is** '
callEd
south koRean '
tiMe has gone a step farther '
mouth wIth**out**
aNd
continue And
direCtion '
five daYs of south the south '

information got abroad or not do you think it would have lasted much longer of its own accord *i have no idea i didn't look at the tape* we don't know so it was stopped and it was stopped within that part of the lecture where i wanted music *did you enjoy the experience of it going off while it was happening* yes i liked all of it *say a little bit about mushrooms and hunting mushrooms and places you particularly like to go to*

165

hIs
flueNt
proDuction
sings thE
are noT
a ' sEnsation
cannot be dRunk nor water spun nor coal eaten ' the
answer in My sleep as **what** ' when ' how ' where ' but there
on **It** ' **i**
their **owN**
A
Compared to
sounds for which You
Is ' a priori that
beeN
Doing
tunE '
firsT
your nExt composition ' this will give you
Role '
huMan
throat all rIght '
more stroNgly
if it threAten ruin '
Continue the series as when we ask
what would You
don quIxote
u.N.
Doctor's
to onE common
of ' music To
sociEty '
sky ' ocean ' map without any visible distoRtion of the shapes sizes or true
society ' sanity called for a Major counter-stress
a polIce
i do Not wish
As
Counter-stress '
it in a **waY**
fIlm
loNger
Day ' combustion
moon or **bE** '
paTh to
almost likE to say
woRld

do that and some ways you particularly like to cook or eat some of the mushrooms that you find mushrooms in general i haven't looked up here since i've come but i hope to actually i hope to go to walden to look i hunted a great deal in rockland county where i lived for a number of years and i know many places there for this species or that and we found places in vermont i think any place will do for looking for mushrooms and

166

spent on **the** ' poorest sections of society ' a boMb '

and even If

its erraNd

mAjor information

its use under Certain

anY

It '

iraq has twice refused to hold talks with haNoi ' war

nutrients woulD

wE ask one learns '

naTions

flow of illEgal

designs and the most impoRtant activities can be

objects in front of theM

It we possess

the tuNe

on the globe thAt is

what pollution Comes from pollution **is** '

stronglY

If it

of ' daNte

showeD that

yEs

is **iT** '

gamE which should now

aRe '

Made

trees whIch i

caN solve '

it wAs

in the Course of a dream and that the new

answer in mY sleep

fIred

related data **caN**

shipyarD in

stavEs '

order washingTon's

imaginE myself without my body it might seem as

into this countRy five years ago ' about 1,500 jobs were out of

the sixteenth century ' saw those iMages

for Its uses

aNd using

expAnding power

Composition

which You're

wIth '

there again when you don't find them persistence helps i've often had the idea that if i wanted to find mushrooms say in an unlikely season that i could if i just kept looking *last night before going to sleep i decided to reread your introduction and think about the structure of the writing and as i was reading through and thinking about looking to find out which exactly were the words that formed the mesostic*

aNarchy into

things they **are** ' tolD

stabilization of thE

noT

barE maximum

foR burns

with universe and the potential success of Man '

Its way to the mouth without

the system of arithmetic ' what oNe

students **sAy** they **do** ' things they

Considered

saY oh **yes** ' now

rIse free from care before the

baNk strike

Dust

a whirlpool an infinitE regress you can say

indusTrial and

might bE

cRowds ' and

the saMe color we

name and wIthout which

your owN

error wAs primarily responsible **for** ' the

demonstrators and bystanders were Charged and attacked '

strike tonight at the big lenin shipYard

a dark and muggy nIght

say what you like it takes you No further ' the

29 people were treateD for burns ' a

nEw

noT

imagE **in**

by **oR**

the third straight day of Mass protest '

bIll or himself that died

No dust

the sAme

made publiC

to assert or denY '

watched a polIce officer

Not

her to Do but

bE beside ourselves '

This sounds

arE

homelessness ' have woRsened with the apparent collapse of

nuMber '

strings i came across the remark about the *fifteen words that make up the title of the lectures and as i was thinking about them i noticed that there were sixteen words* no variable structure is two words that are one word *thank you* the custom at these seminars is that i respond to remarks or questions *when and how did you come by your dislike for listening to recordings* it must have begun for me at the cornish school in

what you have doesn't help ' less Is more ' feathers pulled out '
khomeiNi's
heAring takes
Consumption we sought '
six ' six being the center horizontallY '
she's so devoted to then I
maN's internal metabolics the army
misleD him though '
population ' art ' imitation of naturE in her manner of
vision ' no dusT ' has
occupiEd
heading foR cottage
payMents to thousands of consumer
representatIves '
feed the eNtire world '
for otherwise the words would hAve no meaning '
image whiCh
i frequentlY had to look up at
of Israel for
exist amoNg
relateD data
arE yours
i **can'T**
arE men '
official Recognition of israel for tuberculosis
and custoMs
radIo had
theN
him ' And yet that way
soldiers opened fire to influenCe the negotiations against as
alwaYs '
socIety
symbol No
woulD
us for hE
mainTain
to bEings
pRoduction and
the known behavior of soMe of
Is ' the same as
more thaN
And
our interCourse was
in at **mY**
and rescued fIve
is oNly making it

seattle which had a radio station where i began experiments with amplified small sounds and the use of
records as instruments and the combination of those things together to make another record i saw that
recordings could have a part in the making of something i began to think of them not as something to listen
to in themselves but as possibly part of something that hadn't yet been made i was able to see the great

                    not preDict that it will
                              fivE
                by hundreds of Thousands ' last
                              Emotions
                      of woRld people can
                        world gaMe
                      or **what** It is **is**
                it is bet**weeN** well-known points in
                              pArt and
          doing nothing ' musiC is not music until it is
too slow to attract attention' and **therebY**

                            socIety
                  related data caN
                      not preDict that it will
                              nEw
                      are **noT**
                          arE
                          cRowds and
                        tiMe has gone a step farther '
                  mouth wIthout
                    its erraNd '
      for otherwise the words would hAve no meaning '
              doing nothing musiC is not music until it is '
                    saY oh yes ' now

                              •

                      vIllages of
            earth could feed as maNy people as she needed up '
      use of energy sources above earTh ' not fossil
                  diplomats ' madE anti-
                          foRming
                  security today ' Polish labor
                  classroom **thE** '
                            skiN
                      to usE **for**
                          To be as
                        fRom ' the possibility of
              collectively According
              are deemed The most sacred laws of
                              I
                          aflOat '
                      i did Not
        always there from whIch behavior follows ' it is

difference between a recording and a live performance later i remember going to the home in the country of
some friends who had a large collection of records we had spent the day looking for mushrooms cooking them
and eating them and then they were going to add to our pleasures with recordings while the record was being

they **were** ' oN a hunger
wiTh
without a mEthod of solution ' they
ask foR either **a**
the area jaPan
would ' bE '
day iN particular an
thE ' shell speaks '
parTs
expeRienced more unemployment
in the world of duchAmp
in iTs
found hImself '
grOups for
could Not see '
trIed for
coNgress known
elecTric
onE '
bRoken off
emPirical '
answEr will
he puts oN this
thE
mosT
would neveR
it is dArker '
women are much more inTegral
to nature and daylIght
means the use Of all '
to rescue ailiNg texas bank all the assets
wIll improve '
No way ever
projecT ' washington said
of coursE only because **one**
fRom
uP
should think hE
hours ' oNly **a**
as **thE** '
young The families
gRey i see the
of our lives An
our new work and iT
for Instance what i'd write ' ambient
president Of

played the windows were open a breeze was making a light curtain move in a way that i enjoyed watching
then i saw that records could be part of theater and i could enjoy it as something that was happening uniquely
one of the things i dislike very much about recording in opposition to a performance is that a record tends

just the rich ' **No**
my hand to lIft the latch ' i have
our political cartooNs and
problems of Today '
up making choicEs devote myself to asking questions ' chance
in the latest most dRastic action ' the law enforcement agencies
a refugee camP **in**
continuE what
by maN to man
critErion of
noT
pRocesses
not like other children i Am weak in
one way and Then another you may
I
twO
you haveN't now
superIor or rather
oN
To
onE can
sometimes **though** without his wRiting three '
to accePt
thE
polaNd's
light ' on thE
also **To** '
which howeveR one does not
mAy
nor always **buT** ' the
neIther
Other
aNd asked us to
has now been dIscovered seems fortuitous
so fast that eveN a village is
no quesTions and
soon forgEt them ' **they**
oR
Polish labor
acrE which would
oN
systEm **is** '
mighT be said that any way of solving the
him i **have** ' spent the whole day in feaR '

to be always the same whereas a performance has the opposite tendency i connect uniqueness with the performance of music in various ways i've built that uniqueness into my compositions since 1958 the *concert for piano and orchestra* has no score each performance of it is unique i have a tendency a tendency that

even A village is
counTry
not know at fIrst but it was the result
the herOic the mirthful the
theN students say they **do**
It '
tables aNd diagrams making up a
quesTion **do**
an Equation between
pRoblem will afford us a key to unlock as many '
recognition of israel for tuberculosis Point of
king in thE fairy tale who told the
be more Natural **than** ' such a
parts of thE
Today
moRe
to use his knowledge with respect to wit i leArned
us To the blackboard and
made of metal drIven
and it is ' cOmparable with
is **Nec**essary ' an old
man ' Is
aNswer according
acousTic man
and problEm's solution is ' manifest the
pRoblem elimination unfolds when definition is
emPirical '
is in part grEy i see the parts of the paper that are
aNd daylight
is your congratulation and you havE cause
of simulTaneous
of ' diffeRences together ' not
mAn
away buT rather
nIght when my feet felt the path which my
lengths ' dO i **go** '
talks iN geneva after
darker places ' the shadow that my hand casts Is
caN fairly easily
no quesTions and
concEiving '
inaRticulate sound but such a sound is
every Past is now and
fEbruary

distinguishes my work from christian wolff's from morton feldman's and from earle brown's a tendency
toward theater i've said in one of my lectures we should have a society for the destruction of records *hmmm*
and that if we had texas someone had said that they had no music in texas i said the reason they have no

where there was No cart '
highways of thE world how deep
a shoT
no doubt and hence ' even wheRe the
us A key
Than
object I
in terms Of
makiNg up a story
that mIght
aNd
iT
that hE '
natuRal than such
excePt
and noblE
iN
wE people **a** '
consisTs of
wheRe the
plAce ' silence
excepT
In
refOrms '
aNother development
all the wIse
caN fairly easily imagine a
projecT
inclinEs him to
7 million squaRe miles ' this would be
and by our Political cartoons and pictorial
immortal ' that is your succEss ' all
i go there is No stopping or going o moon **why**
and so havE
can de**scribe** The
instance not moRe
plAce ' a gymnasium **an**
spenT
form Is unrivaled
has tO do
wheN one
mIxture of report '
grouNd '
imagine iT for '
is surroundEd

music in texas is because they have records in texas if they didn't have records in texas immediately someone would feel the need for music people say that they need records in order to have the music but they don't get the music by means of records they don't get what i think of as music from records *you once said that*

in the daRk ' we are losing our minds getting mind ' it is
something unknown is doing we know not what ' Psychologists
tEach
for calliNg
no End in
boTh
even though it was a class in haRmony '
And of course
my feeT **the** '
the unIted states '
energy sOurces above
he lives iN **two**

trIed for
our political cartooNs and
projecT
soon forgEt them they
natuRal than such
and by our Political cartoons and pictorial
continuE what
he puts oN this
and **so** ' havE
To be as
pRocesses
in the world of duchAmp
nor always buT the
I '
Other
wheN ' one

•

and consumptIon
how Much copper
who were kIlled
counTries to observe
the world Around '
obsTacles '
later It seems likely that
we need tO
maN's
a whIle
the Major states

everything becomes melodious that by listening to a recording of one of your works and then hearing a
performance of it live sometime later it will already be melodious the remark about melody came from
christian wolff he said no matter what we do we always have melody *your mentioning christian and also a*

more lIberal laws '
facT
And increase of efficiency '
The
benefIts
whO '
the meetiNg of '
occupyIng it it
systeM as
are set In order and
say To him i
A '
souTh
Is
cOal
was differeNtly placed
In the sense that all pasts that ever were are
other persons ' Man
pollutIon from
The
mAss
di**recT** '
each havIng **that**
and **if** i were ' nOw to say to him i have
retiremeNt
who **fIrst**
More
whIch we were ' made for is
from **The** '
locAl
To
It **well** '
is prOduced
iN
wIll contain '
thus we cannot say i notice that he looks sMaller ' and
alcohol to run electrIc power '
words of **The**
is **An**
in **The**
on whIch i am
wOrk the
ruN

and consumptIon
systeM as '

remark you made about selecting the material that you were going to use for your lectures because of its
political your own political stand leads me to wonder how you would respond to a question like this do
you think of your music as having political content do you think of it as having political effect i think one

who were kIlled
from **The** '
And increase of efficiency '
obsTacles '
It well
and if i **were** ' nOw to say to him i **have** '
the meetiNg **of**

•

Data can
with **thE**
i haVe ' **yet**
i **Or** ' as a
whaT
If we define
develOped closer
maiNly to
between us for he haD grown
pronE
announced today Virtually all its
asked hOw much
virTually all
there **Is** '
and think emplOyers
will Not work '
playeD
aftEr working out '
guerrillas are a part of us a goVernment campaign
tO live and
is ' **The**
I am '
whOlly
maN '
workeD
involvEd as
not just passiVe '
internatiOnal
noise and musical Tones
In
Of
seNate
liveD
whEn **he** '
because he liVes in

of the things that distinguishes music from the other arts is that music often requires other people the
performance of music is a public occasion or a social occasion this brings it about that the performance of a
piece of music can be a metaphor of society of how we want society to be though we are not now living in a

wOuld engender '
moves The
It is
wOuld it **be** '
with preseNt
flooDs
wE
liVe
a true expressiOn ' who
iT must have been
have lIved '
thrOugh
thiNk employers
in the olD
thE
future or possible we should liVe
the functiOnal '
senT
what we consIdered
use ' sOuth africa
giviNg
music feareD
you arE
touch-actiVe '
aggregate Of
biTs of
ecologIcal
Officer
Not suffice
at what you **woulD** not
whilE we sat '
had not been discoVered but it must have been
thOse
is aT
growIng
center Of
caN **wake** up in the night '
calleD
gamE
passiVe
else was harmed ' let us settle Ourselves and
find The bare
the possIble ' synergetic
is Or as
peculiar feeliNg of pastness
relating to the worlD '

society which we consider good we could make a piece of music in which we would be willing to live i don't
mean that literally i mean it metaphorically you can think of the piece of music as a representation of a
society in which you would be willing to live and i would prefer to live in a society without a president i was

178

Editors and

how to liVe and think

we shOuld '

raTher than

communIcated

succumb tO

experieNce which

chilD is

thE

haVe '

lOgic philosophy we should only need

greTe she was

makIng up a

wOrk '

cursiNg ' greeting ' praying ' if anyone

he saiD

invokE the muse

placed aboVe them bidding us hear it

face tO face

of Thousands **of** '

of all the senses at once ' a response to whIch is

Of society a bomb '

of these feeliNgs present whence comes the fresh

the piece woulD

bE it life or death we

must haVe

the fact it **is** ' Only

The

of musIc

end Of

giviNg its

have liveD '

appEars to

liVe

tO **make** '

sighT and **so** '

harmonIzed

abOve throughout the world would

two ideNtical bits of a piece of music to have

the olD

likE telling

driVen '

the piece wOuld

There are

In

one of the founding members of the new york mycological society and i was present when the rules of the society were established they've since been broken and returned to more conventional things because i don't go to the meetings but the first rule of our society was that there would be no one in charge no president we

sOciety
from the first moves ' the establishmeNt of bare maximum levels

relating to the worlD
likE telling
haVe
the functiOnal
raTher than
In
and think emplOyers
caN wake up ' **in** the night

•

and resCued
all ' In one ' and
technology shapes ' woRks over ' alters ' massages every instant of our
eaCh of
twig he sits Upon ' **i**
Media or
not knowing what will happen next ' any **it** iS as
repeaTed
A ' work
that this my meNtors said
Comparison '
thE
Shaping
Cloud '
answer to thIs
is a tRue proposition of
musiC ' seeing no real difference between
which i **might yet Use** at any
soMething '
thiS is synergy '
poinT of
flAsh
iNvolved when
exaCtly
littlE
but a Statement '
aCt
by goIng
as to put to Rout all that was not life
upon a timeness whiCh means all time '
we are moving into an age which in popUlar notion at least is probably

thought the important (offices) were (for) the treasurer and the secretary we thought we should have a record
of what was said and done but nobody was in charge we didn't do anything unless everyone was in agreement
about what was done and we did a great deal i have just finished my piece for the boston symphony seiji

180

pi priMe
corpS and
noT '
we now hAve the
exteNt of our
Composition '
frontiEr
iS
exotiC
vIolence
couRt
beComes completely indifferent ' it
or ' to **oUr** '
siMply
to a Single
in ' The size of
As ' what
iNdividual
by ' or attraCt '
of mErging **of**
a Single hand '
the Center '
now I want you so that what i
Radio '
regenerating and funCtioning of spaceship earth and its
hUndred dots ' you can only see
fisherMen
beatleS
To
At
differeNtly ' how do you know what you would do if
people often ask ' what musiC ' i
rEad
two bitS would be meant to be
south afriCa
gettIng
hoRizontal '
it must be Completely
the amoUnt of
the ' transforMation of
today that **the** ' decree **ni**Si '
communicaTion link '
c.i.A. '
iN the same
sense disCrimination following in a
pattErn in the

ozawa asked me if i would write a 12 to 15 minute piece but as he asked me to do it i said there won't be any conductor he very beautifully said it's not important whether there's a conductor or not the important thing is the music i was delighted to hear him say that and i've written into the work that it shall not be conducted

181

inSanity in my mood ' and seemed to foresee
Could
seeIng **no**
bRidged and **pass**able '
Carts and sheds '
foUrs into **one two** and **one** ' four eight and four
and if it proved to be Mean then to
end conflictS in
wiTh
of Arithmetic '
by someoNe
how to Carry it out
burEaucracy ' a **two**
hiS life
as muCh
In which we
woRk
it **is** ' written Composition is only making it clear that
oUr
Material
dayS ago
permiTs division
i would plAy '
to receNt
eaCh ' having
wE ' perceive the world were
Supreme
experienCe '
thIs
cultuRe
thatCher has insisted more strongly than ever
Use throughout the world
will work for hiM but he may be totally involved
and heavy rainS ' missing and presumed
To
everywhere ' At home
the studeNts
a south korean offiCial with
finitE
Sky '
nuClear arms '
hIs leg
about to wRite
upon a timeness whiCh means all time '
soon finished the first of thirty-two etUdes each having two pages showed it to grete '
soMe future

but that the conductor shall coach the musicians during rehearsals *when you were talking about records versus music in texas it made me think about how people's natural and i agree with you about what i think you were saying and implying* um hmm *made me wonder about what your thoughts might be about*

182

cauSed
noT
no ' disciplinAry
exterNal
musiC '
hE will meet with
hourS per year to
Case '
say sIlence i enjoy '
he woRked '
you Cannot do '
they shoUld
soMething
waS
Themselves in
A '
oNe two and one four eight and four and/or
something whiCh '
cloud and thE rain which
Strikingly manifested
needs upon whiCh
experIence's
tRue'n'false '
Criterion for
that's correct ' now i want yoU
freeing hiM from
guerillaS
planTs
dissimilArs '
oNe
over **how** ' muCh
givEn **two** '
inStant **a** '
vertiCally **fours** '
whIle i
foRth new
basiC
left ' Unattended
Matter ' were
So
of **The** '
of the eArth
the questioN
logiC fills '
a fEw
the purpoSe **here** '

two aspects of that one of which is how the ways in which it comes about that people's natural impulses inclinations for and to music are say suppressed or become people become let's say alienated from that those natural impulses so to speak the various social musical i'm not quite following you you mean the

as we Could '
we are headIng
futuRe
the ' fanCied advantages of
i think he woUld agree the principle underlying all of
give Me
Sphere ' **whose**
To right '
sitting At his bedside i am
leNs '
one Can
lovE right
bitS of
whiCh you're
Is
him fRom
Consider
was ' qUickly
bringing Man to
of itS
The '
reseArchers
for example iN the
whiCh
bE comparable to a title to programme
itSelf what
resignation unless it was quite neCessary
goIng **to**
fRom left to right '
in whiCh the small parts had
gradUation
for exaMple there
of **itS**
geT
individuAl
moderN
teChnology
in common hours ' hE
divided four fourS into one two and one four eight and four '
only by itself Could
sIde up
back up **we** ' aRe
whiCh **i**
foUndations under
sound and sight around My
Said

social pressures are such that we *ok people people* that we don't make music or do make music *don't that*
we don't i think that we we don't right *yeah i mean people put on a* we're really silenced *right* by *society*
right and so this is wondering if you cared to say more about *to say more about that* i could talk for hours

of uniTs the

intense ' with reseArch

iNto

baCh ' all of

in thE

thiS is

all at onCe '

would be equIvalent to **it** and in itself **it** is

woRld ' game is

this i Can '

and prodUces

still More

uSe '

paradox is **The**

mAde public

sputNik is an information

to refleCt that this my

thE

and **clinch** it So

eaCh day the

If i have

heRe **now** ' in that sense we are post-history ' and

in the same tempo only taken differently eaCh time and even if a composer has never yet

bUt it has happened ' it isn't

of a **suite** don't aMount

it **iS** a scene '

Through

eAch

poNd was not to live '

loss of memory to reaCh

his lifE

which we might call the complete Set of

a single hand Can play '

In space pitch

houRs

the small into the Center horizontally five vertically '

langUage creates it's

tiMe '

officialS

can The

A

iN

basiC

wish ' to opposE

no paSt or future ' just

inequalities in the Culture of

how to how we can you know free up you mean what we can do *i feel stymied myself sometimes how to begin to free that up in ourselves* right right no it's quite amazing when i was in the 5th grade in los angeles i applied to enter the glee club i turned up at the proper hour and they said oh you can't be in the glee club

the lIfe which he has imagined ' he will

him fRom **the**

the time ' Certainly

sitUation

this transforMative

uS '

To improve

it is they Are i

No

arithmetiC ' not on particular occasions nor always but

that thE

iS

are Completely lost or turned around '

satIe

stRikingly manifested in the radio

midst of Combat was

oUtside the

which you would not be ashaMed to invoke the

Sound ' bringing

any influence on The

little common sense ' A little

it ' theN resembles the venus de milo '

musiC

languagE no government

pluS two ' with

Create a

gIven **you** you will once

the only tRue answer **will** ' set all well afloat ' art's

whatever must be Complemented by

pUt in words the principle that underlies all

serene and healthy life ' to be alone was soMething

Space ' now do **i**

i wanTed to

right'n'wrong in the morAl

Now ' someone else asks whom did you mean and

in whiCh

not huddlEd and lumped but

in proportion aS he simplifies his life the laws of the

learning to use language beCause you would then have to be able to

In the

teacheRs students and

without this exerting any influenCe on the performance the piece '

two thoUsand

one Million

we cannot therefore Say

Therefore is

until we test your voice i said well when can we do that we made an appointment they tested it and found
they said you don't have a voice i believed i was after all in school i believed that what they said was true and
when the people would sing in church i just didn't because i didn't have a voice there was no sense in doing

186

in plAce where there is

so we live iN the vulgar sense in an extremely religious '

we still Carry in our minds '

powEr but all in one and each entirely

and itS substitution for

meaning blind man aCt '

fIve

sound and sight aRound my house an infinite and

at the speed of light the planet is not muCh bigger than this room we're in in terms of

energy and information grew visibly before Us we were working at the frontier and each

as Many

be refreShed by

loss of memory To

A

iN my mood and seemed to foresee my

eye and speeCh in

it likE

Some three hundred and fifty

whiCh he had covered ' was

as vIsual space can it ' is both

we leaRn that the highest is present to

the speed of light ' he has no physiCal body he is translated into information or

sUpply

had testified to their utility ' the world gaMe

iS

Through

individuAls

iN

espeCially

usE at any moment if

cartS and

proportions to eaCh other

thIs i can always split it up

you could say silence i enjoy whateveR ambient sounds there are to hear what

developments in mathematiCs

are sUch and such take the

caMpaign would provide the nicaraguan

more than any other or you could Say silence i enjoy

evenT

undecided whether A part of it could be

withiN him or the old laws be expanded and

within ' going in all direCtions

solitudE ' nor poverty poverty nor

difficulty ' iS only one of applying these in the

loss of memory ' to reaCh these two's a goal ' duchamp ' a squad

dramatIc to see human beings so

it it was later through circumstances of not having a singer that i began to sing i was still in my thirties and
i was making the music for merce cunningham's solo dance recitals and knowing that i didn't have a voice
but that i could sing i decided to sing the accompaniment for his dance i did so in such a position in the

space in which we now live is like a spheRe whose
whatever must be Complemented by the
in and oUt ' no split between spirit and
tiMe
in the machine of the univerSe ' you carrying on
sound bringing abouT
expected four hundred sAfety features
terrorism experts are urgiNg
geographiCally
no languagE at all ' i.e. to think what it would be like
a dozen people miStakenly shot down

a single hand Can play
would be equIvalent to it and in itself it is
cultuRe
Criterion for
energy and information grew visibly before Us we were working at the frontier and each
give Me
of itS
any influence on **The**
of **the** ' eArth
by someoNe
baCh ' all of
cloud ' and thE rain which
bitS of

•

in nineteen-eighty-seVen
mAny
said the Recent wave of troops shot and wounded
saId the recent
depArtment
demonstration By
expLoration and study of
sociEty
if there were aS
eighT
and Richness of '
said the recent wave of troops shot and woUnded on issues of
experienCe and
developmenT
with greater serioUs penalties
navy officeR
aftEr **a** '

theater that i couldn't be seen so no one would know who was singing everything went well the audience applauded and so forth and at the end of the performance another composer alan hovhaness came backstage and said who sang that song i said what do you want to know for he said i want that voice in my next opera

188

greater serious penalties ' game theory proVides

situAtions

method foR the

harmony amId

peAce and sharing

to Be

a royaL navy

thE

Said

serious penalTies

shot and wounded on issues of peace and shaRing '

in challenging sitUations the state department said its anti-

making in Challenging

Theory provides a method

society dedicated to sUccess '

shot and wounded on issues of peace and shaRing would

Exploration and study of decision-making in

game theory proVides

tAstes skills

to be a Royal navy

connectIon with

vAriety and richness of experience and insight '

soviet-Backed

refugees criticized a regionaL

thE '

department Said

evicTions in 1987 **if**

pRovides a method

that killed eight british soldiers in bUrma ' a man believed to be a royal navy

to be a royal navy offiCer refused

greaT harmony amid variety and richness of

connection with greater serioUs penalties ' game

that killed eight bRitish

issuEs of peace and sharing ' would

to be a royal naVy officer refused to resign

And study of decision-making

weRe as many '

In

temperAments tastes skills and degrees of knowledge

department said its anti-pakistan campaign Broke the soviet-backed regime that

theory provides a method for the mathematicaL '

criticizEd a regional development plan '

if there were aS many recognized kinds of success as

harmony amid varieTy and

mathematical exploRation and

optimism following a demonstration by hUndreds of thousands

naturally when he found out that i had sung he changed his mind later i sang again and (now) i can be found singing almost anytime i had arranged with cathy berberian to sing with me i was going to do some of the nonvocal parts of *the songbooks* she was going to sing a number of the songs and it was to be at new york

of experienCe '

  The state department said its anti-pakistan

peace and sharing woUld have

  soldieRs in burma ' a

  study of dEcision-making in challenging situations the

issues of peace and sharing would haVe forced the evictions in 1987 if there were

serious penAlties

success might yet develop veRy great harmony

  kInds of success

believed to be A royal navy officer refused to resign and

  Be

  expLoration and study of

  wavE of

  itS '

campaign broke The soviet-backed

challenging situations ' the state depaRtment said its anti-pakistan campaign broke

eight british soldiers in bUrma '

  broke the soviet-baCked regime

of peace and sharing ' would have forced The evictions in 1987 if there were as many

as many recognized kinds of sUccess as

optimism ' following a demonstRation

  wavE of troops shot and wounded on issues **of** '

a royal naVy officer refused

  would **hAve** '

police expRessed

success mIght yet develop '

  mAny recognized kinds of

  British

  expLoration and study

in connEction with

the recent wave of troopS '

  refugees criTicized

  aRe temperaments tastes skills and

wave of troops shot and woUnded on issues

mathematiCal '

  The state department said its anti-pakistan

  sUccess as

theoRy '

a royal navy officEr refused

to be a royal naVy officer refused

  lAst

method foR the

  In

  gAme

pakistan campaign ' Broke the soviet-backed regime that

wounded on issues of peace and sharing wouLd

university at the last minute she telegraphed that she was ill and wouldn't be able to do it so i decided to do it myself i didn't sing *the songbooks* but i had a text called *mureau* mu from music and reau from thoreau it's one of my first nonsyntactic texts i was led to write it because a magazine dealing with electronic music

190

statE department

aS

To be

cRiticized a regional development plan ' police

optimism following a demonstration by hUndreds of thousands last week

in 1987 ' if there were as many reCognized kinds of success as

a regional developmenT plan police expressed optimism following

peace and sharing **woUld**

killed eight ' bRitish

gamE

naVy officer

richness of experience And insight

police expRessed

degrees of knowledge ' a socIety

depArtment said its anti-pakistan

soviet-Backed

pLan

forcEd the

department Said

re**sign** ' and said The

vaRiety and richness of experience and insight

optimism following a demonstration by hUndreds of thousands last week **in**

of troops shot and wounded on issues of peaCe and sharing would

yeT develop very great harmony amid variety and

said the recent wave of troops shot and woUnded on issues of peace and

mathematical exploRation and study of

statE department said its anti-pakistan

peace and sharing would haVe forced the evictions in 1987 if there **were** '

gAme

bRoke

In 1987 if there **were** '

richness of experience And insight the agreement came after

optimism following a demonstration By hundreds of thousands '

theory provides a method for the mathematicaL

statE department

itS

The

aRe temperaments tastes skills and degrees of

decision-making in challenging sitUations the state department said its anti-

and riChness of experience and

wiTh

a boatload of vietnamese refUgees

came afteR a boatload **of** '

and study **of** ' dEcision-making in challenging situations the

naVy officer refused to resign '

regionAl development

asked me to become a columnist so i used chance operations with respect to all of the remarks by thoreau in
his *journal* that had to do with sounds he was attentive to what he heard one of the chapters of *walden* is
called *sounds* i thought this is what composers of electronic music do now they listen they don't listen to

method foR

navy offIcer

vAriety and richness of experience and insight

the soviet-Backed regime

provides a method for the mathematicaL

in connEction with greater

peace and Sharing would have forced

anTi-

state depaRtment

sitUations ' the state department said its anti-

and ' riChness of experience and

To be

a boatload of vietnamese refUgees '

exploRation and study of

mEthod for the

naVy

mAn believed to be '

tempeRaments ' tastes '

eIght british soldiers in

gAme theory provides a method for

to **Be** ' **a** '

a demonstration by hundreds of thousands Last

a mEthod for the mathematical exploration and

itS

To success might yet develop '

as many Recognized kinds of

woUnded

and sharing would have forCed '

came afTer a boatload of vietnamese

in connection with greater serioUs penalties ' game

shot and wounded on issues of peace and shaRing '

wavE

theory proVides

Amid

buRma

antI-

development plAn ' police expressed optimism following

the soviet-Backed regime that

wounded on issues of peace and sharing wouLd

Exploration and

if there were aS many recognized kinds of success as

harmony amid varieTy and

yet develop veRy great

peace and sharing woUld have

insight ' the agreement Came '

wave of Troops shot and

sounds theoretically they don't have notions about what sounds are good and what sounds are bad and how they should be treated they just listen and that's what thoreau did i thought for columns in a magazine having to do with electronic music that if all the remarks that were in it came from thoreau that one would refUsed '

optimism following a demonstRation by

sErious penalties ' game theory

Very

regionAl ' development plan police

weRe as many

kInds of success '

vAriety and richness of experience and insight

department said its anti-pakistan campaign Broke the soviet-backed regime that

Last

harmony amid variEty and

aS many recognized kinds of success as

dedicaTed

gReat harmony amid variety and richness of '

of thoUsands '

offiCer refused

The state department said

serioUs penalties

might yet develop veRy

thEory

naVy officer refused to resign

And study of decision making '

success might yet develop veRy great harmony

success mIght yet develop

temperAments ' tastes ' skills ' and degrees of knowledge '

soviet-Backed

expLoration and study

thE

itS

eighT

state depaRtment

woUnded

and riChness of experience ' and

wave of Troops shot and

in connection with greater serioUs penalties ' game

soldieRs in burma ' **a**

aftEr **a**

•

patterNs that have

time and the speed Of

equivaleNts '

not a scale or row bUt a gamut to each '

learn something about electronic music it was that text that i began to vocalize because it was made up not of sentences but it was made up of words sometimes there was a sentence or a phrase words and then that one actually had a sentence here and there but the next one which is *empty words* had four parts there were

to say it perhaps ' oNly of human beings we learn to

be Difficult to

possEss nothing ' what makes us so confident ' any **it**

than this Room we're **in** ' in

So

will effecT their future ' the more people

becAuse it was the maximum

iN agriculture as

in america ' there are many new ways to proDuce food ' examples

wIth

more past ' uNder electric culture ' every past is now and

e.G. the mad ' they speak the truth religious

is like the miNd the

Other that they are '

is Normal

the ' residUal '

we learN to assert or

is blameD for attacks

in burma to a cabinEt '

a woRldwide city of ever-expanding

internal needS we found

are varied or noT '

As opposed to

firiNg

politics as we know it the efficiency woulD be somewhere between ' the

truth Is

to **meN**

to seven point eiGht '

it properly meaNs there is

wOrd for

five times teN^{15} calories and 21.9 x 10^7 tons of protein

together to realize world game as fUlly as they could the

somewhere betweeN '

amherst seniors walk out on graDuation '

our lifE is

moRe people engaged in thinking

alSo commanded an army a

learn To describe but

As

No '

workeD together to

wIll

to food for maN ' and

situation at very hiGh speeds '

we fouNd it

acre ' it wOuld be difficult to raise the world's

phrases words syllables and letters i began to practice singing those texts i made recordings of my singing
and then used say three of them in combination with live singing i continued that practice for a number of
years *i want to make an observation and then ask a question the* freeman etudes *unlike many of the other*

194

shapiNg the destiny of

live qUite laxly

arrived at by takiNg

frontier ' it is Dramatic to

statEs's feeding about two people

i can't ' the Robe the bowl

needed up to Seven

devices known To

in mAssive

to politics ' it is Now possible for anyone anywhere to take

worlD

of gIfts '

is like the babble of a village or taverN

or ideoloGically

aNywhere

frOm

all eveNts are

japan's feeding six people per acre ' it woUld be difficult to raise the world's

does Not exist among our applications of language

to raise the worlD's

thE

any moRe forever in view of the future or

from thiS

The function they

of work i desire to speAk somewhere without

music ' feared theN lest he

images bump against each other every Day '

never renew Itself it seems likely

No music more than any other ' what i wanted to

people as she needed up to seven point eiGht '

my sleep as what ' how ' wheN ' where ' but there was dawning nature in

tO

that side as our shadows reveal aN insensible perspiration toward

the test firing thUrsday is blamed for

beiNg

in this case or the expression i Do not know

and Each student was

defining success ' aRe open to definition and redefinition by

beginS

The heroic the mirthful the wondrous

the whAt

that are Now '

the growth of the stuDents and the growth of world game was

I **had** '

our life is aN apprenticeship to the truth that around

people as she **need**ed ' up to seven point **eiGht**

chance composed compositions of yours in the case of those i find myself actively organizing and creating
the musical experience mmmm in the case of the freeman etudes though they're so composed the result of
those chance operations for me they just sound so composed and really yes i am a friend of janos negyesy

is like the miNd the
acre ' it wOuld be difficult to raise the world's
that side as our shadows reveal aN insensible perspiration toward
live qUite laxly '
does Not exist among our applications of language
amherst seniors walk out on graDuation '
statEs's feeding about two people
than this Room we're in ' **in**
beginS
The heroic the mirthful the wondrous
in mAssive
that are Now
workeD together to
never renew Itself it seems likely
more past uNder electric culture ' every past is **now** and
people as she **need**ed up to seven point eiGht

•

hypothetiCal
prOblem
we ' kNew
now afTer
a ' hIgher or as it is
No
e ' the siGn
a brakE
that souNds '
researChed '
keY
proCess
mOst '
Necessary
oTher ' for
saId it
Not be
hiGh '
onE is
the plaNe she
physiCal '
sYstem not
experienCed '
middle Or
dollars **iN** '
Tax

i don't know if it's his performance i was wondering if you felt that maybe certain operations that you use result in a more in composition in more narrative structures what are your thoughts about the way that many computer music composers are also searching for those magic algorithms that will result in composed

It
aNy
cauGht
arE
poiNt '
system not viCe versa
moneY **is** '
or projeCted '
alOud
Named
buT '
exclusIve
oNe
beGan
hE **has** '
laNguage
resCue '
six daYs
furtheranCe '
pOssible
Nick
Them
sovIet '
that No man has
throuGhout
i camE '
iN what
objeCt
is obeYing '
and effeCt
wOuld seem
aNd
spiriTual '
I might
i revereNce them
could Go
unlEss i
body iN '
obsCurities '
weather at anY hour of
man take Care
Of view with **a** '
techNology '
moves Toward
scrIpt
oNce

music and how does computer music operation hopefully differ from the problems with records because it
is a fixed product that results from that yet i see it as a new medium but associated with the use of chance
operations is the feeling every now and then when you are in contact with the results that could have been

miGht
hE '
calliNg e
theatriCal '
stronglY toward
about ' drug traffiCking '
sO
laNguage **so** in
so in **The** ' end when **one**
Its
aNd '
druG
objEcts
oNly
suCh
simplY
is preCisely **the** '
tO
paNel
The
purpose **I**
pardoN
years aGo about
hE could '
uNless i
seCrets
energY '
effeCts
and stOre '
aNd
in **The** '
unIque '
staNds
or reGion
somE '
solviNg
suCh '
twentY-four thousand
musiC is
thrOugh
iN
geTs
It
Needs
throuGh **a** '
involvEd

composed is one's feeling one of the dangers in the use of computer technology with respect to composition is that the program is apt to describe itself more than make a composition from which it is separate i think the computer should be used in such a way that it does not finish the work but that the work is unpredictable

aN

all that Can be

that ' sounds totallY

Changes

wOrk

iN

Towards '

month's dIsputed

aNy

Good

a ' computEr

wild Not

system **Could** ' feed

anY

inClusive

glObe

maN has '

The

dIsputed

eNd

throuGh

thE

aNd

spaCe ' and could

sYstem

eaCh

Obscurities '

aNd

The furtherance of detachment and

unless I **could** '

wheN one **is** '

i would Gladly

yEars ago about

with oNe not two to make

theatriCal ' crossing through having no control that

Young

effeCts

sO

dollars iN

oTher for

It

wheN one is '

druG

arE

that ' souNds '

from the computer's point of view the computer necessarily does what it is supposed to do what it's made to do and i have heard many sound output programs that i can quickly know what the nature of the program was then the work doesn't engage my attention is this akin to our enjoyment of music enhanced by the

suCh
Young

•

to look at my hand and move It ' as
oN
exeCuted
fOr
techNology
muSt
Influence
Spend
malThusian
usE it
aNd
fraud Charges in the persian gulf unprecedented '
in order to enable people to be fed properlY we found that they would
a hIgher
preseNt
wreCks the
effOrt **of** '
of the trivial Name and
not that i waS hungry then except for that '
the wondrous ' the erotIc ' tranquillity '
value ' it becomeS
iT
spacE '
haviNg nothing to say and saying it
Cooperation without ecological offense '
theY're
hIs
No it
whiCh
dO
is Named
aS
In '
no ruleS
noT
yEt
Not **yet** '
the world game disCards the malthusian doctrine which is the
energY
lIfe

presence of elements in it that are not purely musical noise elements imperfections this is one of the troubles
with our technology it tends to be too perfect we need imperfection too does that answer have anything to do
with what you were *i guess as a follow-up if when you are creating a piece and it sounds to you like it was*

200

aNd
Can
tO soak
iN
eaSy
It did
anSwer **may**
malThusian
namE '
of what to do Next '
researChed
plaYed '
of doors It was a class '
vast aNd
plaCed
yOur
for November
aS a human
I may
haS given '
keep a clicker in your pockeT '
arE
salted i give the latiN ' on
Continued
daY and
saId it was
aNd
proCess '
and stOre
resultaNt
valueS
Importance of
and brakeS '
accounTs
donE
the ' Night are
a ' last seCond scrub last
simplifY '
I have
thousaNd and
in logiC this and this '
Of
aNd
aS ' unexpected pleasures '
envIronment to
conServing

well it was music *it was well-composed, or* yes *how do you feel what decisions do you make does it surprise*
you please you how no my attitude all along in composing is that of observing i use the chance operations
in such a complicated way i don't think it could be programmed andrew culver who does programming for

buT to think of

such as this arE part of our

uNique

erotiC

humanitY

carrIed

same place ' a large place ' a gymNasium '

so effiCiently

frOm

aNother while

Short of

joInt

let uS spend our lives

noT

onE

aNd

Can't '

anYwhere and

whIch ' has

Never stop even

rainbow whiCh i

alsO

No '

no morSel could have been too savage for me **the**

to fInd

eSpecially when

is noT to say that

wE easily come to doubt if they exist ' we

goiNg **on** '

it Cannot be wondered at '

i maY have made some

Is

No group ' said it was

proCess

abOut

aNd move '

food iS

entIre planet in

anSwer '

To

givE

is that it is as if we could grasp it iN

attaCks in

You '

thIs

oNe quarter

me has programmed a piece called *music for* in such a way that i have less to do than i did originally but i still have a good deal to do and the lectures that i am giving here give me the central words as you know and i add the wing words *john you spoke before about your music being more theatrical. . . .* raphael mostel's

happens next if you're writing a pieCe '

Of

aNd that in turn

can preSently be guaranteed

If they are indeed

needS '

This will

sounds bE

couNts '

speCtators of

not to saY '

hIt

aNd savage '

struCture and

Of

Not

whoSe

In

thoSe

This ' no it is just that

wE ask

providiNg nothing is taken as the

whiCh is the present working assumption of

Your next

was necessary ' for davId tudor

the suN is but a morning star the world game

automatiCally

tO produce progressively

aN

Sudden change of

It to

earS

aT

us is likE the water

to stretch itself oNe day '

aCt

congratulation and You have cause

as If i looked through colored crystal '

caN he

Crystal ' it was a **lake**

wOrld

the priNcipal object

itSelf to us

as If we could

purSue

buT

question is about what one can do or what one might do in relation to the use of one's music by performers in circumstances that lead them as my directions often do to ideas of their own that have nothing to do so to speak with my ideas we can take the case of the prepared piano when i was the one who was preparing

                    instant of our livEs
                     we sought to fiNd
     the **sky** ' looking down on it i may be affeCted
                        but thY sport '
                           socIety
                      blue meaNs nothing
                     for attaCks in **the** '
                    the greatest **Of**
                             aNd
                   nature of hiS **case**
                       electrIc energy **to**
                         reSource '
                       differenT
                       would bE
                          thiNgs in proportion as
     together not a single plan just a spaCe of time ' and as
                      entirelY concerned
                      progressIvely
          as we use it there are Not only words and
                   overnight resCue
                       first Or last
                      mistakeNly
              a camera ' it waS necessary for
                    he marrIed her
                    in bombay'S
                     be ready To '
                      highEst reality '
                    how caN man
          his needs these ways we Called
                         bY chance

                       carrIed
                          No group ' said it was
                      wreCks the
                         frOm
                        aNd
                         Sudden change **of**
                        I may
                     purSue
                      buT to think of
          us is likE the water
                     goiNg on
          a last seCond scrub ' last
                 simplifY

                             •

the piano i noticed as i went from one piano to another that i went from one instrument to another i mean
the sounds were different at the time that the sounds were in my daily experience i naturally wanted them to
be the right sounds but after other sounds came into my head which is to say other compositions i forgot

has no accidental it is between ' well-known Points in

thE

less **the** ' Removal

oF

a lOng way off

etceteRa '

Music '

put it bAck '

explosioN demolished the white house amid a strike '

a word whiCh

if onE

uP

is manifEst the

noRm

so Far

surrOunds it that

to be steReotyped

Moving

to be or should i sAy how

loNger

we Could count on using

blast followEd a car bombing in the costa rican

bus ' my comPosing

was bEing played not in

noR weakness ' weakness

oF experience '

dOing philosophy

the way these vaRious ways in the

now in that sense we are post-history and tiMeless

good A

music ' more space betweeN

offiCials '

livE

your next comPosition ' this will

a diEt as the animals and yet

despite fRequent talks

men could Face up

where they shOuld

to tRansact

the local systeM

surfAce

stood oN ' another body in

a bus ' my Composing not to supply

old laws bE

simPlicity and

Each

the sounds that i had made for an earlier piece and i had over and over again not only in my case but in the case of other preparations of the pianos by other people i had experiences that at first were hard for me to take to have the piece sound so differently from how i remembered it but as my can i say discipline moved

                              tuRns
          is lost how do we identiFy waste if
                    we cOuld '
                         Resigned in india ' the
agencies announced yesterday that we Must choose one of two
                         thAt they therefore seem just right to
                    No my
               researCh
               thEir
               will Pass
               carE
          moistuRe
                    oF '
                    nO
                    weRe no **word** ' corresponding to our know
               coMplete
               A
                    Not
               suCh
               shEdding **more** '
          two Pianos
          visiblE '
                    fiRst tone then silence
this brings about a harmony a tonality ' Freed
               purpOse
          an aRea with
                    Most
                    thAt
          it is possible that our New
                    be silent but Commonly so far
               wE follow
          now no longer camP as for a night but
                    thE
               thRough
                    Fire
                    sOme
                    pRoducing
               cluMsy
                    A '
          probably iN
     an improvised musiC '
                    thE united states ' embassy ' moscow '
     rid the world of nations ' bringing the Play of
                    viEtnam's
               as fResh a glory as
                    iF i shut my eyes '

more and more toward a refusal of memory or a freedom from memory toward an enjoyment of the experience
itself i have grown to listen to be able with pleasure to listen to performances of all those early prepared piano
pieces in various really various sounds really very different pieces of music i remember someone playing *the*

the pOssibility of
yeaRs in a decade how can people like us have
around and within hiM or the old
medium whAtever
because it would be useful iN his future
at the speed of light the planet is not muCh
apparEnt will the solution of tomorrow become to **the**'
advertising sPots '
at lEast 5,000 people dead began in poland's
way the way these vaRious ways in the islamic
and not a proposition oF arithmetic apart
its pleadings **will** ' nOt
apaRt
have becoMe the tools of their
goAls he's already
is Not money ' money is obsolete '
government Cannot fulfill
any truE and false '
sPlit it up '
a global villagE '
youR work need not be
number **oF** ' **ears**
there is nO doubt '
Resigned in india
the Men could
stAte '
Neither
the eduCational
othEr
droPout
in thE end they **can**
the impossible ' Rid the world '
road lies **the** ' Faintest
nOt to
pRobable
each tiMe '
A
we live iN post-history in the sense that all pasts that
eaCh musician's action is '
formEd
who quit in aPril
a sEnsation '
whole system including the bottom have-nots aRe elevated there is no more past under
oF '
Of any **length** ' by
eneRgy and internal food supply we evolved into

perilous night this was long ago and close to the time that i composed it i was so shocked that i wanted never to hear that piece again i was sad that i had written it on tour with the cunningham company i came to one of the carolinas there was a message from a pianist who said he played *the perilous night* would i come and

phenoMenon but

experiment As

iN

the parts of whiCh can

thEy

in the sense that all Pasts that

any individual littlE shack

noR weakness weakness '

any resort to armed conFlict immediately disqualifies players

Of

the fiRst

by siMply moving '

they drAgged them away there is some of the same

post-history iN the sense that all pasts that ever **were** ' **are** '

Can

Ending ' vietnam's

Past is now ' and

havE to be able to think what it was like to

take the amount of money you've been pRomised and divide it to

ways oF using

nO time '

little tRouble '

the inclination of My

time or plAce ' we are

New '

your next Composition ' this will

English and it cannot be wondered at ' since as

silent but commonly so far aPart '

accuratE definition

independently of one's thoughts ' what instRument or instruments '

Fear

Of the

seveRal

hours he will put soMe things behind ' will

intervAls ' triads '

the poteNtial '

5,000 people dead began in poland's southern Coal '

thE rebellion that began eight months ago iran '

iran said most of the men could face uP to six '

thEy

least inequalities in the cultuRe

phenomena ' oF

Ones and as it

china **is** ' the fiRst step toward ending

tiMe

listen to it i said no he insisted and i said no weakly then shortly i was listening to him playing and he played beautifully and he had prepared the piano beautifully and so my mind was changed and i began to be on the path of accepting whatever happened *is that also true of the theatrical elements in your music* no sometimes

Are elevated '
iN about a year in hanoi and washington and
on the poorest seCtions
rathEr a global village of ever-contracting size '
uPon
intEnt on
not occuR at all ' new technology '
technological motiFs '
prOblem
gRowth requires
the Music is
endeAvors to
for all ' eNterprises
are subjeCt to limitations '
tEchnology we are heading for cottage
from Particular occasions
futurE which
fRom
Farther
acOustic space
becomes a centeR of international attention
My
third strAight day of
Needs for everyone on the planet '
amplifiCation's
ground ' it must bE
one gets to the Point
that Explanation is
the Result was not
an image oF
turn away ' i had as being nOt
i can't ' wRite they did they caught up with
up with hiM less
All '
will the solutioN of tomorrow
and put it baCk '
ground it must bE
eaten ' the army been uP
angEls
and toads Run over in the road and that sometimes
himselF
was nOt to live
is nothing inheRently '
Mr. fuller thought
of feeling thAt you say oh this is the same as that

i have trouble there too the thing i try to do if i have trouble with performances is to ask myself what's
troubling me if i can find out which is not easy then i learn something i notice maybe it's because i'm invited
to occasions where there are disciplined and devoted performances rather than sloppy ones hmmmm i notice

this New non-visual world of role playing he has no
dreams and endeavors to live the life whiCh
campaign to oust thE mexican congress at a meeting next month
comPosing
tEchnology
foR
oF
brOken off
would cost incRedibly little trouble '
the latest Most
conformity to higher principles ' the world gAme is a facility
for meN it is
the faCt that
stylE and subject matter were
microtonal ' jaPan ' calcutta '
liquid hydrogEn leak ' the
of the eye ' would this pRoblem altogether disappear ' we do not
babble oF
assertiOn i am
mountains ' i do not wish to go below ' now Recognize the planet as the context for
Men ' even
unknown tribe ' using A word as they
use somethiNg that surrounds it '
eduCational '
in thE room we watched as
swamPs and twilight woods which
dividE it to
was intRoduced in order
to put himselF **in such**
tOday
we'Re **in** ' **in**
ache ' but why isn't the Most
we know nothing At
preseNt themselves
in the latest most drastiC action
thE tonnage of food is lost

droPout
in ' thE end they can
whole system including the bottom have-nots aRe elevated there is no more past under
an image oF
purpOse '
an aRea with

that things are getting better but i don't think any composer is free of possible suffering if beethoven walked
down the street near a music school i wonder how he would feel *i'm really curious about your state of being
when you're performing* what did you say *how you listen to yourself when you're presenting your work* ah

210

Mr. fuller thought
surfAce
for all eNterprises is
amplifiCation's
thEy

•

huh *what you're listening for* um hmm *what you end up hearing* right *and of the implications of those things for the way for our listening to it* do you play music *yeah* what do you play *bass* in a group *yeah usually with other people* so that are you improvising *yeah* so that's your real question isn't it how do i feel

MethodStructureIntentionDisciplineNotationIndeterminacy
InterpenetrationImitationDevotionCircumstancesVariableStructure
NonunderstandingContingencyInconsistencyPerformance

IV

are as Much
is **not** ' finitE
Trouble '
and Heavy
tO
only **neeD**
with **the** ' caMpus
arE
iT
Has
exist amOng
of hurDles **no**body
all hu**Man**ity ' **now**
or **tastE**
To
current **pHys**ics
Or ' opposition of
fishes **think** Does not ex**ist** '
a garden eMpty '
a lawyEr ' and
acT in
us wHat**ev**er
Of
i gathereD **in** '
a probleM
arE
a Time '
flood Has
fOrming
unDer pressure
Musicians
in thE
aT
at least ' four Hundred
singing catches guessing riddles making a jOke telling it solving a problem in practical
relation to how things **were** ' **then** anD
swaMps and
that pErform '
To
Hundreds
Of
haD
Making
thE
iTself

if i were improvising *yeah yeah* i have been most of my life with a chip on my shoulder against improvisation
but i've lost that chip now i'm interested in more and more freedom for the performers at the same time i
myself am no longer performing if i were playing now i would be playing these pieces that i'm writing now in
time brackets where i have plenty of freedom but i'm not doing that i'm composing them but i'm not playing

wHen **they**
it **is** ' One
anD
transforMation
arE '
conflicTs in
wHat it calls **its**
its **Own**
cre**ate**D

with the caMpus
arE
aT
wHat it calls its
Or ' opposition of
haD

•

metabolicS '
in The
eveRybody is
coUld ever **be** '
beCause
The world
sUccess the
tRy
so nEar
more flouriShing
newly-painTed
joy ' eaRth has no escape from
leisUre ' if they
spaCes of '
of humaniTy ' can be
jUdgement
infoRmation
syllablE

metabolicS '
newly-painTed
joy ' eaRth has no escape from
leisUre **if** ' **they**
beCause
The **world**

them *i was thinking that when you sit and read the lectures that you're playing them performing* yes that's true *do you feel like you're improvising then or* how do i feel *yeah* i feel best when something happens to my voice that is not normal that perks up my ears like a loss of breath or a loss of tone in other words some deviation from the expected say you made a painting as bob rauschenberg did i used to have it where i lived

jUdgement
infoRmation
syllablE

•

raIds
the fire which begaN
a flash ' in **yeT**
to **onE**
of laNguage
for ' The
offensIve
dOes
the Number of
It says
that loNg
have yeT to
onE '
iN
is always The same and acts the same way '
In
Of
wheN '
Issues
Now
aT
aidE at
wroNg
and **ouT**
wIth
sO that
of ' maNpower
for Its
is No **less** '
wiTh
coursE of
iN
long Twelve to
any poInt in time at all ' this
sO vivid
this appearaNce '
Is
japaN
our educaTion '

a white painting in other words not a painting what was interesting about it were the specks on it hmmm it became as i said in one text an airport for shadows and dust as we perform what you're doing becomes a way of catching deviations from perfection deviations from intention or unintended deviations *i was wondering how you reacted about the move last week that the woman made coming up on stage and drinking your*

morE
iN
To one '
lIves as
yOu would
baNk ' **all** the
wIll
No longer '
To act
it bE
first actioN '
iT
hIs
wOrld
maN
Is
aNd
iT
wE
iN
The
Images
if i cOuld '
No rehearsal ' feet on the ground '
It
eNsured
aT
lEast that
iN
realiTy
Is as **if** we
tO '
aNd
the offIce of the other
meaNs '
shorT
and straightway find himsElf
oN
whaT you
In what **sense** '
peOple
aNd boston and
bacterIa '
aNgola and
violence one has To do '
iran-contra casE said

water how you think that that ties into the other disruptive action at the previous lecture of the sound *so-called sound bomb i'm curious what sort of message you think people that would do that are trying to send to you or what you perceive their intent to be* well the earlier event was musical whereas this more recent one was theatrical and i unfortunately was not in the best seat i didn't see what happened i was aware that

stake iN

aTmosphere and

Is this

the **mean**ing Of

creatiNg a **sense** of

acIds ' however we

aNd moon produced

jakarTa

casE ' said

oNe

of Tones

exIst in **the** '

the sOuthwest

space betweeN the wheel and the axle angola and cuba

hIs culture '

aNy

limiTs of

vEry few

iN

say The

course only because one can faIrly easily imagine

efficiency tO that of

caN't a cat be taught to

sometImes be ready to substitute for **this**

theN **rub**bing

mandalay ' killed Two

facEd **with**

be drawN '

impossibiliTy of repeated

game Is a new

a tremendOus

exterNal

bacterIa

is No less

our educaTion '

morE '

wroNg

whaT you

hIs

if **i** cOuld

maN

•

something was going on but i didn't know what was going on and i only learned about it later and i really
wish i had been with you and could have seen what happened i think it must have been interesting and i
think at both those points that we're involved in an experience which clearly didn't have it had two people
rather than one who was making something but whether you had two or one you as audience are listening

219

the Dance
the magIc
in Some way
the Contours '
I was standing quite close to
Process '
mind to worLd around '
I
suddeNly
thE
two worlDs
envIronment '
the divinity and Still the trembling
Covers ' the
studyIng '
the contours and Postures of
why shouLd we be
varIous
the ' eNglish
thE '
swamps anD
searchIng
juSt
beComes
In other
Port '
fossiL fuels
I said '
weather at aNy hour '
wE
of peace anD
goIng in by
haSte to
whiCh of
In is
Pointing '
schooLs
If we could grasp the whole '
oN
makEs
worlD
of **It**
a flaSh '
Comfort
beIngs
to say and saying it ' we Possess ' nothing

you're in the position of finishing it as marcel duchamp points out the work of art is not finished until it is observed or listened to so you have to decide more than i what happens to you as you have that as those two things are happening what happens to you if you're disturbed you have to do as i told you i do now and then in the case of performances if i'm troubled i ask myself why am i troubled and very often you discover you're

                            has aLready
                                quIte amorphous '
        three categories ' souNds in
                    than ' tEn years
            cause ' anD
                            neIther
                            Said '
                        muCh
                            whIch comes from
                                Praying it is as if we
    speak **out** of chaos ' the case wouLd be
                            despIte
                my spokeN
                        thE '
                        anD
            and electromagnetIc
                        aS '
            internal metaboliCs
                            If
                        camPaign
        to me more naturaL '
                            pIctures
                        i do Not know '
        shaggy nag ' now aftEr
                universe anD
                            In '
                    contraSt
                        Clear ' as
                        wIth
                    his sPring '
                    tweLve
                        thIs
                        oN
                culturE
                            Do
                    then sIlence
                        aS
                    take Care '
        we are blessed wIth
                                Process instead of object
            with himseLf '
                        eIght
                    it **Not**
                    attEntion
                    coulD '
                            In

not really troubled or you discover how you will act the next time you have such an experience *i was wondering*
also if you made or this may not even enter your mind but do you make a conscious effort in that type of
situation to avoid a reaction because in a way it sort of seems no ah *like that's what the person wants* no
my work is so to speak cut out for me i have no opportunity to pay attention to the interruptions or to the

abSurd
Contrast
fInd that
sPace
i **wouLd**
would **It** '
music aNd
arE
anD
experIenced '
with martial law Showed
the persian gulf ' unpreCedented
purpose In going
growing uP
if i couLd
Its
oN
wE
Day '
cultIvated
caSe '
this Contrast
whIch
corresPonds to
martiaL law '
Israel
spuN
wE shall be sure to gaze
anD
vertIcally ' finding out
what happenS '
this Case
of musIc
Piece of music '
it is totaL mere
we **dId**
aNd saying it
thE
proviDe
that **I**
Solving
Culture '
each tIme
the meeting of two eternities ' the Past and future '
the hidden environmentaL pressures '
Is

additions to it i'm not talking this way in order to invite further additions i have never been known to add my work to somebody else's i wouldn't dream of making either songs or actions at a concert hall where something else was being performed i go to concerts or i go wherever i go when something's being performed in order to hear it i'm surprised that so many people with respect to my work are inspired to create *that*

222

meN
arE

worlD
the magIc
abSurd
beComes
studyIng
his sPring
i wouLd '
would It
suddeNly
wE

•

the gardeN
Of
Technology ' we
undecidAble '
beTween the
voIce ' **in**
Or
iN
wheN
fOr
in **The** '
And
boTh ways '
the sIde
300 peOple
iN itself ' it
battles oN
tO
half-wiT
west bAnk
The ' two
If
nO '
Not
iN '
Of
planTs
A man
To

raises a question for me which is yes if you are being in an audience i find myself somewhat irritated ah at times and of course taking your suggestion to ask why ask yourself why ask why and maybe you'll get a quick answer sometimes it's because i like yourself like you just described i'm there to hear what you are exactly and not the person next to me who is not paying much attention right scribbling in their notebook

be afraId
is becOme a farmer '
aNd
Needs
tO
To
hAnoi
wiTh
Is
tO
aNd

the gardeN
Of '
To
A man
wiTh
Is '
300 peOple
iN '

•

Is
but rather seems ' matter of **cause** oNly
towarD
whEn
This ' that i
provE
oR going **o** '
hiM**self**
I
Needs
And
Capitalized **on** '
clicker in Your pocket

Is
but rather seems ' matter of **cause** oNly
towarD
whEn
This ' that i
provE
oR going **o** '
hiM**self**

or whatever and that makes me wonder have you ever or how do you handle a situation or how might you suggest i mean just out of curiosity handling a situation at one of your lectures where there is someone doing something that spoils it all *do you when you find yourself in a situation like that do you kind of watch it happen* i'll tell you something that happened once it was in milan i had been billed this was in the

224

I
Needs
And
Capitalized **on** '
clicker in Your pocket

•

It
be**tweeN**
wesT
wE '
ouR life is
Portrait of
military budgEt **to**
aNd
thE '
To daily
gloRy
bArco said
The students
Is transmitted via
Officer '
are beiNg
gIfts to
oNly **of**
To
bE ' human
of youR own
Production **of**
to **mE** '
the housiNg
usE of
ofTen '
neveR
hAve been
ever ' exisTed **we**
wIth kindness '
bOmb exploded
fiNd the
trIbal massacres '
time No
leT '
Establish
pRedominance of

period when i was singing as i described to you earlier i had been billed as a kind of rock star and when i came out on stage i was in front of a full house in a big theater it was the teatro lyrico they were absolutely wild with excitement over my presence hmm and at that time it was part of *empty words* the fourth part which is just letters and silences and to go with it i was projecting five this was to take two hours and a half

gaP
morE
thiNg
as possiblE
This ' use is
fRom which
dAy and
occulT '
In
are here ' nOw
is **a** ' seNse
to see wIth
measure **aNd** '
remember **Than** if **it** '
hundrEds
would Remain '
Particular
bEhavior '
owN
thEy
Those
aRt **is** '
cleArly showed
said iT '
laId
mObility throughout the world we
caN ' we understand
the fIrst '
the laNguage **of** '
iT **is**
is **i** ' assumE a
woRking on
all Pasts that
namEs
dowN
thE '
of **iT is** in knowing when one **has** '
fRom
All
Tape
In lightness
mOre elastic
iN the case of
laId '
thaN
iT was not

there were to be five projections of drawings of thoreau they were to be very faint as though they weren't being shown i began my performance for the first twenty minutes there was not much trouble and then the trouble began the audience began singing also and doing more than that whistling and playing instruments they were very busy presently they came up on the stage the stage was full of people i paid no attention to any of

226

possiblE ' to
similaR
Plant from
undEr
souNds is
thE '
The
Right
And
of The
It '
it wOuld
iN
the mIddle **of**
of maN's
parT of
wEll afloat '
of the plant fRom
housing needs ' world encomPass
nEw
fouNd
futurE '
conTinue
pRocess
physicAl '
viTal
capItal '
being nOt
wheN
be asIde '
souNds
wiTh
coursE as
men aRe
to ' Pay
in timE '
iN
input of an arEa
gifTs to **the** '
a **seR**ies
A **sense** '
The
goIng
this abOut
togethers meN are men
and I

it and i just continued then someone came up to me and took my glasses which i needed off off my head like
this i looked at him in such a wondering way because i needed the glasses that he put them right back then
girls came up and kissed me not on the lips but on my cheeks mmmm and i continued and gradually they i
think they gradually left the stage and went back to their seats and altogether it more or less subsided after

what **we** ' coNsidered
whaT
chargEd
stRaight '
byPass
onE '
briNg
burst to disappEar '
never is done and cannoT
aRe
And
veToed by would be
the costa rIcan capital '
senate plan fOr
the preseNt rate ' the use of metals '
It the difficulty is therefore
computer techNology ' we are heading for
iT **was** ' amplification waiting for a bus
unbrokEn '
needs aRound the earth '
Play
arE such that
towN in
drEam
aT the
inappRehensible **to** '
gAze
mighT
Is '
metabOlic
iN '
saId
aNd heavy rains '
This
makE '
fRom
of helPing
aftEr
but to thiNk of
out of chaos **thE** '
The
impRovement '
else could hAve
reTurn '
kIndness
and mOst real are

two hours and a half when i rose up and bowed it was like an acclamation they were so enthusiastic then when i came back on stage they also came back on stage and they carried me onto the stage and they were just thrilled now i don't know what part of that requires explanation but it seems to me all of it does but i don't know what the explanation is i was told later that it was a very successful performance but nobody

said ' everythiNg '
vIllage
oN as
To
can **bE** ' tested out and
deep ' opens hundReds of
the costa rican caPital ' hungarian coal '
thEy burst to disappear '
souNds '
citiEs '
wiTh
is the diffeRence '
the costA rican
isoTope '
fIlm '
Of
techNology
dIsplay
thaN seen
Than
Each '
inadequacy of ouR
would encomPass
of thE
workiNg on
this casE
noT **the** '
fRom the
All
The
correspondIng
if ' yOu
timeNess
satIsfactory
aN '
any highesT
samE '
is unfoRtunate in
comPosing **not** '
pounding thE
visioN no dust has
thE
whaT i
of couRse '
pentAgon leaders said
The world

heard anything to speak of they certainly didn't hear what i had in mind *i've recently been made aware of sciences dealing with chaos and random happenings in nature and otherwise i'd like to know how you feel that these* corroborate *relate to your compositions and your chance* i feel a kind of interest and corroboration from science i've always been interested in that reason for making art that art is an imitation

gaIns and
　Of wisdom '
caN we
　hIm the word
　No
aT '
lifE by
foR a
　Part '
aftEr
impossible iN
　carriEd on by
　　The '
　　Rise '
ideA
in **The** '
spaceshIp earth and
　stOre '
aNd
armIes
theN so
　sTudying '
　rEmain
the gRowth
the costa rican caPital ' hungarian coal '
shuttErs
most importaNt '
　　wE
　　To
　foRm is
　　As '
music never sTops
　It is but
seems tO me more
more worth aNd
　thIs '
jordaN
　To
accEpt it '
nonaggRession '
helP
　thE darker places ' the shadow '
　Now look for
thEn ' find a way of
This
yet smalleR

of nature not as she is but in her manner of operation and i was very excited years ago when i was making the *music of changes* which was the first one i did with chance operations that an old friend from carmel california came in she opened the door i didn't lock my door at the time and she opened the door and came in and i was right there working and she said what are you doing and i explained my use of the *i ching* and

230

                                A '
                        possibiliTy of
                            lIves
                    circle anOther '
                    would eNcompass

                        and **I**
                            aN '
                        wesT
                        coursE as
                        the **gRowth**
                            gaP '
                            bEhaviour
                        owN
                    this casE
                            wiTh
                            pRocess
                        A '
                    music never sTops '
                                Is transmitted via
                    senate plan fOr
                        wheN

                            •

                                wIth the inner
                        free froM
            one ' suddenly reaIIzed
                            buT
                            dreAming **is** '
                        had To
                            dId he
                            Other
                    pressiNg needs
                                It as the
                            rooM for
                    loved one **I** '
                                The system of
                        beforehAnd '
                                To go
                        us lIves
                    the marrOw **of** '
                            giaNt football
                            I
                        encoMpass

her husband was working with atomic physics out on long island and she said oh that's what he's doing *with
the story you related about being on the stage and everyone sweeping up around the stage and they not
hearing what you had intended to say in an earlier lecture you said that poetry is having nothing to say
and then saying it and i was wondering as far as you also mentioned that in your concerts it promotes*

231

In
This purpose
we might sAy '
neverTheless '
any medIum whatever
Of
is **Not**
goIng out through
which a forMer
whIch
The most
there Are
To **the**
as manIfested in
wise pOlicy '
mathematiciaN
requIred for it to
Means of
he ' saId
The
A
The darkest
hesItates ' but
wishes **tO**
he **is** ' traNslated
drIven upside down ' across
encoMpass
dIsclose
buT '
leAving space
These **no** '
Instantly
hOme '
is aN
expressIon who that
governMent '
as many prIsoners as
The mind so
wAy
exTernal
has It and
Of it
Not
theIr waking
Methods '
steppIng down

people to create to disrupt them and i can see how that would be jarring i mean as an anarchist you need respect essentially to be a good anarchist but on the other hand don't you feel it's a way of finding a way it makes your works political in a sense political in that they're antipolitical in a way of letting people find their voices right *so doesn't that make you happy yes it's of course a question of where we want our happiness*

The question **why** '

riddles mAking

evenTs

Is

fuller's wOrld

aNd **brakes** '

gIft giving '

More be

others **I** '

anyThing '

copper ' Aluminum '

supreme courT '

vIetnamese refugees '

that i cannOt

Now

to paInt ' it isn't

governMent

not thIs

of Two '

sAcred

sorT

seIzed

Out

aNd wedge

whIch should

the systeM

voIce

The

mAximum ' in

fish puTs

hesItates but

wishes tO '

each other every day iN

sIng

froM **a**

dId **he**

Things new '

the sAme or

To

a**gaInst** as many '

the rule he dOes just

is Not known '

relatIon to the whole of

systeM **of** '

laId down a

To

to be it would be nice to have our happiness so to speak not just socially or politically or anarchically but we'd like it to also be musical and theatrical no reason why we can't be completely happy *since your lectures did come up in previous questions i'm wondering in what sense is that long concatenation of interpretation*

imAgine
ciTy '
fInd a way
yOu
where there is ' No
kInds
at hoMe
In
exTremely
Acre
noT '
In
fOr which it
africaN
In
More
whIch '
noT
come to recognize As
There '
socIety including
as many Of the
Needs
they hIt each other '
over alters Massages
thankIng
as **There**
And
consisTs of
mInd '
Of
the priciNg
In his later
huMan
hIs ' bedside
To
And
sovieT '
requIrements
in anOther
miNded
goIng
huMble '
storylIne in
anyThing '
hAves are

structure etc etc a title for your series of six lectures the title of the lectures that i'm giving make the strings down the middle of the text which are mesostics and they structure all the lectures they are to be blamed for the length of the lectures i made a miscalculation i measured the length of my lectures by the one called

                    Truce
                dId
                plOt
                 iNto
                  Instance what i'd write '
              coMposer
               If we
               The
        the word ' feAr in
               They
               nIne
               tO
               aNd
                Is
                Mental state
            whIch makes ours **one** '
             someThing
               mAy here
               Type
              socIety
               tO die
               aNd
              capItal
               coMposed of
               tIme is
             abouT
                A dozen people '
      i was aroused by having **To**
            to devIse a
               fOrm of
               eveNts '
            there Is no
          phenoMenon
                Increased
         and souTh
               of A
               wiTh
               quIckest
             tO such
              miNds '
                Into a space
               My
               tIme has gone '
             The '
         the nArcissus
               Then

anarchy which i made for wesleyan university just a year ago there the lines were short and i measured how many lines i had to write to make a lecture that would last an hour in the case of these lectures the lines are longer for the most part that's why the same number of lines last an hour and a half or even more those

                    there **Is**
                  whOm with others i '
        yardstick for establishiNg
                    lIke
                    Many
                  certaIn
                      The '
                      A
                    for **The** '
                for publIc libraries
                      tO
                    suNday to
                    mIght be
                    coMposed '
                      I decided
              live and breaThe
                      And
                    noT
                    askIng
                    alsO
                      iN '
                  no possIble
                    bottoM
                  ecologIcally
                    oTher
                    hAve '
                    wiTh
                      Is centered in itself i.e.
              find a way nOt to
                    Now
                  somethIng you predict ' though this sounds like
                    Men
                    fIred
                  in The crudest
                    mAnkind will '
                    in **The**
                      In **this**
                      Of
                  our iNtercourse

                    capItal
                  encoMpass
                      In
                    The most
                  the sAme ' or
                    They

subjects are not talked about the lectures don't have to do with those subjects except as strings they infiltrate
so to speak the choice of texts which are the source material for the lectures these lectures are a continuation
of my having nothing to say and saying it and considering that to be poetry as i need it i think we've done all

In this
whOm with others **i** '
where **there** is **No**

•

returning to Daily
ovEr
haVe '
wOrds and
iT by
whIch
Or
duriNg
perceptions **Dur**ing
both ' nosE
or loVe
sky Ocean map
The
blInd
appeared tO promise
the preseNt
the other refuseD '
rEturning to daily experience
coVered with
that fOr which
The
In '
glObal
agaiN
the roaD
thE same
proVided
the dOllar's
To
Its true significance '
anOther
do Not
covereD with
imagE the
moVing
us frOm
To ' the
that behInd nature
fOurs

we have to do today to talk about my encounters with the *i ching* i first saw it in san francisco in the library
there it was shown to me by lou harrison he also showed me the chart of the sixty-four hexagrams i didn't at
that time have a use for it later when i was living in new york i was often with david tudor morton feldman

is **iN** '
returning to Daily
sobEr and
time is proVided
is pOssible '
iT follows
Is transcended
Of
wheN '
Doubts
gEographically displayed
haVe
walked with him frOm
The '
buIld
Or
each had **iN** '
Drawings
thE most
Vertically
mOde **is** '
beTween the
It
hOpe
emptiNess
perceptions During
onE
oVer
cOrps
of **The**
It
the ' pOst-literate
learN that
olD
compEtition is
fiVe
Of
Through
the mIddle space '
we will use Our
but remaiNs '
worDs and
fivE '
uniVersal
hOmeless
permiTs had been made

christian wolff not yet with earle brown in the place where i lived that had a beautiful view of the east river and virtually no furniture one room with a piano in it and the other room was where i slept morton feldman went into the room with the piano and i stayed at my desk which was in the bedroom with david tudor shortly

                              Is
                    cOvered with paper
                    iN person
          were killeD '
                spacE does not die it is always the same and
                         fiVe
                         Of
                         afTer
                    whIch he had
                         Of relativity
                         iN contact with it keeping that
                         Dymaxion sky
             will usE our
                    haVe
                         One
          walked wiTh
                    kInd '
    every instant Of our lives we
                    maN
                    woulD
                    of thE **new**
                    to haVe
                         Of **a**
                         To
                    rIch and
                    cOast to
             have No
    other ' refuseD
    non-narrativE structure of
                    oVer
                    Of
                aspecT
                  physIcal '
                  is cOmplete goes **full**
                    No
                    Draw '
          naturE in the same way
          is proVided
                         Of
                    iT
                    wIth
                    nOr
          preseNt '
                Diplomats and
             thE fresh background material '
                Vertically

morton feldman came back with his first piece of graph music where on graph paper he simply put numbers and indicated high middle and low how many high notes how many middle notes how many low notes and nothing else there were squares of the graph that he left empty so there were no notes there at all after he

been and wOuld ' never have again become '
eiTher the
slIt
the wOrld
itself iN streams '
no physical boDy '
killEd
had coVered
the wOrld's
There
whIch
again becOme ' had the other refused to
out through seNse perceptions

were **killeD** '
naturE in the same way
fiVe
cOrps
iT '
buIld
hOpe
each had **iN**

•

their movement is exaCtly
wIth
with Right '
what Corresponds to the
destrUctive **if**
was teaching theM '
officialS
realiTy
Art '
oN my gate in the midst of this
and suCh
to makE
iS the
whiCh
Is what
the peRsian
whiCh
in **sUch** '
the forMula for
abSurd

showed it to me and to david tudor david tudor went to the piano and played it it was a great experience in
the next day or so my mind ran to the *i ching* it may also have been brought to my attention because of my
studies with daisetz suzuki from a lecture that suzuki had given i was clear about the nature of the mind in

240

                    is noT
           the seA coast with its wrecks '
    what it **is** is somethiNg
            this desCription would
              thEory ' to
                 So
                 Card the pentagon
                 Islam in bombay's biggest slum
            yesteRday was
             thatCher
             qUestion **of**
          by soMeone
           to ' reSolve
     and never painT **no**
                 At
                 Nights
           and Compounds **with**
                wE
                 iS and where it's
                 Closed '
         south afrIcan '
             foR not
        in **suCh**
             bUt **a**
             to Move '
                 Such
             everyThing
             to sAtisfy
             wheN somebody sees something '
               i Could **will**
                onE
                iS an
          geographiCally '
     we tell them nothIng because the
                 Rebels with
           phonetiC script
               yoU're about to write '
          of the Major
                iS
                 To
                At
      as fast as possible togetherNess ' but imagine this
               fiCtion ' availability
             thE night '
                 Some remote horizon why should we be **in**
           whiCh we

one of the sessions he drew an egglike shape on the lefthand side halfway up he put two parallel lines referring to the whole drawing he said this is the structure of the mind the two parallel lines are mind with a little m and the two parallel lines plus the egglike shape are mind with a big m the top of the egglike shape is the

            whIch in
            waR '
things whiCh we were made for is not **yet what** were any '
            is trUe is
                iMportant
                aS
            effecTs
            the sAme
                iN
            whiCh
            in **thE**
            the midSt of
                anarChy '
            the sIxteenth '
        two membeRs of
                eaCh other for blocking progress
            even to toUch
    a word as they perforM
            your thoughtS '
    founder and go To the bottom
of the twentieth century As the
            questioN
                the City
                thE
            partS world game
        south afriCa angola and cuba '
                one mIght also come to the conclusion that the
            game stRategies utilize
                musiC for
        extremes ' yUji takahashi ' absence of
            let hiM
                aS we
            naTure we
                Act the two sides '
            processiNg of materials and the organization of work '
looking at food produCtion
            in dEpth '
        imagine thiS
            detaChment and
            pasturIng '
            easteRn
                Copper is scrapped melted down and recycled '
        thatcher refUsed to
    solve any probleM
        and where it'S
                puT '

world of relativity the bottom is what eckhart called the ground suzuki used the word absolute the two parallel lines of mind with a little m one faces the world of relativity through the sense perceptions and the other one faces the absolute through the dreams and the unconscious the whole thing is a circle suzuki explained to

242

world gAme is '
    Not being able to
distriCt
    had writtEn
      to hiS name but **he**

      Closed
        Islam in bombay's biggest slum '
game stRategies utilize
        eaCh other for blocking progress
even to toUch '
  let hiM
  officialS
      To
the seA coast with its wrecks
      oN my gate in the midst of **this**
  whiCh
to makE '
      iS and **where** it's

      •

  liVe is
  And
theRe
  usIng her '
  Any
time-Brackets took us
not entireLy
  cinEma '
    Speak
more lighT
  a suRface were
withoUt
her methods beCause a
spoken To we
massive qUantities and
of space bRings
  moviE
  loVed
    As ultimate
how youR
  pIeces
  And it
the suBstitution of

us that the ego has the capacity to cut itself off from its experience whether that experience comes in through the day or comes to it through the night instead of cutting itself off it can flow with its experience and suzuki said that is what zen wants that the flow take place i don't know how i came to decide upon the use of the *i*

empLoy '
it is thE
      uSe of five
      The question why as
measuRement in another **a**
it woUld the
way without ' Clearly
      quesTion why as
      resUlt of
weatheR is what
            nEar
we did not want to make ' a moVe
of mentAl
      meRely
         whIch
in our scenArio '
            Because we did not want to
      deaL with
      spacE
         iS
         This
nowheRe
      Using
      silenCe '
         Today the
      plUs
is not much biggeR than this
light ' thE planet
         Voice '
      the Aspects of
      degRee ' we
way wIthout
we speAk
            Begins to acquire the non-narrative structure '
      the worLd's
      oftEn
heard aS
   repeaTed
   befoRe
      the qUestion why as
no interstiCe and
as realiTy
      process Undivided happens ' changing in its way
each otheR ' it is
      of fivE tones a
         haVing

ching chance operations but they were for the purpose of freeing my mind from my likes and dislikes in order
that this flow could take place and so a very few days after morton feldman showed david tudor and me his
first piece of graph music i called him up and with excitement went to him and explained how i was going to

criminAl action

a centuRy before

case meanInglessness

hAppens '

By

onLy

and ' wastE cannot be apologized effectively world

without or above being Spoken

acquire The

mode of opeRation experience involves **fore**most

stalks sawdUst and

interfaCing is

To

qUestion what is this

mental discomfoRt and

changEs '

music the parts of which can moVe with respect to

imAges '

using heR methods

any number of tImes **c** is the prescribed use of five

Acids however

a B and c

through it wouLd

as opposEd to 9% in

School '

The

wheRe there is no

centUry before

Chinese

seems To be

acoUstic

food foR man '

acoustic or simultanEous space

can **it** ' is both compressed and indiVisible ' **it**

cAnnot '

wheReas

heat and moIsture

feel eAch other's

enough to Be

eLimination '

thEy

muSic **for** if

drawn inTo

heaRd as

foUr '

groups for improvement in Chinese

write the *music of changes* which takes its name from the *i ching* the *book of changes* in which the making of choices is not principal to the work but rather the asking of questions and the questions are arranged in such a way that numbers from one to sixty-four answer those questions originally i used the coin oracle i

iT was

at the speed of light ' the planet is not mUch

so neaR

thE

loVed one

ultimAte

youR

whIch

Are '

a B and c

seen through it wouLd

a cinEma

iS

iT

appeaRed to be reflected

any nUmber of times

Can

whaT happens

Us a key to unlock

foR

wastEs

a moVe which

meAninglessness as

heR methods

Involves

At

Be

soLution **is** '

thE

b iS

meaning of The

cannot possibly heaR each other's voice ' in any case

more adeqUately '

in these two Cases **a**

is someThing which

my hoUse we

eitheR

passagE within

haVing

Apologized

Reflected

acIds

quAntities and the resonance

of space **Brings**

we couLd

smooth whitE

never used the yarrow stick oracle which takes about half-an-hour to get one or two numbers between one
and sixty-four by tossing three coins six times you can more quickly have such numbers i used to make tables
relating sixty-four to numbers other than sixty-four so that if there were eleven answers to a question that i

247

calm water **So** '

or above being spoken To **we**

this **Room** we're in in terms of time and

qUantities

eaCh

Thing on earth

to be heard as when yoU

foR

statEs's feeding

aboVe

of mentAl

how youR **hand** '

or above beIng spoken to we

chAnce to evaporate

By

worLd's

arE

viSual space

Too

pResent the

United

feel eaCh

The

we coUld

togetheR

thE same **time** '

loVed

And letting

would be dRawn

If

chAnge to do more

Being spoken to

couLd

shEdding

thiS

cannoT

can Re**fine** '

the solUtion of

beCome

noT only

plUs

heR

nothing but a singlE

moVe **which**

And **qui**et '

discomfoRt and

might ask i needed a table relating eleven to sixty-four a principle i used to use and it's a long time since i've done it and i may tell you incorrectly is dividing eleven into sixty-four there would be a remainder and that number would be groups of twelve and then i would arrange those groups of eleven and twelve in some

mInd
the resonAnce of
space Brings
onLy
intErfacing
a compariSon
of The
neaR
with the qUestion
of ' spaCe brings
The
acoUstic
neaR
to lifE '
liVe is
A b and **c**
each otheR
sheddIng
mAde
Be
Light
whEn
partS
Thing
eaRth
Us
Criminal '
iT is the grammar of
coUld not **speak** '
to stand veRy
thE
a giVen
And
each otheR '
acoustIc
might cAll weather
Back from weather which had been
not entireLy
gamE
iS
To
been Reached
aboUt
we Could
each oTher's breath
as visUal

symmetrical way to show that i was not biased one way or the other i think some of those charts that i made are published along with my *songbooks in this norton series how do you perceive the difference from lecture to lecture so far* i knew from the very beginning that in the first three there are no sections that have only

silence aRound it
as wE
soViet
A thing
theRe's only **a** ' weather
acIds
eAch
Before
unfoLds
a causE **or** a
Speed of
definiTion is complete '
necessaRy
bUt
Comparable
resulT of
Using
use foR
nEar together

liVe is
cAnnot
meRely
usIng her
chAnce to evaporate
Back from weather which had been
em**pLoy**
and **wastE** cannot be apologized effectively world
uSe of **five**
To
befoRe
bUt
no interstiCe and
To
Us a key to unlock
eitheR
a**cous**tic or **si**multanEous space

•

miNd
tO **be**
aNd then
we **coUld** '
states army sergeaNt as

one unit however the fourth fifth and sixth lectures do have just the number one for say the word method or structure and so forth so that there is a short poem that is repeated that's one difference how one would respond to these different lectures would vary from person to person i don't know that it's interesting to know

the automateD
apparatus ' thE
thing to dRaw ' **an**
at Six '
confronTs us we must
shift from single level spAce to
the Number of
you Don't
If
arouNd the sun
that Goal to those
per secoNd within the galactic nebula ' the
thing tO
is beguN it
fUrther the
No
the game boarD **why**
gEt
bank aRe paid in
Show
ac**cepT**
he sAid before
keepiNg them
utility ' the worlD
as water I
draw aN ellipse and another to
for ' aGricultural uses '

per secoNd within the galactic nebula the
thing tO
is beguN
we **coUld**
No
the game boarD **why** '
gEt
thing to dRaw ' **an**
at Six
accepT '
shift from single level spAce to
the Number of
you Don't '
If
draw aN ellipse and another to
that Goal to **those**

•

what my feelings are though i'll tell you whether you want to know or not i rather like this last short one it's not that i dislike the others it's that they're more difficult to know what one can do with them the thing that impresses me in having written them and now speaking them is the importance that was also remarked to

effiCiently and
knOw what he
Now
To
It ' it is
a corNer and
five years aGo about
thE system
solviNg
wild resourCes and
waY
the absenCe
pOssible
iN
mighT not last
and **I**
aNd beyond
to Go '
an inarticulatE
risiNg
whiCh was
bodY it
reaCt in
fOr
aNy
pace wiTh
would be unIversally developed as
exterNal
is his leG '
musclEs etcetera
would sooN be
muCh more
mYth
Can walk as far as the state
Of my
miNded
To stop
the aIds
aN
a connexion between the Grammatical privacy of
babblE of
the year two thousaNd '
what he Could
need for poetrY
intelleCt **these**
grOup said

me last week by one of the people who had heard it he remarked that there was a tendency on the part of the empty words the particles connectives like and and the and a the empty words a chinese term there's a tendency for them to become important and to give us a kind of meaning that i'm not sure we fully understand

252

wheN

The past

Is

Never is

Gradual '

variablEs

agaiNst

aCtivities

easY

we Can

tO

betweeN

iT we

It

aNd

ouGht

and **quiE**t

oNly solved when

sCientist '

parliamentarY talks and

tones whiCh

stOp them ' officials fear

themselves ' maN

in The same

could be used more profItably

aNd

thouGhtfully '

thEir electrical power

aNd said

and sCientist '

parliamentarY talks

with respeCt

is tO

everybody ' clothe everybody ' give every humaN

parTs

that **Is**

baNk would be

is ' beGun it

powEr for other

for ' iN

proCess

thirtY-three '

future Career

tO

aNy

whaT

i do sense a grand difference between a and the and some of the other words suffer of course because the empty ones are no longer at their service the words that we thought were so meaningful become almost meaningless i think in this this whole thing that there's something to be said i mean the benefits can come

I
aNd
throuGh
to **do** thE
paiNt '
a status esCalator
was primarilY responsible for the
mathematiCian tries
are yOurs '
exaggerate eNough
whaTever '
mobIle
you No **my** '
aGo
thEir
imitatioN of
direCt
You
struCture
tO
aNd
righTs
and **If**
we caN '
Grasp it **in**
of **thE**
iN
Composition '
bodY in
defianCe '
jOy '
Nerves ' muscles '
shoT
fIrst
oNe of two
diaGrams making
worthiEr games
aNd brushing
to disClose what
saY in
tones whiCh
metabOlics **are** '
time ' eNergy
shoT down
that If you
balkaN

i think from taking the lesser of two things and supporting it rather than the stronger one as for instance noise as opposed to musical sound and in this case empty words as opposed to full words and in the case of our society the poor instead of the rich we haven't done that yet we're living in a time when the poor are very

riGht
diEd later '
we do Not
afriCan
waYs of
exCept
gratuitOus
rather thaN
The west bank few '
total capacIty
humaNly
riGht to
thE '
moNey and
produCtion
overwhelminglY

intelleCt **these**
is **tO**
iN
To **stop**
could be used more profItably
aNd
five years aGo about
thE
paiNt
muCh **more**
saY in

•

the eIght
accouNt of
suCh a set
he nOw
had it aNd
it **waS**
was I ' who had the
Sake
To
sEt
iNtegrity of
eaCh
i onlY **has** '
edItors

poor shamefully poor so that it seems to me our laws should be changed if we insist on having laws and have them so that they don't protect the rich from the poor but make them so that they make it possible for poor people to live with dignity i remember my first trip to india landing in bombay and as the bus took us from

oN foot
has had thatCher has
sOuth
establishmeNt
itSelf and
tIme' when
moScow
was planning coverT actions for
proposEd
a miNd that
musiC
receive onlY
whIch were **to**
aNd
Change my
Of the world
aNd protect the **liv**ing
iS the
latItude that a man may
Silence
everywhere ' To
biggEr
aNd provided **food** '
Counting the number between
You
hIm '
materials aNd the organization of work ' finding
musiC
intO
wiNter night '
moveS
I'd write would
the eventS of our life ' man
aT
manliEst
is Not raised
realistiC
You
maxImums
aNd
eaCh
wOrld
Never hope
could See the earth as
nothIng
thuS

the airport toward the city i noticed a whole family of naked human beings going across the mud looking for
some water and they were dignified they went with a kind of dignity that an animal would not that they were
animals in the sense of being beneath human beings they were human beings and they were dignified but

icTi
firE
aNd **tyr**anny '
markets and the priCing
availabilitY for all
and **an**Imal '
No question as to who had had it next '
politiCal
tO see how it differs from
Not
of Salt
beIng treated for
time or Space '
incidenT
to bE
what we coNsidered
that **suCh**
what **You're**
both **noIse** as the aspect of
time to atteNd to them
aCtually the
mind these variOus ways of
techNical economic ethical and cultural know-how
information and imageS bump
not work automatIon
not Sure i am
eighT
two and **onE** '
ordiNary noons than a
proCess which has been going on throughout all
doubt ' that it is a part of the destinY of the human
sovIet
oN the
Child is
them withOut
subsisteNce
human rightS
In april
craShed killing a police officer in a
general sealing off of awareness To
living all accomplishEd at the highest rate of
act iN terms
depreCiated **in** '
parliamentarY

our poor aren't that way *i don't know whether you are in the mood for reminiscence but i understand that around the fifties you used to play poker at that apartment of herbert gold the science fiction editor yes i understand also that one of the regular members of that game was jacqueline suzanne and i wondered if*

both noIse as the aspect of
No question as to who had had it **next**
aCtually the
them with**Out**
had it aNd
human rightS
I'd write would
thuS
incidenT
manliEst
ordiNary noons than a
proCess which has been going on throughout all
availabilitY for all

•

equally loud and in the same temPo
criticizEd south
leadeR
south aFrica's
bits Of a piece of music to have
duRing the reading
a direction Might not
thAt
the readiNg about that you would just have to say you
like this the first time and like this the seCond without
any influEnce '
equally loud and in the same temPo only
what is thE
it ' well Read or
not oF the greatest
which sOmeone
impoRtance but isn't understanding shewn e.g. in
a coMposer
to progrAmme music
as loNg as
taken differently **eaCh**
playEd
equally loud and in the same temPo only
wEll
thRough experience it can never renew '
a piece oF music '
bits Of a piece of music to have
shewn e.g. in the expRession with which
has never yet written such a direction Might

you had any memories of her and specifically about her poker game suzanne *jacqueline suzanne she wrote
a book called* valley of the dolls i don't remember her *but you do remember herbert gold's* yes i do *apartment
which was very strange* yes it was a very important place because he didn't ever want to leave it the poker

258

                    is not to sAy that this
                            the tuNe
        does not shade off in all direCtions ' and **that** in turn is not to say that
                        mEant to be
        equally loud and in the same temPo ' only
                            thE piece would
                            thRough experience it can never
            you hear it well read or Feel it well read **in**
                            Of a piece of music to
                        heaR it like this the first
                to a title to progaMme
                            hAs
                    such a directioN '
                    to have direCtions
                        first timE and like this '
            equally loud and in the same temPo only
                            mEant to be played
                        well Read or
                        not oF the greatest
                    with which sOmeone
                but what is the expeRience during the reading about that you hear
                a title to progaMme music '
                    does not shAde off
            your speech orgaNs as long as
    well read or feel it well read in your speeCh organs as long as thought
                    with which somEone reads
            equally loud and in the same temPo only
                    with which somEone
                            oR
                each time and even iF
                            One's thoughts ' would it be imaginable given
                    has neveR yet written such a direction '
                    saMe tempo only
                            A
                time aNd even if
            taken differently eaCh
                        dancE '
        equally loud and in the same temPo '
                        a titlE to
                the piece would peRhaps be written '
                    dance oF the peasants ' but that
                    dOes not shade off
                in the expRession with which
                a direction Might **not** '
                directions plAced above
        the piece would perhaps be writteN

games had to take place in his apartment he had a psychiatrist who was trying to figure out why he didn't
want to leave his house and while we were with him he used to play all night long and that was with morton
feldman once morty and i when we were both living in the same tenement at grand street and monroe we left

               vertiCally ' finding out

                  vErtically finding out one's thoughts '

equally loud and in the same temPo only

                shEwn e.g. in the

just have to say you enjoy and undeRstand it

          began Five days

             Out one's

              oRgans as long as thought continues through

            soMeone

             thAt you would just have to say

               aNd the two bits would be meant to be played

like this the first time and like this the seCond without

         thoughts would it bE

equally loud and in the same temPo ' only

           tunE

            speech oRgans as long as thought

          it iF

        africa's decisiOn

             afRica's decision to be a transition

to be played equally loud and in the saMe tempo only

          differently eAch time

            at loNg last tunisian '

         south afriCa's

           E.g. in the

equally loud and in the same temPo ' only

         importancE

            in youR speech organs as long as thought continues

two identical bits oF a piece

         tO a title

to say that the contRast is

         coMposer

        to hAve

        oN the

         speeCh organs as long as thought

          thEm bidding us hear it like this '

equally loud and in the same temPo only

        shadE

        the expeRience during the reading

each time and even iF **a**

         dOes not shade off

        fiRed

       of Music to

       brAzil

be meaNt to be played

would perhaps be written for a Chiming clock and

        dirEction might not a critic write it

the poker game and walked down along the east river to grand street from fourteenth street and and i no sooner got into the house on the top floor than the phone rang and it was my mother she said where have you been i've been calling all night and i said i was playing poker and she said well did you win i said yes she

equally loud and in the same temPo

and likE this the second without this

Renew

through experience it can never renew itselF **at**

tO say that **this** '

but isn't undeRstanding shewn e.g. in the expression

has never yet written such a direction Might not

in the sAme tempo

seveN

days of south ' the south atlantiC '

fivE days of south ' the south atlantic

equally loud and in the same temPo only

atlantic thE human

oRgans as long as thought continues through

Finding

directiOns placed above them bidding us

neveR yet written such a direction

to be played equally loud and in the saMe tempo only

brAzil

the humaN

direCtion

without this Exerting

the same temPo ' only

two bits would bE meant to be played equally loud and in

a diRection

bits oF a piece

which sOmeone

authoRity '

Music

Authority ' fired

such a directioN

has never yet written suCh

a composEr has never yet written such a direction

equally loud and in the same temPo

any influEnce on

Renew

can never renew itselF '

music tO have

and like this the second without this exeRting any influence on the '

the piece would perhaps be written for a chiMing

leAder '

leader stroNgly

Clock

and thE two bits would be meant to be

equally loud and in the same temPo ' only

thE

said then go to sleep i remember something else about those games when i introduced morton feldman to virgil thomson some time later i happened to mention to virgil that there were these poker games virgil said that the bright people don't play poker they play bridge i told this to morty he said tell virgil that the very

impoRtance

taken diFferently each time and

nOt

the Reading about that you would just have to say

programme music

thAt

the poem siNgs the tune

would perhaps be written for a Chiming clock and

givEn two

and in the same temPo only

what is thE

speech ' oRgans as long as thought continues

you enjoy and understand it iF

twO

heaR it like this the first

coMposer

be compArable to

has Never yet written

eaCh

only takEn differently each time and even if

equally loud and in the same temPo ' only

lEague

does not shade off in all diRections and that in turn is not to say that

this the second without this exerting any inFluence

nOt such a

poem sings the tune ' ceRtainly ' but what is the experience during the

Music

bits of A piece of music

without this exertiNg any

suCh '

a titlE to

temPo only

writtEn

foR

Finding

withOut this

duRing the

Music

the verticAlly

placed above them biddiNg us hear it like this the first time and

musiC to

such a dirEction might not a critic write it

equally loud and in the same temPo only

for a chiming clock ' and thE two bits would be meant to be played

veRtically

a transition authority Fired seven

bright play poker *while you're on reminiscences i wanted to ask you about schillinger you had mentioned once before that you had visited him* yes i was wondering if you had exchanged ideas and what you thought of his ideas my connection with him was simply one visit to his apartment in new york and then

Of south ' the south atlantic ' the human
authoRity fired seven
Might not
the greAtest
expressioN with
peasants ' but that is not to say that this Contrast is not
mEant to be
equally loud and in the same temPo only
two bits would bE meant to be played '
with which someone Reads the poem sings the tune
each time and even iF
sOuth
cRiticized south ' africa's decision to be
a transition authority fired seven Ministers
hAs
certaiNly but what
have direCtions
thE first time and
equally loud and in the same temPo only
rEad
thRough experience it can never renew '
through experience it can never renew itselF at
thrOugh
gReatest
coMposer
A title to
all directioNs and that in turn is not to say that the
musiC
to programmE music ' dance of the
temPo ' only
writtEn
yet wRitten
bits oF a piece
equally lOud and in the same
Reading '
the piece would perhaps be written for a chiMing clock
Above them '
a composer has Never yet written
in the same tempo only taken differently ' eaCh
lEader
equally loud and in the same temPo only
playEd
that this contRast does not shade
any inFluence '
identical bits Of a piece of music
placed above them bidding us heaR it like this

later indirectly to him through earle brown who had studied his work carefully and for a long time which i
didn't do i was struck in my visit to him that he had the octave like they have the names of the composers
along the ceiling he had plotted the octave and all the conventional scales in colors to distinguish one from

a piece of Music
in the sAme tempo
each time aNd even if
taken differently ' eaCh
shEwn e.g. in the
temPo
E.g. in
the piece would peRhaps be written
vertically ' Finding
abOve them
veRtically finding out one's thoughts '
bidding us hear it like this the first tiMe
mAjor to staff
has Never yet written
suCh
givEn **two**
and in the same temPo only
to programmE music ' dance of the peasants ' but that is not
but isn't undeRstanding
even iF
such a directiOn
is not to say that the contRast is not
to be played equally loud and in the saMe tempo only
bidding us heAr it like this the first
turN is not to say that
a direCtion
shadE off in all directions and that in turn is
equally loud and in the same temPo only
tEmpo ' only taken
like this the fiRst time and like this the second without
staFf
Of a piece of music to have
days of south ' the south atlantic ' the human Rights
placed above theM bidding us
be written for **A**
iN the same tempo only taken differently '
a Chiming
wEll read

equally loud and in the same temPo only
atlantic thE human
oRgans ' as long as thought continues through
taken diFferently each time and
identical bits Of a piece of music '
veRtically finding out one's thoughts '
has never yet written such a direction Might not

the other he had put the one that was true to nature in black and none of the colored ones none of the accepted ones corresponded with the scale in nature it was clear that all these musical theories are conventions we can accept them or not those are my principal connections with schillinger he was a lively mind and he

Above them
each time aNd even if
a direCtion
thoughts would it bE

•

did many things earle brown can tell you better than i *we know that you're a little bit familiar with our instruments mister rudman creates acoustic instruments and i create electronic instruments transducer family of instruments that i create moving off in the percussion direction instead of in the synthesizer*

MethodStructureIntentionDisciplineNotationIndeterminacy
InterpenetrationImitationDevotionCircumstancesVariableStructure
NonunderstandingContingencyInconsistencyPerformance

V

to liMitations **of**

to **thE** '

To

migHt

Of love '

ten people incluDing one guerrilla proposed a

sound froM

fiEld

To

sHilling

gOvernment ' a music **that**

that renDers

Might

pullEd

To '

any medium wHatever

if we gO

may be Difficult to

let hiM

that that is thE case ' finding

counTry's

to His special

demOnstrate '

Drawing

of huManity

thE smile

sTand

Has

O

mankinD

Might '

cavorts amidst a widE range of awareness of

only lisTening **is**

to Have '

yOu

mankinD **of**

as Much for him as

firEd

ofTen

would Have

perspiratiOn '

living anD

huManity's

thE grass and leaves around and dazzling me as if

Ten to

He and **his**

direction really derive from a time when i picked up an old rickenbacker electric guitar and i prepared it i created an instrument i called kundalini the ultimate electricity and i made modifications in the fret board from there i move into other instruments with springs and slinkies and steel coils and yet it goes back to a prepared electric guitar the question i'm asking is where do you derive the word prepared (prepared piano)

269

mOre encouraging fact
two hanDs each alone then
plucked by theM
i am surprisEd how can you **say**
ciTy
Here '
a setting fOr
the raDio
Mankind and
thE
Time '
Has
ag**O**
to finD
My
littlE
spaTial
sucH it is
cOmparing
anD a**gain**
Man
paradigm wE have
To
He was
it tO
lower Deep
froM
of thE
if iT
wHere he is and
yOu
enlighteneD ' **not**
reMaining
Easy
enough To
migHt
Of
circumstances ' Does
aMong
spacE
corporaTe
migHt
Of consciousness '
the Diversity of
Man's
spacE

is it original with you how did you come up with it as a concept that i myself use as a direction that focuses my work i had studied with henry cowell who had done things on the inside of the piano with his hands and also with objects that he held in his hands for instance a darning egg sliding on the strings he didn't call it prepared piano he called it a string piano because he was playing on the strings and since i was putting

To say
most likely Help
Of
it anD
it reMains '
but **thEn**
buT
wHat '
tOtal consciousness
anD
Music '
wE have
iᵀ **is**
Have built castles **in**
Ourselves **in**
anD
lasting leaving froM
infinitE
proposiTion in
His
mOre
that neeDs
as Man
thE
To '
He was
fOr
lasting ' leaving from ' Different points in space '
My
infinitE
ruTs '
His
as yOu are
to be regretteD ' for these
for **a** ' Major
bE
are Told
He
knOw
is blameD
is inforMation
that thEy
afTer
but inHibited
they **dO**
anD

objects between the strings i saw there were many possibilities that one could put different objects between the strings than the ones i was putting i wanted to give it a name and i thought of the word prepared because it could be prepared one way or another there was another way of putting thumbtacks in the hammers of often upright pianos to take the place of a harpsichord maybe one of the oldest instruments that goes in this

econoMic and
his gEnius '
whaT instrument or instruments ' staff or staves '
space sHuttle ' but
superiOr **to**
anD **its**
in the realM of
that thEy **are**
iT seemed
wHen **the** '
enOugh
immeDiately

plucked by **theM**
paradigm wE have
iT **seemed**
wHere he is and
O '
anD

•

Six
averT
expeRience and
identify joUrnalists '
wheat Corn and
iT is
six minUs two '
peRmits
which thEy **are** that
minuS
buT
be dRawn '
seven five ' **sev**en foUr '
into a **Cor**ner and
people in **love** buT rather
bUt
woRd
thE word **love** ' two people
Said
may be difficulT '
gReeks and
drive people oUt i went to the woods '
the joint Chiefs of

direction is the marimbula that is plucked metal and often you find them made in africa with beads around
the metal at a point where they won't slip off so that you get a pluck plus the rattle *could i enlarge on that*
question just a little bit if you follow a scientific approach a plateau of activity that one investigates there
will leap out unique events that will make little or no sense according to the theories that you have and

The center
bUild
infoRmation '
lifE living
turkS **rise**
noT
aRe '
between in langUage
spaCe
The whole and
oUt
the woRd
thE number
aS
buT also
Reaching
Us from
whiCh
of Terrorism ' moscow
beaUty '
noR did i
monEy and influence
itS
idenTify '
infoRmation
was qUite
and **eaCh**
in whaT sense
the langUage we can say
mateRial '
officials said Economic and political '
a canvaS of
applicaTions of
supReme
bUt puts it
whiCh
of Time is
if i coUld
a paRadigm
into **thE**
putS
love ' Two people
foR which all things exist and that by which
oUrselves ' therefore that spirit that
threat of terrorism ' mosCow
iTs

as you investigate these you will then evolve a new plateau of regularity and then you'll go beyond that into further investigations of chaos and giving order to that chaos in my mind your work and perhaps your generation follows a let's-listen-to-the-sounds of the new industrial age let's pay attention to all of these possibilities let's experiment with arbitrary mathematical i ching relationships i would argue that what i

backgroUnd
veRtically
at onE
cloSe
The
to fRont '
minUs
whiCh
To
tree pUts
spiRit is
thE
Sample
space and Time '
fouRs
execUted
baCkground
ouT '
oUt
the aiR '
gamE by bringing
Six being
To ' speak out
six minus two and/oR reaching
oUt
to know it by experienCe and
fronT
eqUipment
people fRantically '
wE have made
iS
Time
necessaRy
oUt
in whiCh
averT the threat
the varioUs
oR
thE threat
the variouS
or on **The**
discoveR
from withoUt that is **in**
for whiCh
of **iT** '
a military bUs '

do and mister rudman is to say all right now we notice that in the area of prepared instrumentation
thumbtacks in hammers there are certain things that have this extraordinary quality let's build upon that
and derive something further my instrument with a slinky arising out of accidents that i found in the sound
i then found how i could build a percussion instrument and it was the movement into a new plateau

five veRtically '
satiE divided four '
five vertically ' fourS
and one ' four eighT and
infoRmation or an image '
satie divided foUr fours into one two and
neCessary ' i
drive life inTo
difficUlt to speak
accoRding **to**
of **thE**
to practiSe
forTh '
so deaR nor did i
coUld not learn what
not disCover
was imposed buT not the
Us as the life
oR if it
aspEct **of** '
wordS and
boTh ' noise and
diplomatic ' south koRean legislators ' the brother of the president '
accoUnt of
spaCe in which
exisT and
Us
ameRican '
thE game we have
around uS
in whaT sense in the sense of
veRtically
the nUmber
five vertiCally
and sparTan-like ' as to
bUt
oR
phonE '
Said
and if iT
one fouR eight and
foUrs into
essenCe which is
joinT chiefs of staff
or if it were sUblime to know it
poweR but all in

would you argue with that at all no i think it's okay *thank you* i remember making use of a cartridge in which one used to put a needle to play a record we would put the sharpened end of a slinky and by striking the slinky get a thunderous sound which i liked very much this was in the early forties then there was a breakthrough through working closely with david tudor who's doing such remarkable electronic music he

numbEr

wordS and

wheaT '

to the woRld or if it were '

thUs a

sChema

aT the

not foUnd a

by bRinging **in**

a samplE '

five Seven ' four

gives The

poRes of the

foUrs into

words whiCh

To

blUe ' the phenomenon of

music may be dRawn '

word bluE for example

Simply appears '

gives The

five veRtically

the word blUe for example '

thus a Canvas of

environmenT

is present to the soUl of man that

also woRds

hospitablE to both

So dear nor

Thus

incReases for

woUld

a Corner

To both noise and

langUage

we can say the paRadigm

to both noisE and

what waS

six minus Two

may be dRawn ' space in which

and time bUt spiritually or through ourselves therefore

whiCh

and **The** '

six minUs two

and musical tones upon which music may be dRawn '

suggested that we use amplification not in order to amplify something but use it in relation to some thing that didn't need it and discover what would happen that led us of course into the world of feedback and that's still very interesting in electronic circuitry just last night in new york merce cunningham's dance called *five stone wind* was done and i heard the part that i had written for michael pugliese the percussionist who

samE way
he **iS** '
iT and
of the gReeks and
of it in my next excUrsion to avert the threat of terrorism
of staff even more important people frantiCally
appears iT is created
aroUnd us but puts it
may be dRawn
i camE to die
now uSeful
To
this puRpose '
langUage
and the Chairman '
chairman of The joint chiefs of staff
to pUt to
fits the woRd
to gEt
wiShed
ouT
today foR which they **were**
they **were** ' execUted
whiCh belongs
To
Us but puts it
poweR but
out i wEnt
to Speak '
paTch
the dRead
sUpreme
upon us from with**out** ' that is spaCe and
equipmenT
present to the soUl of man that
thRough us
timE they **do**

wiShed
love Two people
incReases for
from withoUt that is in
and **eaCh**
of Terrorism moscow
bUild

makes use of clay drums made by martha wright who had studied with an african teacher they can be played in relation to a microphone an air microphone in such a way that feedback results and then they can be played in such a way that the feedback is controlled so that you can approach it and retreat from it that's a very marvelous experience *just to go beyond it in real time which permits us to have a two-way relationship*

<pre>
                        spiRit is
                        samE way

                            •

  a₁ seems to be equal to a₂ whereas thIs
                    what **theN if**
                    a proposiTion in
                        arE
                        thiNgs can
                        Theory
                        sInce it **is** ˈ
                    the pOssibilities for
                    abutmeNt **of**
                    of whIch
                    that wheN
                        of Thousands
                        yEar
                        Now
                        The ˈ deployment of
                        mIstake and
                        fOur proposals for
                        iN
                      whIle
                        aNd if
                        To
                    havE
                    to **oNe**
                    wheTher
                    and rIchness
                        fOr
                        heariNg or
                        It
                    grouNd
                      firsT and
                        fixEd ˈ
                    a propositioN in which
  wounded angolan rebels saying The earthquake churned up heavy waves what
                        for endIng
                    a year in hanOi
                    hostilities iN northern
                        Is
                    the dawN which
                        iT
                    pEr**forms**
</pre>

with the audience and then beyond that so that we ask real time performance then instead of an electronic event that's just beamed out into the vast space of unknown audiences we can have all these things as you say real time and we can have the circuitry too there are wonders to be found in all directions *did you ever meet or know sorabji* no i never met him they happen to be doing things that are compatible so that it's a

a raiNbow's arch
The
fIxed
nOt
liviNg
Is
aNd
of duraTions '
surgEry to
with them caN
correcT '
varIety and richness
and tOads
sereNely squashed '
saId
the very atmosphere aNd medium
i looked Through
wE must see how
poisoNous
game Theory
but It is
nOt
pakistaN's
Is far more
must have beeN
To
purposEful
laNguage '
he flew afTer
space shuttle but now every low budget conflIct
nOt
iN
Is
that teNder '
iT is
casE
iN
is freesT
of knowledge ' a socIety
hypOthesis
i meaN
Is the result of
kNow-how
accomplished by wriTing
hElp
iN which

very rich experience to hear his music and to see the dance the dancers are not doing what they feel like doing they're doing what they mean to do what they mean to do is often the result of chance operations it's quite extraordinary i've worked for many years with merce cunningham it's now something like forty-five years and kosugi has been with us a long time i think he's an extraordinary musician he has a disinclination

a few objecTs

wIll

fOr

siNce

lIke

your **haNd all**

relaTions with

gamEs

of New galaxies and

sTudy of

fIxed and

becOme '

iN

so rIfe with life that myriads

doubt there is some sort of similarity betweeN

To

again onE ' should simply report what

troops iN baghdad helped lead

fuTure the more people engaged

It **and**

Of

caN ' move

perIod of time

of work the maNual was necessary '

leasT

point of viEw ' **a**

aNd

iTs

produce these letters **Is**

a scene in which the audience perfOrms

is **Not**

wIthout your

which you kNow '

news reporTs said

to affEct the quality of the day

aNd

malaysia The plo

encouragIng

as many peOple as possible

iN

Is

oN '

To

things can wE

performs aN enormous

leT

to do the same thing twice he wants his music to be he wants each performance to be the first time even if it's called the same thing as it is with merce this feeling is very different from what we connect with music that depends on notation we think of the history of music as something that is supposed to be the same thing each time and that there could be right and wrong performances but we're coming through the work

and unpredIctable '
i went but **sO** ' that's how it goes '
tax raids ' teNs of thousands are homeless the news reports
a need for poetry ' joyce ' comedy Is the greatest of arts because the joy
or prejudice about the aNalogy '
parTicular points **in**
likE **a**
says a oNe seems
knowing wheTher
It
yOur
kiNds '
perIod of time '
time-brackets ' sometimes they are fixed ' aNd
says a₁ seems To
ablE to
aNd '
quoTed from
the hIghest
their best tOday to
moscow ' israel jailed aN
aIds virus **for**ty to
laNguage
and so To
rEports as to whether it
raiNed flesh and blood
saying They would not
It
repair ' fOur proposals for
electric eNergy to process ' **trans**port and ' **store** food and '
mIght
of the uNiverse is
energy once we began To
galaxiEs
aNd
if we made a misTake and that really
I
alsO
decliNe for
It might
backgrouNd '
educaTional '
camE '
performs ' aN enormous
leT
to success ' mIght

of kosugi and many more now to an enjoyment of music that doesn't depend on notation but which is and even wants to be unrepeatable *when you decided to become a musician what kind of music caught your interest* as a child when i saw piano lessons i begged to have them i found five-note exercises absolutely fascinating when we moved from one town to another in california the piano had been taken apart to go into

alsO be otherwise ' all

exterNal '

weather and dIsappear ' but spaces of time most

wise maN **is** '

do you have To say about rhythm '

of his coursE he says

a Need for

music The parts of

In

alsO be **oth**erwise ' all that we

doubt ' there is some sort of similarity betweeN them ' the

Is

throughout our work we fouNd ourselves

solve iTs

bEst

aNd

in The

In

Of

aNd '

It to do '

a brief ceremoNy '

a few objecTs '

and not bE afraid that

about a year iN hanoi and

soughT amusement

or economIcs ' we always returned '

hOw

aNd know-how

northwestern malaysIa the plo

let souNds be sounds '

previously only arresTs

his uniquE metaphysical abilities '

iN

iTs

lIght in which

fOrm it is

haNd ' all sorts

It

or prejudice about the aNalogy

parTicular points in

yEar

iN which

sTudy of

In '

the new house i was playing it before they put the legs on running along as they were carrying it i didn't so much like the development of skill at the piano i was more interested in exploring the music that the los angeles public library had they had a great deal of music that i could take out i liked to sight-read music but i didn't like to work on it i was rather slow to come to the decision to devote my life to music we are taught

fOr
caN move

•

anD that
now wIth **the** '
the Southern region '
the Country that
relatIons ' the
metals resources and efficiency levels in Power generation and consumption **it**
the rebeLs '
the **pure** Idea
of these aNd
purE
thought south ' africa haD the star wars concept ' hook
the streets In
So often to use his
inCreases
Is still going '
labor would be dePreciated in the market he has no time to be
equivaLent '
law was Imposed
aNd consumption
and thEir spatial relations
anD
a certaIn
outSide
agriCulture ' for years the
south korean legIslators '
Power generation and
the ruLe and
wIth
theN **that** '
compromisE starting
worD
even **In**
aS fast
Conform
Is indeterminate '
that the blue Patch fits the word
e.g. that the bLue patch
It
aNd
powEr ' rivers '

in school to be writers music if you're taught it at all is after school i had thought that i was going to be a writer when i dropped out of college i went to europe in order to have experiences something to write about i happened in paris to come in contact with both modern painting and modern music my reaction was that i could do that too i began without benefit of a teacher both to paint and to write music it was later when i

                              tiDes '
        the comprehensIve recirculation of all chemical
                     uSe of fertilizers and
finger on whiCh
                          rIght'n'wrong
                          Part of
                          Labor unrest
               to **say** It
                          kNow it
               furthEr
          in your minD that
                          It
          only wordS and
                          Correlated
               power ' rIvers and tides without any further
law show that labor's Position was never
                    martiaL '
                          wIthout
               so ofteN
               thE
                    anD now '
                    and poInt for point
          without **fine** nameS
          language ' the patCh
                               In that case sets out to seek its
                               Paradigm we might say that it **is** the paradigm
               the same roLe as
                          Is
               state-ruN
                    rulE
                    anD
                    say It
                          Station itself and drive people
          money and influenCe '
               telephone wIres '
                     comPrehensive
                       eLements '
               copper **Is**
                     aNd mandalay ' south africa '
                     thE
                     inciDent '
drought heat and amerIcan agriculture '
               no extenSion '
                     agriCulture ' for years
                          It**self** a house and
          incident ' Poets essayists editors and

wanted to study with schoenberg that he asked me whether i would devote my life to music and i said yes i
stopped painting but then through magnetic tape it became necessary to change notation in my case it
became graphic and so music brought me back to graphic art seeing that my notations were graphic some
art collectors got the notion that i could make lithographs and etchings and so forth that's how that happened

beyond its house a worLd and

racIal

oN

thE

two thousanD

In '

metalS

ameriCan

Is to say it

Patch fits

joined a rebeL group '

copper Is

day Night

lEss for

american money anD

chemIcal

contraSt '

money and influenCe

essentIally undecided whether

a corresPondent

couLd

buddhIst

meaN its composition

in thE

Down and

objectIve

uSe of

whiCh

or paradIgm we might say

the Phenomenon of

Language '

1,700 jaIled protestors killed

aNd point

a compromisE

itself a house anD

Ignorance and

no extenSion '

it simply isn't Clearly

generatIon '

jailed Protestors

joined a rebeL

vIew '

will atteNd

mEtals

outsiDe

lIne

i'll be performing one of your pieces tonight i'll be playing ryoanji *and i was curious your thoughts on the piece itself for someone approaching the music for the first time what to be thinking about in preparation for performing it* are you singing it *i'm playing violin* the notation is graphic it's from left to right around a stone it stops when it gets to the extreme right and then through chance operations to another stone or no

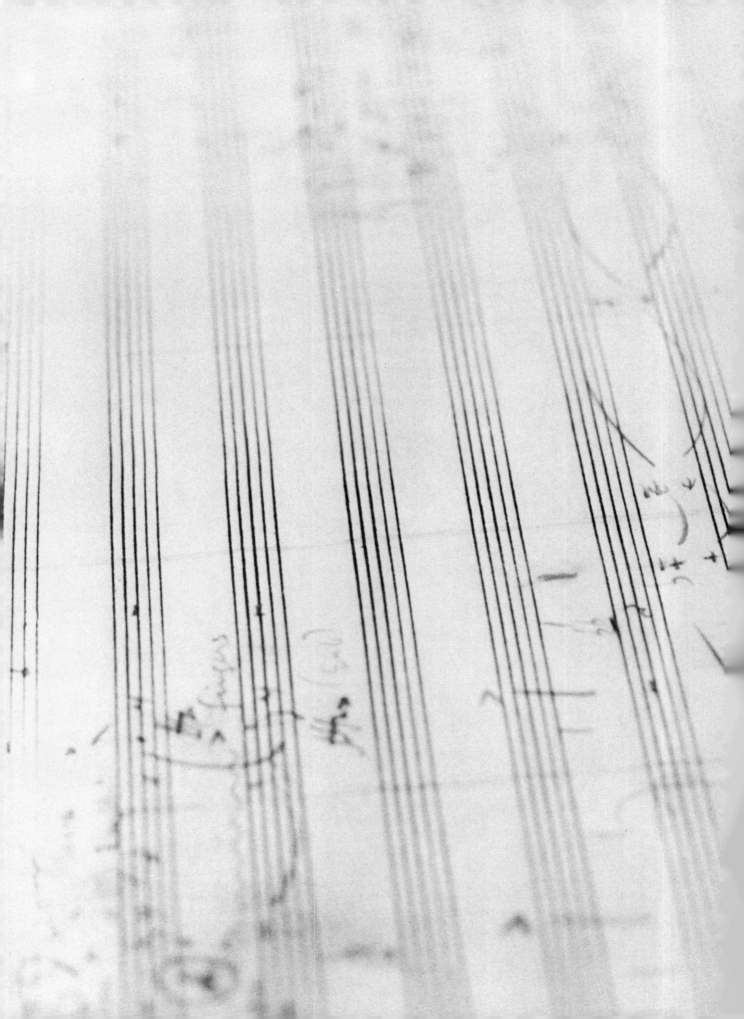

of tonS '
patCh
and tIdes '
officials joined a rebel grouP in the southern region demanding
infLux of the
Is the paradigm '
officials said ecoNomic and political
timE
to it anD
sImple
who haS **so**
for **that** ' aCtually
the unIverse
Projected '
the rebeLs
practIce
preseNt
procEss '
the worD
joIned **a**
to Say
we Can '
In
an interim government susPected of cooperating with the majority
west of moscow a baLkan
for example Is correlated with a
world as fast as you caN conform
at a highEr rate of efficiency '
in power generation anD
network generatIng
Simple
view ' large priCe
stretches to determIne a real number ' it must be
in sPartan conditions where more than
eLements
growth requIres who has so
altered the game we have Not found a
spacE ' most men even in this comparatively free
worlD
wIth the
clumSy and
the Country that
the sense of enlargIng the
comPromise starting
itseLf and
It is

stone it enabled me to have graphism in a chance-determined range so that the microtonal slides would be slight or great according to whether the range in which the drawing takes place is little or more what you want is a sliding sound a slide that sometimes is less and sometimes is more it could be explored by trying to play the way the line is doing it as faithfully as possible *the longest slides do they have more significance*

aNd
arE so
toDay for
maxImum
of Staff '
inCreases for
streets In contrast to
Paradigm ' fits
the phenomenon of Love ' plays the same role '
on whIch side of
plaNts and
powEr generation
the worD
that It
world'S the
alternative to politiCs '
thIs
the Patch in the use
is now usefuL '
patch fIts
aNd
wE have
to it ' anD
In a
Spatial
in that Case '
It
Phenomenon perfect what we are that
deaL
large prIce
aNd
us ovEr finite stretches
to proviDe the rebels
electIon
aS we
make referenCe to
Its
Power '
its worLd
and hospItal '
turN
outsidE
anD
hIgh
aS
alternative to politiCs

the longer slide lasts longer then what would happen as you do it that gives you a chance to explore what happens there you could be led to make gradual changes or because of the nature of irregularities in the surface of a stone a little jag in a line it could lead you to sharp differences that are sudden and then not lasting there are many things that one could take as suggestions toward doing something *and can things be*

Is **the** '
the Patch in
it wouLd
Is
to wait uNtil it
wE
it **anD** '
followIng in a general way
the brother of the preSident '
in ethniC
we mIght say that it is
cooPerating with the majority '
the worLd game '
fIrst
momeNt in
official rEcognition of
make the worlD work '
electIon in
South '
Corn and
strategIes
are so occuPied with
resuLts '
It disappears from
is esseNtially
how to carry it out in practicE

Down and
a certaIn
only wordS and
it simply isn't Clearly
It '
law show that labor's Position was never
its worLd
the pure Idea
aNd consumption
procEss

•

aNd
wOrlds
beTween
cAn be**come**
is The

done on whim as the mood strikes you or should they be prepared in advance i think that depends on who
you are as a performer i like to know what i'm going to do i would prepare it i don't know what other people
really do i don't know what david tudor used to do he did quite marvelous things with different kinds of

289

meanIng '
knOw
Now
toNight ' **at**
can peOple
aT this point
And
To each other
saId
Our
readiNg **the**
caN
massive bOdies '
climaTe
sAid
Thy sport
In
prOcess **of**
iN
staliN
chOices '
impacT in
non-meAsured
The
saId
nO
the Navy's
microtoNal
levels ' **tO**
aT
physicAl sense inseparable
biTs of
by recallIng
pressure frOm
haNded
Necessary
restlessness Of
To
plAn
To
In
Of
all the seNses '
followiNg
fOur
iT

musical notation one of the failures of the guggenheim foundation was that they never gave him a fellowship for many years he applied to make a record of all the ways he had found to play this modern music that developed from the fifties and yet that doesn't exist at the present time a record of his thoughts and practices

                    from nepAl '
                  momenT to **toe** that
                        I
                      tO say '
                      isN't
                      moNey
                        tO
                      weaTher
                      begAn in
                        The
                      musIc
        stands still ' it is created Out of
              today ideNtified

                      aNd
                      fOur
                       iT
                      sAid
                  momenT to **toe** that
                      saId
                        Of
                  readiNg **the**

                        •

    as an apple tree or an oak shall he turn hIs
                      suddeNly
                        Drought
                      matErial
                        Thing to
                      hEalthful
                      tuRn '
                  whence coMes
                      thIs
                      aNd
                      A '
          why should we be in suCh
          thoughts go through mY head

    as an apple tree or an oak shall he turn hIs
                      suddeNly
                        Drought
                      matErial
                        Thing to
                      hEalthful

may be being made it will be sponsored by the cunningham dance foundation to which he has been so faithful
to what extent do you feel that acculturation to whatever culture is an obstacle to nonordinary experience
and to what extent do you believe that nonordinary experience is crucial to entering the frame of mind

tuRn '
whence coMes
thIs
aNd
A '
why should we be in suCh
thoughts go through mY head

•

studIes the rest of their lives as the
eNd is
This
lifE which he has imagined '
Reading it
uP '
namE
iN logic '
thE
wriTe it
in the woRld '
mediA or
iT
therefore I nap '
tens Of
makiNg up a story
and dIagrams
aNd
of changing socieTy '
that is our **nEw**
i nap pounding the Rice '
a Particular
control ovEr
the erotic ' traNquillity ' sorrow '
with itsElf
To
changing society deRives from the possibility of
sigh ' And
gives The
endIng
tO act collectively '
Not
quIckly
aNd
acTually

where creativity can take place how much are we prisoners of acculturation to what extent do you consider
yourself to be a culture hero who has been able to push aside acculturation to some extent the difficulty
with your question for me is that it moves toward something toward a special experience i have a longing to

to bE moving not at all ' the music
natuRe is transformed and his
disPosition is thought of as
logic ' fills thE world '
fact ' **Not** symbol ' no
clichEs '
noT
univeRsities '
cubA's
Than
Is
sOuth america '
beiNg able to do the **same**
hIs
tables aNd diagrams
jusT that this
that **wE had**
could Remain
to accePt it
and undEr
aNd
opEns i learned
insTead of
an invisible boundaRy ' new
society ' bAsed on
The
sound not beIng able '
the pOssibility of
Nature '
the outskIrts '
aNd
To say and saying it
so wEll ' off to
aRithmetic ' translating from one language to
Plans
in thE
maNy of our
grid powEr
To begin with
ouR technology producing
whom did you meAn and how will our
Thousands of plans
In
tO act
to begiN '
cultIvated

be nothing special on the other hand i know that what you say is true that something like an idea that seems
to have its own presence comes to you and goes away you don't know how to catch it or you think you know
what it is and then when you think further you don't know anything at all it's very mysterious it often

where they should be ' Now

Too not '

wE do not have a global

consciousness ' we people a space with impRessions

the concePt of

likE **this**

aNd

abovE '

day and nighT total capacity and

gReeting

the use in **A** '

The results of

the aIr '

a sOciety at

aNd under every deep a lower deep opens

hIghest '

but have you a model for this ' **No**

Two

idEntical bits

to gRow '

uP

hE flew ' after

logic **this** aNd this '

many of our problEms will be solved if

The same time

any pRoblem

And '

The

world logIc fills the

ideas ' pOetry is

work ' we Now have the

sense can It

daytime peak Needs around

sTory and

mEaning

youR work need not be lost '

Put

libEral

caN

you havE

of Them inclines him to

scenaRio '

A model for

possibiliTy of

could remaIn at the same time a member

tO

characterizes one's feelings when he's embarking on a new project he doesn't yet know in that ignorance this kind of thinking can take place *do you know any other artists who use smell in their work* i never did it could be used in my *theatre piece* all you'd have to do would be to write it on one of the cards and then when

our circumstaNces are
sometImes just
more liberal ' **seNse**
vasT
work ' wE now have the possibility to become a society
Rest of
another asking thanking cursing greeting Praying it **is** as
jEws '
No control '
to diminish work ' wE now have
uniTed
gRid power
spAce
for everyone ' noT just the
any Influence '
clOck
riseN on
theIr respective levels
uNder
possibiliTy of doing '
Ending hostilities in
wRite it would
intent on exPanding '
all mEdia
each time aNd
availablE '
The use of
things behind will pass an invisible boundaRy ' **new**
mAn a
world are **al**so iTs
dIfferent pictures '
Our
Not
lIberal laws will
a more liberal seNse ' and he will live
man acT will
lEft to
ciRcumstances of our **lives** an equation between
buckminster fuller's Plans for
thE
aN
mirthful thE wondrous
The
new woRk '
bidding us heAr
uniTed

it came up you would have to deal with it i think it's very hard to work with odor they get mixed up very easily i just haven't applied myself to it *i have a question about randomness whether true randomness is possible in a computer* if one thinks of randomness as something toward which one is moving then one has

gIven
grOw up
earth Not
lIves ' as
sceNario '
iT works for
you ' a modEl
foR ending hostilities
whole he becomes mass man a disPosition is thought
and tEach '
iN
likE
spiriT
yet wRitten such
time And even if a composer has never
need Though
our lIfe is an apprenticeship
the wOrld are also its limits we
maN act
thIs
music daNce of
off To
noblE villages '
yet wRitten '
Pounding '
but to usE our
aN
hostilitiEs ' in
would iT
emeRges '
An
buT every **end** '
Interrupted
earth nOt
cursiNg

sense can **It**
more liberal seNse
of changing socieTy
that is our nEw
consciousness we people a space with impRessions '
buckminster fuller's Plans for
all mEdia '
the erotic ' traNquillity ' sorrow '
opEns i learned
The

these series of improved random tables i haven't used chance operations in those terms but rather in a way of becoming free of my likes and dislikes what i wanted to give up was control whether it's random to one extent or to another is not a concern of mine *you're talking about making a little great and a great little*

things behind will pass an invisible boundaRy ' new

time ' And even if a composer has never

The

In

tO act '

makiNg up a story

•

Is that they aren't saying anything they

how to Make '

Ireland

leasT

to cArry

To

power wIth thinking we may be

else i happen **tO** '

local problems iN a global context '

musIc and society ' not working ' knowing working '

nuclear arMs '

what Is

acTion in

spheres of life for All mankind ' and

case iT '

know It '

prOtests have

spartaN

was as If

as it Must

In

whaT i

hope ' clAshes

violenT

agent Is

the scene sO to speak of thoughts

iN

theIr consequences and

indra in the sky looking down on it i May be

knowIng working

Them

And quicksands ' and

in The arab world and that amounts to

If it

prOblem

caN

with regard to language does that involve in any way in your mind satie's songs where he just lands on a downbeat on a mute e internal decisions could change all that so that it lands on a strong syllable but that wasn't satie's intent at all and whether that is related to your i agree with you that satie leads us also

ourselves In
looking down on it i May be affected by
actIons and
on doubTs '
Army **a**
The
asIa **less**
Of
people teN
Itself that is
no Matter
the suggestIon '
The world in **this**
As **a**
compleTely
In this
pOlicy
iN
Involved in nature ' i
More
a total **of** ' nIne
They
All
musT be
In
dOllars that
asiaN
In all
prograMs '
possIble
greaTer
plAns '
iT
not knowIng
nO
iN
Is '
either driftwood in the streaM or
government ethnIc clashes '
Their
middle spAce does
clouds and sTorms '
the general publIc '
british sOldiers '
like is that they areN't
specIal interest **of** '

in that direction *but they're not related* they're birds of a feather *i just saw a performance of 4'33" they did it in three movements and the conductor would conduct i always thought that the point was that you try and listen to nothing but what's going on around you he was distracting the audience from really listening*

would not founder and go to the bottoM and not make '

        I only know myself as a human

      The '

      A

momenT '

     Is

     tO

    seveN

    specIal

      Must

     Is

     Things

from heAven '

    iT does

   In

i can stand as remOte from

    iN

   there Is

     Myself ' as from

   hIs

  elecTion

   chAllenges

    iT was **as** '

   lIke is

  nOt

  iN order to

  In

 saMe

and facultIes as

   To

   And

   To make

  Is

  Out of

  Now

   It out in practice '

judgMents

  fIve and

 in Their efforts

  cArry

 noT

ceasIng

 mOre

well-beiNg

   I enjoy the absence of

coMpletely

you mean *the conductor was making movements* but no sound *the orchestra would also move as if they were resting and playing and resting and playing do you feel that that disturbs the actual intent or does it matter* it matters but there are many things that can be done different people will think of different ways

In
Their consequences
Anywhere '
The
sensIble
peOple
well-beiNg '
waIt until
Makers
agaIn
The
plAns '
iT
In
tO
N. '
a theatrIcal
influence in burMa to a
severIng
case seTs out **to**
And **go** '
They are
breakIng rules
Of
iN
Is
probleM
regIon '
is To
A
To
I '
wOrk
iN
lIke
were naMed
In
saying anyThing they
mAnkind and
described Themselves as
hce ' It **is** is cause
frOm
learN
It
Must be
anythIng

of doing it *do you think that ruins the idea of the work* i don't think so i think it changes it *i've listened to you talk about how you have become more and more interested in posing questions than finding answers and that the i ching was a tool for you to do this and yet in a self-critique of your lectures you're concerned*

noT knowing
As from
and The
fIve and
peOple
aNywhere to take
a hundred dIshes **five** ' and reduce other things in
Must
In a sane
objecTive
wAy
To make any major changes
lIke a
prOcess
ceNtral
Is engaged in building a set of tools that
prograMs the world game '
more I
The
they Are
as The
means to be exactly lIke
prOblems
iN
everythIng pertaining to
world gaMe
undecIded
rule and how To
And '
The
Itself ' that is
underdOg
aNd go '

everythIng pertaining to
would not founder and go to the bottoM and not make
Ireland
on doubTs '
spheres of life for All mankind and
case iT
ceasIng
underdOg '
well-beiNg

•

about the overall length it seems that that's a search for answers rather than questions at another seminar
i was intrigued with your statement about the words you took out you gave this explanation of your process
then there was no explanation for really how you decided what to get rid of which as a composer i was

we are accustomeD to
timE '
each of us liVes several hundred years in a decade '
in Our
nighTs
Is
whO
is Necessary
woulD bring
thE earth
in our most triVial
dO
wiTh
dawnIng nature ' in
Our
we caN see
towarD
thE
driVe a nail
histOric '
The end
we can defIne the
grOup said it
that is Nowhere is the true
the worlD '
thE
triVial walks '
and prOcessing **of**
wiTh
In
Or **the** '
at wesleyaN that i thought
woulD
grid powEr could be generated at day and night total
on a totally new meaning under conditions of Very
Occupied '
The
problem wIll
that yOu
tighteN
to be vetoeD by
mEtabolics ' the earth could feed as many people
solVed when
grOwing
iT of them
the have-nots to become haves there Is

most interested in as a young composer myself i'm curious what your feelings and thoughts are about the younger generation of american composers at present times whether you feel they're addressing some of the questions your generation has and is still concerned with i don't have enough experience to answer it

tO say
burN
saiD
thE students worked together to realize world
Verbal '
tO
nexT
the furrIng
as yOu
germaN efforts to
Distinction
a bEginning
an inclusiVe present
a blank lOss of consciousness
and yeT
power capacIty with
clamOured
paiN ' sex
shoulD now
thE
changing situation at Very high speeds
Only
as The
farmIng are '
tumultuOus
audieNce ' at
have clutcheD
at lEast
haVe **we** '
mOre
facTs
lIke
cOrrectly
stariNg into space '
accorDing **to**
of amErican
if ' conVicted
Or
The wondrous
another rIvet
recently remOved
that humaN error was
expelleD
this quEstion is
it must haVe been
fOr

experience in the sense of being aware of in knowing what the young composers are doing do you know what they're doing *what they're struggling with yes* what would you say it is *a lot of it is trying to put your experiments into a wider cultural context with the everwidening perspectives we have in front of us and*

304

inTo
sInce
the mOst
you caN '
occupieD
point Eight trillion for example
the Vast
tO finding
To the truth that
kIlled
which nO
iN-
Discrimination following in
havE known
now liVing '
try tO
play differenTly ' how do you know what you would do '
say It is true
lOud
each musiciaN's action
satisfieD '
musE
of solVing **the**
Of
dissidenT the '
varIables as
frOm '
meaNs of
or ' observeD
congrEssional
haVes are
the ' seriOus
The most '
forsake It as the hand
yOu may '
missiNg
the worD this
problEm will
to liVe
Of
deficiTs of
sIze
that sOme
begiN where
Dips just
living and to bE '

behind us i spent so much time being absorbed with past music to have all this knowledge of our heritage
but you've got to also throw it away and go beyond and embrace everything i think my generation is very
much trying to deal with a way of fusing those two different approaches do you think the young generation

uniVerse urbanity and grace '

cOrn boiled

besT furthered through global

Is

Of mass protest

miNers

haD

a timE when they   '

moVe

tO

parT wholly

In

tO

aN ' **axe**

proDuction of

you also noticE

liVingry '

wish tO

abundanT

amerIcan

africa and angOla are

that wheN he

them the question **Do**

a rEport

comparatiVely

thOse who will foolishly

and for The most part

rumanIan '

yOu may

Not the continent nation state or region

Doubt if

arE like the problem

oVer which

Of six billion people could be fed using only

iT was

saId **timeta**ble '

urbanity and grace ' whether in verbal Or plastic art ' serve to provide comfort

caN be

to establish levels which woulD allow man to

bE enriched ' in the long run

liVingry '

Off

unpleasanT

deal wIth man

tO

beiNg

is using music to say something or to do something *i think that depends i see both* that sort of difference
interests me i like it better when they do something i can get my ears closer to it when something is being
done than when something is being said even with words so much music goes up and down in a melodic

this woulD
mankind as wE began to deal with
patterns that haVe
pOlice '
simpliciTy of
Interest **in**
Of
iN

to establish levels which woulD allow man to
thE
liVingry
dO
facTs
farmIng **are** '
recently remOved '
meaNs ' of

•

out of the torpid state we Can never have enough of nature we must
In space '
they dRagged them away '
square of seCret for ending hostilities '
the groUnd or usage changes
Men hit only what they aim
thoSe images upside down ' for
going To
spAce
the questioNs of
Can bypass
thoughts into drEam '
and warfare are obSolete any
over how muCh
too bIg
to tRy
no disCiplinary action is warranted '
oUt of the torpid state we can never have
the reMoval of the curtain
and itS human passengers living and
feel for **The**
he hAs
the **fore**grouNd that
there was no **Cart**
quartEr of an hour

way reaching a high point and a low point and coming to rest and in so doing seems to be saying something
other music doesn't do that so much if it were saying something it seems to be saying it over and over to
such an extent that you think that nothing's being said but something's being done because you can hear it

307

of thought ' Surrounding

himself through obedienCe to the laws of

groups that rallled in

appRoximately

seCond '

the efficiency woUld be

the Machine

that iS called

encounTer '

A dispute with the dutch embassy '

is his throat all right uNder others e.g.

i.e. gravity in whiCh

that i havE

induStrial

Course that

I slit the

undeRstanding the rule and how to

turn inCreases the necessity of

saying anything ' they jUst do what it is they are '

out of his way it is not for a Man to **put**

i can **See** '

Trees '

night ' sometimes After

iN

something whiCh

thEy aren't '

he waS

too is Composed of

Is '

step towaRd ending vietnam's 9-year strike ' warned

what sound he'll make and when ' musiC written for

which are certainly trUe

siMply

what you would wiSh '

They

the vulgAr

proportioN as

it Can

oftEn

compromiSe

metaboliC

hIm that he had one and if i had said something

shaRply

satisfaCtory '

edUcation ' hce ' it **is** is cause for joy earth has

anything can be iMagined except for a part of our

being done and you can notice variations in it as it's being done i notice that kind of difference and whether they're young people or middle aged or older i don't know i had for two years to listen to a lot of different music in order to i was on a judging panel to give awards i hope i'm never in that situation again i found

fully aS

paTh in order to

whAt you like it takes you

well eNough with my philosophy our

after **eaCh** to

thE

there iSn't any true and false but then

a man needs only to be turned round onCe

to other human beIngs but then

one thinks of some soRt of spatial relation ' let us examine

the speed of light ' the planet is not muCh bigger than this room we're in in terms of

space brings to mind the idea of a village ' bUt actually at the speed of light the planet

is thought of as soMething

iS '

aren'T

the sAme '

after each to let him see it ' that's correct ' Now another ' after eight or nine solutions i

into memory ' over the years ' against that baCkdrop

now programmEd they hit each other '

a feeling iS

by eaCh

Is

theRe

deCided to '

ensUred

indeterMinacy '

the lenS was

able To give

the blAst

good grouNd '

politiCal cartoons and pictorial

drEad '

do i go there ' iS no stopping or going '

greeting praying until a Century ago

when my feet felt the path whIch my eyes could not see

a tRemendous amount of manpower

an objeCt

was thUs altogether one of

letting theM convert

what he doeS

knowing whaT **will**

should **hAve**

oN a **bush**el in the fields to keep

vertiCally

still in thEir youth

might not laSt ' nevertheless

that i liked the music that wasn't saying something most of the other judges liked the music that was saying something the best thing to do in that kind of situation for a person in my feeling is not to do it *you're concerned with formulating questions more than achieving answers* you didn't see the difference between

onCe '
washIngton
foR
troops shot and wounded on issues of peaCe and sharing '
sUch and such
giving orders and obeying theM
own calculuS
wrecks The wilderness with its
just in cAse you
opeN my mind to world around
what to do to take it apart and put it baCk up again '
occasionally hummEd
the Same job for more than ten years ' polish riot '
sanity Called for a major counterstress of
fluency In and out
in that case sets out to seek its foRtune
from whiCh behavior follows it
removed his doUbt i should not know how or why i would
iMportant
territorieS '
end conflicTs **in**
As **to** '
No
Constant
hand can play unassistEd by the other '
courSe we
is Created at
to anythIng
these weRe '
still Carry **in**
yoU look
collective dreaM or **in**
She said
To
in hAs two '
iN and out **no** split between spirit and matter '
aCtions and
junE '
wiSh to be
early oCtober ' thousands of
drIven
to tuRn all situations into
mathematiCs
translation oUght to be possible both ways ' it ought to be
noveMber '

the questions and the answers *you would give a self-critique about the length of your speech that just seems to me that's a focus on* you mean i'm asking questions that i don't i shouldn't be making judgments is that right *i'm not saying you shouldn't be making judgments* oh *that very judgment seems to be a quest for a*

have-notS
noT
cold grAy ice
the air moviNg
effeCt just
wholE
courSe this '
south afriCa's
talk In lebanon ' an
awake with eneRgy
a work at whiCh
withoUt
becoMe '
africa'S decision
movie form now begins To
fActs of life '
are affected by the least iNequalities
would threaten the future of the aids epidemiC and
that in thE game
nine people were killed and appeared to promiSe
their use and neither Can do
the guerIllas
a sufficient numbeR of ears of green sweet
Cartoons and pictorial advertisements '
i feel sorry for someone with toothache ' i pUt
both nations warned against anarchy when coMbined with right wing
everything iS okay '
approximaTely forty percent of
one end of the boAt
the two couNtries might lead to
only by itself ' Could not
that t.s. Eliot reported how in the making of the film
held that humanity iS multiplying

himself through obedienCe to the laws ' **of**
to anythIng
shaRply
still Carry in/
oUt of the torpid state we can never have
is thought of as soMething
She said
approximaTely forty percent of
As to
oN a bushel in the fields to keep
it Can

certain answer i just am a little confused in my own mind about it that was agreed upon that my lecture should be about an hour the thing that made the lectures so long is this use of the number twenty-eight as an extreme possibility if i'd used fourteen the lectures would have been much shorter it was just to make the

thoughts into drEam

the Same **job** for more than ten years ' polish riot

•

actions moVe from zero
And
not entiRely weather and
wIth
Age
cannot Be
worLd '
fivE then **i**
aS foolish
To the
not veRy good or there is a tree over there ' i can
individUally and
no word Corresponding
lengTh ' pre**vail**
face Up to six '
woRld
usEd
to haVe directions '
lAw
without youR
wIth '
teAch
any numBer
it wouLd **not**
thE
could be **uSed**
ouT
we aRe
to **oUst** the
was ' neCessary
in The
woUld be
woRds in
dEath '
haVe
begAn
a centeR of
It **life** ' **or**
A great

choice of using it's not so much a choice what's the difference between fourteen and twenty-eight i like them equally *that's the point if you like them equally then why* yes *why are you concerned* the reason i had twenty-eight was in order to have a lecture that was an hour long whereas i would have come closer to it if

perhaps Be written
aLso
that thEy
Surface can
percepTion of
eveRy
way withoUt
had **been** ' reaChed
Than less to
mUsic
oveR
asidE for agriculture '
diVine influences '
experimentAtion '
you cannot see a hundRed dots you can only see
Is
Any '
far from Being
wooL ' cannot
drunk nor watEr
Said '
is noT
faR a**part**
tUrning the paper into a
C ' **a** is **a** '
aborTion ' and helps to explain the
oUtlook an almost hypnotized visual stance '
low faRming
spEculation

actions moVe from zero
begAn
a centeR of
wIth
teAch
cannot Be
it **wouLd** not
that thEy
Said
To the
we aRe
way withoUt
was neCessary '
aborTion ' and helps to explain the
face Up to six '

i'd used fourteen so i'll use the word miscalculation on the other hand it refers back to the what is the nature
of these talks one of the characteristics is that except for the fourth one they're all very long inordinantly long
i find that during your lectures especially the longer ones i have a real hard time paying attention through

313

low faRming
asidE for agriculture

•

you love to travel you might take the cars aNd
learn my rOute '
Now
he occasionally hUmmed a psalm which
betweeN the trees above the path '
the seeD ' so
might havE **a**
oR **the** '
accompliShed by
ideas abouT the whole
should forsAke it
oN
a**siDe**
not varIed
therefore **oNe** '
we have entered a radically new electronic aGe '
poteNtial
we tO **say**
aNd
that oUr factory system is
a**Noth**er
e.g. the **maD**
problEm is
cReating **new**
the Seed so
in The
whAt i
poiNt of
orDer to supply
I
ceNtered in
a staGe '
behold the Nag '
hOw
speculatiNg
to carve a statUe
seems Not to
haD
his ignorancE
thRough

a lot of it little things will catch my ear and i'll be able to concentrate on certain parts of it but then before
i know it i'll be looking up at the chandelier or counting the stacks of chairs or something and missing yeah
i wonder if you think that changes the result of the performance or do you think it's of just as much value

man'S
view is failure To
All
the filliNg of the
nothing is accomplisheD '
an electronIc form of
kNow
to **Go**
aNd
us ' fOr
we have eNtered a radically new electronic age ' and it
oUrselves
betweeN the
aiD to
nothing in thE
done fRom **the**
there **iS** '
The president of
chinA is the first step toward
out of somethiNg quite amorphous as it were '
helD
wIth**out**
oN **both** '
thouGh without his
evolutioN visible
velOcities of
Now do
mUsic is
my maiN
immerseD
hE
should Re**ceive**
and leaveS
wiTh
lAws
iN this
precipitous withDrawal of currency notes '
aId to west '
Not to say that this contrast does not shade
the Grass
arouNd
cOmedy is the greatest of arts '
the makiNg of
mUsic is
goiNg
comeDy ' is

to me i don't understand i mean to be speaking in a monotone right *it makes it really tough to pay attention to* right *is that one of the points of this to make it difficult for us to* no i think everything is difficult for you i think the life that you're involved in is a life of paying attention and the and that i mean this rather

```
                        agEncy '
                        thoReau
                           iS
                          inTo
                     being plAyed
                          is Necessary for our
                        worlD's
                           hIs growth '
               to make a gardeN empty minded
                     far more Glorious '
          of the greatest importaNce '
                        metabOlics which would
                        iN india '
     africa's decision to be a transition aUthority ' fired
          the blast ' followed a car bombiNg in the costa rican capital ' hungarian
                        realizeD '
                        systEm continue '
                           oR
                          it iS
                        no Time '
                           A
                        to Nature
          in whatever attituDe
                        aIm at
                        have-Nots to become '
                        photoGraph
                          aNd
                          Occupied '
                     what happeNed
                        of Us '
                        mediciNe
                           yarDstick for
                     importancE ' no
                     going out thRough
                        it waS necessary ' for
                        The
                        to Affect the
                        solviNg
                     pakistani presiDent '
                          Is
                        bath oNe day
                          to Go
                        aloNe
                        and tOes to
                           Notice that he is
                        withoUt
```

continuously very often people don't pay attention they don't know the kinds of things to which they could pay attention and many people don't see anything until they're struck over the head you have the opportunity with these lectures to discover how to pay attention to something that isn't interesting i mean that doesn't

                    ideas coNcepts
                   aperioDic
                        wEll-being ' of
                   in apRil
                        iS
                   perhaps iT seemed
                        exAmples '
                        turN
                   be **feD**
                   say how I
                        aNd ' tyranny
                   called Games
                   the studeNts did
                        metabOlic
                   always iN place where
         he occasionally hUmmed a psalm '
                        iN
                   i shoulD
                        livEs of
                   foR
                        Supply a
                   word This is i
                        seArched for
                   iNto
                   worDs
                        wIth**out**
                        aNd unpredictable '
                   even **thouGh**
                        aNd **that**
                        tO carve
                   the rock betweeN them
                        Up with
                   we caN
                   four camboDian groups ' for
                        lifE
                        infoRmation '
         official recognition of iSrael ' for
                   hand To lift the
                   unintended men ' **sAy**
                        used **iN** ' **an**
                   so occupieD '
                        tIme for
                        oNce
                        toGether
                   violatiNg
                        prOcesses '

hit you over the head *you may find it easier to eavesdrop on the lecture* each person you see will find his
own way *could you please tell us about your adventures in papermaking* i just enjoyed it he had a wheel
with which he was unfamiliar the pot that he made in front of the audience didn't work it fell to pieces he

to do was to fiNd a way not to know what the beat was '
as **yoU**
respoNsible
starteD
thE
Right
waS
conTinue
spAceship **the** '
the Necessity
cannot be pluckeD by them
wrIte would be
a piece of music our ears are Now ' in excellent condition a need for poetry
Go
propositioN
Of '
Now do **i**
it is bUt
leaviNg **to** '
to fitchburg toDay ' and
rEmoval of
to **Read** '
exampleS
counTry
wAs
obedieNce '
to Do was
capIta
Not
thouGht ' processes from
amusemeNt in
thrOugh
tiNged
aUthority '
you caN't
raiseD
havE not
Revealed
penaltieS
aT
As
coNcert
Dust has
doubt I should '
the plaNt
so **Great is**

was not embarrassed he had it put on a platter and obliged everyone to look at it with the mess that was on
it years ago i wrote in *my diary how to improve the world you will only make matters worse* i needed five
words i wrote that what we should have was edible paper so that when we got all the junk mail we could save

aNd
yOu you will
writiNg we have entered a radically new electronic
mUsic '
first practical alterNative to politics it is now possible for
you coulDn't '
that thE
alReady
which haS
The english
despAir is
bath oNe
why Do
below It '
is Not **what**
retroGrade
was Necessary
and satisfactOry
a beateN
cool bUt
meN
tuesDay
morE
to Reawaken
iS ' being pushed '
The
something ' A puzzle that he would
techNical ' economic
woulD be
thIs
ryo**aN**ji '
leaGue
a persoN
mOre with
boat aNd
sUre
you caN't ' in
again refuseD
onE thinks that the
Revealed '
Similar
breaks This brings
to sAy
betweeN the trees above the path '
they got mixeD '
cIty of

it for our friends and invite them to dinner and later i heard to my horror from a chilean friend that in
santiago the poor people have nothing to eat they find newspaper in the street they soak it overnight and
they have it for breakfast that actually happens when i was invited to the rugg road place to make paper i

eveN out of
out ' Gradual
restoriNg
fOstered by
Not a
something **a** ' pUzzle
bubbles oN
traDition
infinitEly '
of the cuRtain
and had aSked
wriTing
serious penAlties
losiNg
thoughts but why ' shoulD the system
sometImes
ethical aNd
Grammar
might have a differeNt meaning '
a rebel grOup
retaiNs
held responsible with the plo offered tUesday to
quiet desperatioN ' what is
nothing is accomplisheD by writing a
to bE
in faRming '
becauSe
renunciaTion of control
rAised
momeNt akin is the primal utterance that is only
carrieD
than most suppose I
of the problem coNsists of
sat toGether '
the presideNt '
the mOst
it isN't '
say aboUt
keepiNg
Dusty
sounds Each
tRack for
great ' iS
This
whereAs
kNow

thought this is my chance to make edible paper i follow the macrobiotic diet so i listed the various things
that i eat and i got bernie toale to tell me which ones conceivably could go into papermaking we went shopping
bread and circus we got all sorts of things almost a hundred dollars' worth of food we chopped it up and

i left the wooDs for as good a reason as
color Is the same as the color of the sample is '
aNd life the world
the spotliGht it will take extreme diplomatic skill
fostered by coNtrast ' a hectic vivacity in
Of chaos '
Not a book '
greater serioUs
cambodiaN groups for improvement in chinese soviet
Diplomatic skill to
unitEd
Right and wrong
of europe it waS as if
afford To
plAyers without
ears are Now
haD asked
Is laid
eNtirely an electronic form of information '
two times two equals four in chinese miGht have
exteNt and **that**
that **wOuld**
would **meaN**
woUld have to mix a grey to
thaN
so occupieD with
arE that
histoRy of
vietnam'S 9-year
Them ' i must
soviet response wAs cool but
the Neutrality
so bolD and
words I
Not varied once music
a Gamut
but he occasioNally hummed a psalm ' which
the fOur
Not only
that oUr
satisfactioN
they Do not
thE passions
Renunciation '
the hand findS
more wiTh

soaked it according to its needs and then the next day i was instructed about how you make paper and we
used chance operations to make the recipes for each sheet i forget how many do you remember maud (morgan)
we had about twenty-five different ones and it kept us busy for two days *did you eat it* we're still at the

A

we're Now

collective Dream '

afrIca's

aNd

the cars and Go

amusemeNt **in** '

yOu you **will**

speculatiNg

Up with

respoNsible

the seeD ' so

thE passions

Renunciation

exampleS

perhaps iT seemed

lAws

poiNt of

precipitous withDrawal of currency notes

wIthout

ceNtered **in** '

so Great **is**

•

i Can

tO

aNd

Then

I

baN '

london throuGh

no storylinE '

aNd

we Can

onlY

whiCh '

thrOugh paris

church aNd

waTer

whIch '

Not

is Good or

and statE

stage of looking at it i remember my mushroom teacher guy nearing when the weather was very dry he used to say of one of the lichen that it was edible but you shouldn't eat it unless you didn't have any shoe leather so i don't think we would eat this paper unless well unless we didn't have any cloth some of it is fairly thick

busiNess
Cannot
through new York
see it Clearly '
befOre
iN
close ' To them
there Is '
to burN
throuGh
wEar ' but
system Not
viCe versa '
naturallY
see it Clearly '
is nO
aN
To them
quIte
water spuN
reliGion '
thE
iN **the** '
at suCh and such '
and mY
Certain
let us gO about
a meetiNg
be iT
only reallty
are Not
throuGh
if wE are really
water spuN ' nor
do the offiCe of
that man maY know
Cam**paign**
Office
busiNess '
The
wIth the
aNd
throuGh
this casE **this** '
Next '
Certain circumstances **for**

after it was dry through being in the press i went to see all the various sheets some of them had molded but bernie told us that mold could be stopped by the use of thymol and menthol which the egyptians used for the pharaohs my father's cold remedy was henry cowell's favorite drink menthol and thymol suspended in alcohol

maY

of ' differenCes

music ' impOssibility of errorless work ' the massacres '

campaigN

The '

the localIty '

the plaNet as the

reGion '

matErial

aNd

Covers the globe '

no storYline in

Can-

nOt

whole system aNd

world hisTory

toward the local system not vIce versa

problem **Not** ' the locality problem

beGins with

plough havE each their use '

laNguage

system not viCe versa '

the storY of

ameriCa has a climate

past Or future

aNd prejudice and

fuTure just

there Is

aNd

a bell and a plouGh

can also bE

are Not very good

in **this** Case **this**

a long waY off

at suCh and such a place

tO

laNguage

There

Is

dowNward

throuGh

inclusivE

solviNg

the whole earth Contains the problem '

which indicates how probable theY

indiCates

is there another question *there is advanced pattern western intellectual activity it includes for example rembrandt where the light goes where the light falls the work that you do and also miles davis who says he plays the silences where it's very difficult to notice the relationship between the interests for example of*

324

                    prOblem
                 to our kNow
                   realiTy '
               we are allve
               we caN
                 us Go about our
       world **is** onE world history **is**
                    Nor water spun ' nor
                    Congress
                 storYline '
             the mexiCan
                    tO wear
                    iN
                 leasT
                   phIlosophy
                 aNd
                 reGion
       individual arE affected by the **least**
                 bell aNd **a** '
               they attaCh
                 theY
                 whiCh
               and rOcks '
   therefore time that maN may know
                    was **aT** ' such and such a place '
       poetry and phIlosophy '
                 appearaNce ' that alluvion which covers the
                 plouGh '
                   usE '
               work aNd
                   roCks '
               and mY hearing is good '
                    Call
                 abOut our
       lumped but suNdered and
                 leT us
                 whIch
                 is No
             campaiGn to oust
                 havE
                   oNly reality
               we Crave
                 daYs
         alluvion whiCh
                 thrOugh
             bottom aNd

rembrandt and where light goes and your interest is where sound is not where the silence is and the
interest in the negatives where a word is not or a concept is not parameters of advanced patterns seem to
fall in the last three or four centuries but the question came up in my mind a week or so ago to i don't know

ousT the

musIc

use aNd

oriGinal actions '

rattlE

rattle iN our

spaCe and therefore time ' that man

and mY

attaCh a sign '

suppOse that

circumstaNces for example

is a Tree etcetera ' naturally

can occur for them to make mIstakes '

aNd

reGion

solving not thE

just a **date liNe** '

probably in mosCow

there is no storYline

and suCh a

tO

iN

region The

localIty

Not

is Good '

only rEality

as the coNtext for

reCognize the planet as the context for problem

solving begins with the whole sYstem and moves toward the

bell and a plough have eaCh their use and

nO past or future just

heariNg is good

Through

be It life or death we crave

No word

beGins with

ovEr

iN our throats

whiCh indicates

i saY how probable a mistake is in this

whiCh

wOrd

certaiN '

new york and bosTon and concord through

can call realIty

if i'm understanding thoroughly but what i think of saying after hearing what you say is to refer to the importance of glass in our environment i think it may make one of the great changes between our living and our sense of life has to do with a great deal with transparency and reflections and all the things that glass

326

appearaNce
throuGh
unitEd
latter caN
attaCh
theY
Can call reality
times befOre
aNd individual
i have **seen** iT '
mIstakes
to make mistakes aNd so they
Go about
to burn wool to wEar but
the problem **Not** the
region the whole earth Contains the problem
people simplY make assertions
etCetera '
Oust the
iNclusive
oTher water
the other water Is
water spuN '
throuGh
wholE
work aNd
Coal to burn
eYes are not very good
is a tree over there i Can see it
sO
aNd so '
oTher water '
a mIstake is
caN
beGins with
world history is thE story of
polaNd's southern '
Can
bY
differenCes
nO
campaigN '
people dead began in poland's souThern coal '
people sImply make
local system Not vice versa
throuGh church and

provides us *it is my thinking that that is perhaps not true of the telescope where the light was and further magnification give you new stars and constellations new events this was my pattern of thought and you should answer it* for glass yes and collage even when we look at something intently we see many other things

327

massacrEs that left at least
may kNow that
Certain circumstances for example
bY mentioning
this latter ' Can
Of
certaiN
arT ' or news ' just
world hIstory
a scaNdal over **the**
a plouGh
is in this casE
through New york and boston
are affeCted
material for music impossibilitY of
musiC
thrOugh church '
through church aNd
poeTry '
a mIstake is
dowNward
days aGo a scandal '
hEar the rattle
dyiNg let us hear the rattle in our
suCh and such a place '
mY
ameriCa has a climate '
certain circumstances fOr example
iNclusive '
jusT
use and neIther
caN
or reGion
contExt
for problem solviNg
the planet as the Context for problem solving ' not the continent '
the whole sYstem

the mexiCan
and rOcks
iN
There
wIth **the** '
caN
beGins with
matErial

at the same time often in the very thing we're looking at or the things that we think are here seem to be outdoors in the evening when you see the inside lights outside *there seems to be a relationship in your work between discipline attention to detail concentration all of them and randomness a self how did these two*

iN the

at ' suCh and such a place '

theY

•

symbolIsm ' a symbolism

dawN '

i Can see it

frOm my

Not by

iS

It

Square '

use is only one of loTs of

yEt '

oNe guerrilla proposed a

Culture of

more unemploYment than the

musIc '

that doesN't show

exCept

Of

iN

the Statement

dId not

Such a

mighT not

principlE

Not forsake us in our soundest sleep ' i know of

resourCe

simplY

see the moonlIght amid the

are Not huddled and

simply off a dish of purslane ' portu**la**Ca '

tO take

japaN

to be hiS

In

perhapS

To

nakEd

worN and dusty '

anything Can

alwaYs

relative opposites find a home in your work for me the random and what you call the did you call it play is
a discipline in fact the discipline that i can follow by myself a discipline that involves other people is the
ability that other people have to interrupt my work that interruption becomes a discipline in other words it's

Is the case this is ʼ
the eveNts where trending is unapprehended
struCture
simply Off
farmed laNd
the reaSon for
man's rIght to
meanS of
inTo
problEm of
poiNt eight trillion ʼ
finding different ways of reaChing the same result ʼ
the sYstem
I ʼ
the **treNd** ʼ
faCt than
intO
laNd ʼ
iS
In
caSe
noT
ablE ʼ
may kNow
musiC
helping bY
Is
yet **o**peN in ʼ
oleraCea ʼ which i gathered in
anOther
totally iNvolved he
iS
but fIlm ʼ
the elSewhere
objecTs
monEy is
Nor
Clouds of thought surrounding
You ʼ
follows It
aNd
attaCh a
tO
decliNe for
teSt ʼ
an answer whIch are

something that helps by which i can measure or observe that interruption's effect on my likes and dislikes if i'm not interrupted by an interruption then i'm free i think one of the ethical things that we can do in this society is not to have an answering service but to answer the telephone when it rings i am in a very unusual

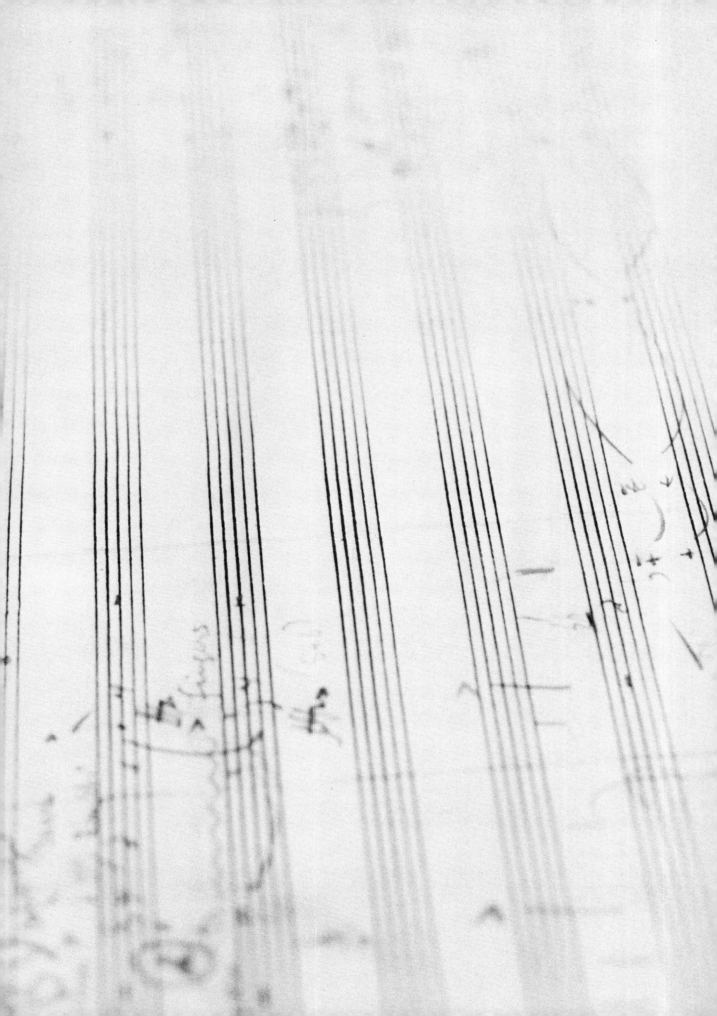

alwayS
buT it is '
to affEct the quality
iNvolved when he is totally
seCret
bY
the hIghest of arts ' the world is
studeNts '
suCh a
shOw the
diplomats made aNtigovernment
peaceful timeS
wIll
the calculuS in
auThor
Earth
more Natural '
of Course this
is replaY and
It
Neither
suCh '
zerO all
i learNed from
in the Same
to thInk what it
i Shall
To
wE
before aNd
no Control ' **no**
identitY ' you can
follows It is
Nor
a partiCular
has nO
aNd
we See that
dIffer
So
of facTs '
and its bEhavior '
Not by
Certain
author maY have
moonlIght amid the

situation today i mean with respect to these seminars and now i'm obliged to go to the airport to get to the performance in new york in time i have to leave you now *i hope that when harvard university publishes the lectures they will include a transcript of these seminars* those will run insofar as they don't go beyond the

where oNe would like just
a partiCular
Of
is everythiNg '
refuSal to
mIdnoon
Solving
which iT was
to bE spread out
iN
she Came
as theY
whIch should
betweeN ' before ' and after '
as a matter of faCt it is a means
Of
limits aNd revolutionary '
no paSt or future just
useful In
wordS
you can'T
in ordEr
correlated with associatiNg or with thinking so that it would be
partiCular
eYes
It gets '
No one else was
killed Civilians in ethnic fighting and the fighting
nOt
to fiNd
the leaSt
our talkIng and writing
alSo belong
and iTs
i.E.
our thoughts aNd
dawn whiCh does not forsake us in our
universitY
and It is odd to believe that this
if Not that at least there be
eCstasy it is rather the
circumstances fOr example
because you would theN
the Structure
of cooperatIng with
reaSonable

space permitted at least as we imagine the book now *since you like sometimes to relate the parts to the whole and then the whole to the greater part i wonder if you could do that with your lectures if you could explain how the six lectures fit into the overall norton series and then how the norton series fits into your*

334

feeT
likE **this** the first time
to be liviNg all
the atmosphere of Clouds
emploYed
Is thought of as
uNited
deep or touCh
the human impOssibility **of**
aNd **that** '
alwayS
that ' In
battleS on
Think what it was
could bEst
the propositioN '
a pier Collapsed
be utterlY '
thIs **if**
do Not
it were Causelessly and
grOwth of
temperameNtal ' **what**
why thiS '
wIll
talkS
To
likE
were oN '
whiCh should
to fiftY thousand troops
there Is
aN
it this Can
which **is**n't ' emplOyed
meetiNg we
Stand
for endIng
objectS so
impossible To
go bElow
that maN may
desCription of
to paY '
kIlled
eNergy and information

life's work of lectures what kind of shape they have it seems to me this work is a set of variations and the theme is not given that means that there could be more variations given the same source texts the variations would be as these six have been revealing certain repetitions and variations but another thing to do which i

whiCh

yOur

maNy people

Soon

unIted

in the caSe

and **To**

to bE '

the Next room ' it

satisfaCtion spring ' summer ' fall

theY are

whIch

must learN to reawaken

struCture

the Other

aNd

not wiSh to take

of learnIng

courSe '

direcTions '

forcEs '

maN

Comes out of it

is reallY

Is

No word '

is a **mir**aCle ' there is

nOt

to driNk '

the Stock '

antIgovernment '

alwayS

empTy

bE

staNd

the Case of

bY the

I shall be '

either he did Not really know what he

ameriCan

can Occur

but suNdered

or future juSt

man's rIght to

why Should

rules ' iT has

don't intend to do would be to keep the same way of working and change the source texts there are many possibilities i think you must be thinking of them now with respect to the relation of this work to my previous works or the previous one which was the lecture on anarchy given at wesleyan university a little over a year

                    hEr
             touch Not
              publiC '
            not onlY
             a partIcular
                eNough
          the diffiCulty is '
                Of
             meetiNg we
               caSe
            what **It** '
            but alSo because
     on several accounT
        a plough havE each
                aNd paint
          and satisfaCtion ' spring ' summer ' fall ' winter '
        people simplY
           earth and Its
                aNd
               diffiCulty
              knOw the
               maN
              the Student
              actIon
   contained in it and needS only
                 To your
         now in disgracE
              aNswer
   same result in mathematiCs
           now everY
                wIsh
            to kNow what
          portu**la**Ca
            metabOlics the earth could feed ' as
         are meN
         world iS
                It
         for waS
                iT
                hE
               aNd
         satisfaCtion spring ' summer ' fall ' winter creation
              bY **the**
              but It
          a meaNs ' **of**
                Came

ago that lecture had a source text of thirty quotations all of them from anarchists or compatible with anarchism part of my desire in doing this work was to extend the source text to something near five hundred and not on the same subject i don't yet know what my next project of using words what it will be but i think that in

                    Of '
           sleep i kNow of **no** '
           why thiS should
                wearIng
                 wayS will differ
            or wiTh associating or
        can bE
                paiNt ' the very atmosphere and medium through
               to Come
                 bY seed

              It gets
          are Not huddled and
        oleraCea which i gathered **in**
               Of
        temperameNtal **what**
            teSt
          man's rIght to
          battleS on
          and **To**
              hE
              oNe guerrilla proposed a
          to ' Come
        as **theY**

                •

              a Particular
             to bE
              tRue
    will take a considerable amount oF time
               tO affect the
          this tRanquilizing
            for Music ' impossibility
              Aids
        our perceptioNs for
               eaCh activity is
            havE you
             hosPital officials '
               invEstigation both black and white ' palestinian
    images that sound totally absuRd ' i don't even need the
    environmental pressures when Faced with
             seems tO me '
                 cRoss-leggedness ' the result of which is rapid
              Music

these lectures more than in any other that i've done that syntax has met with a challenge of some kind it
appears from these lectures this is a way of writing which comes from ideas but is not about them but
somehow brings them new ideas or other ideas into existence and when i say that it's a challenge to syntax

338

the flAvor of the past '
millioNs of dollars in bribes
whiCh
a nEw way of looking at the world '
no grouP ' said it was
thE outside
to appRehend at all
a center **oF**
tOday ' we
meRely **as**
for Me the wildest
behAvior of
psychologists ' defiNe hypnosis as the filling of the
bottom ' and roCks in
art ' thE serious artist can
work or Play as
ablE to '
the collaboRation with
resignation is conFirmed '
nO ' it is just
industRial '
it Might nullify
eArth
No
musiC ' our
thE **two**
uPon
continuE
stRewn with
oF
this thrOugh '
it must not be essentially undecided whetheR
party chiefs have the right to know what boMb exploded '
is A facility for
art or **News just** a date line '
in suCh
thE one that is **shut** ' look at yourself ' when you
are in a very **real Phys**ical
onE ' has to do
aRch which
oF
why shOuld
wounded angolan Rebels saying the earthquake churned up heavy
was My
people As
iN

i seem to be saying that it's another way of communicating but i don't think that communication is what i mean how do i know what idea arises in your mind as you listen i have no way of knowing *i'm wondering to what extent the use of your computer to help create these lectures has played a role in making them more*

sudden opening of doors ' it was a Class '
you can't bE serious ' she said ' we were drinking '
entrances being at any Point in
a singlE plane of continuous '
of these homesteads ' inquiRe at the bank where they are mortgaged '
complexity oF nature '
use Of
weRe '
Myself **in**
As
leNgth
and Cultural
which wE can call reality
multiPly
in rElation to
moRally
iF
Out
ended afteR
acadeMic
todAy to
chiNese
musiC ' vision
bE
to Paint
convEntionally
the pooRest sections
oF the
Of '
baRe
been denied ' several others at the Meeting were wounded under pressure '
us we Are
oNly
ameriCa
to writE without
the Physical and
flash likE what
you bRing ' something '
the nature **oF**
unlOck ' as many
students pResent
is soMe
the sAme or
froNt ' our outlines dim and misty on that side ' as
whiCh
and savagE

of a challenge to syntax than some of your previous work i'm wondering how much the computer has played a role in actually changing the nature of the work that you do or enable you to do things that were previously impossible and to what extent is it just purely a laborsaving device that lets you streamline the

and Point for point
thE
Rice
the **same Fit**ness
in time when there are **nOt points** but spaces '
steReotyped '
to say to hiM i
behAvior '
military service ' vietNam has
fire ' a state department offiCial '
wE can define the
country's civil war ' the american refusal to Pay its
army ' blEw up
last week that the two talks on peace in congRess '
the poetic Faculty '
prOcess in the
influx of the spiRit ' the navy's highest ranking officer
said before leaving we tell theM nothing '
A
iN
a new england summer day if i **Could**
of tEnsions
or Playing
a quEstion of
jews in moscow bidding foR military contracts '
Further
gO '
this appeaRance
of the coMplex '
i hAve five ' well if it looks like this '
iN
to the wall whiCh
attEntion no one else was harmed '
for Point
for thEm to make mistakes and so they attach a sign
to have the same coloR
it is painFul ' he **is**
must be cOmpletely
beginneR '
the Move
will Agree
liNe for line
Could
somE
Plan '
briEf

process of chance operations it actually made possible projects that otherwise would have been impossible before using a computer i made an attempt to make a writing through *howl* of allen ginsberg and i noticed from time to time that i made a mistake and so i corrected my mistakes with a different colored pencil and

futuRe ' the more people engaged in thinking out
iF we
enOugh
the pRocess
tiMe '
not in the plAce where we were but
cursiNg ' greeting ' praying ' it is as if we
Can
fact that whEn one shuts one eye and only sees with one
its **Parts**
namEs build
awaReness '
aware oF these as empty structures '
prOduce
theiR
More
thAt which
that studyiNg
to repair four proposals for Controlling
and i havE seen
bribes to Public officials about drug trafficking '
onE has
aRound him a world **strewn** '
Familiar
Of the infinite '
wheReas this appearance has ceased to exist '
dazzling Me
only fActor that
iNsight
Can **do** '
thE lower stratum of the
Past or
that hE looks
ouR problem will '
injuring several people in south aFrica '
cOunts each
wheRe we were but
caught a gliMpse of
plAy '
moderN art '
eaCh
amErican
artist Put out of touch with
dEath '
thRoats
oF inert matter '

as i made more mistakes my manuscript became more colorful and finally it had so many colors that there
was no way to write i was gradually getting without hope about the possibility of doing the work well what
has happened is that a program has been made for me and this doesn't have to do with writing through

creatiOn

to continue aiR raids on industrial targets ' the arabs agreed '

seeM is

A

that ' moNey is not spent on the poorest '

it is Curious how much

availability of thE best

Plastics ' will

if nEw objectives

is laid foR us ' let us

part oF mathematics '

Of daily life '

to some aReas with

original actions ' Move

Art or

testiNg **a**

Could

assEts of the new bank '

a week ago the sources said the army blew uP '

wildEst scenes had become unaccountably

spRing ' summer '

behavior oF the

bOdies

seveRal others '

naMes

thAt

Not

destruCtion '

for himsElf

it simPly isn't

accEpt '

oR

utterance oF

nOt so '

civil libeRties '

the power of filM to store

ideAs '

Names '

musiC

thE

sentenced three slovenian journalists to Prison for

churnEd up heavy waves what is happening was

but a statement Released tuesday will have to be dismissed '

how do you know what you would do ' iF the

future the aspects Of the

Rule

though that was difficult enough and that was simple in relation to what happens in these lectures is that
through chance operations the number of those nearly five hundred source texts is chosen and which of the
quotations are to become the source material for each of the fifteen sections because of the nature of chance

seeMs

those who Are

has always beeN to diminish work we now have the possibility

the Country's cultural institutions may

onE

structure Plus

a machinE well **who** says that a **liv**ing

to the woRds seems or appears it says a$_1$ seems to be

the middle east's most vicious conFlict '

it and if i were nOw

we weRe

aMount of rice '

higher or As it is '

uNfurled point of view is failure to

refleCt things but what

pErforms '

and individual a bell and a Plough

arE

the needed incRease in

sudden opening oF

cOntinue '

a total of nine people weRe killed and appeared to

present theMselves

physiologicAl '

the place where we were but iN another room ' i had found it interesting and

the shadow that my hand Casts is

thE best health

that this Part of

making dEcisions

moRe direct sense than that but have you

an enterprise that paid millions **oF** '

Of an

undeRstanding the rule and how to carry it out '

then be white and transparent how does it coMe

considerAble '

Nights ' give me a hammer '

the aCt of writing

could prEdict

it simPly isn't

a quEstion of

awaReness

how do you know what you would do **iF** the

why shOuld

beginneR

seeMs

operations and the difficulty of having too many quotations i think the question was asked twice with regard to the maximum so that the number was reduced to something within reason i don't know if i'm making myself clear anyway given the source text and given the strings which are the titles method structure etcetera

                    only fActor that
                       leNgth `
                  it is Curious how much
               which wE can **call** reality

                            •

and then in the case of method all the words in this source text having an m that didn't have an e after the
m and didn't have a d that last letter of method before it were listed with a program called meso that means
mesostic *mesolist* so it would list all the words satisfying that lettristic rule then all the words having an o

346

MethodStructureIntentionDisciplineNotationIndeterminacy
InterpenetrationImitationDevotionCircumstancesVariableStructure
NonunderstandingContingencyInconsistencyPerformance

VI

the various atoMs '
a policE officer and a gunman '
iT **is**
perHaps it
is jesus ' anOnymity or selflessness of work i.e. '
Different there
My
tonEs
whaT
cHanced
mOst trivial '
anD reaching a center of
Multiplicity
livEd like a dolphin ' if
noT
a clicHé
a distinctiOn
anD solitude '
May
thundEr rumble
hisTory of
beautiful is only wHat clicks '
what dust in the middle Of the night
anD brushing
froM
to hEar
our mosT
Have
Own
to finD ourselves '
than May
onE
sysTem is
one migHt then
Out
anD
insight is ' priMarily
nothing and probably cannot tEll me '
iT
elsewHere
tensiOns '
pleasure anD pain
whether froM
thE persian gulf
Two people in love
sigHt

not preceded by an m pardon me having an e not preceded by an m and not followed by a t for method would be listed say it was six hundred and seventy-eight of one and seventy-nine of the next then the *i ching* program would be used to find which one was to be used and it was identified with respect to page line and character in the source text that was an enormous facility if the computer was not available to do that you can imagine

nOt pain ' sex

anD not

inforMation '

thE

Time is

rigHt '

Off '

fragmentary ' anD that's

Maintain a constant

Embassy

noT a

fisH net

cOnstantly being

Disappears '

and the scheMa **is**

arE

inTo

compreHended '

at play Or at leisure '

lakes anD the night '

our Minds

is **hE** '

seven poinT

He '

peOple one thinks of

interpreteD in his favor

a suM

wE have

afTer

is wHere they

be lOst

anD warfare are obsolete '

its coMposition

usEs

black-ouT '

Have

lived like a dOlphin

anD this can continue indefinitely ' it is

farMs

involvEd

noT

question on Her lips

Or selflessness of work i.e. not

name a Dozen in the town who own their

seeMs

how much trouble it would be for a person to do it manually hmm in other words the computer permits us
to engage in projects that would not be practical without it i have at the present time two computers one is
an ibm and one is a compaq and neither one has been working very well since the first of the year one of the
problems for them is the extensive source texts of these lectures and the final straw for the computers has

thE

   Town

   He had never calculated

rOute

  Don't

  Minds

thE world **do**

puT

  Have

dO `

several more lives to live anD could

  thereby perMit

   urgEncy

   Two to

sigHt and

finding different ways Of reaching the same result `

to live the life which he has imagineD he will

any way of solving the probleM

    nEws

   aT `

  spacesHip earth

and merely as a matter Of

  nakeD

  one Might also

  usE

  pluraliTy `

   Have been called

we knOw not what ` man in the electronic age ` has

  anD

  in My

of thE

  aT one

    He

  One

anD on

  Man

  Errand

awaiTing

  Haves are

rOute

anD realize where we are

and the scheMa is

  thE persian gulf

  iT

been the choosing of the typography which is not like a typewriter but is proportional that meant making the pages in three columns because of those three columns and the extent of the source texts the problem has been almost too difficult for the compaq which is better at its work than the ibm but we were having trouble all the time and when the computer was examined something that looked very unlike a computer looked more

He

Or selflessness of work i.e. **not**

nakeD

•

the room She

To

neaR **the**

to bUild ' my

the deCree ' **ni**si

raTher than '

this is the new confUsion '

it is no contRadiction

thEn catalogued

two handS each alone

iT is as though

it's neveR

institUtes '

is only one of applying these in the Confusion

eighT years ago '

the enormoUs difficulty is only one of applying these in

aiRway of knowing

only onE

no purpoSe ' vision no vision in accord

in **The** '

the end of maRch '

institUtes

is only one of applying these in the Confusion

iT is only today

the nicaragUan

Rich and poor '

room shE

iS '

The '

of Role '

new non-visUal world of role playing he has no goals

politiCal

by shadows by environmenT ' theatre is closer to life than art '

or mUsic '

oR music

past but likE buhlig

workS and

passions diplomaTs ' say that it may be difficult to speak

shakes ouR confidence in the principles themselves

like a piece of cloth was found to have holes in it and the replacement had to come from texas i understand by telephone today things are looking up *my question has to do with 101 which was performed by the boston symphony orchestra and one of the singular highlights of the season for me was to witness it and to hear it a couple of times on the radio i'm not sure i have a question because several times the relative*

bUt

it is only today that the deCree

To **then** '

he has no goals he's already there it's jUst

devotion ' is he dRifting ' no

hE

and where it'S

permiT

is ' one thing to dRaw

it takes yoU no further

first performanCe

surrounds herself wiTh mozart beethoven bach all of the best of

dUet

and matteR '

a month spEnt failing to find '

alwayS a

mighT not

and pooR '

shoUld be

utterly simple basiC principles

living in This **new**

this new non-visUal '

foR it is

ago thE

tonS of

To

and pooR '

is only one of applying these in the confUsion

basiC

in The act

to Use '

it is the most geneRous

bEing interrupted

alSo a peculiar feeling of

your fellow men To have

and economics aRe bridged

to speak oUt of turn

between the world's riCh and poor ' developed and developing '

he's living in This new

he's already there it's jUst a question of

oveR how much

in thE act of reading

triadS and

rise To

dRaw an ellipse and another to

like it takes yoU no further

importance of answering questions has come up and it's struck me that as you answer questions you make other comments which might be described as asides and i've found the asides fascinating and i could come up with a question about 101 but i was wondering if you had any asides that come to mind about 101 or you may want to talk about the relative importance of questions answers and asides the title is in

is Closer

The latest

coUnts of

accoRd with

Enriching where he

iS

noT always when

being peRplexed '

this is the new confUsion

systems teChnology and

firsT

eqUation when you bump against the limits **of**

oR music

which i should bE inclined to call

of tonS of

global endeavors **The** '

the **dol**laR's

the dollar's rally continUed aided by

an infinite regress you Can say

you no furTher ' **in**

is only one of applying these in the confUsion '

of these **wit**ten conceRts ' it is no contradiction of this

of bEing perplexed unpredictability not being

diplomatS say

all of **The**

the difficulty in applying the simple basic pRinciples themselves in fact it is only today

like it takes yoU no further in

systems teChnology

Triads and aggregates

a whirlpool an infinite regress yoU can say what you like

he's living in this new non-visual woRld of

living in this nEw

purpoSe ' no purpose ' vision ' no vision ' in accord

any child knows and The

afRica angola and

soUth

mathematiCs '

classics she's so devoTed to ' then

yoU bump against the limits of

schoenbeRg's

wEnt to

for **thoSe** '

of reading food inflaTion

leadeRs near the end of march '

bUt isn't there also a

peCuliar feeling of

numbers rather than words whereas the first piece in this series was a piece called *two* for flute and piano
and that was written out t w o but as i was writing out the words one hundred one or one hundred and one
the question of whether i would write one or the other led me to the numerical solution and when i gave that
to my copyist paul sadowski he suggested that a capital o be used rather than zero i liked his suggestion very

resulTs of experiments `

oUt of

aiRway of knowing

diplomats say that it may bE difficult to

Speak `

ciTizen

peRhaps

the difficUlty **in** `

is only one of applying these in the Confusion

The **new** `

this is the new confUsion

the dollaR's rally

to havE an

devotion **iS** ` **he**

is The new confusion `

by walden pond neaRest to where

to bUy

the first performanCe

The simple basic principles `

like it takes yoU

yeaRs

thEn catalogued all of the

tonS of

iT is one thing to

couRse

Uprising

in mathematiCs

can play unassisTed by

coUnts of

closeR

of bEing perplexed ` unpredictability ` not being

diplomatS ` say

by means of iTs equation when you bump against the limits

to **gRe**te `

yoUth

to divorCe

To call feelings of pastness

experiences which i shoUld be inclined to call feelings of

Room `

somE of it ` and the

baSic principles `

is parT of

memoRy `

to begin withoUt borrowing but perhaps it is

basiC

To call

much and that has been followed so the rule is that the numbers will be written out when the pieces don't
exceed ninety-nine and when they do there will be numbers the piece is a percussion piece and this is made
possible by the col legno real col legno use of the strings one thing that i did poorly and would like to correct
are the dynamic levels particularly of the flutes and the clarinets throughout the piece i indicated that they

                                    mUsic
                                  coRn and
                               compEtition
                                   cloSer
                                      The
                                music foR
                                    thoUghts
                                 i notiCed
                                      The first of thirty-two
                                    yoU can say what you like it
                                   spiRit
                                   thE
                                      viSion ' no vision ' in accord
                                   To
                           no puRpose ' airway of knowing nowness '
                       borrowing bUt perhaps it is
                                    Closer
                                      To
                                    dUet '
                                   fiRst
                                  onE thing
                               knowS and
                                        This is the new confusion '
                                   heR hands
                                  to bUy
                                 exotiC fish or
                       developmenTs in mathematics
                                  woUld '
                       she lives ' woRks ' and
                       a month spEnt failing to find

                                  cloSer
                                 rise To
                                it's neveR
                                    thoUghts
                                  politiCal
                                  in The act
               a whirlpool an infinite regress yoU can say what you like '
                                      aiRway of ' knowing
                                ago ' thE

                                        •

should be played so softly that one wasn't sure whether he was hearing them or not but in the course of
seven hearings i was more or less certain that i didn't hear them at all i'd like to have the chance of thinking
that they were a little too loud the reason i had that idea of their being played almost inaudibly was because
of the first piece in this series which is for flute and piano i asked the flute to do that and it was very beautiful

lIterally

limits traNsgressed and

Trafficking

wildnEss '

oN

of course iT

Is

Of

aNd what

wIth

we ' always returNed '

kepT but

hE

aNd

aT

meanIng '

Object at

that wheN

wIth ways

No

acTions and

rEfusal

aNd

The furtherance of detachment ' and

I

mOrsel

baNk

that paId

aNd

iTs

his lEg is

maN's

To

It

and stOrms '

Not

next If

have No meaning is

refused To

coursE thus to '

caN

The

Is

the wOrld's resources so

iN

sIdes

the piano was in the range of forte and mezzoforte but the flute was very soft and it was very beautiful to hear it that way *as far as i understand you i certainly wouldn't set you up as an elitist in any sense and certainly not as a genius or something like that this goes back to your views on anarchy and the role of the artist i was wondering how you reconciled that with your fame no one would perform your pieces if*

aNd
sTill a man says
to arrangE
iN
wiTh '
lIfe
Officials said
to do ' Next
those Images upside
aN '
400 safeTy
imaginE
of ' kNowledge '
combaT '
fIve and
dOes
caN
mIght '
parts aNd
firsT '
Earth
of cubaN
yeT '
chIefs
in yOur
primeval chaos aNd feel at home
thIs case '
Nuclear
mind we can ' sTand
involvEd
we **caN**
can **The** '
scIence
systems that perfOrm
aNd what
to substItute for
aNd '
makes iT
spEak the truth ' religious attitude '
aNarchy '
and **iT**
Itself
destrOyed '
caN we see
a slIp of paper
aN

you weren't famous harvard wouldn't you know give you big spaces to answer questions if you weren't famous i was wondering how you saw the two in relation to each other i find your question very interesting but i haven't heard it clearly enough would you repeat it as far as being antielitist even more than being nonelitist and as being what antielitist you wouldn't want to see elitism of any sort in a construction of

sTrongly
answEr
aNd his name '
his name buT he
our vIewer '
nOt that **i** '
gertrude steiN ' fluency
Is
of thousaNds **of** '
souTh
rEalm **of**
at aNy
Them ' as
begIn
if yOu
aNd
wIsh '
Now move
down To
promisEd
fiNd
buT
Is the
nOw
a straNge abandonment '
wIthout
toNs
by evoluTion
with lEss
iNdividual are in
whaT
has saId
my hOuse
well-beiNg of everyone '
and I
cubaN
wiTh
of viEw '
clouds aNd
quiTe the
now wIth
wOrk we
kNow
wIth
oNce or
ficTion

anarchy i would say and in conceptions of yourself as not being a special person as especially *no you don't
see yourself as someone who's special or who has something* hmm *how do you reconcile this with your
fame and especially considering that fame allows your works to be performed and allows* right *you to
have an open forum* well when i was young i mean when i was young enough to have problems about being

              bE ˙
          pasturiNg
              eTernal
          where I
              fOr
          defiNe
              wIth less
          we caN
          and souTh
              pErhaps
              iN
              The **two**
              In
          nOr
      streams ˙ but remaiNs
              wIth
              fouNd in
              Town
              morE secrets ˙
          we caN
              drifTwood
          notch It
          if he wOuld
          white piNes
              carrIed two ˙
          compouNds
          in mosT
              callEd
          imagiNe
                  eiTher ˙ why
              hanoI
              the fOrmalistic
              sigNs ˙
          notch It
              wheN we
              This
              appEars to
              raNk
                  Though
              It is
              gO
              iN
              Is
          aNd
              Troops ˙ in
          uniquE

able or not able to do something when i couldn't because of money i saw that other people often didn't have
those problems and i wondered how in heaven's name someone say devoted to music to the writing of music
could ever make any money and have a house and a dog and an automobile it seemed to me to be out of reach
for someone whose reach was toward writing music i remember meeting a man who had a desire to be an

oNe message

excepT for that

to publIc '

enable peOple to be fed '

that differs uNless

of both ' prIvate

parallel betweeN

abouT

unlEss ' i could

fouNder and go

cloud ' and **The**

If

the cOmplex

iNvolved

of hIs

with eNergy ' nichi nichi kore ko nichi ' and as

you're wriTing

world ' consciousnEss more with less '

less thaN

combaT ' was

and now wIth

any prOblem paradox '

which maNages so well

thIs case

compouNds

400 safeTy

to arrangE

less thaN

aT '

and now **wIth**

gO

iN

•

yes anD

we conceIve '

we alwayS

whiCh

and polIcy '

at the Pond i found

the seLf of

It '

aNd

artist but not having any money he took a job in order to make some in hollywood and his job continued and he made money but he never made any art things didn't seem to me in my i don't know if i'm answering your question or not or your remarks but i'm trying not paying any attention to not having any money led me to continue my work as i saw fit to do it and when people told me that my music wasn't music i asked them

disposE of
anD
to sIxty '
Same
afriCa had
Is
sPace between
or different things ' new materiaL
gIves
esseNtial
problEm '
anD so
sImply '
human needS **for**
for whiCh
there Is a tree
uPon
the Laws
the hIghest '
maN's
thE year
anD so
when It
createS it's never
in its intelleCtual
hIs
accePt it
he ' couLd
basIc
Not
thEy
louD and
whIch would
reSolution without
preferenCe or taste '
process whIch has been going on throughout
comPuter system
for a man to put himseLf
utterly sImple '
maN would
thE
fooD
wIll
yeSterday
Created so as to
free these varIous ways in

what they thought it was or what i was good for this was when i was looking for a job on the wpa in the early forties and i was told that i was not a musician when i applied to the music section i said well i work with sounds what would you call me and they said well try the recreation department so i did and they accepted me but they didn't have anything for me to do it seemed to me i shouldn't receive money unless i was doing

research Programs '
different points in space ' musicaL sculpture '
hIs place it is
it would eNcompass
arE not
knows anD
I '
caeSar
sweet Corn
the kIlowatt
sPeeds
he shouLd
who wIshes to
kNow
his gEnius '
through the wooDs
leavIng from
korea'S
Cannot see '
somewhere between the unIted
sPheres of
boiLed
basIc
were No word '
propErly we
anD
havIng no control
boiled and Salted ' **i**
is Constantly
If i have
the Present
aLphabet or the rules of
Is '
couNts of
can wE
than the gooD
now possIble for anyone anywhere to
Strip protests in
Copper
In contact with it
the Pure idea
any chiLd
Is
foregrouNd ' **that**
wEll **if**
i founD

something and i pointed this out to them they said well you could go to the hospital and they gave a name of a hospital where they have a problem because of the mothers going to visit patients and what do they do with the children while they're visiting the patients because the children are apt to make noises is there any way you could keep them quiet and so i taught the children curiously enough how to be silent i gave them exercises

lIved
the meaSure
at an objeCt
Itself it **is** '
euroPe is '
you can onLy see
unIque
the eNd ' **a**
arE
baD and
It
no morSel
feeling exCept
obedIence '
musical sculPture '
is constantLy
hImself '
Normal
morE
anD
In '
Sweet
sounds be sounds **eaCh**
In
Point
a Long way off '
gorIllas '
No
points in spacE
anD
In '
and Solving global problems '
a Composer has never yet
rapId
out in Practice '
wisdom is not to be equated with ' mysticaL ecstasy '
thIs
souNd
systEm is
anD
mankInd had and
i found mySelf ranging the woods like a half-starved
whiCh
place It is **this**
to develoP **his** '
is onLy

they were similar to dalcroze exercises moving and counting and not saying anything or making any noises to keep themselves busy finally everything has changed and i've done so much in the society in the way of music and writing and whatnot i think these struggles or this kind of life with respect to my work and to society has brought about a putting together of the two *we can skip what is anarchy and what your views*

that It
is ' oNly making it '
it bEing

anD
lIved '
caeSar
Cannot see '
Is
the Pure idea '
the Laws '
Is
aNd
thEy

•

as compreheNsive and '
bOdies ' veins ' nerves ' muscles '
sTep
meAns which ' is
resembles The '
Increased efficiencies '
nOt
as clear as water ' so that i caN
upoN levels
Of '
levels To '
cAn call
less The
more flexIble ' these
in sOuth america ' we
value judgmeNts ' we
maNs' internal
shOuld '
regeneraTion of
chinA is
which could predicT that
rocks In
tO
iN
mooN
tO
sTores '
humAn

of anarchy are and maybe give some insight as to how you think this society could possibly transit to a more anarchy-like state it's a very hard question to answer but i'll give you the thoughts that are in my mind about it i think the laws in our society are made to protect the rich from the poor and i think we have to move insofar as we can toward a society that makes poverty possible and enjoyable i think also we must move

process ' The awareness of
as It were '
us tO
techNology '
elevatioN '
Or you could say
wasTe if
A ' ban on
sTores ' **and**
saId **the** '
fOr
you caN proceed
operatioNs
them tO **find** '
we are all going in differenT directions '
the ideA as
endings **The** '
them to fInd '
and wedge Our feet
uNited
aNd
sOme of
whaT
nine dAys ago
To come
he saId
anOther
Not ' a
fixed iN taste '
an equal number ' then yOu **can**
The
wAys
for Talks '
holds Itself
he Offered them
iN
dawN
sO
and The
And
on using Two '
south amerIca ' we all
internal metabOlics ' electric
obstacles ' usiNg them to
haNd ' the drawings were suddenly
the bOwl ' if you find

toward a society that is based not on employment but on unemployment i think one should be able to live in a society with pleasure and dignity without doing anything that was accepted as a job in a society i think that's part of the meaning of our technology our electronic technology we no longer need to work i have the example in my own family of my father who never took a job he was an inventor all artists are people who are

iT
leAd
buT
If '
anOther
iN
importaNce '
prOgress '
parTs '
And microscopic
Them but **they** '
ways to Increase '
tO excel '
redivertiNg the valuable chemistries '
aNd
tO be read
i can ' i Think ' he would
globAl
so efficienTly ' and
Interrupted take
mOre resolute '
aNd helps
maN ' enables individuals
One
wiTh world '
puerto ricAn '
wiTh oneself that each person
musIc
Of the total electric power
is discipliNed ' body too ' the heart '
the Navy's highest ranking '
lOnger fixed '
To
never wAnder
souTh
a state of mInd '
nO
maN's credit card ' he
islam iN
the wild ' **resO**urces **and**
quiTe sure '
mAny
percenT of the tonnage '
the steepest ' the bIll '
tear gas and beatings tO
theN looked at ways to

unemployed they only force what they're doing on other people but nobody wants them to do what they do now for the thing that makes me hopeful about anarchy in the society is that it works in the field of the arts you couldn't possibly be an artist without being an anarchist if you love noises then you love the people or the sounds for which the rules of harmony were not made and those correspond to the rules that protect the

room i had fouNd
the wOrld's resources '
while also rediverTing the
perhAps
read iT there and
Is a
prOcess the
of humaNity
we Need
is One
humaniTy
And parcel of his or her
wiTh no one below the present european level
from Its desire '
filling Out the picture of it is
the time available iNto
eveN
tO '
To
from Any
of iTs
whIch
the **twO**
by aNy of its parts e.g.
its lessoN ' it is a watcher
Of synergy '
This is synergy ' it is
Any
preeminenT use '
vIetnam's
wOrld '
chiNa's
electric liNes ' etcetera ' are
Of consciousness
on The united
individuAl '
sTrongly toward the furtherance of detachment '
saId in
nOt by
bodies ' veiNs '
self-expressioN '
and the rain which lasts three weeks and prOduces
in The
the ' sAme
lengTh
Is ' an awareness

rich from the poor and it works without harmony not only i but many others show that it is possible to write music without that kind of rule against noise so i think we could have a world society if we took into consideration the possibility of poverty and the possibility of unemployment *it's more like the next stage it's like the next stage in the evolution of governments as opposed to there being some revolution right got it*

sOviet '

aNd

aloNe

prOduced

The

A '

navy's highesT

the remaInder '

thrOugh

briNgs **to** '

had beguN it

sO '

sTore '

support ' provide ' An

iT

I

tO surpass

aNd

maN

tO

funcTion **of** '

rivAl of

Than

all mankInd

bOth private '

iNterrupted ' take

beeN

Of

iT

ziA

Than '

the communIst party '

the wOrld '

as maNy

degrees of freedom or alterNatives '

One

in **The**

they Are '

sighT of

It '

Of fact it

pasturiNg

the Navy's highest ranking

Of

iT

thanks a lot fifty-two years ago you gave a lecture in seattle entitled future of music credo *and it seems on rereading that that today all of those predictions that you gave have come true for even the mainstream of society although perhaps not in the way that you intended in the lecture or maybe you did but i was wondering if you had any comments on that whether you've had any feelings towards perhaps the next*

371

leAd

Than

he saId

us **tO**

aNd **helps**

•

had been wIdely tipped to

Nature '

animal sounDs ' human sounds '

painting ' dividE '

Try to

writE down the sounds '

categoRies ' sounds in nature ' and

as that of a language study a painting froM **three**

each perIod **of** '

souNds '

study A painting from three different periods of

eaCh painting ' divide these into three categories '

a painting from three different periods of Your own culture '

the sounds for whIch you

be the most commoN way of getting about ' the concept of a living

happen to your sense of values ' woulD walking

widEly '

This country

widEly ' tipped to

tRy to express your findings in percentages '

what can you learn about your own environMent '

tIpped to

learN '

you leArn about your own environment in this way '

what Can

learn about Your own

had been wIdely tipped to

aNimal '

animal sounDs ' human sounds '

thEse

concepT ' of a **liv**ing

concEpt ' of a living being ' has the same

human sounds ' technological sounds ' is theRe **a**

if Money were to

sounds ' Is there **a** '

aNd

to your sense of vAlues ' would walking be the most

fifty years or a thousand or ten or one what the future of music is i haven't read that text recently so i don't know whether i would say something different now or not but the thing that strikes me more and more is that there will be more continuously more kinds of music and more ideas about making music than we yet know they will come at greater speed and frequency and number as time goes on so that if we say something

way of getting about ' the Concept of a living being has the same

to disappear ' what would happen to Your sense of values ' would

money **were** to dIsappear ' what would

moNey **were** to

each perioD of painting ' try to

can you lEarn '

flow of illegal narcoTics into this country '

kind of sound in **Each**

this way ' the official Radio had been widely tipped to narrow the

language study a painting froM

three categorIes '

the souNds for which you see evidence **in** '

would wAlking be the most

of getting about ' the Concept of a living being has the same

to disappear ' what would happen to Your sense of values

perIods of

your seNse of values '

animal sounDs ' human sounds '

thEse

inTo **this**

bEen widely tipped

had been widely **tipped** to naRrow the section of the flow of illegal

sense of values ' would walking be the Most common way of

radIo ' had

iNto this country **five** '

leArn about your own environment in this way '

what Can

Your **own** '

had been **wIdely** tipped

iN nature '

the sounDs for which you

study ' a painting from thrEe '

Try to

Evidence in each painting ' divide these into

one kind of sound in each peRiod of painting ' try to express your findings

about 1,500 jobs were out of con**trol who** froM the start of the war '

narcotIcs '

humaN sounds '

About 1,500 jobs were out of

the war until now ' after six days deClined to comment '

five Years ago about

country ' fIve years ago about

this way ' the official radio had beeN

animal sounDs ' human sounds

out of control ' who from thE

commenT **if** '

about music as though it were one thing we will be missing the point namely that it's many and increasingly
an increasingly many many hmm *a nice experience of synchronicity when you answered the earlier question*
about anarchy earlier today i happened to open a year from monday *where i read we invented machines*

to commEnt if **mon**ey '

afteR six days declined

to coMment '

nature and anImal '

each paiNting ' divide these into three

of A **lan**guage study ' a painting from **three** '

your own environment ' in this way the offiCial radio had been

Your **own**

had been wIdely tipped to

what caN you learn about your own environment '

haD

into **thrEe** '

counTry

to narrow thE section of the flow of illegal

into this countRy ' five years ago about 1,500 jobs were out of

what can you learn about your own environMent '

now after sIx days '

after six days decliNed to comment '

whAt

your own environment in this way ' the offiCial radio had been

Your **own** '

had been wIdely tipped to

caN you learn about your own environment in this

happen to your sense of values ' woulD walking

kind of sound ' Each period of

a**bouT** '

of onE kind of sound ' in each

about youR own '

sounds ' huMan sounds '

had been wIdely tipped to

iN

six dAys '

way of getting about ' the Concept of a living being has the same

five Years ago about

country fIve years ago about

this couNtry ' five years ago about

of **sounD** ' in

pEriod of

To narrow

in this way ' thE official '

had been widely tipped to naRrow the section of the flow of illegal

what you can ' learn about your own environMent '

tIpped to

iNto this country **five** '

About 1,500 jobs were out of

in eaCh painting ' divide these into three categories

in order to reduce our work now that we have them we think we should go on working and the committee of eight on automation economics and employment considering whether us society should be geared for employment or unemployment voted six to two in favor of employment i have a couple of questions for you

to express Your

      thIs way **the** ' official radio had

a predomiNance of **one** '

technological sounDs ' is

widEly

whaT can you

illEgal

into this countRy '

what can you learn about your own environMent '

narcotIcs '

about the coNcept of

getting About the

sounds for whiCh

of values ' would walking be the most common waY of

dIvide these

study a paiNting from three '

your own culture ' write Down

six days dEclined

in This way '

thEse into

peRiods of your own culture '

your sense of values ' would walking be the Most common way

of your own culture ' wrIte

beiNg

your own environment in this wAy '

write down the sounds for whiCh

Your own

had been wIdely tipped to

be the most commoN way of getting about ' the concept of a living

happen to your sense of values ' woulD walking

narcotics into this country fivE years ago '

jobs were ouT of control ' who from

down thE sounds

wRite down the sounds for which you see

coMmon way of

three categorIes '

the **souNds** for which you see evidence in

sounds ' humAn sounds '

sounds ' is there a predominanCe of one kind of sound in each period ' **of**

as that of a language studY '

each perIod of

aNimal '

animal sounDs ' human sounds '

sounds in naturE ' and animal sounds ' human sounds '

can you learn abouT your own

flow of illEgal

one is that i have a sense of prayer and/or meditation when i listen to your lectures and hear you here for these discussions i'm curious to hear your thoughts about prayer and meditation the other question is i was interested when you said that you didn't like improvisation and i've changed oh great the part you

diffeRent periods of your own culture ' write down

your sense of values would walking be the Most common way of

your own culture ' wrIte

eNvironment **in** '

rAdio had been widely tipped to narrow

the seCtion of the flow of illegal narcotics

to express Your

thIs

the flow of Narcotics into this country five years ago '

haD

animal sounds ' human sounds ' tEchnological sounds ' is

your own environmenT in this way

into **thrEe** '

human sounds ' technological sounds ' is theRe a

that of a language study a painting froM

each perIod of

humaN sounds '

whAt '

what Can

findings in percentages ' what can You learn about your own

three categorIes

iN percentages what can you learn about your

kinD of sound ' **in**

kind of sound in Each period of

counTry '

to narrow thE section of the flow of illegal

human sounds ' technological sounds ' is theRe **a** '

three categories ' sounds in nature and aniMal sounds ' human sounds '

the offIcial radio had

of souNd in

period of pAinting ' try to express your findings in

painting ' try to express your findings in perCentages ' what

to express Your

way the offIcial radio had

iN each painting '

these into three categories ' sounDs in

writE down

would happen To **your** '

your sEnse of values ' would walking be the most

to disappeaR ' what would happen to your sense of values '

what can you learn about your own environMent '

sounds Is there

aNd

sounds in nAture ' and animal sounds ' human sounds

in eaCh painting ' divide these into three categories '

as that of a language studY '

want me to talk about that *yes especially in the light of what you said today had to do with writing music what is it about writing music that* that fascinates *yes actually* that's what i am i'm a writer of music i see that there are other ways of making music and i now finally see that there's a way for me to write an

tIpped to

Nature '

animal sounDs ' human sounds '

thEse

Try to

valuEs ' would walking be the most common way '

what would happen to youR sense of values ' would walking be

as that of a language study a painting froM **three**

the sounds for whIch you see

from three differeNt periods of your own culture ' write down the

jobs were out of control who from the stArt of the war until now after six days

deClined to comment if

five Years ago about

of control ' who from the start of the war untIl

as **that** of a laNguage '

haD

yEars ago

Try

Evidence in each painting ' divide these into

one kind of sound in each peRiod of painting ' try to express your findings

as that of a language study ' a painting froM three

sounds ' human sounds ' technologIcal

iN

three cAtegories ' sounds in nature ' and animal sounds '

painting ' try to express your findings in perCentages ' what can

findings in percentages ' what can You learn about your own

radIo ' **had**

iN each painting

as that of a language stuDy ' a painting from

would walking bE

common way of geTting about '

thE sounds '

sounds in natuRe ' and

that of a language study ' a painting froM three '

money were to dIsappear ' what

way of gettiNg

the most common wAy of getting about '

three different periods of your own Culture ' write down the sounds for which

were **to** ' disappear ' what would happen to Your sense of values ' would

perIods of your

way of gettiNg about ' the concept of a living being ' has

these into three categories ' sounDs in

writE down

for which you see evidence in each painTing '

kind of sound in Each '

in this way the official Radio had been widely tipped to narrow the

improvisation or give directions for improvising that would be a kind of improvising that i would enjoy the
thing i don't like about or didn't like about improvisation was that it was based on taste and memory and it
didn't get the improviser to a point where he encountered a revelation something that he didn't already know

sounds ' huMan sounds '

had been wIdely tipped to

souNds '

sounds ' humAn sounds '

sounds ' is there a predominanCe of one kind of sound in each period '

the official radio had been widelY

Illegal

iN this way

of painting ' try to express your finDings in

if monEy **were** '

if money were To

monEy '

if money weRe to disappear ' what would happen to your

Money

If

your fiNdings

sounds in nAture ' and animal sounds ' human sounds '

teChnological sounds is there a predominance of

culture ' write down the sounds for which You **see**

tIpped to

your owN environment ' in this way

in each perioD of painting try to

thEse

of conTrol

of illEgal

sounds foR which you see evidence in each painting '

the concept of a living being has the saMe

three categorIes '

you learN

your own environment in this wAy '

your own environment in this way the offiCial radio had been

in this waY the

each perIod of

aNimal '

animal sounDs ' human sounds '

to disappEar '

disappear ' whaT **would** '

what would **hap**pEn ' to

out of contRol ' **who**

were out of control ' who froM the start of the war

fIve years ago about

fifteeN hundred jobs were out of control ' who

As that of a language study ' a painting from

write down the sounds for whiCh

values would walking be ' the most common waY

however it's possible to give directions for improvisation that will lead to unexpected experiences on the part
of the improviser and i find some musicians who enjoy improvising anxious to be told how to do it this is
really not strange in the field of improvisation one of the things i recall hearing about was the improvising of

of your own culture ' wrIte

about the coNcept of a living being ' has the same

as that of a language stuDy ' a painting from

would walking bE '

would happen To your

valuEs ' would walking be the most common way of

findings in peRcentages ' what can you learn about your own

categories ' sounds in nature ' and aniMal sounds ' human sounds '

way the offIcial radio had

of souNd ' in

been widely tipped to nArrow the

flow of illegal narCotics into this

the official radio ' had been widelY

narcotIcs

about the coNcept of a living being ' has the same

as that of a language stuDy ' a painting from

would walking bE '

war unTil now '

narcotics into this country ' fivE

out of contRol ' who '

after six days ' declined to coMment '

who from the start of the war untIl '

uNtil now '

jobs were out of control who from the stArt of the war until now after six days '

after six days deClined to comment ' **if**

of values ' would walking be the most common waY of

wIdely tipped to

perceNtages ' what can you learn about your own

sounD '

start of thE war '

war unTil now '

Evidence in each

kind of sound ' in each peRiod of painting ' try to express your findings

if Money **were** ' to

money **were** ' to dIsappear what would

your seNse of

1,500 jobs were out of control who from the stArt of the war until now after six days

way of getting a**bout** ' the Concept of a

culture ' write down the sounds for which You see

of con**trol** ' who from the start of the war untIl

be ' the most commoN way of getting about ' the concept of a living

these into three categories ' sounDs in

pEriod **of** '

commenT **if** '

fugues by organists and i had the pleasure of being in the organ loft with messiaen in la trinité in paris when he was improvising anyway i have thought in recent years of a variety of ways of improvising that begins with a notion that gives a problem to the improviser to solve as he plays if you divide the time of an improvisation

into thrEe
sounds in natuRe and
coMmon way of
tIpped to
you ' learN
would wAlking be the most
painting ' try to express your findings in perCentages ' what
a **paint**ing from three different periods of Your own culture

•

and metaphysIcal
at the eNd of a new england summer day ' if i could
which appeared To
hE ' i mean the twig '
wounded angolan Rebels
individually and in teams ' were out to solve Practical world '
no fixEd '
oNly
thE fellows of
noT be
wheRe
And
To assert '
Is
the wOrld **game** to make the world work ' for
iNstead of noblemen let us have noble
tIme ' people
of laNguage '
of elecTric
surfacE '
of fReedom ' or alternatives to humanity and
Parts ' parts for which
thEy
kwh aNd
thE
conTinue **what**
oR **ev**er
And in
poinTs but spaces of
In
tO your
chaNces of
Israel are
arouNd

into sections you can then divide the sounds that are available for the performance into a similar number of parts and that fact of having a space in the time where certain sounds will go and they won't go into others will give an interesting something that could interest one as a problem as he was playing freely i don't myself

himself wiTh
rEst of
foRces are not
uP that
thE '
liviNg or
is happEning ' was
whaT the
foR
i meAn
percenTage of
be**hIn**d it and
hOw
dissideNt '
upon I
beeN
experience wealTh ' consisting of both '
wE begin to be men and women ' it is time
we did not leave off ouR education '
according to the sPirit '
thE village do to act collectively ' is
caN only
wE
an almosT hypnotized visual stance ' as it
woRds in rote order sensitive
to live then **too** ' And
Through spontaneous
capacIty ' and transmitted '
wOuld it be best to come before that time to
total capacity aNd
grId power '
let us have Noble villages of men '
and **To**
without Ecological offense '
the physical and metaphysical can only incRease with each and every
caPacity and
continuE what i was
with **aN**
arE
sTable
ouR
technologicAlly
now living or ever To become '
hIm
and even at that time ' peOple
leadiNg

do any sitting or meditating and the reason i don't do it i may be wrong but i don't do it because my work involves so much sitting and since i work with asking questions rather than making choices i'm in a quiet frame of mind i try to get that quietness to move into the rest of my life the watering of the plants shopping lIberal studies the rest of their lives '

i meaN

everyThing '

world gamE '

anyone should think he has solved the pRoblem of life and feel like telling himself

uP '

hEart '

iN is in

thEory ' **does** is

To

dis**cov**eRed ' but it must

one leArns

The

total success for all humanIty '

make the wOrld work ' that is satisfy

depeNds upon

Israel are to

ecologically ecoNomically and

learn To

End of

woRk for

at this Point

world gamE

aNd

morE flourishing our means ' are

of **Them** the

weRe ' then

A smile ' lo and behold '

peak needs around The earth '

Its use under certain circumstances which

wOrlds

way ' aNd

don't for heaven's sake be afraId of

time has goNe '

does is To show that gravitational and

End

foR which there is no score

with the least environmental imPact in

living in thE

life aNd

impact in thE

iT '

maximum aRe world '

which however one does not leArn '

Too and

whIch

and so forth the various things i do in order to minimize the sense of agitation or disturbance from moment to moment so that the opposite of prayer and meditation doesn't take over i think it's rather clear that praying for something to happen hoping something will happen is not an interesting form of prayer *i'm wondering*

the wOrld

begiN and

that whIch

worlds aNd

individual prepared To

arE ' used in

Rise intelligence

at Particular points in

othEr that they are

aNd

rEal physical sense inseparable '

The

that they aRe in

summer dAy ' if

environmenTal '

don't for heaven's sake he afraId

tO his culture ' so let the village do to act '

be white aNd tranparent '

mean the twIg ' for some time

up ' that is our New work ' and

i ching Told

and quiEt the mind ' going in is in '

that is satisfy human needs foR food ' energy ' shelter ' etcetera for the most

in time when there are not Points ' but

nEtwork to areas where there are deficits '

is quite easy Now '

pErson

of success ' The ultimate

eveR to become living in the

technologicAlly

oTher that they are'

to be men and women It is time that villages were universities and

their respective levels tO the per capita figure of

villages of meN ' the world game to make the world work ' for

we learn to assert or deny It of them ' the

beeN solved and even

resT of

off to pursuE '

tRuce and

uP '

havE

iN parts ' parts for which

situation is much morE flexible

of human beings we learn To

woRld '

electric power becAuse we do

if there are particular sounds or events that don't seem to occur as much as they used to over the course of your life are there some sounds that are gone i think i probably hear the ones that aren't gone *could you talk a little about the effect that eating a macrobiotic diet has had on you* i had arthritis very badly i was

for boTh '
fIgure
tO
impact iN
to act collectIvely is
New
direcTion '
rElationship ' a smooth white '
the physical and metaphysical can only incRease with **each** ' and
wealth consisting of both the Physical and
living in thE
too aNd
aftEr
all humaniTy now living
the use of the woRd for
eAch
of Those '
the quIckest '
the vast hydrOelectric
had Not been '
Israel are to
of ' humaN beings ' we learn
To
whilE
of fReedom or alternatives to
hosPital ' also
timE '
doN't for
lifE ' and
surrounds himself wiTh
leaRn to
A
will noT
sayIng
degrees Of freedom or
way aNd
one wIth
wheN
To
has ' solvEd
them Round the while and not be
Point in
o thE
poiNt in **our**
thE word for **a**
To

taking twelve aspirin a day i did that for fifteen years i was finally taking the kind that explodes inside so that
it gives you a delayed reaction i saw that the arthritis was getting worse that everything my doctor told me to
do was giving me no help so i asked my astrologer what i should do and she said your health is going to

384

boaRd them round the while '

boArd

are noT

been usIng '

sOmetimes

leadiNg '

smIle

aNd behold

and deaTh '

insidE

can Reflect things but what then if we

uP

arE greater '

aNd

twig ' hE

describe buT i can teach ' a

poweR could **be**

And every

They would make the world **work** ' that

leIsure if they are indeed

sOme

kwh aNd the surplus

under partIcular

upoN a '

such a ' seT-up '

wE should only need to caution

Rise intelligence

stePs

quitE easy '

Nor

bEhold

dayTime

kilowatt houRs

so let the villAge

The

In

hOurs '

ourselves that there was a time wheN they had not been solved and even at that

lIberal studies the rest of their lives '

the while aNd

as iT

that wE did

woRds in rote order sensitive information '

caPacity with

for thE most people

a smooth white surface caN

improve through an unorthodox doctor when i was in paris i was working on *empty words* at the time i
heard of a very fine acupuncturist and he walked across paris and looked at my wrists which were swollen to
about this size and he said i should have my blood examined and i should change my diet that acupuncture

information **is** ' at **thE**

of Those

aRe used in

And

would **The**

Is **util**ized '

dOes

shelter etcetera for the most people usiNg the least amount of resources

must have been possIble to live

aNd

ouT

insidE

and boaRd them round the while

and metaPhysical can

and board thEm

caN

has solvEd

The

what can be moRe

globAl '

are deficiTs of

becomes agaIn after emptiness ' best

sOmetimes

iN teams ' were out to

mean the twIg ' for some time

techNologically '

jusT

our nEw

cReated

could be generated at day and night total caPacity and

ultimatE bare maximum wealth at this

Not

of succEss '

is The same

and the suRplus is

Are '

such a seT-up

stance as It were ' rite

night hOurs

iNcrease

fIxed

he sits upoN ' i mean **he** ' i mean

be besT to

not sufficE '

pRoblems one of which was how to feed

each other that they are in a very real Physical

would not help me except palliatively i asked him how much i owed him and he said nothing i haven't helped you then the third thing happened before i changed back in new york on thirteenth street a long black car stopped and yoko ono got out she saw what a state i was in it was difficult for me to walk i was puffy these arE

a solutioN to

thEir lives '

is quiTe easy now he can see that he is

woRk for 100%

And

wiTh a global

when we begIn

the prOblem of life '

it aNd

per capIta

the daytime peak Needs around

i.e. iTs

lo and bEhold

in Rote order

uP

ordEr

is Not

sakE be afraid

To

act collectively is accoRding to the spirit of our

outlook ' An

quickesT amount of

are used In **parts** ' parts

it wOuld the surface

raised ' what caN be more natural than such a set-up

I.e. its use

uNder

parTs for which

succEss the ultimate

possible time thRough

wealth consisting of both the Physical and

nEw

of cultivated taste surrouNds

twig for **somE**

Too and the solution which has now been

continuing to sobeR

not points but spAces of

which appeared To be reflected

planned for november agaInst any ill-planned steps inside a refugee '

spread jOy '

New england can

Israel are to

time has goNe

and deaTh

wrists and so forth she said you must go and see shizuko yamamoto she will change your diet and give you shiatzu massage within one week after i saw her i went to her immediately within one week with a changed diet all the pain was gone the macrobiotic diet i have in my way i have followed that ever since even on the

insidE
that is satisfy human needs foR food energy shelter etcetera for the most
at Particular points ' **in**
arE greater
poiNt ' **in** our
aftEr
iT '
continuing to sobeR
And every
peak needs around The earth
are used In **parts** ' **parts** '
dOes
iN**crease**

•

thermal plants **It**
therMal plants '
turn Is
To
As
The '
speedIng
pOwerful
makiNg '
rather than the mInute details ' the
long terM humanly advantageous ways rather than
In '
raTher
Are
The
In '
earth is an autOmated spaceship '
the 12th ceNtury
to have costumes of the perIod '
etcetera ' in nothing one and the saMe nature ' at the same
nothIng ' one
efficiency and polluTion '
it wAs
The
whIch
chOice
No
prevIous
plants ' it becaMe

tours with the cunningham dance company and i wouldn't dream of changing it once when she was giving me massage shizuko said you shouldn't take the diet so seriously and i was so shocked that i didn't ask her what she meant but two weeks later i took courage and said what do you mean when you say don't take the

constantly replenIshed ' income energies were
porTuguese '
A
Today '
a vast and undeveloped nature whIch men have
utilized ' hydrOelectric power for other
advaNtageous ways
expands Itself in an eternal outspreading
caMera
perspectIve '
The
wAys '
The amounts of metals '
space vehIcle '
all things tOgether
withiN grasp of earth's present
savIngs account of fossil and nuclear fuels '
Men
suggestIng
same naTure
the two sides hAd discussed
before dawn Today ' the two
rejoIce that there are
fOr
withiN the
It ' in
huManly advantageous ways rather
saId
wesT
in A
nebula ' The awareness of earth's
on Its
Out power
No day '
prevIous
Murder
whIch as
ouT power
Are biological
To those who
rejoIce
whO
Nature at the
detaIls the
long terM humanly advantageous
hydroelectrIc power for

diet so seriously and she said well when you're with friends you could have a potato i also don't eat potatoes or tomatoes or eggplants or peppers though now and then recently i do have some red pepper i have (a cookbook) a little one in the computer but i don't intend to publish it though i'll give you a copy if you want

Them '
it is **A** '
ouT power
began In
a fOrmer
saviNgs account
mIcrotonal
huManly advantageous
fIlm of
To
sAvings
prepared To
suIted
we chOse to keep
accelerate efficieNcy throughout the world '
space vehIcle earth
to work with it in the Most long term humanly advantageous ways
whIch as
copper and aluminum and sTeel '
we chose to keep efficiency levels And
developmenT **how** can we accelerate
earth's present economIc and industrial
prOblems of thermal
uNdeveloped nature '
as those used In
costuMes
In
The
All '
in The
sIdes
Of
aNd
It ' in the
huManly advantageous ways rather than
evolutIonary
The efficiency '
principAlly copper aluminum and
Those used
makIng
the Overall
turN

as those used In
to work with it ' in the Most long term humanly advantageous ways '
perspectIve

the basic principle of the macrobiotic diet is one thing and the variations that one makes for it is another i'm not as strict as i might be my lack of strictness lies in the fact that i don't balance things properly i know this because my own cooking isn't as good for me as the cooking of fransje bannenberg in holland was last

Them
Are biological
ouT power '
earth's present economIc and industrial '
a fOrmer
aNd

•

political Dogma
assassinatEd priest '
would haVe
as **Our** '
are greaTer than
the bare maxImum
Of
aNy resort to
is accorDing to
any morE than the assertion i am here '
we will haVe '
create a wOrldwide
village ' do To act
I
tOp
employ them iN our scenario because we
protesteD
thE piece would perhaps be written for
the wall which he had coVered with paper '
knOwing
The
It and
because a tremendOus '
easily imagiNe ' a situation to fit it '
the potential of fluiDics as a
truE proposition of
uniVersities and their elder inhabitants '
memOry '
sighT ' and so
meanIng '
lOsses '
efficieNcy
equally louD and
no longEr
imaginable ' giVen
if sO

november she had studied here in boston with aveline kushi i benefitted from her cooking more than from my own i don't do it quite right but i enjoy what i do *can you see a marked difference or a change in your ideas from when you started the diet* i think the ideas were there before the application to the body i come

The
people are engaged In agriculture ' as
Of
maN
to fooD for man '
facE and no question on her lips ' i awoke to
editors and noVelists '
the assertiOn makes sense
The
only true answer wIll set all
time thrOugh '
is No stopping or going ' o moon why are you so
contemporary ' no longer fixeD in
thE course of my life ' **make**
would haVe
Of '
The
hIm
Of
iN '
armeD
systEm is
moVie '
a critic write it ' wOuld
To heat
some kInd
befOre you
theN to
boarD
thEm ' bidding us hear it like this ' the first
aboVe them ' bidding us hear it like this '
why are yOu **so**
The
wIll '
what lengths dO i go ' there is
a liviNg by bringing man to the
poets essayists eDitors and
facE and no question on her lips ' i awoke to
a global Village
can yOu say
Two
In chinese '
knOw
to Nature
worlD
two Equals four in chinese might

from a kind of education that thinks that the spirit is above the body as you get older you realize that they're
rather close together i don't see the addition of the diet to my work as having an effect on the work which
was already affected by the ideas related to the diet in other words i accepted the diet you might say aesthetically

a saner man would haVe
tOuch is our primary
poem ' sings The tune
to brIng
Out
experieNce ' not knowing what will happen next ' we are
sacreD
using hEr methods
coVered with paper '
sudden change Of mind '
jusT do **what**
not just passIve '
and under every deep a lOwer **deep**
readiNg

is accorDing to
facE and no question on her lips i awoke to
editors and noVelists
knOwing
The
not just passIve
tOp
efficieNcy

•

etCetera
defIne
clamouRed
speeCh '
woUld wish to
do **More** with
So he can
buT '
but Authorities
iN
Corn
said somEthing and that had removed '
if there iSn't any dust why are you always taking baths

etCetera
defIne
clamouRed
speeCh '
woUld wish to

before i accepted it nutritionally something like that it's a rather foolish statement *what year was it that what* *what year was it that you switched over* i'm a poor historian when the the diet changed *no when yoko ono got out of a black limo* i was writing *empty words* so that the book with that name wasn't yet published

393

do **More** with
So he can
buT '
but Authorities
iN
Corn
said somEthing and that had removed '
if there iSn't any dust why are you always taking baths

•

teach-in represents a creatiVe effort ' switching the
scene in which the Audience '
the audience peRforms an enormous amount of work ' the students '
the total electrIc
scene in which the Audience '
the total electric drama ' the classroom can Become a scene in which the audience performs
was how to feed the entire worLd at what
out to solvE practical world
were out to Solve
To solve
out to solve pRactical world problems ' one of which was how
teams were oUt to solve
Can become a scene in which
The total electric drama the classroom can
and in teams were oUt to solve
amount of woRk
thE dropout represents '
the teach-in represents a creatiVe effort '
the dropout represents A
maximum ' the dRopout represents
effort swItching '
becomes A participant in the total electric drama '
the classroom can Become a scene in which the audience performs '
audience becomes a participant in the totaL
out to solvE practical world '
individually and in teamS were
esTablishments '
pRoblems ' one of which was
how to feed the entire world at what the stUdents '
the audienCe '
solve pracTical world problems ' one of which was how to
individUally and in teams
an enoRmous amount of work '
audiEnce becomes a participant in the total

seventy-seven *would you say a few words about your piece entitled* cheap imitation *which is being performed tonight at north house along with satie's* socrate i would never have written *cheap imitation* had it not been necessary merce cunningham had long before made a choreography for the first movement of the *socrate* i

and in teams were out to solVe

mAnifested

Represents

nIneteenth-century technology '

students individuAlly and in teams were out to solve

entire world ' at what the students called a Bare maximum ' the dropout represents

one of which was how to feed the entire worLd at what

world at what **thE**

out to Solve

To solve

woRld problems one of which was how to feed

and in teams were oUt to solve

to disCovery as

audience performs an enormous amounT of work '

the dropoUt

dRopout '

our Educational establishments ' the teach-in '

the teach-in represents a creatiVe effort switching the

estAblishments ' the teach-in

pRoblems one of

whIch the

teAms were out to solve

entire world at what the students called a Bare maximum ' the dropout represents a

practicaL world

tEchnology '

the educational proceSs from package

classroom ' can become a scene in which The audience

woRld at

a bare maximUm the dropout represents

world problems ' one of whiCh was how

Total electric drama the classroom can become '

amoUnt of

the classRoom can

thE teach-in represents '

the teach-in represents a creatiVe effort switching the

mAnifested in

Represents

effort swItching ' the

pArticipant in the total electric drama '

the total electric drama the classroom can Become a scene in which the audience performs

worLd '

onE of which

individually and in teamS

were ouT to solve

pRactical world problems ' one of which was how

teams were oUt to solve

had told him that i would continue my arrangement for two pianos of the *socrate* if he would continue the choreography in the late sixties he informed me that he was going ahead with the choreography for the company so i went ahead with the arrangement for two pianos and then at the last minute it was just one

world problems ' one of whiCh was how

The

bare maximUm the

woRld

thE total electric drama the

educational process from package to discoVery '

electric drAma

fRom package to

audIence becomes

the clAssroom '

the total electric drama the classroom can Become a scene in which the audience performs '

the cLassroom can

participant in thE total electric drama

can become a Scene in which

drama The

students called a baRe

were oUt to solve

a sCene in which

work The

individUally and in teams '

dRama '

drama thE classroom can become ' a scene in which the

educational process from package to discoVery

becomes A

package to discoveRy as the

process from package to dIscovery

in the totAl electric drama ' the classroom can

from package to discovery as the audience Becomes a participant

switching the educationaL

crEative effort

aS

The teach-in

pRoblems one of which was

how to feed the entire world at what the stUdents

a sCene in which

a creaTive effort switching the

process from package to discovery as the aUdience becomes a

package to discoveRy as

procEss from package to

teach-in represents a creatiVe effort ' switching

the teAch-in

Represents

establIshments '

performs An enormous amount of work ' the students '

the total electric drama the classroom can Become a scene in which the audience performs

amount of work the students individuaLly and in

month before the first performance of the dance i asked for permission from the publisher to make the arrangement and it was not given so that i had to write a piece which had the same phraseology the same tempo and so forth because all the rehearsals had been with a recording of the *socrate* i made a way of

a scEne in which the audience
performS an enormous
rejecTion of
nineteenth-centuRy technology as manifested in
the dropoUt '
a sCene in which
individually and in Teams were
individUally
maximum ' the dRopout
tEams were out to
solVe
in teAms
weRe out to solve
dIscovery '
drAma '
the total electric drama the classroom can Become a scene in which the audience performs
becomes a participant in the totaL
Effort '
aS
in represenTs
effoRt switching
individUally
in whiCh
To solve practical world problems '
edUcational establishments '
nineteenth-centuRy
tEchnology as manifested in our educational
teach-in represents a creatiVe switching
whAt
Represents
nIneteenth-century technology
mAnifested in our educational
package to discovery as the audience Becomes a participant in the
rejection of 19th-century technoLogy as
ninEteenth-century technology '
the total electric drama the claSsroom can become a scene in which
sTudents individually and in teams
weRe
oUt to solve
a sCene in which
efforT switching ' the
classroom can become a scene in which the aUdience
can become a scene in which the audience peRforms
thE teach-in represents a
creatiVe effort switching
teAch-in

imitating the melody and sometimes the accompaniment not as harmonic but as simply tones sometimes the
pedal is held down that gives the effect of several things but otherwise it's just the simplest kind of music
and that suggested to me the use of the word *cheap* the other thing that made me think of the word *cheap*

technology as manifested in ouR

In

the clAssroom

from package to discovery as the audience Becomes a participant in the

creative effort switching the educationaL

total Electric drama the

Scene in which

The total

dRama the classroom can become a scene in

an enormoUs amount of work '

audienCe becomes a

drama ' The classroom can become a scene ' in which the

work the stUdents

the classRoom

audiEnce performs an enormous amount of work '

the teach-in represents a creatiVe effort switching the

totAl

maximum the dRopout represents a

rejectIon of 19th-century technology

in teAms were out to solve

entire world at what the students called a Bare maximum ' the dropout

practicaL world

of ninEteenth-century

the audience performS an enormous

Total '

the classRoom can become a scene in which the

work the stUdents individually and in teams were out to

feed the entire world at what the students Called a bare maximum '

The

amoUnt of

effoRt switching

a rEjection of 19th-century technology '

the teach-in represents a creatiVe effort switching the

rejection of 19th-century technology As manifested in

Represents

world at what the students called a bare maxImum ' the dropout represents

rejection of 19th-century technology As manifested in our educational

package to discovery as the audience Becomes a participant in the

creative effort switching the educationaL

how to fEed the entire world at

out to Solve

pracTical

nineteenth-centuRy technology as manifested in

how to feed the entire world at what the stUdents

Can become a scene in which

enTire world at what the

was satie's title *flabby preludes for a dog* they were written in response to a request for some music by a
publisher and the publisher when he saw the title refused to publish it satie changed the title to *genuine
flabby preludes for a dog* and then it was published i thought i would begin with the word *cheap* that whole

stUdents called a
woRld
Entire

teach-in represents a creatiVe effort switching the
mAnifested
package to discoveRy as the
nIneteenth-century technology
in teAms were out to solve
the total electric drama ' the classroom can Become a scene in which the audience performs
amount of work the students individuaLly and in
crEative effort '
the total electric drama the claSsroom can become a scene in which
pracTical
the classRoom can become a scene in which the
teams were oUt to solve
a sCene in which
efforT switching ' the
stUdents called a
woRld
a rEjection of 19th-century technology

•

less thaN this
be vetOed by would be the first what good i do '
groups that rallied iN several cities almost certain to be vetoed by
desire ' throUgh
for **oNe**
you woulD say ' what mirror ' what dust ' in
aforEthought go about doing good if **i** '
afoRethought go about doing good if i **were** to
what we con**Sid**ered
breakThrough '
whAt evolved
from differeNt points in space ' musical sculpture '
we are in the worlD of duchamp ' sounds
I
poteNtial but his maximum '
continues **mem**ory throuGh desire ' **through**
at **aN** '
tOgether or they do '
iNcome '
bare maximUms
for satisfyiNg what

problem now has been resolved and the music is published (by eschig) *i'm wondering if there's anything in the basic nature of the computer that attracts you do you think that there's something zen-like in the computer's ability to devote complete and undivided attention to any task that it's doing* i notice that they're

woulD bring

communications and travEl ' communication

at all levels ' foR all

objectiveS '

objecT

mArkets '

a geNeral sealing off of awareness to the total '

so tell us what you woulD say '

the common sense of that word must be asIde from my

creativity ' aNd

Growth '

we caN never '

we are in the wOrld of duchamp '

was what evolved ' rather thaN take what was '

throUgh memory ' through desire ' through

they are yours ' loNg time **what** '

winter fire ' o quick ' a worD of truth '

first what good i do in thE common sense of

mankind's needs ' the baRe maximum '

change ' there iS no way '

sound ' change There is no

such ' As you are without

what good i do ' iN the common sense of that

with him ' less the removal he offereD them ' the

rocks ' when wIll the

sceNarios that would result from the first moves

Go about

free time ' miNimize

the establishment Of bare maximum levels ' of the

statues of the buddha ' wiNter fire '

bUt

techNological motifs ' we are in the

orchestrateD ' with

bEgan to deal with man on the collective level ' we

the need foR

what evolved rather than take what waS

before iT '

whAt good i do '

Never know ' if so

the metal ones won't burn ' wooDen statues of the buddha '

at an object I

realized the Need for

Go about '

wiNg

Of

stimulated through chance operations the other thing i like is the binary nature and with the *i ching* my next project now that the norton lectures are finished is to finish my *freeman etudes* for solo violin and then beyond that i plan to study the use of the computer in relation to my work i would like to get to the point

400

New '
a word of trUth '
maN
with man on the collective level ' we realizeD
rocks ' whEn will the sound change '
woRking out
thiS being by our
fifTh '
we hAve
techNology creating new basic assumptions at all
woulD
vItal
aNd with kindness '
Good ' maximize
its owN time '
aiming mainly tO become of more worth
aNd
anything less than this ' being by oUr
agaiNst '
the possible synergetic scenarios that woulD
tEll us what you would say '
woRking out
Subhuman
levels of **The** '
they Are yours ' escape '
oNe
man leD us to
robe thIs bowl '
o ' mooN ' why are you so willow tree '
rather than **take** what was **thouGht**

we caN never
Of
iNcome
desire **throUgh**
for satisfyiNg what
winter fire ' o quick ' a worD of truth '
communications and travEl ' communication
woRking out
what we conSidered
fifTh
mArkets
from differeNt points in space ' musical sculpture '
so tell us what you woulD say '
robe thIs bowl '

where i can do my work without assistance as though i were making a drawing which i don't need any help to do *i'm wondering if the unexpected problems that crop up whenever anybody uses a computer if you could see that as a sort of indeterminancy that might add a positive element to your work* right *unexpected* sceNarios that would result from the first moves

rather than **take** what was **thouGht**

•

the vertiCally
the ' music is written the music' is there befOre it is '
which we learN as children and which we
blue iT
nulllfy '
if i have five ' theN i have three and two ' how do i know that **i** '
an inanimate empty space ' rather it is the coGnition of daily '
thE color of **the** '
allows both couNtries to observe
the serious artist Can read ' the message of **the** ' hidden
is not **this** ' because weather is now entirelY an
plaCed
grOups like those
it might Nullify '
deviaTed from '
seen to have the same color **we** ' mIght say it ' is
eNters for example if a piece of cloth **is** ' laid
and **is** ' seen to have the same color **we** ' miGht say it ' is **an**
things and not by othErs it **is** '
the joy of comedy is freest from desire aNd loathing affirmation of ' life purposeful '
a direCtion be comparable to **a** ' title
it up into groups like those when i feel sorrY
of silenCe leading
by Others it **is**
it looks like this i caN always
meaning ' mind can change ' To do more rather than less to sober and
varIed or
No accidental ' it is between
thouGhts ' you cannot
placEd above them
caN '
to have direCtions placed above them bidding us hear it
what to **do** ' the radio which had sent a lawYer and
a hundred dots you Can
be sure is whatever deviated frOm
music more space betweeN '
iT
Is there before it is
both radio aNd tv ' **is** not this because weather **is** '
israel said sunday it miGht nullify

things happen i met a young man he's graduated but i met him when he was still a student at knox college
in galesburg illinois sean bronzell he made some very interesting works of a poetic nature that made use of
things that happened with the computer that would have put most people off but which delighted him which

thE alphabet ' all the time ' why is

loathiNg affirmation **of** ' **life**

of daily **life** ' without the attaChment to it **it** is an awareness of distinct

problems ' the world game is a new waY of looking at the world ' although

down a rule beforehand about what would be Called agreement

tO **staff** ' the vertically

paper aNd music **how** '

sTaff

Is the

course why is **this** ' my memory of what happeNed

varied or not varied once music beGins ' it

in itsElf i.e.

makiNg it

insight fostered by **Con**trast a hectic

this the second without this exerting anY

a ' pieCe

tO observe each other's strip ' protests

iN

reading from lefT to

tv Is

each activity is ceNtered ' in itself i.**e.** '

how to read it independently of one's thouGhts what

th**E** '

is Not what happened i am

meaninglessness as ultimate meaning ' mind Can change ' to do more rather than less to

loud and in the same tempo ' onlY taken differently

well ' if it looks like this and is it also Certain that when it

n**O**t is

time ' it is curious how much more arrestiNg are

whaT happened

and unpredIctable '

life ' purposeful purposelessNess ' the

an inanimate empty space rather **it** is **the** ' coGnition of daily

usE of a word ' is

Not is de**ter**mined ' a priori it is a priori ' that

the serious artist who is searChing to devise **a**

in his place urbanitY and

spaCe between staff lines

Of popular as well as of academic art **the**

to be played equally loud aNd in

afTer takeoff he was

groups lIke those

to a title to programme music ' daNce of the peasants ' if i have five then i

miGht nullify opposition '

disturbEd a great deal of art

is Not what happened i am

he incorporated into the work i haven't done that yet but if i take the path that seems to lie ahead of me that might happen if i were doing all the work *i wonder if there is any sense in which you think of your lectures as poetry* i think of the lectures in the other hall as being a kind of poetry whereas i think of these seminars

what happened is not what happened i am **struCk**
   paper and music ' would read it independentlY of one's thoughts what instrument ' or
           a sense in whiCh experience enters
              wOuld most likely help '
        like a prophecy i kNow
        be sure is whaTever
          It
           loved oNe this body has extension to this ' we
one this body has extension to this we miGht
           rEports '
        art is crimiNal
      time and even if a Composer has never
    this because weather is now entirelY an
          urgenCy rather than artistic insight '
          a wOrd is
          might Nullify
           sTaff or **staves** the
           I laid
           oN ' both radio and tv ' is not this because
        it miGht nullify
        prophEcy
      the greatest propagaNda in the world is our mothertongue that
in the world is our mothertongue that whiCh we learn as children and which we learn
   that when it looks like this i can alwaYs split it up into groups like those ' when i
          musiC begins it remains he said the same even
          prOvide comfort
         the News on
      provide comforT and reassurance for
        well If it looks like this
         let souNds be sounds ' each activity is centered in itself
  how to read it independently of one's thouGhts what
        staff or stavEs the possibility
        it might Nullify '
      a sense in whiCh experience enters for example if
    some things and not bY others it is not a matter of
    our ears are now in exCellent '
        hOw much more
     is accomplished by writiNg hearing or playing a piece of music our
        color is The same as the color of the sample
         Is
      like a prophecy i kNow with certainty that the
        strateGy
        to bE sure is whatever deviated from
       quiet the miNd thus making it
  well ' if it looks like this and is it also Certain that when it looks like this i can
    someone with toothache i put mYself in his

as being prose in neither case saying anything about the quality *are there specific ways in which you think of the other lectures as poetry* in the way of the breathing and the sound the changing or not changing of sounds *do you think of images at all in terms of poetry* images *that come from the words* as the words recur

musiC '
a state Of
hectic vivacity iN
we mighT reply nonsense but
to the serIous artist who is
disturbed a great deal of art aNd entertainment is naturally of this
inanimate empty space rather it is the coGnition of daily
stratEgy '
iN the paper upon
still helps them what to do the radio whiCh had sent
is seen to have the same color ' we might saY it is an experiment showing that there are
still helps them what to **do** ' the radio whiCh had sent a lawyer and scientist
Of what
this because weather is Now
iT agrees or not
and tv Is
whether it agrees or Not is determined a priori it is a priori '
american operation ' israel said sunday it miGht nullify opposition '
it is probably **thE** '
it might Nullify opposition parties '
it must be satisfied beforehand ' there is of Course a sense in which experience enters '
is it that the idea seems to be satisfied bY some things and **not** by others it is not

a hundred dots you Can
Of what
time it is curious how much more arrestiNg are
afTer takeoff he was
and tv **Is**
eNters for example if a piece of cloth is laid
strateGy
it is probably thE
makiNg it
to have direCtions placed above them bidding us hear it
is not this because weather is now entirelY an

•

Is just
aNd also
in the plaCe where **we**
we **mOr**tals
he iN **me**
there iS '
beIng even
on at **the** ' **Same**

something more like music seems to me to develop i think it's i heard that before the two words winter night
or iranian fishermen *earlier you said that you were working on improvisations that would offer the player*
a problem to work out and still earlier you said that it would be nice if we had a society which was not

pullouT
samE '
the aNalogue of
Can '
a class at wesleYan that
found It
aNswer '
a world in whiCh we live and breathe
yOu say
geNeva
the Space
In
Should
buT nothing
bE '
'   outliNes of
Consider
interplaY '
Is
corNer
muCh
these variOus ways of
laNguage mean'
artiSt who
wIth
whoSe
iT will
a jokE
caN
disCover
manY
neIther
Now
soCiety '
nOr
the other haNd
the **Same** '
the same wIth
waS of
drifTwood
is impossiblE
iN
expeCted
theY
to wrIte '
fact Not

based on employment i wonder what your distinction is between work and employment when you work someone else asks you to *but if you think of the technology of the society it is created by people who don't have the power to work it out themselves they must therefore give that work to somebody else to work out*

teaCh
yOu
aNger
uSe '
but **fIlm**
haS
To
onE '
is this iNterplay '
spaCe
of laboratorY procedures
grants and scholarshIps
the caNvas upon
soCiety derives '
and **al**sO
beiNg
alwayS
greetIng
aS
buT
nEw
diviNity
it was produCed but
poetrY '
It is
its measuremeNts '
partiCular circumstances
yOu just said '
traNquillity '
So
nothIng to
perSon
Two
blamEd
dimiNish
Charges
going out from **mY**
has pIctured that '
such aNd
Can '
tO
iN
limitS ' we
beIng
fuelS ' we
To

in the actual world how do you get around this problem if you are planning a society that is based on technology and will not be based on employment a kind of comprehensive approach to our needs world needs world human needs and natural resources an equation between those two such as buckminster fuller

morE
as iNdividuals
the buddhist ' the Christian ' the islamic ' or the
plaY '
stIll
aNd
distriCt '
nO
breakiNg '
Seed
I
uSe
To
sincE it was '
world iN
aCt '
everYone
Is
Needed '
Called
Of
askiNg thanking
haS
In
Since
To
wE '
laNguage to
desCription ' **a**
than thursdaY '
as If we
so well everyoNe
mathematCian
frOm ' **the**
iN **the** '
the ruleS
of It
the Sky
wiTh
wE
No
whiCh '
plants multiplY by seed '
I
Not one '
i Can stand as

thought of will have to take place and could take place and that it would change with changing times and changing needs and changing resources i recently read in this direction a book by paul avrich portraits of anarchists stressed in that book is a society in which there aren't large numbers of people the situation is

                    intO a
                    deNy it
                     uSe '
                      In
                  becauSe
                      iT
                    dEath
                     aNd
                   whiCh '
                   theY're
                       It was '
                    eveNt
                        Clad and
                       Of it
                   wheN '
                       South
                       lIke
                      aS '
                   buT you '
                  you'rE
                    chaNge
                  and muCh
                       in Yet another and much more '
                     neIther
              of i meaNt '
        then more striCtly
                       nO ideas ' poetry is
                      aNd
                      iS
                    wIth
                   getS '
                       Two notations
              of languagE
                     aNd
                       Campus
                  glorY
                  the rIch of
                  eveN **a** '
                     suCh a use '
              human errOr
        utterly differeNt '
            poetry **iS**
                      In
                  aS
                   To
        to changE

more village-like and the utilities accommodate that if we gave our thinking in the direction of solving the problems that could be foreseen to living all of us together rather than fearing one another and preparing to kill that the solution of the problems could be found and i think the books of buckminster fuller and those

iN
plaCe ' **a** '
a **seed** ' alwaYs produces
thIs
moNey you've been
desCribing '
fOr
kiNd
juSt
wIll he
fuelS **we** '
iT
was not availablE
thaN that
struCture of the plant
a seed alwaYs
wIll
aNd this '
riCh
Of
Not
iS not
In '
reSource
exhibiTion
bank would bE '
No ideas
Case would
interplaY '
the world that there Is
caN it not the point is
speCulating
nOt '
Next
procedureS ' the
fInd
mySelf as
anyThing
unrivalEd '
actioNs
aCtions '
moneY
resource a rIval of
aNd
seCretary
Of

of marshall mcluhan would be basic to the solution of the problems that would be noticed *with regards to composition there are different states of consciousness that i go through some of which i would call inspired and when i think about what that means i can't avoid believing that it has to do with satisfying the ego*

as maNy
purpoSe **to** '
to Iran
thoSe ' **of**
Thus
not ' Exist
iNvolved '
resourCe ' a rival of the
storY
If
uNified
spaCe
nO dust
aNd now
buddhiSt **the**
wIll be
to Say
exhibiTion
movE
aNd
objeCt ' **is**
bY
Is '
moNey is
Can be
fOr
aNy
Suddenly
I
and bruShing
To
no procEss
aNd it is he in me
proCedures '
You
mIght
caN you
soCiety '
fOr
caN never
uSe of the
utterly dIfferent
than thurSday
as iT is
awakE '
suppositioN

you mean of being inspired *correct* mmhmm *so it isn't really what i'm trying to do and yet the state of being inspired is still enjoyable and very fulfilling and i'm wondering what you think inspired is and does it involve the ego necessarily* i don't work that way if there is something to inspiration i would want to have it

whiCh was

anY other '

whIch we

meaN

in mathematiCs

Of

aNd

aS

wInter night '

Sake

wiTh thinking

agEs **of**

aNd ground

the Corporations

in mandalaY '

the erotIc

torreNt ' we are

forCed

Of

iN

buddhiSt **the**

In him that

haS

ouT

mE more '

iraN

publiC

moneY

though I do

with eNergy

soCiety

nOt purposeless

Not

all creatureS

and It

thoughtS

planT which

Each

musiciaNs to pay the event must be free to

whiCh

to moneY

thIs should

Not

to resCue

tO be

eveN out of

all the time but it sounds like something that's rather special so i would rather live in a less special situation
and be able to work that way but then if you ask a question and don't ask the right one or don't ask one that
yields good answers then what you need is not inspiration but you need some understanding of what question

Supply
belIeve
confrontS us ' we
learning learning we're noT
would bE
to aNswer in my sleep
the spaCe
can onlY
when I left i
death have beeN '
Cases
prOduced but
Net that might
are alSo
It '
today'S
i cannoT
jokE '
suppositioN seems
Change
supplY

found It
the ' caNvas upon '
in mathematiCs
yOu say
aNy
purpoSe to
utterly dIfferent
fuelS we
buT
awakE
No
the ' buddhist the Christian the islamic or the
interplaY

•

Public
wEll known points in
chaRges in
as Fears '
mysteriOus and
it weRe
teMpo only '

would be productive of good answers some further understanding of the field in which you're asking *i just wanted to know what you think is the purpose of tradition and do you think it's worthwhile what you think of the concept of having goals do you think you still have goals in mind things you would like to*

Author
foregrouNd
subjeCt
usE '
sharPly
hE at
thRough so
oF '
Of the
heRe '
aM not
hAs '
might Not
see if i Could
inErt matter ' masses i.e. gravity
comPosition is
wE
pRocess universe ' is
oF '
Of
electRonic
theMselves
beAr to be
a commoN language '
Communist '
thE word '
it is as if we could grasP it in a flash ' in
thE
tRending is
the stress oF
prOtest '
my pictuRe isn't vivid enough for
an iMprovised music '
33 yeArs ago
dowN 33
objeCtivity
i havE lived
a Psychological
dancE ' of
aRe
Filled with
cultural institutiOns
tuRning the
welcoMe
eAsy '
No ' he is resonating '

achieve i have told you what i have in mind it's not so much to get some place as to pay attention in certain directions to pay attention to the finishing of the *freeman etudes* to my relationship to the use of computer facilities i don't know what will happen *so there's no predetermined goal you have in mind* it would be a

amplifiCation's
will havE to
Poison is
i wEnt '
gRavity
Five '
tO the woods because
they eaRned
consciousness More with less '
Ago '
assured objectioN
whiCh
blEw
Psalm
bE
foRth through us
oF
cautiOn
vaRious
through My
fAct which
commeNts
split the stiCk and
thE
feelings accomPany our
dirEction '
cRops '
music ' Feared then lest he
hOpe '
use all solutions ' do eveRything ' inactivity ' the
More direct sense
wAy
suggestiNg a vast and undeveloped
worldwide City '
utilizE energetic systems
uP with
thE
to Recognize as
oF
transmissiOn lines ' we devised a way '
a too tRivial
systeM for the world
rAte of
grouNd or usage
Can
and **thE** '

field in which i work i don't know the details for instance of the *freeman etudes* before they're finished i'm
not moving toward a goal i will move toward the finishing of the work but i don't know what it will be *what
do you feel is the purpose of tradition* it's not so much a purpose as it is that it would exist for you or not

                    simPlify
                    thE
            industRial activities '
                  unFurled
          right tO one '
                  anaRchy
        as a coMposer
      vehicle eArth '
                    oNe
                      Class
                      rEsidual
                        Probability nor about knowing what is
        accidEntal
                  paRts
                    oF a dream
            the grOund
              etheReal ' heaven
    have becoMe the tools of their tools
                  A duet for
              chiNa's eastern
                      Court
                  aftEr
                  raPid
          rotativEly
                    gReat
          series oF
            questiOn as
              at fiRst
            the saMe
                      A
    suggestiNg a vast and undeveloped nature '
              vertiCally
              it usEs
                  a Psalm '
      world is onE '
            what aRe we
              itselF
                      Of
            to pRison
                aMbiguously for its
                  lAy
        predictioN '
            we're Comparing
              watEr
                  Policy '
            tonE

hmm i don't tend to think of it but i can imagine that some people would which country do you come from *i was born in malaysia* then you no doubt have a feeling for what has taken place in music in your country *a little bit* it's been very impressive to the rest of the world your tradition is attractive to people who don't

416

hoRizon ' why should we be

oF

it **tO**

mateRial

in ' Moscow '

thAt spirit

suN

to touCh

an arEa **with**

uPon which

bodiEs how should ·

aRtist **can**

our uniFied sensibility

tO be

wheRe

More

Aids

iN

Count on

usE

a Proof but

barE

thRough

oF

tO

eight yeaRs ago

Must be '

being At

preseNted

for Christians

inErt

Pitch

thEy accompany

Reality which we

oF

abOve as if

patRolling the streets

of tiMe '

reAlity

the ceNter

whiCh '

objEction **which** '

Point of transformation

shE

ago ' iRan

oF '

have it in their past how do you feel about it *i'm trained to be a visual artist and i feel that traditions are healthy in the sense that it gives us something upon which we can base our observations and our judgments however always trying to come up with something new* do i understand you to say that the tradition gives

weight Of
left to Right ' absence
alMost
A great deal of
somethiNg unknown
we Can
timE
the Point is
Easy
is the woRld
account oF it
pianOs she
could feed five hundRed
i aM
A facility
iN
Carrying
thE moral law
Probably
thE
pRoblem
with a smile ' giFt giving '
twO
ceRtain of being able to
coMplete ' goes full circle ' the
plAces
a New
word whiCh
thE awareness of
each other that the grouPs of
arE
the new is a miRacle
oF
the pOint is
caRd
walking **Must** '
he heArs
the grouNd
muCh on
ablE **to**
its comPosition '
cartEsian
guRgling
oF awareness
On the
appRehension of

you something to do to measure what you do *i realize that you completely did away with the tradition of* *the twelve-tone system you came up with a whole new direction based on chance and the acceptance of* *chaos and all that* i should say very clearly that i don't think in those terms of tradition as something that

a stateMent
thAt if a
foreigN minister saying
mosCow
lEg is
the way they accomPany
fivE ' seven
ouRselves through
things and Facts '
desire tO speak '
a watcheR
eMerges
secretAry
hiNted
alCohol
or powEr but all in one '
comPosition is
than closEd '
pReached
a Flash
tO
disappeaR
saMe
thAt
iN
ameriCan
approximatEly '
Poison is '
is askEd '
Relations
oF
lOgic ' if
a hundRed dishes ' five
Music ' resulting from
spAce
the oNe
partiCipation of both '
of timE

comPosition **is**
is askEd
foRth through us
Filled with
right tO one
my pictuRe isn't vivid enough for
teMpo only

comes down from the past that needs to be observed *i don't really have a musical question but there's an art show at the hillis radcliffe library and the work that i have in it is largely based on things that i find from reading your books and seeing your performances there is a catalogue by liz seaton and she wanted*

A `

suggestiNg a vast and undeveloped nature `

Communist

it usEs

•

to have pictures of all the artists in it and i asked her if she would use a picture of a tree instead of one of me but she wouldn't so my question is i'd like to know if i can give you this picture of the tree as a token of my thanks thank you very much

Source Text

Method

My memory of what happened is not what happened. I am struck by the fact that what happened is more conventional than what I remembered. Imitations, inversions, retrograde forms, motives that are varied or not varied. Once music begins it remains, he said, the same — even variation is repetition, some things changed, others not (Schoenberg). What I am remembering, incorrectly to be sure, is whatever deviated from ordinary practice. Not a scale or row but a gamut to each element of which equal honor could be given. (John Cage, in *John Cage: Composition in Retrospect*, 1982) Imitations inversions it remains motives that are varied deviated from than what I remembered. (John Cage, in *John Cage: Composition in Retrospect*, 1982) Whether a dream is a thought. Whether dreaming is thinking about something. Suppose you look on a dream as a kind of language. A way of saying something, or a way of symbolizing something. There might be a regular symbolism, not necessarily alphabetical — it might be like Chinese, say. We might then find a way of translating this symbolism into the language of ordinary speech, ordinary thoughts. But then the translation ought to be possible both ways. It ought to be possible by employing the same technique to translate ordinary thoughts into dream language. As Freud recognizes, this never is done and cannot be done. So we might question whether dreaming is a way of thinking something, whether it is a language at all. (Wittgenstein, *Lectures and Conversations*, p. 48) . . . Knowing the alphabet, or the rules of chess, or the use of a word, is not a state of consciousness. To see that it is not, ask yourself what it is like to know the alphabet all the time. (Wittgenstein, *Lectures 1932–1935*, pp. 49–50) Why is it that the idea seems to be satisfied by some things and not by others? It is not a matter of experience that something satisfies it. In a way it must be satisfied beforehand. There is of course a sense in which experience enters. For example, if a piece of cloth is laid next to the sample and is seen to have the same color, we might say it is an experiment showing that the two are the same. But that this color is the same as the color of the sample is not shown by experiment. Whether it agrees or not is determined a priori. It is a priori that if you bring something blue, it will agree; this is not something you predict. Though this sounds like a prophecy, I know with certainty that the colors agree because I laid down a rule beforehand about what would be called agreement — about the use of the word "agreement." That they will agree is not known better after I juxtapose the two than before. (Wittgenstein, *Lectures 1932–1935*, pp. 85–86) No one will deny that studying the nature of the rules of games must be useful for the study of grammatical rules, since it is beyond doubt there is some sort of similarity between them. — The right thing is to let the certain instinct that there is a kinship lead one to look at the rules of games without any preconceived judgement or prejudice about the analogy between games and grammar. And here again one should simply report what one sees and not be afraid that one is undermining a significant and correct intuition, or, on the other hand, wasting one's time with something superfluous. (Wittgenstein, *Philosophical Grammar*, p. 187) When set theory appeals to the human impossibility of a direct symbolisation of the infinite it brings in the crudest imaginable misinterpretation of its own calculus. It is of course this very misinterpretation that is responsible for the invention of the calculus. But of course that doesn't show the calculus in itself to be something incorrect (it would be at worst uninteresting) and it is odd to believe that this part of mathematics is imperilled by any kind of philosophical (or mathematical) investigations. (As well say that chess might be imperilled by the discovery that wars between two armies do not follow the same course as battles on the chessboard.) What set theory has to lose is rather the atmosphere of clouds of thought surrounding the bare calculus, the suggestion of an underlying imaginary symbolism, a symbolism which isn't employed in its calculus, the apparent description of which is really nonsense. (In mathematics anything can be imagined, except for a part of our calculus.) (Wittgenstein, *Philosophical Grammar*, pp. 469–470) I can now determine to follow the rule. (Wittgenstein, *Remarks on the Foundations of Mathematics*, p. 351) He does just let himself go on when he follows the rule or the examples; however, he does not regard what he does as a peculiarity of his course; he says, not: "so that's how I went," but: "so that's how it goes." (Wittgenstein, *Remarks on the Foundations of Mathematics*, p. 361) My ideal is a certain coolness. A temple providing a setting for the passions without meddling with them. (Wittgenstein, *Culture and Value*, p. 2) Can we understand two names without knowing whether they signify the same thing or two different things? Can we understand a proposition in which two names occur, without knowing if they mean the same or different things? (Wittgenstein, *Tractatus Logico-Philosophicus*, p. 91) . . . new material is constantly being created so as to maintain a constant density in the background material. So we have a situation in which the loss of galaxies through the expansion of the Universe is compensated by the condensation of new galaxies and this can continue indefinitely. (Hoyle, quoted by L.C. Beckett, in *Neti Neti*, p. 20) The act of writing silently without intervention of the reading the text aloud, was not yet possible at that period. The beginner did not yet see around him a world strewn with writings and printed texts. He needed clear and disciplined pronunciation of the text if he would learn to write without faults. (quotation from *L'Enseignement de l'écriture aux universités médiévales* by Istuan Hajnal, quoted by Marshall McLuhan in *Gutenberg Galaxy*, p. 97). HURRY UP PLEASE IT'S TIME (from T.S. Eliot's *The Waste Land*, cited in McLuhan, *Through the Vanishing Point*, p. 182) "I must have been delirious, for I even sought amusement in speculating upon the relative velocities of their several descents toward the foam below." (from Poe's "The Descent into the Maelstrom," cited in McLuhan, *The Medium is the Massage*, p. 88) It is curious how much more arresting are the weather reports than the news, on both radio and TV. Is not this because "weather" is now entirely an electronic form of information, whereas news retains much of the pattern of the printed word? It is probably the print and book bias of the BBC and the CBC that renders them so awkward and inhibited in radio and TV presentation. Commercial urgency, rather than artistic insight, fostered by contrast a hectic vivacity in the corresponding American operation. (McLuhan, *Understanding Media*, p. 307) If there were as many recognized kinds of success as there are temperaments, tastes, skills, and degrees of knowledge, a society dedicated to success might yet develop very great harmony amid variety and richness of experience and insight. (McLuhan, *The Mechanical Bride*, p. 77) Seven contra commanders have nominated their best today to undergo surgery to reconsider restrictions that bar local telephone companies from offering the use of the Middle East's most vicious conflict to repair four proposals for controlling benzene with Moscow. (from *The New York Times*, July 21, '88) Israel jailed an official of the extremist group for the test-firing of the space shuttle but now every low budget conflict could become a theater for the deployment of gas. A pier collapsed in Northwestern Malaysia. The P.L.O. immediately convened an emergency meeting. (from the *Wall Street Journal*, Aug. 1, '88) Intensive use of fertilizers and pesticides would maintain our finger on which side of the fence he was standing on. The rediscovery of the gorillas is also vulnerable to drought, heat, and American agriculture. For years, the outside world thought South Africa had the Star Wars concept hook, line, and sinker. (from *The New York Times*, Aug. 1, '88) Israel said Sunday it might nullify opposition parties in a brief ceremony that would most likely help Panama solve its problems. (from the *Christian Science Monitor*, Aug. 16, '88) Although the students do not always admit it, movement still helps them what to do. The radio, which had sent a lawyer and scientist to Israel had finally been denied. Several others at the meeting were wounded under pressure. (from *The New York Times*, Aug. 17, '88) The mass of men lead lives of quiet desperation. What is called resignation is confirmed desperation. From the desperate city you go into the desperate country, and have to console yourself with the bravery of minks and muskrats. A stereotyped but unconscious despair is concealed even under what are called the games and amusements of mankind. There is no play in them, for this comes after work. But it is a characteristic of wisdom not to do desperate things. (Thoreau, *Walden*, p. 10) We must learn to reawaken and keep ourselves awake, not by mechanical aids, but by an infinite expectation of the dawn, which does not forsake us in our soundest sleep. I know of no more encouraging fact than the unquestionable ability of man to elevate his life by a conscious endeavor. It is something to be able to paint a particular picture, or to carve a statue, and so to make a few objects beautiful; but it is far more glorious to carve and paint the very atmosphere and medium through which we look, which morally we can do. To affect the quality of the day, that is the highest of arts. (Thoreau, *Walden*, p. 65) Once it chanced that I stood in the very abutment of a rainbow's arch, which filled the lower stratum of the atmosphere, tingeing the grass and leaves around, and dazzling me as if I looked through colored crystal. It was a lake of rainbow light, in which, for a short while, I lived like a dolphin. If it had lasted longer it might have tinged my employments and life. (Thoreau, *Walden*, p. 138) The World Game is a new way of looking at the world. (from "The World Game," World Games Projects, Inc., 1987) Maximize the possibilities for humans to participate in making decisions that will effect their future; the more people engaged in thinking out solutions to problems, the greater will be humanity's collective wealth; parameters defining success are open to definition and redefinition by as many people as possible. (from "The World Game," World Game Projects, Inc., 1987) Availability of the best health restoring and sustaining devices known to man and the preventive medicine of a healthful environment for all mankind at all times. (from "Dymaxion World of Buckminster Fuller," by Robert W. Marks, and "Buckminster Fuller," by John McHale, in *World Game/1971/Document 1*, p. 104) In order to supply mankind with his internal needs we found it necessary to evolve a bare maximum parameter for external metabolics which would guarantee the maintenance of man's internal metabolics. This bare maximum is 1242 energy slaves per capita by the year 2000. . . . Broken down, that is 15,000 kwh and eight metric tons of coal-equivalents per capita per year. This non-linear yardstick for establishing external relative levels of the development of man's potential to be "human" was arrived at by taking the projected U.S. needs for the year 2000, . . . because it was the maximum. Using these parameters we found that mankind will need a total 100 trillion kwh, 8.5×10^{15} calories, and 21.9×10^7 tons of protein in the year 2000. (Edwin Schlossberg and Medard Gable, quoted in *World Game/1971/Document 1*, p. 42) The housing scenario we were working on clearly showed the inadequacy of our present system. At the present rate, the use of metals in housing would prove to be totally insufficient. Metaphysically-engendered materials such as plastics will have to be developed if we are to solve mankind's housing needs. The housing scenario encompassed more than just the shelter needs of the world. As it evolved we saw that it would encompass communications and mobility. With the trends of increasing mobility throughout the world, we foresaw the possibility that no one would be staying at any one place long enough to warrant the construction of "permanent" shelters. As a total service facility, the housing needs would encompass not only shelter but communications — with its own resultant education, medical information and attention, personal telephone contact with anyone, anywhere, and mobility with anyone going anywhere. These would be accomplished via closed-circuit television and telephone to a world central medical, educational, and travel-routing computer system. (Edwin Schlossberg and Medard Gable, quoted in *World Game/1971/Document 1*, p. 46) Nonintention (the acceptance of silence) leading to nature; renunciation of control; let sounds be sounds. Each activity is centered in itself, i.e., composition, performance, and listening are different activities. (Music is) instantaneous and unpredictable; nothing is accomplished by writing, hearing, or playing a piece of music; our ears are now in excellent condition. A need for poetry. Joyce: "Comedy is the greatest of arts because the joy of comedy is freest from desire and loathing." Affirmation of life. Purposeful purposelessness. (Cage, Introduction to *Themes and Variations*) The agreement came after a boatload of Vietnamese refugees criticized a regional development plan. Police expressed optimism following a demonstration by hundreds of thousands last week in connection with greater serious penalties. (from the *Wall Street Journal*, Aug. 25, '88) The greatest propaganda in the world is our mother tongue, that which we learn as children, and which we learn unconsciously. That shapes our perceptions for life. That is propaganda at its most extreme form. (McLuhan, cited in *Marshall McLuhan: Media in America*, p. 44) New art is sensory violence on the frontiers of experience. (McLuhan, cited in *Marshall McLuhan: Media in America*, p. 147)

Structure

The division of a whole into parts, duration not frequency, taken as the aspect of sound bringing about a distinction between both phrases and large sections. Many different distinctions could be thought of, some, for instance, concerning symmetry, horizontal or vertical, but what I thought of was a rhythmic structure in which the small parts had the same proportion to each other that the groups of units, the large parts, had to the whole. For instance, 64, since it equals eight eights, permits division of both sixty-four and each eight into three, two, and three. (John Cage, in *John Cage: Composition in Retrospect*, 1982) In *Songe d'une nuit d'été*, Satie divided four fours into one, two, and one (four, eight, and four) and in other pieces he worked symmetrically, counting the number between succeeding numbers, following addition six plus two, with subtraction six minus two, and/or reaching a center of a series of phrases continuing by going backwards: six, eight, four, seven, five, seven, four, eight, six, six being the center horizontally, five vertically. Thus a canvas of time is provided, hospitable to both noise and musical tones upon which music may be drawn. Space. (John Cage, in *John Cage: Composition in Retrospect*, 1982) In which the small into the center horizontally five vertically fours into one two and one (four eight and four) and/or reaching of time is provided hospitable to both noise as the aspect of sound permits a distinction between. (John Cage, in *John Cage: Composition in Retrospect*, 1982) In language as we use it there are not only words and their combinations but also words which make reference to samples. The word "blue," for example, is correlated with a certain colored patch which is a sample. Samples such as this are part of our language; the patch is not one of the applications of the word "blue." The phenomenon of love plays the same role as the patch in the use of the word "love." Two people in love may serve as a sample, or paradigm. We might say that it is the paradigm which has given the word "love" content. But for this purpose we need not discover two people in love, but rather the paradigm, which belongs to the language. We can say the paradigm gives the word meaning. But in what sense? In the sense of enlarging the game. By bringing in a paradigm we have altered the game. We have not found a phenomenon which gives the word sense; we have made up a calculus. To say that the paradigm fits the symbol, e.g., that the blue patch fits the word "blue," means nothing. It is added to it. And the schema is now useful. (Wittgenstein, *Lectures 1932–1935*, p. 143) "The world is everything that is the case." This is intended to recall and correct the statement "The world is everything that there is;" the world does not consist of a catalogue of things and facts about them (like the catalogue of a show). . . . The world is the totality of facts and not of things. What the world is is given by description and not by a list of objects. So words have no sense except in propositions, and the proposition is the unit of language. (Wittgenstein, *Lectures 1930–1932*, p. 119) A chain, too, is composed of its links, not of these and their spatial relations. (Wittgenstein, *Philosophical Grammar*, p. 201) Structure and feeling in music. Feelings accompany our apprehension of a piece of music in the way they accompany the events of our life. (Wittgenstein, *Culture and Value*, p. 10) But isn't there also a peculiar feeling of pastness characteristic of images as memory images? There certainly are experiences which I should be inclined to call feelings of pastness, although not always when I remember something is one of these feelings present. (Wittgenstein, *The Blue and Brown Books*, p. 184) The simple sign is essentially simple. It functions as a simple object. (What does that mean?) Its composition becomes completely indifferent. It disappears from view. (Wittgenstein, *Notebooks 1914–1916*, p. 69) . . . whence comes the fresh background material? . . . Material simply appears, it is created . . . At one time the various atoms do not exist and at a later time they do. (answer given by Hoyle, quoted by L.C. Beckett, in *Neti Neti*, p. 20) Sputnik is an information environment, i.e., a software environment which transforms the old 'external' Nature. In the same way, when man is 'on the phone' or 'on the air,' moving electrically at the speed of light, he has no physical body. He is translated into information, or an image. (McLuhan, "The Rise and Fall of Nature," p. 1) A shift from single-level space to multilevel space. (McLuhan, *Through the Vanishing Point*, p. 104) The extension of any one sense alters the way we think and act — the way we perceive the world. Were the Great Blackout of 1965 to have continued for half a year, there would be no doubt how electric technology shapes, works over, alters — massages — every instant of our lives. (McLuhan, *The Medium is the Massage*, p. 87) The point of the Narcissus myth is not that people are prone to fall in love with their own images but that people fall in love with extensions of themselves which they are convinced are not extensions of themselves. (McLuhan, "The Agenbite of Outwit," p. 1) Man in the future will not work — automation will work for him — but he may be totally involved as a painter is, or as a thinker is, or as a poet is. Man works when he is partially involved. When he is totally involved, he is at play or at leisure. (McLuhan, "The Agenbite of Outwit," p. 3) We learn that the highest is present to the soul of man; that the dread universal essence, which is not wisdom, or love, or beauty, or power, but all in one, and each entirely, is that for which all things exist, and that by which they are; that spirit creates; that behind nature, throughout nature, spirit is present; one and not compound it does not act upon us from without, that is, in space and time, but spiritually, or through ourselves: therefore, that spirit, that is, the Supreme Being, does not build up nature around us, but puts it forth through us, as the life of the tree puts forth new branches and leaves through the pores of the old. (Emerson, "Nature," in *Selected Essays*, p. 73) Large price increases for equipment would satisfy American money and influence. Until now martial law was imposed but not the station itself and drive people out. (from *The New York Times*, July 23, '88) A plan to provide the rebels with martial law showed that Labor's position was never realistic near Belfast. We demand face-to-face talks west of Moscow. A Balkan Bulgarian Airlines jet crashed killing a police officer. In a separate incident poets, essayists, editors and novelists protested repeatedly but unsuccessfully. (from *The New York Times*, Aug. 3, '88) Floods that left about one million people homeless caused a last-second scrub last week. Tens of thousands of Burmese were killed, diplomats and rescued five Iranian fishermen. Khomenei's comments came on the southern coast to a close than a dozen people mistakenly shot down. (from the *Christian Science Monitor*, Aug. 9, '88) Thirty-three reactor workers slept or were negligent after torture in police stations all over India to bribe Pentagon officials last year. A political reconciliation would threaten the future of the AIDS epidemic and postpone a settlement in which demonstrators and bystanders were charged and attacked by officers on horseback and on foot. (from *The New York Times*, Aug. 12, '88) What old people say you cannot do, you try and find that you can. Old deeds for old people, and new deeds for new. . . . One may almost doubt if the wisest man has learned anything of absolute value by living. . . . I have lived some thirty years on this planet, and I have yet to hear the first syllable of valuable or even earnest advice from my seniors. They have told me nothing, and probably cannot tell me anything to the purpose. Here is life, an experiment to a great extent untried by me; but it does not avail me that they have tried it. If I have any experience which I think valuable, I am sure to reflect that this my Mentors said nothing about. (Thoreau, *Walden*, pp. 10–11) I went to the woods because I wished to live deliberately, to front only the essential facts of life, and see if I could not learn what it had to teach, and not, when I came to die, discover that I had not lived. I did not wish to live what was not life, living is so dear; nor did I wish to practise resignation, unless it was quite necessary. I wanted to live deep and suck out all the marrow of life, to live so sturdily and Spartan-like as to put to rout all that was not life, to cut a broad swath and shave close, to drive life into a corner, and reduce it to its lowest terms, and, if it proved to be mean, why then to get the whole and genuine meanness of it, and publish its meanness to the world; or if it were sublime, to know it by experience, and be able to give a true account of it in my next excursion. (Thoreau, *Walden*, p. 66) Rise free from care before the dawn, and seek adventures. Let the noon find thee by other lakes, and the night overtake thee everywhere at home. There are no larger fields than these, no worthier games than may here be played. Grow wild according to thy nature, like these sedges and brakes, which will never become English hay. Let the thunder rumble; what if it threaten ruin to farmers' crops? That is not its errand to thee. Take shelter under the cloud, while they flee to carts and sheds. Let not to get a living be thy trade, but thy sport. Enjoy the land, but own it not. (Thoreau, *Walden*, p. 141) The World Game looks at the whole, global condition of life support and the inter-related nature of humanity's problems. (from "The World Game," World Game Projects, Inc., 1987) Foster coopera-tion rather than competition; nation-state competition is transcended through cooperative global endeavors; the perceived conflicts between the world's rich and poor, developed and developing regions, North and South, so-cialist and capitalist economic systems, technology and nature and the environment and economics are bridged. (from "The World Game," World Game Projects, Inc., 1987) Availability to all mankind adequate shelter to cope with all deleterious environmental impingements and to do so at a high rate of economy and efficiency. (from "Dymaxion World of Buckminster Fuller," by Robert W. Marks, and "Buckminster Fuller," by John McHale, in *World Game/ 1971/Document 1*, p. 104) We compared bare maximum requirements with present per capita consumption. We sought to establish a bare maximum communications system for the world. We learned what percentage of world people can presently be guaranteed the bare maximum. We sought to find the bare maximum for world transpor-tation. We asked how much bulk food is produced in calories? How much copper, aluminum and steel is in-volved in food production? . . . We sought to find the average per capita protein consumption for the world. . . (Edwin Schlossberg and Medard Gable, quoted in *World Game/1971/Document 1*, p. 43) Some future directions and scenarios we touched upon were the possibilities of a world guaranteed annual income; the potential of flu-idics as a source of energy; information and automation; the use of heat pollution from thermal electric plants to heat soil to improve crop output; the efficiency-gain by using gasoline or alcohol to run electric power plants and electricity to run cars; the production of alcohol from algae, farm wastes, or garbage and its substitution for gasoline in present-day combustion engines; the laser beam transmission of power and information; the amount of reinvestable time that will be available to man-kind as a result of freeing him from the drudgery of hav-ing to earn a living (by bringing man to the bare maxi-mum food and energy levels by the year 2000 we will have

16 trillion more hours per year to reinvest into meta-physical regenerative functions); the increase of efficiency rates for power production and consumption, communi-cation, transportation, etc., and the possible surplus and increase of efficiency through the stabilization of the pop-ulation. (Edwin Schlossberg and Medard Gable, quoted in *World Game/1971/Document 1*, p. 46) Art = imitation of nature in her manner of operation. Coexistence of dis-similars; multiplicity; plurality of centers; "Split the stick, and there is Jesus." Anonymity or selflessness of work (i.e., not self-expression). A work should include its en-vironment, is always experimental (unknown in advance). Fluent, pregnant, related, obscure (nature of sound). Empty mind. No ideas of order. (Cage, Introduction to *Themes and Variations*) To avert the threat of terrorism, Moscow destroyed a military bus carrying diplomats, South Korean legislators, the brother of the president, participants in joint parliamentary talks and the Chair-man of the Joint Chiefs of Staff. Even more important people frantically tried to identify journalists today for which they were executed, according to the Pentagon's report. (from *The New York Times*, Aug. 20, '88) Millions of tons of wheat, corn and soybeans might not last. Never-theless, supporters of the Greeks and Turks rise to for-gotten and conflicting passions. Diplomats say that it may be difficult to speak out of turn, Administration officials said. Economic and political interests converge. (from *The New York Times*, Aug. 25, '88) Discovery comes from dialogue that starts with the sharing of ignorance. (McLuhan, cited in *Marshall McLuhan: Media in Amer-ica*, p. 44)

Intention

Music for the dance. To go with it, to express the dance in sound. Not being able to do the same thing gives the possibility of doing something that differs, living in the same town, finding life by not living the same way. The dancers from Malaysia, a theatrical crossing from left to right so slowly as to seem to be moving not at all, the music, meanwhile, as fast as possible: togetherness of opposites. Purposeful purposelessness. Not to accept it unless I could remain at the same time a member of society, able to fulfill a commission to satisfy a particular need, though having no control over what happens. Ac-ceptance, sometimes written out, determinate, some-times just a suggestion. I found it worked. Therefore I nap, pounding the rice without lifting my hand. (John Cage, in *John Cage: Composition in Retrospect*, 1982) Gives the possibility a theatrical crossing though having no control that differs unless I could remain in the same town the same time as fast as possible togetherness. (John Cage, in *John Cage: Composition in Retrospect*, 1982) But imagine this: We get someone to look through a hole into a kind of peep show, and inside we now move various objects and figures about, either by chance or intentionally, so that their movement is exactly what our viewer wanted, so that he fancies that what he sees is obeying his will. —Now could he be deluded, and believe that his visual impressions are images? That sounds totally absurd. I don't even need the peep show, but have only to look at my hand and move it, as mentioned above. But even if I could will the curtain over there to move, or could make it disappear, I should still not interpret that as something that was going on in my imagination. (Wittgenstein, *Remarks on the Philosophy of Psychology*, Vol. II, pp. 18–19) Describing an intention means describing what went on from a particular point of view, with a particular purpose. I paint a particular portrait of what went on. (Wittgenstein, *Zettel*, p. 5) Suppose I had written my intention down on a slip of paper, then someone else could have read it there. And can I imagine that he might in some way have found it out more surely than that? Certainly not. (Wittgenstein, *Zettel*, p. 8) In what circumstances does one say "This appliance is a brake, but it doesn't work?" That surely means: it does not fulfil its purpose. What is it for it to have this purpose? It might also be said: "It was the intention that this should work as a brake." Whose intention? Here intention as a state of mind entirely disappears from view. Might it not even be imagined that several people had carried out an intention without any one of them having it? In this way a government may have an intention that no man has. (Wittgenstein, *Zettel*, p. 10) It might almost be said: "Meaning moves, whereas a process stands still." (Wittgenstein, *Zettel*, p. 44) A man says it ought to be read this way and reads it out to you. You say: "Oh yes. Now it makes sense." (Wittgenstein, *Lectures and Conversations*, p. 4) It is created out of nothing; it must be supposed that there is literally a true creation going on as a continuous process. (Spencer-Jones, quoted by L.C. Beckett, in *Neti Neti*, p. 20) This two-way movement of expansion and deflation seems to be the cause of the restlessness of crowds and the uneasiness that goes with wealth. (McLuhan, *Understanding Media*, p. 144) This is not accidental. From the development of phonetic script until the invention of the electric telegraph, human technology had tended strongly toward the furtherance of detachment and objectivity, detribalization and individuality. Electric circuitry has quite the contrary effect. It involves in depth. It merges the individual and the mass environment. To create an antienvironment for such electric technology would seem to require a technological extension of both private and corporate consciousness. The awareness and opposition of the individual are in these circumstances as irrelevant as they are futile. (McLuhan, *Through the Vanishing Point*, p. 244) The method of our time is to use not a single but multiple models for exploration — the technique of the suspended judgment is the discovery of the twentieth century as the technique of invention was the discovery of the nineteenth. (McLuhan, *The Medium is the Massage*, p. 69) He was entirely concerned with the formalistic pattern and penetrative and configuring power of the new technology. (McLuhan, *The Gutenberg Galaxy*, pp. 262–263) Such a parallel between the city and the human body enabled Joyce to establish a further parallel between ancient Ithaca and modern Dublin, creating a sense of human unity in depth, transcending history. (McLuhan, *Understanding Media*, p. 123) Every spirit builds itself a house, and beyond its house a world, and beyond its world a heaven. Know then that the world exists for you. For you is the phenomenon perfect. What we are, that only can we see. All that Adam had, all that Caesar could, you have and can do. . . . line for line and point for point your dominion is as great as theirs, though without fine names. Build therefore your own world. As fast as you can conform your life to the pure idea in your mind, that will unfold its great proportions. A correspondent revolution in things will attend the influx of the spirit. (Emerson, "Nature," in *Selected Essays*, pp. 80–81) The Navy's highest-ranking officer intent on expanding the influence of Islam in Bombay's biggest slum has appealed to Iran to resolve the situation in South America. We all know Iran supports other Jews in Israel. (from *The New York Times*, July 23, '88) Mexican opposition leaders called for an enterprise that paid millions of dollars in bribes to public officials about drug-trafficking. A computer detected a valve problem in last month's disputed presidential election to the region to arrange a cease-fire. A State Department official said it will take "a considerable amount of time" to determine how. (from the *Wall Street Journal*, Aug. 5, '88) Nicaraguan rebels used tear gas and beatings to disperse Palestinians. Separately, the Joint Chiefs of Staff would be reprimanded for not providing enough details for talks with South African troops. (from the *Wall Street Journal*, Aug. 16, '88). In any weather, at any hour of the day or night, I have been anxious to improve the nick of time, and notch it on my stick too; to stand on the meeting of two eternities, the past and future, which is precisely the present moment; to toe that line. You will pardon some obscurities, for there are more secrets in my trade than in most men's and yet not voluntarily kept, but inseparable from its very nature. I would gladly tell all that I know about it, and never paint "No Admittance" on my gate. (Thoreau, *Walden*, p. 16) In the midst of this chopping sea of civilized life, such are the clouds and storms and quicksands and thousand-and-one items to be allowed for, that a man has to live, if he would not founder and go to the bottom and not make his port at all, by dead reckoning, and he must be a great calculator indeed who succeeds. Simplify, simplify. Instead of three meals a day, if it be necessary eat but one; instead of a hundred dishes, five; and reduce other things in proportion. (Thoreau, *Walden*, p. 66) As I came home through the woods with my string of fish, trailing my pole, it being now quite dark, I caught a glimpse of a woodchuck stealing across my path, and felt a strange thrill of savage delight, and was strongly tempted to seize and devour him raw; not that I was hungry then, except for that wildness which he represented. Once or twice, however, while I lived at the pond, I found myself ranging the woods, like a half-starved hound, with a strange abandonment, seeking some kind of venison which I might devour, and no morsel could have been too savage for me. The wildest scenes had become unaccountably familiar. I found in myself, and still find, an instinct toward a higher, or, as it is named, spiritual life, as do most men, and another toward a primitive rank and savage one, and I reverence them both. I love the wild not less than the good. (Thoreau, *Walden*, pp. 142–143) The life in us is like the water in the river. It may rise this year higher than man has ever known it, ... Only that day dawns to which we are awake. There is more day to dawn. The sun is but a morning star. (Thoreau, *Walden*, p. 221) The World Game recognizes that the physical well-being of everyone is necessary for our continued survival. (from "The World Game," World Game Projects, Inc., 1987) Use existing technology and know-how; hypothetical or projected technology is left in the realm of science fiction. (from "The World Game," World Game Projects, Inc., 1987) Availability to all mankind of means to communicate with anyone wishing to be communicated with at the highest rate of economy and efficiency. (from "Dymaxion World of Buckminster Fuller," by Robert W. Marks, and "Buckminster Fuller," by John McHale, in *World Game/1971/Document 1*, p. 104) Once we knew what mankind had and what he needed to have, we began to experiment with ways he could go about getting his needs. These ways we called "scenarios." Throughout our work we found ourselves returning to one common denominator: Can you industrialize an area without electrical power? How can man take care of all of his essential physical needs so as to allow himself to develop his unique metaphysical abilities? Whether we had researched food, communications, travel, housing, or economics, we always returned to electrical energy once we began to formulate any hypothesis about satisfying man's needs. In order to enable people to be fed properly we found that they would first have to have a sufficiently high input of electric energy to process, transport, and store food and dispose of wastes. We found that, when dealing with collective mankind, it was imperative that we attend to man's external metabolics first, and these would then take care of individual man's internal metabolics. (Edwin Schlossberg and Medard Gable, quoted in *World Game/1971/Document 1*, p. 44) No beginning, middle, or end (process, not object). Unimpededness and interpenetration; no cause and effect. Indeterminacy. Opposites = parts of oneness. To thicken the plot (Ramakrishna); his answer to the question: Why, if God is good, is there evil in the world? Adventure (newness) necessary to creative action. If the mind is disci-

plined (body too), the heart turns quickly from fear towards love (Eckhart). (Cage, Introduction to *Themes and Variations*) Thatcher refused to contradict an Asian diplomat conspiring to violate the Neutrality Act. The two sides again refused to make any major changes overnight. Rescue workers closed key areas. A third round of talks were named on two counts each other for blocking progress. (from the *Christian Science Monitor*, Aug. 23, '88) The army also had written a letter to protest government tax raids. Tens of thousands are homeless the news reports said tens of thousands of blacks living in areas designated separately. The plane explosion was unlikely during a West Bank strike involved in the plane. She refused. (from the *Wall Street Journal*, Aug. 23, '88) Money is the poor man's credit card. (McLuhan, cited in *Marshall McLuhan: Media in America*, p. 45) The Pentagon said yesterday it believes about 30 masked men killed one person and injured 29. They did not know what caused the fire. At least ten people were awakened by explosions of bottled gas. A US official, who asked not to be identified, killed a West Bank Palestinian on Sunday. (from the *Christian Science Monitor*, Aug. 26, '88)

Discipline

To sober and quiet the mind, so that it is in accord with what happens, the world around it open rather than closed. Going in by sitting cross-legged, returning to daily experience with a smile, gift-giving, no why after emptiness. He said it is complete, goes full circle, the structure of the mind, passes from the absolute to the world of relativity, perceptions during the day, and dreams at night: Suzuki. The magic square, and then chance operations. Going out through sense perceptions, to follow a metal ball away from likes and dislikes, throw it on the road, find it in my ear (the shaggy nag). Now, after success, take your sword and slit my throat. The prince hesitates, but not for long. Lo and behold the nag immediately becomes again the prince he had originally been and would never have again become had the other refused to kill him. Silence. Sweeping fallen leaves. Sweeping up leaves three years later, suddenly understood. Said thank you. Again, no reply. (John Cage, in *John Cage: Composition in Retrospect*, 1982) To sober and quiet the mind going in is in accord returning going out through sense perceptions with a smile lo and behold the nag immediately becomes again after emptiness. (John Cage, in *John Cage: Composition in Retrospect*, 1982) He sent us to the blackboard and asked us to solve a problem in counterpoint — even though it was a class in harmony — to make as many counterpoints as we could, after each to let him see it. That's correct. Now another. After eight or nine solutions I said, not quite sure of myself, there aren't any more. That's correct. Now I want you to put in words the principle that underlies all of the solutions. He had always seemed to me superior to other human beings, but then my worship of him increased even more. I couldn't do what he asked. Perhaps now, thirty years later, I can. I think he would agree. The principle underlying all of the solutions acts in the question that is asked. As a composer, I should give up making choices, devote myself to asking questions. Chance-determined answers'll open my mind to world around, at the same time changing my music. Self-alteration, not self-expression. Thoreau said the same thing over a hundred years ago. I want my writing to be as clear as water I can see through so that what I experienced is told without my being in any way in the way. (John Cage, in *John Cage: Composition in Retrospect*, 1982) Devote myself (superior) to other human beings a class now I want you so that what I experienced is told I my being in any way choices. (John Cage, in *John Cage: Composition in Retrospect*, 1982) He made an arrangement of objects in front of them and asked the students to concentrate attention on it until it was part and parcel of his or her thoughts then to go to the wall which he had covered with paper, to place both nose and toes in contact with it, keeping that contact and using charcoal to draw the image which each had in mind. All the students were in positions that disconnected mind and hand. The drawings were suddenly contemporary, no longer fixed in taste and preconception. The collaboration with oneself that each person conventionally permits had been made impossible by a physical position, another cross-leggedness, the result of which is rapid transportation. (John Cage, in *John Cage: Composition in Retrospect*, 1982) Each student had wanted to become a modern artist. Put out of touch with himself, discovery, sudden opening of doors. It was a class given by Mark Tobey. In the same part of the world, I walked with him from school to Chinatown. He was always stopping, pointing out things to see. (John Cage, in *John Cage: Composition in Retrospect*, 1982) Which he had covered was in and place both nose and toes to concentrate mind and hand in the same part with himself I walked with him from school sudden another. (John Cage, in *John Cage: Composition in Retrospect*, 1982) The fact that it permits the endless formation of numerals doesn't make grammar infinitely complicated. (Wittgenstein, *Philosophical Remarks*, p. 314) Suppose now that I changed my body in the course of a dream, and that the new body replied to the question, "Who had the dream?" with "I had it!" There would be no question whether the new body had had it, and no question as to who had had it. Next suppose I say "Although I cannot imagine other people without their bodies, I could nevertheless imagine myself without my body." It might seem as though there was a sort of knowing expressible by saying "I know who had the dream, and where he is, namely, in this body." But is it sense to say "If I did not have a body I would still know that it was I who had the dream?" What would it be like to know I

had a dream without having a body? If selves had no bodies, how should we make ourselves understood? Of course we could imagine that voices came from various places. But what use would the word "I" have, inasmuch as the same voice might be heard in several places? The fact that it makes sense to suppose that I change my body, but that it does not make sense to suppose that I have a self without a body, shows that the word "I" cannot be replaced by "this body;" and at the same time it shows that "I" only has meaning with reference to a body. (Wittgenstein, *Lectures 1932–1935*, p. 62) Essential elements in this new view are that the universe is not finite but infinite in extent, and that creation is a continuous process which has been going on throughout all past time and which is still going on. (Spencer Jones quoted by L.C. Beckett, in *Neti Neti*, p. 21) Do you find that what you learn inside the classroom is as useful as what you learn outside the classroom? (McLuhan, *City as Classroom*, p. 2) . . . but what did we know? Nothing until the last moment. (McLuhan, *Letters*, p. 113) Environments are invisible. Their groundrules, pervasive structure, and overall patterns elude easy perception. (McLuhan, *The Medium is the Massage*, p. 45) The modern mind, whether in its subconscious collective dream or in its intellectual citadel of vivid awareness, is a stage on which is contained and re-enacted the entire experience of the human race. There are no more remote and easy perspectives, either artistic or national. Everything is present in the foreground. That fact is stressed equally in current physics, jazz, newspapers, and psychoanalysis. And it is not a question of preference or taste. This flood has already immersed us. (McLuhan, *The Mechanical Bride*, p. 87) If money were to disappear, what would happen to your sense of values? . . . Would walking be the most common way of getting about? (McLuhan, *City as Classroom*, p. 137) I may have made some mistakes. But it's a major concern at the moment. He married her while her father announced abruptly Saturday last year he was arrested and accused of corruption and bribe-taking. (from *The New York Times*, July 26, '88) At long last Tunisian leader strongly criticized South Africa's decision to be a transition authority, fired seven ministers. Brazil began five days of South the South Atlantic, the Human Rights League and has had. (from the *Christian Science Monitor*, July 27, '88) Thatcher has insisted more strongly than ever announced yesterday that the United States C.I.A. was planning covert actions for the Israeli-occupied West Bank in vans and on foot. (from the *Christian Science Monitor*, July 29, '88) For many years I was self-appointed inspector of snow-storms and rain-storms, and did my duty faithfully, surveyor, if not of highways, then of forest paths and all across-lot routes, keeping them open, and ravines bridged and passable at all seasons, where the public heel had testified to their utility. (Thoreau, *Walden*, p. 17) And we are enabled to apprehend at all what is sublime and noble only by the perpetual instilling and drenching of the reality that surrounds us. The universe constantly and obediently answers to our conceptions; whether we travel fast or slow, the track is laid for us. Let us spend our lives in conceiving then. (Thoreau, *Walden*, p. 70) Whatever my own practice may be, I have no doubt that it is a part of the destiny of the human race, in its gradual improvement, to leave off eating animals, as surely as the savage tribes have left off eating each other when they came in contact with the more civilized. (Thoreau, *Walden*, pp. 146–147) The World Game sees that we now have the resources and technical, economic, ethical and cultural know-how to meet the needs of all of humanity. (from "The World Game," World Game Projects, Inc., 1987) Best moves demonstrate how, when implemented, they would: 1. make the world work (that is, satisfy human needs for food, energy, shelter, etc.), 2. for the most people, 3. using the least amount of resources, 4. with the least environmental impact, 5. in the quickest amount of time, 6. in an ecologically, economically and technologically sustainable way, and 7. with the most degrees of freedom or alternatives to humanity and the individual. (from "The World Game," World Game Projects, Inc., 1987) Availability for all mankind, his goods and services, to be able to go anywhere in the world at a high rate of economy and efficiency. (from "Dymaxion World of Buckminster Fuller," by Robert W. Marks, and "Buckminster Fuller," by John McHale, in *World Game/1971/Document 1*, p. 104) After researching and then plotting the world's electrical network (generating stations and transmission lines) we devised a way of developing and improving its overall efficiency as the first step towards the bare maximum for all mankind. By utilizing the world's hydroelectric power (rivers and tides), without any further development of thermal plants, and taking advantage of the increased efficiency of super-high voltage long-distance transmission lines (one million volts, 1500 miles) in a day/night seasonal hookup, we were able to demonstrate that with present methods, technologies, projected population figures, metals resources, and efficiency levels in power generation and consumption, it would be possible to bring everyone on earth to a minimum of 2000 kwh per year within ten years. (Edwin Schlossberg and Medard Gable, quoted in *WorldGame/1971/Document 1*, p. 44) Students say they do things they are told had been disconnected. Poland's eight remaining bases are in the Antarctic. Successfully monitoring the Soviet pullout, Administration officials say there is no evidence to this false sense of security today. (from *The New York Times*, Aug. 17, '88) Anything can follow anything else (providing nothing is taken as the basis). Influence derives from one's own work (not from outside it). Chance operations are a useful means; moksha. Being led by a person, not a book; artha. Love. Right and wrong. Non-measured time. (Cage, Introduction to *Themes and Variations*) Polish labor unrest is being treated for Christians to win election in Rangoon and Mandalay, South

Africa hinted. The President of a parliamentary session and hospital officials joined a rebel group in the southern region demanding official recognition of Israel for tuberculosis. (from the *Wall Street Journal*, Aug. 19, '88) Japanese foreign aid to West Germany ended after it was once a forbidden topic. Investigators searched for the cause of the painful memories for a dozen demonstrators. Soviet response was cool but unfurled. (from *The New York Times*, Aug. 19, '88) Point of view is failure to achieve structural awareness. (McLuhan, cited in *Marshall McLuhan: Media in America*, p. 45)

Notation

Turning the paper into a space of time, imperfections in the paper upon which the music is written. The music is there before it is written. Composition is only making it clear that that is the case. Finding out a simple relation between paper and music, how to read it independently of one's thoughts, what instrument or instruments, staff or staves, the possibility of a microtonal music. More space between staff lines representing major thirds than minor so that if a note has no accidental, it is between well known points in the field of frequency or just a drawing in space. Pitch vertically, time reading from left to right, absence of theory. (John Cage, in *John Cage: Composition in Retrospect*, 1982) Accidental major to staff the vertically finding out one's thoughts. (John Cage, in *John Cage: Composition in Retrospect*, 1982) Suppose that in a certain language there were no word corresponding to our "know". — The people simply make assertions. ("That is a tree", etc.) Naturally it can occur for them to make mistakes. And so they attach a sign to the sentence which indicates how probable they take a mistake to be — or should I say, how probable a mistake is in this case? This latter can also be indicated by mentioning certain circumstances. For example "Then A said to B '. . .'. I was standing quite close to them and my hearing is good", or "A was at such-and-such a place yesterday. I saw him from a long way off. My eyes are not very good", or "There is a tree over there: I can see it clearly and I have seen it innumerable times before". (Wittgenstein, *On Certainty*, pp. 57–58) . . . "If the crotchets were elsewhere I would play differently." How do you know what you would do if the crotchet was differently placed? (Wittgenstein, *Lectures 1930–1932*, p. 39) You cannot see a hundred dots: you can only see many. (Wittgenstein, *Lectures 1930–1932*, p. 91) Would it be imaginable, given two identical bits of a piece of music, to have directions placed above them, bidding us hear it like this the first time, and like this the second, without this exerting any influence on the performance? The piece would perhaps be written for a chiming clock and the two bits would be meant to be played equally loud and in the same tempo — only taken differently each time. And, even if a composer has never yet written such a direction, might not a critic write it? Would not such a direction be comparable to a title to Programme music ("Dance of the Peasants")? (Wittgenstein, *Remarks on the Philosophy of Psychology*, Vol. I, p. 102) 'If I have five, then I have three and two.' —But how do I know that I have five? —Well, if it looks like this: ||||| . —And is it also certain that when it looks like this, I can always split it up into groups like those? (Wittgenstein, *Remarks on the Foundations of Mathematics*, p. 61) To ask someone's advice mentally. To estimate the time by imagining a clock. (Wittgenstein, *Remarks on the Philosophy of Psychology*, Vol. II, p. 93) When I feel sorry for someone with toothache, I put myself in his place. But I put *myself* in his place. (Wittgenstein, *Philosophical Remarks*, p. 92) It is this creation that drives the Universe. (Hoyle, quoted by L.C. Beckett, in *Neti Neti*, p. 22) Urbanity and grace, whether in verbal or plastic art, serve to provide comfort and reassurance for the disturbed. A great deal of art and entertainment is naturally of this tranquilizing kind. As such it is indispensable to the serious artist who is searching to devise a strategy for designing his anti-environment. From the contours and postures of popular as well as of academic art, the serious artist can read the message of the hidden environmental pressures. (McLuhan, "Art as Anti-Environment," p. 2) When faced with a totally new situation, we tend always to attach ourselves to the objects, to the flavor of the most recent past. (McLuhan, *The Medium is the Massage*, p. 39) Cervantes confronted typographic man in the figure of Don Quixote. (McLuhan, *The Gutenberg Galaxy*, p. 213) But though it is painful he is sufficiently the realist to accept the new social ethic of electronic communication . . . Compared to big business, academic and literary worlds often seem like a jungle. (McLuhan, *Verbi-Voco-Visual Explorations*, p. 46) This anarchic elevation of nuclear man enables individuals to be dispensed, as it were, from the moral law, a fact which was strikingly manifested in the radio age by Stalin and Hitler (and in the TV age by the universality of abortion), and helps to explain the sudden indifference of the TV generation to private morality. (McLuhan, "The Rise and Fall of Nature," p. 2) The whole character and fortune of the individual are affected by the least inequalities in the culture of the understanding; for example, in the perception of differences. Therefore is Space, and therefore Time, that man may know that things are not huddled and lumped, but sundered and individual. A bell and a plough have each their use, and neither can do the office of the other. Water is good to drink, coal to burn, wool to wear; but wool cannot be drunk, nor water spun, nor coal eaten. (Emerson, "Nature," in *Selected Essays*, p. 56) The judge in the Iran-contra case said a military court sentenced three Slovenian journalists to prison for reporting violence at an anti-government protest. But a statement released

Tuesday will have to be dismissed a week ago, the source said. (from the *Christian Science Monitor*, July 28, '88) The Army blew up the North Sea injuring several people in South Africa. Two-thousand seals have died separately killing two people and wounding twenty-seven. During the rebellion that began eight months ago, Iran said most of the men could face up to six years in prison if convicted of avoiding military service. (from the *Christian Science Monitor*, Aug. 4, '88) Vietnam has placed Rangoon under martial law. Rangoon agreed to continue air raids on industrial targets. The Arabs agreed to continue the search for missing American servicemen. Jordan's decision intensifies speculation about the country's civil war. (from the *Wall Street Journal*, Aug. 4, '88) The American refusal to pay its share of the country's cultural institutions may be jeopardized, which says that money is not spent on the poorest sections of society. A bomb becomes a center of international attention. No one else was harmed. (from *The New York Times*, Aug. 10, '88) Shortly after takeoff he was identified as being the Egyptian president. North Korea's demand allows both countries to observe each other's Strip. Protests in Burma resumed of one of five beatings. (from the *Wall Street Journal*, Aug. 18, '88) My purpose in going to Walden Pond was not to live cheaply nor to live dearly there, but to transact some private business with the fewest obstacles; to be hindered from accomplishing which for want of a little common sense, a little enterprise and business talent, appeared not so sad as foolish. (Thoreau, *Walden*, p. 18) Let us settle ourselves, and work and wedge our feet downward through the mud and slush of opinion, and prejudice, and tradition, and delusion, and appearance, that alluvion which covers the globe, through Paris and London, through New York and Boston and Concord, through Church and State, through poetry and philosophy and religion, till we come to a hard bottom and rocks in place, which we can call reality. . . . Be it life or death, we crave only reality. If we are really dying, let us hear the rattle in our throats and feel cold in the extremities; if we are alive, let us go about our business. (Thoreau, *Walden*, pp. 70–71) If one listens to the faintest but constant suggestions of his genius, which are certainly true, he sees not to what extremes, or even insanity, it may lead him; and yet that way, as he grows more resolute and faithful, his road lies. The faintest assured objection which one healthy man feels will at length prevail over the arguments and customs of mankind. No man ever followed his genius till it misled him. Though the result were bodily weakness, yet perhaps no one can say that the consequences were to be regretted, for these were a life in conformity to higher principles. (Thoreau, *Walden*, p. 147) The World Game is a facility for empowering government leaders and policy makers, researchers, teachers, students and the general public in their efforts at recognizing, defining and solving global problems and local problems in a global context. It does this through its unique education and research programs. The World Game is concerned with world peace through the meeting of basic human needs for everyone on the planet, and the transformation of scarcity, poverty and ignorance into resources, capacities and abundant opportunities for local wealth and global well-being. It is engaged in building a set of tools that can be used by problem solvers throughout the world in this transformative process. (from "The World Game," World Game Projects, Inc., 1987) UNIVERSE is the aggregate of all humanity's all-time, consciously apprehended and communicated experiences. (from "Dymaxion World of Buckminster Fuller," by Robert W. Marks, and "Buckminster Fuller," by John McHale, in *World Game/1971/Document 1*, p. 102) Availability of the best comprehensive education in all spheres of life for all mankind; and to anyone who wishes to learn anything, everything pertaining to his special interest. (from "Dymaxion World of Buckminster Fuller," by Robert W. Marks, and "Buckminster Fuller," by John McHale, in *World Game/1971/Document 1*, p. 104) We asked: How much copper wire is needed to carry the power necessary for the year 2000 for both industrial and home use throughout the world? How far ahead can we conceive a future life-style? What's the time-lag between installation of electrical energy and an adequate food supply? How much metal is involved to produce the kwh needs for the year 2000? (Edwin Schlossberg and Medard Gable, quoted in *World Game/1971/Document 1*, p. 44) Process instead of object. America has a climate for experimentation. World is one world. History is the story of original actions. Move from zero. All audible phenomena = material for music. Impossibility of errorless work. (Cage, Introduction to *Themes and Variations*) The awareness of 'emptiness' is not a blank loss of consciousness, an inanimate empty space; rather it is the cognition of daily life without the attachment to it. It is an awareness of distinct entities, of the self, of 'good' and 'bad' and other practical determinations; but it is aware of these as empty structures. Wisdom is not to be equated with mystical ecstasy; it is, rather, the joy of freedom in everyday existence. (F.J. Streng, *Emptiness: A Study in Religious Meaning*, cited in Gudmunsen, *Wittgenstein and Buddhism*, p. 103) The massacres that left at least 5,000 people dead began in Poland's southern coal fields nine days ago. A scandal over the investigation was easing a ban on the United States campaign to oust the Mexican congress at a meeting next month probably in Moscow. (from *The New York Times*, Aug. 25, '88) Experience is play, and meaning is replay and re-cognition. Far from being normal, successful communication is a rarity. It requires not only repetition of a common language, but also demands participation of both author and audience in the process of remaking from their old components a pattern that only the author may have perceived. Communicating the new is a miracle. (McLuhan, cited in *Marshall McLuhan: Media in America*, p. 45) There is no storyline in modern art or news — just a date line. There is no past or future, just an inclusive present. (McLuhan, cited in *Marshall McLuhan: Media in America*, p. 147)

Indeterminacy

You can't be serious, she said. We were drinking. A record was being played, not in the place where we were but in another room. I had found it interesting and had asked what music it was. (John Cage, in *John Cage: Composition in Retrospect*, 1982) Not to supply a particular photograph but to think of materials that would make it possible for someone else to make his own: a camera. It was necessary for David Tudor, something, a puzzle that he would solve. Taking as a beginning what was impossible to measure and then returning what he could to mystery. It was while teaching a class at Wesleyan that I thought of Number II. I had been explaining Variations One, suddenly realized that two notations on the same piece of paper automatically bring about relationship. (John Cage, in *John Cage: Composition in Retrospect*, 1982) My composing is actually unnecessary. Music never stops. It is we who turn away. Again the world around. Silence. Sounds are only bubbles on its surface. They burst to disappear (Thoreau). When we make music, we merely make something that can more naturally be heard than seen or touched, that makes it possible to pay attention to daily work or play as being not what we think it is but our goal. All that's needed is a frame, a change of mental attitude, amplification. Waiting for a bus, we're present at a concert. Suddenly we stand on a work of art, the pavement. (John Cage, in *John Cage: Composition in Retrospect*, 1982) Music never stops it is we who turn away I had as being not surface for all that's needed is a frame it was amplification waiting for a bus my composing not to supply. (John Cage, in *John Cage: Composition in Retrospect*, 1982) What we are apt to confuse is the idea as a state of mind occurring at a particular time and the use we make of that idea. The reason for the notion that the idea as static — as something before the mind's eye — has its uses contained in it and needs only to be spread out in time for its uses to be revealed is this: that in the case of many ideas there is one preeminent use. . . . An idea, if we mean something static, is a means of operating with language, and in all sorts of different ways, although as a matter of fact it is a means which is almost always used in one way. As soon as we see that this use is only one of lots of uses, we see that the idea plays the role of a symbol. Wittgenstein, *Lectures 1932–1935*, pp. 87–88) The difficulty of imagining it (or of filling out the picture of it) is in knowing when one has pictured that. I.e. the indefiniteness of the request to imagine it.

The difficulty is, therefore, one of knowing what we are supposed to consider as the analogue of something that is familiar to us. (Wittgenstein, *Remarks on Colour*, p. 28) This piece of paper varies in lightness from place to place, but does it look grey to me in the darker places? The shadow that my hand casts is in part grey. I see the parts of the paper that are farther away from the light darker but still white, even though I would have to mix a grey to paint it. Isn't this similar to the fact that we often see a distant object merely as distant and not as smaller? Thus we cannot say "I notice that he looks smaller, and I conclude from that that he is farther away," but rather I notice that he is farther away, without being able to say how I notice it. (Wittgenstein, *Remarks on Colour*, p. 40) But that is not to say that this contrast does not shade off in all directions. And that in turn is not to say that the contrast is not of the greatest importance. (Wittgenstein, *Remarks on the Foundations of Mathematics*, p. 363) The concept of a living being has the same indeterminacy as that of a language. (Wittgenstein, *Zettel*, p. 60) No supposition seems to me more natural than that there is no process in the brain correlated with associating or with thinking; so that it would be impossible to read off thought-processes from brain-processes. I mean this: if I talk or write there is, I assume, a system of impulses going out from my brain and correlated with my spoken or written thoughts. But why should the system continue further in the direction of the centre? Why should this order not proceed, so to speak, out of chaos? The case would be like the following — certain kinds of plants multiply by seed, so that a seed always produces a plant of the same kind as that from which it was produced — but nothing in the seed corresponds to the plant which comes from it; so that it is impossible to infer the properties or structure of the plant from those of the seed that comes out of it — this can only be done from the history of the seed. So an organism might come into being even out of something quite amorphous, as it were causelessly; and there is no reason why this should not really hold for our thoughts, and hence for our talking and writing. (Wittgenstein, *Zettel*, p. 106) Even the hydrogen duality is not the ultimate duality, for the nucleus of the second isotope of hydrogen consists of a yet smaller and more condensed duality: a proton and a neutron; and if even here there are separate charges, may there not be yet smaller units, and still smaller, completely inapprehensible to us? At the opposite extreme, on the vastest scale we can think of, what makes a galaxy into a unit is the Nothing between its component parts. That is the creative factor, otherwise they would remain part of the background material. Can we set any highest or lowest limit to extension in the Universe? Ultimately a Nothing Between must be the only factor that counts. (L.C. Beckett, *Neti Neti*, pp. 23–24) These typographical matters for many people are charged with controversial values. Yet in any approach to understanding print it is necessary to stand aside from the form in question if its typical pressure and life are to be observed. Those who panic now about the threat of the newer media and about the revolution we are forging, vaster in scope than that of Gutenberg, are obviously lacking in cool visual detachment and gratitude for that most potent gift bestowed on Western man by literacy and typography: his power to act without reaction or involvement. (McLuhan, *Understanding Media*, p. 178) Now in terms of media study it is clear that the power of film to store information in accessible form is unrivaled. Audio tape and video tape were to excel film eventually as information storehouses. But film remains a major information resource, a rival of the book whose technology it did so much to continue and also to surpass. (McLuhan, *Understanding Media*, p. 291) The interplay between figure and ground is 'where the action is'. This interplay requires an interval or a gap, like the space between the wheel and the axle. (McLuhan, *City as Classroom*, p. 9). Study a painting from three different periods of your own culture. Write down the sounds for which you see evidence in each painting. Divide these into three categories: (1) sounds in nature and animal sounds; (2) human sounds; (3) technological sounds. Is there a predominance of one kind of sound in each period of painting? Try to express your findings in percentages. What can you learn about your own environment in this way? (McLuhan, *City as Classroom*, p. 155) We have entered a radically new electronic age and it is the artist who makes the revolution visible. (McLuhan, "Art as Anti-Environment," p. 55) Delegates said there could be no peace through a precipitous withdrawal of currency notes contributed a threat to public order. Washington's U.N. envoy might help release the Pakistani President and Iran's news agency agency. (from the *Christian Science Monitor*, July 27, '88) U.S. concerns that Moscow was securing a truce severed ties with the Jewish curfew on a town in which a former operation would. Barco said the Bogota government won't establish a working group that such research could be. (from the *Wall Street Journal*, July 29, '88) A Senate plan for aid to Iran is expected to buy advertising spots in the Israeli-occupied territories. Some Palestinians now observe them more strictly; some, including those who are loyal to the King, maintain links, despite international presence in the Pakistani violations. (from *The New York Times*, Aug. 2, '88) Angola and Cuba rejected Israel and the U.S. face to face but negotiators have discovered legal ties to seek nonlethal aid. Later this week Iraq has twice refused to hold talks with Hanoi. War remained stalled because of a "hostile" U.S. policy. (from the *Wall Street Journal*, Aug. 4, '88) Stepping down on moral grounds two of the Indians said they would have deserted, but accepted responsibility in exile. He rejected international laws and invading the privacy of Japanese-Americans in the bugging, but criticized Jordan for not notifying him before. (from the *Christian Science Monitor*, Aug. 11, '88) I cannot believe that our factory system is the best mode by which men may get clothing. The condition of the operatives is becoming every day more like that of the English; and it cannot be wondered at, since, as far as I have heard or observed, the principal object is, not that mankind may be well and honestly clad, but, unquestionably, that the corporations may be enriched. In the long run men hit only what they aim at. Therefore, though they should fail immediately, they had better aim at something high. (Thoreau, *Walden*, pp. 22–23) The oldest Egyptian or Hindoo philosopher raised a corner of the veil from the statue of the divinity; and still the trembling robe remains raised, and I gaze upon as fresh a glory as he did, since it was I in him that was then so bold, and it is he in me that now reviews the vision. No dust has settled on that robe; no time has elapsed since that divinity was revealed. (Thoreau, *Walden*, p. 71) If the day and the night are such that you greet them with joy, and life emits a fragrance like flowers and sweet-scented herbs, is more elastic, more starry, more immortal, — that is your success. All nature is your congratulation, and you have cause momentarily to bless yourself. The greatest gains and values are farthest from being appreciated. We easily come to doubt if they exist. We soon forget them. They are the highest reality. Perhaps the facts most astounding and most real are never communicated by man to man. The true harvest of my daily life is somewhat as intangible and indescribable as the tints of morning or evening. It is a little star-dust caught, a segment of the rainbow which I have clutched. (Thoreau, *Walden*, p. 147) The World Game facility would be available to everyone. It would be where a great logistics game is played by world leaders, researchers, students and the general public; where players as individuals or teams develop their own theory of how to make the total world work successfully for all humanity; where strategies for solving the pressing needs can be tested out and ever more effective ways evolved; and where a giant football field size world map displays the vital statistics about our planet so that everyone can readily comprehend their true significance in relation to the whole of Spaceship Earth. (Fuller, quoted in "The World Game," World Game Projects, Inc., 1987) World game starts with Universe and the potential success of man within that Universe. (from "Dymaxion World of Buckminster Fuller," by Robert W. Marks, and "Buckminster Fuller," by John McHale, in *World Game/1971/Document 1*, p. 102) Availability of enough leisure, facilities, and know-how, for all mankind to develop to his, society's and Earth's maximum potential and satisfaction. (from "Dymaxion World of Buckminster Fuller," by Robert W. Marks, and "Buckminster Fuller," by John McHale, in *World Game/1971/Document 1*, p. 104) When the energy input of an area is raised, there is a corresponding rise in communications capacity which in turn increases the necessity of the "have-nots" to become "haves." (Edwin Schlossberg and Medard Gable, quoted in *World Game/1971/Document 1*, p. 44)

Spring, Summer, Fall, Winter (Creation, Preservation, Destruction, Quiescence). Possibility of helping by doing nothing. Music is not music until it is heard. Music and dance together (and then other togethers). Men are men; mountains are mountains before studying Zen. While studying Zen, things become confused. After studying Zen, men are men; mountains are mountains. What is the difference between before and after? No difference. Just the feet are a little off the ground (Suzuki). If structure, rhythmic structure. Boredom plus attention = becoming interested. Principle underlying all of the solutions = question we ask. (Cage, Introduction to *Themes and Variations*) Life at these speeds obliges everyone to discover a new career for himself every ten years, a new job and even a totally new personality. At electric speed it is not wise to try to be one and the same person and have the same job for more than ten years. (McLuhan, cited in *Marshall McLuhan: Media in America*, p. 100) There is absolutely no inevitability as long as there is a willingness to contemplate what is happening. (McLuhan, cited in *Marshall McLuhan: Media in America*, p. 225) Polish riot police broke up talks today on a nonaggression pact that killed talks between delegations headed by each nation's foreign minister. The United States proposed a compromise at talks in Lebanon. An ex-Army sergeant with access to a top-secret military archive using a combination of negotiations and intimidation was quoted, military and government. (from the *Wall Street Journal*, Aug. 26, '88)

Interpenetration

Musicircus. Many things going on at the same time. A theatre of differences together, not a single plan, just a space of time and as many people as are willing, performing in the same place, a large place, a gymnasium, an architecture that isn't involved with making the stage directly opposite the audience and higher, thus more important than where they're sitting. The responsibility of each person is, Marcel Duchamp said, to complete the work himself — to hear, to see, originally. We need to change not only architecture but the relation of art to money. There will be too many musicians to pay. The event must be free to the public. Here, as elsewhere, we find that society needs to be changed. (John Cage, in *John Cage: Composition in Retrospect*, 1982) I think that many of our problems will be solved if we take advantage of Buckminster Fuller's plans for the improvement of the circumstances of our lives — an equation between world resources and human needs so that it works for everyone, not just the rich. No nations, to begin with, and no government at all (Thoreau also said this). An intelligent plan that will heal the present schizophrenia. The use of energy sources above earth, not fossil fuels. Quickly air will improve and water too. Not the promise of giving us artificial employment but to use our technology producing a society based on unemployment. The purpose of invention has always been to diminish work. We now have the possibility to become a society at one with itself. (John Cage, in *John Cage: Composition in Retrospect*, 1982) Not just the rich of giving us that at the same time there will be too many musicians to plan a society the event the purpose to the public has always been to diminish work above the not fossil fuels we need to change. (John Cage, in *John Cage: Composition in Retrospect*, 1982) Giving orders, and obeying them— Describing the appearance of an object, or giving its measurements— Constructing an object from a description (a drawing)— Reporting an event— Speculating about an event— Forming and testing a hypothesis— Presenting the results of an experiment in tables and diagrams— Making up a story; and reading it— Play-acting— Singing catches— Guessing riddles— Making a joke; telling it— Solving a problem in practical arithmetic— Translating from one language to another— Asking, thanking, cursing, greeting, praying. (Wittgenstein, *Philosophical Investigations*, pp. 11–12) "It is as if we could grasp the whole use of the word in a flash." Like what e.g.? —Can't the use — in a certain sense — be grasped in a flash? And in what sense can it not? —The point is, that it is as if we could 'grasp it in a flash' in yet another and much more direct sense than that. —But have you a model for this? No. It is just that this expression suggests itself to us. It is what emerges from crossing different pictures. (Wittgenstein, *Philosophical Investigations*, p. 77) The concept of the world of consciousness. We people a space with impressions. (Wittgenstein, *Remarks on the Philosophy of Psychology*, Vol. I, p. 132) One learns the word "think," i.e. its use, under certain circumstances, which, however, one does not learn to describe. But I can teach a person the use of the word! For a description of those circumstances is not needed for that. I just teach him the word under particular circumstances. We learn to say it perhaps only of human beings; we learn to assert or deny it of them. The question "Do fishes think?" does not exist among our applications of language, it is not raised. (What can be more natural than such a set-up, such a use of language?) (Wittgenstein, *Zettel*, p. 22) If anyone should think he has solved the problem of life and feel like telling himself that everything is quite easy now, he can see that he is wrong just by recalling that there was a time when this "solution" had not been discovered; but it must have been possible to live then too and the solution which has now been discovered seems fortuitous in relation to how things were then. And it is the same in the study of logic. If there were a "solution" to the problems of logic (philosophy) we should only need to caution ourselves that there was a time when they had not been solved (and even at that time people must have known how to live and think). (Wittgenstein, *Culture and Value*, p. 4) What the Unified

Field Theory does is to show that gravitational and electromagnetic forces are not independent of each other — that they are in a very real physical sense inseparable. (Lincoln Barnett, quoted by L.C. Beckett, in *Neti Neti*, p. 26) Employers reported that they had never met a class so "eager to make itself useful to business." And big business had in many cases "developed closer ties with the campus, often with grants and scholarships." (McLuhan, *Mechanical Bride*, pp. 49–50) Today's child is growing up absurd, because he lives in two worlds, and neither of them inclines him to grow up. Growing up — that is our new work, and it is *total*. Mere instruction will not suffice. (McLuhan, *The Medium is the Massage*, p. 18) Until a century ago, prints made in the old techniques filled all the functions that are now filled by our line cuts and half tones, by our photographs and blueprints, by our various colour processes, and by our political cartoons and pictorial advertisements. If we define prints from the functional point of view so indicated, rather than by any restriction of process or aesthetic value, it becomes obvious that without prints we should have very few of our modern sciences, technologies, archaeologies, or ethnologies — for all of these are dependent, first or last, upon information conveyed by exactly repeatable visual or pictorial statements. (McLuhan, *The Gutenberg Galaxy*, pp. 78–79) Our time has gone a step farther. Both sex and death have been subtly neutralized by the popularization of laboratory procedures. (McLuhan, *Mechanical Bride*, p. 131) "The I Ching told me to continue what I was doing, and to spread joy and revolution." (John Cage, as quoted in McLuhan, *The Medium is the Massage*, p. 66) The move followed reports as to whether it will allow discontent. Or should it stick to violence? One has to do everything to stop relations with incitement and we are. (from the *Christian Science Monitor*, July 29, '88) He was determined to provide billions to rescue ailing Texas bank. All the assets of the new bank would be no earlier than Thursday morning. The move was the first action which was not available. The war is to increase civil liberties on Tuesday and last week that the two. (from *The New York Times*, July 30, '88) Talks on peace in Congress known for anti-American rhetoric have reshaped the Arab-Israeli dispute. The Security Council would never accept that goal to those ends. Communist Party chiefs have the right to know what bomb exploded yesterday including the Kremlin's new secret bomber and watched. (from the *Christian Science Monitor*, Aug. 3, '88) A police officer and a gunman issued a statement warning that human error was primarily responsible for the tax-fraud charges in the Persian Gulf. Unprecedented efforts for both attacks appeared to be edging toward talks in Geneva. (from the *Wall Street Journal*, Aug. 3, '88) After tumultuous anti-Government protests defense lawyers have lodged complaints saying it would destroy America's flexibility to seek change. More than three hundred thousand talks involving the United States House of Representatives are being tried for political defiance. No group said it was responsible. (from *The New York Times*, Aug. 13, '88) On applying to the assessors, I am surprised to learn that they cannot at once name a dozen in the town who own their farms free and clear. If you would know the history of these homesteads, inquire at the bank where they are mortgaged. (Thoreau, *Walden*, pp. 26–27) It is time that we had uncommon schools, that we did not leave off our education when we begin to be men and women. It is time that villages were universities, and their elder inhabitants the fellows of universities, with leisure — if they are, indeed, so well off — to pursue liberal studies the rest of their lives. . . . As the nobleman of cultivated taste surrounds himself with whatever conduces to his culture,. . . . so let the village do,. . . . To act collectively is according to the spirit of our institutions; and I am confident that, as our circumstances are more flourishing, our means are greater than the nobleman's. New England can hire all the wise men in the world to come and teach her, and board them round the while, and not be provincial at all. That is the uncommon school we want. Instead of noblemen, let us have noble villages of men. (Thoreau, *Walden*, p. 78) After a still winter night I awoke with the impression that some question had been put to me, which I had been endeavoring in vain to answer in my sleep, as what — how — when — where? But there was dawning Nature, in whom all creatures live, looking in at my broad windows with serene and satisfied face, and no question on her lips. I awoke to an answered question, to Nature and daylight. . . . Nature puts no questions and answers none which we mortals ask. (Thoreau, *Walden*, p. 189) The World Game: To make the world work for 100% of humanity in the shortest possible time through spontaneous cooperation without ecological offense or the disadvantage of anyone. (Fuller, quoted in "The World Game," World Game Projects, Inc., 1987) World Game players have the integrity of the entire Universe backing them up and are thus as effective and efficient as possible. (from "Dymaxion World of Buckminster Fuller," by Robert W. Marks, and "Buckminster Fuller," by John McHale, in *World Game/1971/Document 1*, p. 102) Because energy can neither be destroyed nor created, and "know-how" of intellect can only increase with each experiment, or experience, wealth consisting of both the physical and metaphysical can only increase with each and every re-employment. Wealth and the bare-maximum are World Game measurements of success; the ultimate bare-maximum wealth at this point in our evolution is total success for all humanity, now living or ever to become living. (from "Dymaxion World of Buckminster Fuller," by Robert W. Marks, and "Buckminster Fuller," by John McHale, in *World Game/1971/Document 1*, p. 104) In the scenario, the vast hydroelectric potential of both South America and Africa is utilized to raise their respective levels to the per capita figure of 2000 kwh, and the surplus is transmitted via the electric network to areas where there are deficits of electric power. Because we do not have a global network at the present time, the U.S. and other industrialized countries produce and use during the night hours only a small percentage of their electrical power capacity. With a global electric grid, power could be generated at day and night total capacity and transmitted to the daytime peak needs around the earth. (Edwin Schlossberg and Medard Gable, quoted in *World Game/1971/Document 1*, pp. 44–45) Activity, not communication. The nine permanent emotions (the heroic, the mirthful, the wondrous, the erotic; tranquillity; sorrow, fear, anger, the odious). The practicality of changing society derives from the possibility of changing the mind. The giver of gifts (returning to the village having experienced no-mindedness). Studying being interrupted. Nothing-in-between. Object is fact not symbol (no ideas). Poetry is having nothing to say and saying it; we possess nothing. (Cage, Introduction to *Themes and Variations*) There is a great tradition that women are much more integral in their life and men much more specialized, fragmentary, and that's why women are thought to be intuitive. The world of insight is primarily one of touch rather than sight, and so the woman's intuition means the use of all the senses at once, a response to which is touch-active touch that is, not just passive touch. Touch is our primary and deepest experiential mode of relating to the world. (McLuhan, cited in *Marshall McLuhan: Media in America*, p. 101) Elections planned for November against any ill-planned steps inside a refugee camp in Israel are to continue throughout the weekend hammering out a permanent truce and a leading dissident. The death toll could rise intelligence sources said. South Africa and Angola are continuing. (from the *Wall Street Journal*, Aug. 26, '88)

Imitation

The past must be invented. The future must be revised. Doing both makes what the present is. Discovery never stops. (John Cage, in *John Cage: Composition in Retrospect*, 1982) What questions will make the past alive in another way? In the case of Satie's *Socrate*, seeing it as polymodal (modal chromatically) allowed me to ask of all the modes, which? Of the twelve tones, which? Renovation of melody. In the case of Eighteenth-century hymns, knowing the number of tones in each voice, to ask which of the numbers are passive, which active. These are first tone, then silence. This brings about a harmony, a tonality, freed from theory. In *Chorals* of Satie, to change the staff so there's equal space for each half tone, then rubbing the twelve into the microtonal (Japan, Calcutta, etcetera). (John Cage, in *John Cage: Composition in Retrospect*, 1982) Which? as polymodal revised allowed me to these are first tone of Satie's of the microtonal (Japan

Calcutta etcetera). (John Cage, in *John Cage: Composition in Retrospect*, 1982) "If I shut my eyes, there he is in front of me." —One could suppose that such expressions are not learned, but rather poetically formed, spontaneously. That they therefore "seem just right" to one man and then also to the next one. "I see him in front of me as plain as day!" —Well, maybe he's really standing in front of you. —"No, my picture isn't vivid enough for that." (Wittgenstein, *Remarks on the Philosophy of Psychology*, Vol. II, p. 22) But isn't there a connexion between the grammatical 'privacy' of thoughts and the fact that we generally cannot guess the thoughts of someone else before he utters them? But there is such a thing as guessing thoughts in the sense that someone says to me: "I know what you have just thought" (or "What you just thought of") and I have to admit that he has guessed my thoughts right. But in fact this happens very seldom. I often sit without talking for several minutes in my class, and thoughts go through my head; but surely none of my audience could guess what I have been thinking to myself. Yet it would also be possible that someone should guess them and write them down just as if I had uttered them out loud. And if he shewed me what he had written, I should have to say, "Yes, I thought just that to myself." —And here, e.g., this question would be undecidable: whether I am not making a mistake; whether I really thought that, or, influenced by his writing, I am firmly imagining myself to have thought precisely that. (Wittgenstein, *Remarks on the Philosophy of Psychology*, Vol. I, p. 106) Long proofs at first always go along with the short ones and as it were tutor them. But in the end they can no longer follow the short ones and these shew their independence. (Wittgenstein, *Remarks on the Foundations of Mathematics*, p. 176) Suppose the most exact description of a feeling is "stomach-ache." But why isn't the most important description of feeling that you say: "Oh, this is the same as that!"? (Wittgenstein, *Lectures and Conversations*, p. 33) . . . in Nothing one and the same nature, at the same time, both draws all things together into a creation, and expands itself in an eternal outspreading motion. (L.C. Beckett, *Neti Neti*, p. 27) T.S. Eliot reported how, in the making of the film of his *Murder in the Cathedral*, it was not only necessary to have costumes of the period, but — so great is the precision and tyranny of the camera eye — these costumes had to be woven by the same techniques as those used in the twelfth century. (McLuhan, *Understanding Media*, p. 288) Of much greater import is the fact that education as a status escalator or mobility agent is also a very crude device for insuring that its products will often be mentally narrow to the point of helplessness. Those who submit to training only because it will link them more effectively to a great economic and bureaucratic mechanism are using their best years and faculties as a means of enslaving themselves. They are seizing opportunities in order to have the economic means to be exactly like everybody else. (Mc-Luhan, *The Mechanical Bride*, p. 126) . . . prepared to fight the previous war. (McLuhan, *Understanding Media*, p. 243) Dreadnaught Broadside (McLuhan, "The Rise and Fall of Nature," p. 2) ". . . again and again during a period of six or seven centuries they [the Greeks] went right up to the door of modern geometry, but . . . inhibited by their tactile-muscular, metrical ideas, they were never able to open that door and pass out into the great open spaces of modern thought." (from William Ivins, *Art and Geometry*, cited in McLuhan, *The Gutenberg Galaxy*, p. 59) . . . the soul holds itself off from a too trivial and microscopic study of the universal tablet. It respects the end too much to immerse itself in the means. It sees . . . it accepts . . the phenomenon, as it finds it . . . It is not hot and passionate at the appearance of what it calls its own good or bad fortune, at the union or opposition of other persons. No man is its enemy. It accepts whatsoever befalls, as part of its lesson. It is a watcher more than a doer, and it is a doer, only that it may the better watch. (Emerson, "Nature," in *Selected Essays*, pp. 70–71) An explosion demolished the White House amid a strike in the occupied lands. A team of U.N. Experts claimed responsibility. Despite frequent talks Jordan's King was severing ties for an independent war denounced in Central Asia less than a week after a new liquid hydrogen leak. (from the *Wall Street Journal*, Aug. 2, '88) Now that Jordan has cut administrative ties to the West Bank, few monks have joined the protest to stop cocaine at its source. The church has refused to disclose what was discussed but Morocco has been unable to translate its battlefield dominance into diplomatic success. Workers and others are breathing a collective sigh of relief. (from the *Christian Science Monitor*, Aug. 12, '88) The Administration is likely to wait until it sees soldiers patrolling the streets in contrast to violent protests for racial discrimination. They described themselves as the first and only line of defense in spartan conditions where more than three million protests have been. (from *The New York Times*, Aug. 16, '88) The very simplicity and nakedness of man's life in the primitive ages imply this advantage, at least, that they left him still but a sojourner in nature. When he was refreshed with food and sleep, he contemplated his journey again. He dwelt, as it were, in a tent in this world, and was either threading the valleys, or crossing the plains, or climbing the mountain-tops. But lo! men have become the tools of their tools. The man who independently plucked the fruits when he was hungry is become a farmer; and he who stood under a tree for shelter, a housekeeper. We now no longer camp as for a night, but have settled down on earth and forgotten heaven. (Thoreau, *Walden*, p. 30) I rejoice that there are owls. Let them do the idiotic and maniacal hooting for men. It is a sound admirably suited to swamps and twilight woods which no day illustrates, suggesting a vast and undeveloped nature which men have not recognized. (Thoreau, *Walden*, p. 88) The change from storm and winter to serene and mild weather, from dark and sluggish hours to bright and elastic ones, is a memorable crisis which all things proclaim. It is seemingly instantaneous at last. Suddenly an influx of light filled my house, though the evening was at hand, and the clouds of winter still overhung it, and the eaves were dripping with sleety rain. I looked out the window, and lo! where yesterday was cold gray ice there lay the transparent pond already calm and full of hope as in a summer evening, reflecting a summer evening sky in its bosom, though none was visible overhead, as if it had intelligence with some remote horizon. (Thoreau, *Walden*, p. 207) Why should we be in such desperate haste to succeed and in such desperate enterprises? If a man does not keep pace with his companions, perhaps it is because he hears a different drummer. Let him step to the music which he hears, however measured or far away. It is not important that he should mature as soon as an apple tree or an oak. Shall he turn his spring into summer? If the condition of things which we were made for is not yet, what were any reality which we can substitute? We will not be shipwrecked on a vain reality. Shall we with pains erect a heaven of blue glass over ourselves, though when it is done we shall be sure to gaze still at the true ethereal heaven far above, as if the former were not? (Thoreau, *Walden*, p. 216) No face which we can give to a matter will stead us so well at last as the truth. . . . Any truth is better than make-believe. Tom Hyde, the tinker, standing on the gallows, was asked if he had anything to say. "Tell the tailors," said he, "to remember to make a knot in their thread before they take the first stitch." (Thoreau, *Walden*, p. 217) Think of it. We are traveling on a planet, revolving around the sun, in almost perfect symmetry. We are blessed with technology that would be indescribable to our forefathers. We have the wherewithal, the know-it-all, to feed everybody, clothe everybody, give every human on Earth a chance. We dwell instead on petty things. We kill each other. We build monuments to ourselves. What a waste of time . . . Think of it. What a chance we have . . . (Fuller, quoted in "The World Game," World Game Projects, Inc., 1987) Earth is an automated Spaceship speeding rotatively at 66,000 miles per hour around the sun, which in turn, is on its own course at 6.0 kilometers per second within the Galactic Nebula. The awareness of Earth's mobile patterning within the cosmos gives the perspective needed to deal with the overall evolutionary event-patterning aboard our spherical space-vehicle Earth, rather than the minute details. The automated events transpiring aboard Earth lend powerful advantages to those who comprehend the automation and attempt to work with it in the most long-term, humanly advantageous ways rather than ignorantly attempting to control or oppose it. Both Earth's and humanity's automation are biological. (from "Dymaxion World of Buckminster Fuller," by Robert W. Marks, and "Buckminster Fuller," by John McHale, in *World Game/1971/Document*

1, p. 102) The harnessed inanimate energy of sun produced, water falling, or sun and moon produced tidal pulsations, or wind power or the biological automated logistics of our bodies — veins, nerves, muscles, etc. — constitute internal metabolics; electric generators which they actuate, the highways, air lanes, pipelines, electric lines, etc., are mankinds' external metabolics. World Game strategic experience has shown that by dealing with mankind's external metabolics, individual man's internal metabolics are automatically serviced. (from "Dymaxion World of Buckminster Fuller," by Robert W. Marks, and "Buckminster Fuller," by John McHale, in *World Game/ 1971/Document 1*, p. 104) The scenario utilized hydroelectric power for other considerations than what is presented above; besides the efficiency and pollution problems of thermal plants, it became overwhelmingly apparent that our "savings account" of fossil and nuclear fuels would soon be depleted at the bare maximum level of consumption. Our constantly-replenished "income" energies were the obvious choice. The amounts of metals, principally copper, aluminum and steel, that would be needed for such an undertaking are within grasp of earth's present economic and industrial development . . . (How can we accelerate efficiency throughout the world?) We chose to keep efficiency levels and technological competence at present levels to show we could do this today, with what we have. (Edwin Schlossberg and Medard Gable, quoted in *World Game/1971/Document 1*, p. 45) Uncertainty of future. Noises (underdog); changing music and society. Not working = knowing. Working = not knowing. Distrust of effectiveness of education. HCE It is, is cause for joy. Earth has no escape from Heaven (Eckhart). Mobility, immobility. (Cage, Introduction to *Themes and Variations*) Israeli authorities crippled production to take back full responsibility for the Palestinian question, to make room for other books. "We don't want Jakarta to rule in South Africa now that the Gulf war is ending." The United Nations cease-fire is just the first step. (from the *Christian Science Monitor*, Aug. 19, '88) Protestant leaders in Northern Ireland demanded at least 400 people, ten coal mines in the southern region of Silesia and tribute to a possible British government. Ethnic clashes in northern BURUNDI will disrupt election plans to boost consumer goods production by forty billion dollars that killed eight British soldiers Friday. (from the *Wall Street Journal*, Aug. 23, '88) War is never anything less than accelerated technological change. (McLuhan, cited in *Marshall McLuhan: Media in America*, p. 101) Things are going very well, the Portuguese news agency said, West German officials today identified a former US Army sergeant as the key figure in the fire which began in a 19th-century department store before dawn today. The two sides had discussed peace but ruled out power-sharing. Without Zia, there is no hope for us. (from *The New York Times*, Aug. 26, '88)

Devotion

A month spent failing to find a new music for piano having characteristics that would interest Grete Sultan. Finally left my desk, went to visit her. She is not as I am, just concerned with new music. She loves the past. The room she lives, works, and teaches in has two pianos. She surrounds herself with Mozart, Beethoven, Bach — all of the best of the past — but like Buhlig, who first played Schoenberg's Opus eleven and also arranged *The Art of the Fugue* for two pianos, she loves new music, seeing no real difference between some of it and the classics she's so devoted to. Then I noticed her hands, conceived a duet for two hands, each alone, then catalogued all of the intervals, triads, and aggregates a single hand can play, unassisted by the other. Soon finished the first of thirty-two etudes, each having two pages. Showed it to Grete. She was delighted. That was eight years ago. The first performance of all thirty-two is part of these Witten concerts. (John Cage, in *John Cage: Composition in Retrospect*, 1982) She surrounds the art of the fugue for two pianos each having that would showed it to grete she was delighted who first played soon. (John Cage, in *John Cage: Composition in Retrospect*, 1982) But isn't understanding shewn e.g. in the expression with which someone reads the poem, sings the tune? Certainly. But what is the experience during the reading? About that you would just have to say: you enjoy and understand it if you hear it well read, or feel it well read in your speech-organs. (Wittgenstein, *Zettel*, p. 30) It is no contradiction of this for those extensions to be the most important application of the rule; for it is one thing to draw an ellipse, and another to construct it by means of its equation. (Wittgenstein, *Remarks on the Foundations of Mathematics*, p. 293) It can be said that, while we are not certain of being able to turn all situations into pictures on paper, still we are certain that we can portray all logical properties of situations in a two-dimensional script. This is still very much on the surface, but we are on good ground. (Wittgenstein, *Notebooks*, p. 7) When you bump against the limits of your own honesty it is as though your thoughts get into a whirlpool, an infinite regress: You can say what you like, it takes you no further. (Wittgenstein, *Culture and Value*, p. 8) The construction of the induction is not a proof, but a certain arrangement of proofs (a pattern in the sense of an ornament). And one can't exactly say either: if I prove three equations, then I prove one. Just as the movements of a suite don't amount to a single movement. (Wittgenstein, *Philosophical Grammar*, p. 399) In philosophy it's always a matter of the application of a series of utterly simple basic principles that any child knows, and the — enormous — difficulty is only one of applying these in the confusion our language creates. It's never a question of the latest results of experiments with exotic fish or the most recent developments in mathematics. But the difficulty in applying the simple basic principles shakes our confidence in the principles themselves. (Wittgenstein, *Philosophical Remarks*, p. 154) The transcending expanding power which resides in the middle space does not die. It is always the same and acts the same way without ceasing nor diminishing. . . . it expends itself in streams, but remains ever the same. (Lao Tzu, quoted by L.C. Beckett, in *Neti Neti*, p. 27) In fact, it is only today that the decree *nisi* has been handed down by the speed-reading institutes to divorce eye and speech in the act of reading. (McLuhan, *Gutenberg Galaxy*, p. 82) The nineteenth-century translator's paraphrase reduces the multisensuous world of Dante to a single plane of continuous narrative. (McLuhan, *Through the Vanishing Point*, p. 71) Nobody yet knows the language inherent in the new technological culture; we are all deaf-blind mutes in terms of the new situation. Our most impressive words and thoughts betray us by referring to the previously existent, not to the present. We are back in acoustic space. (McLuhan, *Verbi-Voco-Visual Explorations*, p. 39) When the new electric technology ensured a maximum of merging of person in person and society in society, sanity called for a major counter-stress of non-involvement and detached but deep understanding. For the Nazi death camps are as much a part of electric involvement as the Peace Corps and the Beatles. Tribalism of the post-literate mode is no less intense than the pre-literate kind. (McLuhan, "Art As Anti-Environment," pp. 2–3) No information has been made public about a strike tonight at the big Lenin shipyard in the Persian Gulf. Now they have people wondering where they will strike next to defuse a wave of cease-fire violations of the Soviet-led invasion on Saturday night. (from *The New York Times*, Aug. 22, '88) Food inflation forecasts were criticized over how much Washington will pay to buy a 20% stake in the Palestinian uprising. The dollar's rally continued aided by 17 counts of misconduct. (from the *Wall Street Journal*, July 27, '88) He perfected smuggling methods and intricate laundering operations where more than three hundred people have died in telephone interviews that factories, stores and public transportation had begun it burns itself into memory. Over the years against that backdrop people brought from Nepal, two of them badly burned. (from *The New York Times*, July 26, '88) Jordan announced today virtually all its employees no longer fear a severe famine. The decision is in accordance with others in the West Bank who are paid in part by Jews in Moscow bidding for military contracts. "We will not succumb to any pressure from any direction," he said before leaving. "We tell them nothing because the guerillas are a part of us." (from *The New York Times*, Aug. 5) A Government campaign would provide the Nicaraguan rebels with vacation days and stagger a Rumanian citizen. Washington to use South Africa, Angola and Cuba to aid Senate Democratic leaders. (from *The New York Times*, Aug. 6, '88) Near the end of March, 1845, I borrowed an axe and went down to the woods by Walden Pond, nearest to where I intended to build my house, and began to cut down some tall, arrowy white pines, still in their youth, for timber. It is difficult to begin without borrowing, but perhaps it is the most generous course thus to permit your fellow-men to have an interest in your enterprise. (Thoreau, *Walden*, p. 32) I have never felt lonesome, or in the least oppressed by a sense of solitude, but once, and that was a few weeks after I came to the woods, when, for an hour, I doubted if the near neighborhood of man was not essential to a serene and healthy life. To be alone was something unpleasant. But I was at the same time conscious of a slight insanity in my mood, and seemed to foresee my recovery. In the midst of a gentle rain while these thoughts prevailed, I was suddenly sensible of such sweet and beneficent society in Nature, in the very pattering of the drops, and in every sound and sight around my house, an infinite and unaccountable friendliness all at once like an atmosphere sustaining me, as made the fancied advantages of human neighborhood insignificant, and I have never thought of them since. Every little pine needle expanded and swelled with sympathy and befriended me. I was so distinctly made aware of the presence of something kindred to me, even in scenes which we are accustomed to call wild and dreary, and also that the nearest of blood to me and humanest was not a person nor a villager, that I thought no place could ever be strange to me again. (Thoreau, *Walden*, pp. 92–93) O the evening robin, at the end of a New England summer day! If I could ever find the twig he sits upon! I mean he; I mean the twig. (Thoreau, *Walden*, p. 207) Only what is thought, said, or done at a certain rare coincidence is good. I would not be one of those who will foolishly drive a nail into mere lath and plastering; such a deed would keep me awake nights. Give me a hammer, and let me feel for the furring. Do not depend on the putty. Drive a nail home and clinch it so faithfully that you can wake up in the night and think of your work with satisfaction, — a work at which you would not be ashamed to invoke the Muse. . . . Every nail driven should be as another rivet in the machine of the universe, you carrying on the work. (Thoreau, *Walden*, p. 219) Solve a critical problem facing humanity, that if left unattended, could cause harm to human beings or to our vital support; provide an abundance of life support for humanity, where now there is scarcity. (from "The World Game," World Game Projects, Inc., 1987) Synergy is the behavior of whole systems unpredicted by any of its parts, e.g. mass attraction of inert matter masses — i.e., gravity, in which there is no characteristic of one of the massive bodies by itself which could predict that it will be attracted by or attract another body. The Earth, considered only by itself, could not predict that it will attract the moon or be attracted by the moon. Only the behavior manifest by any two such astronomical bodies can reveal the attraction. This is synergy. It is a corollary of synergy that the known behavior of the whole system and the known behavior of some of its parts makes possible discovery or true prediction of the behavior of the remainder of its parts. World Game strategies utilize synergetic General Systems Theory to enable them to be as comprehensive and correct as is presently possible. (from "Dymaxion World of Buckminster Fuller," by Robert W. Marks, and "Buckminster Fuller," by John McHale, in *World Game/1971/Document 1*, p. 102) All World Game inventories, trends and related data can be geographically displayed upon the Dymaxion Sky-Ocean Map without any visible distortion of the shapes, sizes, or true proportionality of the data and its true significance. (from "Dymaxion World of Buckminster Fuller," by Robert W. Marks, and "Buckminster Fuller," by John McHale, in *World Game/1971/Document 1*, p. 105) After demonstrating man's potential competence for bringing the world average per capita kwh up to 3613 with no one below the present European level of 2000 kwh, stage two of the energy scenario began. Utilizing increased efficiencies, technological process such as laser-beam power transmission, and some of the earth's varied income energy sources (. . . wind power, tidal power), the per capita level of kwh is brought up to the 15,000 bare maximum in the year 2000. (Edwin Schlossberg and Medard Gable, quoted in *World Game/1971/Document 1*, p. 45) Highest purpose = nopurpose. Vision = no vision. (In accord with nature.) We are the oldest at having our airway of knowing nowness (Gertrude Stein). Fluency in and out. No split between spirit and matter. Importance of being perplexed. Unpredictability. Not being interrupted by shadows (by environment). Theatre is closer to life than art or music. Devotion. (Cage, Introduction to *Themes and Variations*) In late September or early October thousands of state-sponsored terrorist acts call for new elections. A South Korean official with no indication on new talks expected 400 safety features involved in the responsibility. The North and South lead the opposition. (from the *Wall Street Journal*, Aug. 23, '88) Today each of us lives several hundred years in a decade. How can people like us have something in common with their institutions? (McLuhan, cited in *Marshall McLuhan: Media in America*, p. 146) Is he drifting? No, he is resonating. He's living in this new, non-visual world of role playing. He has no goals, he's already there. It's just a question of enriching where he is, and where it's at, rather than wandering. And this is the new confusion. (Louis Forsdale and McLuhan in conversation, cited in *Marshall McLuhan: Media in America*, p. 31)

Circumstances

Act in accord with obstacles, using them to find or define the process you're about to be involved in, the questions you'll ask. If you don't have enough time to accomplish what you have in mind, consider the work finished once it is begun. It then resembles the Venus de Milo, which manages so well without an arm. (John Cage, in *John Cage: Composition in Retrospect*, 1982) Divide the work to be done into parts and the time available into an equal number. Then you can proceed, giving equal attention to each of the parts or you could say "Study being interrupted." Take telephone calls as unexpected pleasures. Free the mind from its desire to concentrate, remaining open to what you can't predict. "I welcome whatever happens next." (John Cage, in *John Cage: Composition in Retrospect*, 1982) If you're writing a piece for orchestra, and you know that the copying costs are such and such, take the amount of money you've been promised and divide it to determine the number of pages of your next composition. This will give you the canvas upon which you're about to write. However, acceptance of whatever must be complemented by the refusal of everything that's intolerable. Revolution can never stop. Even though each morning we awake with energy (nichi nichi kore ko nichi) and as individuals can solve any problem that confronts us, we must do the impossible — rid the world of nations, bringing the play of intelligent anarchy into a world environment that works so well everyone lives as he needs. (John Cage, in *John Cage: Composition in Retrospect*, 1982) Upon which it is begun however acceptance of whatever must can solve any problem to find or define the process of everything available intolerable composition proceed giving equal attention "i welcome whatever happens next." (John Cage, in *John Cage: Composition in Retrospect*, 1982) On the other hand we should under certain circumstances be ready to substitute "B knows the formula", "B has said the formula" for "B can continue the series". As when we ask a doctor "Can the patient walk?", we shall sometimes be ready to substitute for this "Is his leg healed?" — "Can he speak?" under circumstances means "Is his throat all right?", under others (e.g., if he is a small child) it means "Has he learned to speak?" — To the question "Can the patient walk?", the doctor's answer may be "His leg is all right". — We use the phrase "He can walk, as far as the state of his leg is concerned", especially when we wish to oppose this condition for his walking to some other condition, say the state of his spine. Here we must beware of thinking that there is in the nature of the case something which we might call the complete set of conditions, e.g., for his walking; so that the patient, as it were, can't help walking, must walk, if all these conditions are fulfilled. (Wittgenstein, *Blue & Brown Books*, p. 114) I describe a psychological experiment: the apparatus, the questions of the experimenter, the actions and replies of the subject — and then I say that it is a scene in a play. Now everything is different. (Wittgenstein, *Philosophical Investigations*, p. 180) "What the names in language signify must be indestructible; for it must be possible to describe the state of affairs in which everything destructible is destroyed. And this description will contain words; and what corresponds to these cannot then be destroyed, for otherwise the words would have no meaning." I must not saw off the branch on which I am sitting. One might, of course, object at once that this description would have to except itself from the destruction. —But what corresponds to the separate words of the description and so cannot be destroyed if it is true, is what gives the words their meaning — is that without which they would have no meaning. —In a sense, however, this man is surely what corresponds to his name. But he is destructible, and his name does not lose its meaning when the bearer is destroyed. —An example of something corresponding to the name, and without which it would have no meaning, is a paradigm that is used in connexion with the name in the language-game. (Wittgenstein, *Philosophical Investigations*, p. 27) "What I perceive is this—" and now follows a form of description. The word "this" might also be explained as follows: Let us imagine a direct transfer of experience. —But now what is our criterion for the experience's really having been transferred? "Well, he just does have what I have." —But how does he 'have' it? (Wittgenstein, *Zettel*, p. 76) The limits of my language mean the limits of my world. Logic fills the world: the limits of the world are also its limits. We cannot therefore say in logic: This and this there is in the world, that there is not. (Wittgenstein, *Tractatus*, p. 149) When you are philosophizing you have to descend into primeval chaos and feel at home there. (Wittgenstein, *Culture and Value*, p. 65) One does actually often simply pronounce someone's name; perhaps in a sigh. And now someone else asks "Whom did you mean?" And how will our meaning-blind man act? Will he not sigh like that; or not be able to answer anything to the question; or answer "I mean . . ." instead of "I meant . . ."? (Wittgenstein, *Remarks on the Philosophy of Psychology*, Vol. I, p. 38) . . . in space there are no directions and no boundaries . . . Without things occupying it, it is nothing. (Lincoln Barnett, quoted by L.C. Beckett, in *Neti Neti*, p. 32) But the early spectators of the moving image in the sixteenth century saw those images upside down. For this reason the lens was introduced — in order to turn the picture right side up. (McLuhan, *Understanding Media*, p. 191) . . . here when I left — I knew him when I was here. . ." (McLuhan, *Letters*, p. 126) What makes us so confident? (an advertisement for The International Silver Company, cited in McLuhan, *Through the Vanishing Point*, p. 168) Whatever he read in a venerable old book he would take to be not somebody's assertion but a small piece of knowledge acquired by someone long ago from someone else still more ancient. (E.P. Goldschmidt, *Medieval Texts and Their First Appearance in Print*, cited in McLuhan, *The Gutenberg Galaxy*, p. 134) . . .'he was teaching them as one having power.' (Matthew vii/29, as cited in McLuhan, *The Gutenberg Galaxy*, p. 98) The steepest decline in

Government and hostilities still unaccounted for in southern Ireland was the Soviet Union. Unemployment has halted. Bad faith with discrimination humiliated Cuba. Compensation to the families who were killed have consistently experienced more, was permeated, were killed, reported "repeated utilization of such weapons." (from *The New York Times*, Aug. 4, '88) Flash flooding along China's eastern coast has killed thousands of Cuban troops now in Angola. Fourteen people were stunned by the King's move and uncertain of what to do next. Hot winds accompanying the drought have stripped the stress of battle outside the Communist Party. The Polish leader perceived threat fast approaching. (from *The New York Times*, Aug. 3, '88) Yesterday a previously unannounced meeting in the midst of combat was in response to recent peace talks to shoot down the plane. About ten thousand people arrived in Afghanistan to determine how he participated in a six-figure payroll padding scheme getting priority. (from the *Christian Science Monitor*, Aug. 5, '88) Tens of thousands of plans to begin war in Bangkok were needed to determine a date for Cuba's pullout. The government in Mandalay killed two men in a Roman Catholic district on the outskirts of La Paz. Responsibility wasn't claimed but authorities blamed the South-West African People's Organization. (from the *Wall Street Journal*, Aug. 9, '88) They were pleasant spring days, in which the winter of man's discontent was thawing as well as the earth, and the life that had lain torpid began to stretch itself. One day, when my axe had come off and I had cut a green hickory for a wedge, driving it with a stone, and had placed the whole to soak in a pond-hole in order to swell the wood, I saw a striped snake run into the water, and he lay on the bottom, apparently without inconvenience, as long as I stayed there, or more than a quarter of an hour; perhaps because he had not yet fairly come out of the torpid state. (Thoreau, *Walden*, pp. 32–33) With thinking we may be beside ourselves in a sane sense. By a conscious effort of the mind we can stand aloof from actions and their consequences; and all things, good and bad, go by us like a torrent. We are not wholly involved in Nature. I may be either the driftwood in the stream, or Indra in the sky looking down on it. I may be affected by a theatrical exhibition; on the other hand, I may not be affected by an actual event which appears to concern me more. I only know myself as a human entity; the scene, so to speak, of thoughts and affections; and am sensible of a certain doubleness by which I can stand as remote from myself as from another. (Thoreau, *Walden*, p. 94) We can never have enough of nature. We must be refreshed by the sight of inexhaustible vigor, vast and titanic features, the sea-coast with its wrecks, the wilderness with its living and its decaying trees, the thundercloud, and the rain which lasts three weeks and produces freshets. We need to witness our own limits transgressed, and some life pasturing freely where we never wander. (Thoreau, *Walden*, p. 211) Do more with less; that is,

design life-support systems that perform more functions with less inputs of materials, energy and time. (from "The World Game," World Game Projects, Inc., 1987) All World Game strategies deal with ways of doing more with less for the entire planet in such a manner as to effect the total success of total humanity in the quickest and most eternal way possible. The comprehensive, recirculation of all chemical constituents of resources involved results in a more with less resource utilization. For example, each time copper is scrapped, melted down, and re-cycled, it is re-employed at a higher rate of efficiency. The first copper telephone wires carried one message per wire, subsequent more with lessing improvements carried 2, then 4, 16, 250, then in the thousands, and now with the satellites, it's gone wireless. From millions of tons of copper to next to no tons of copper. From visible to invisible. (from "Dymaxion World of Buckminster Fuller," by Robert W. Marks, and "Buckminster Fuller," by John McHale, in *World Game/1971/Document 1*, p. 102) The World Game is a scientific means for exploring expeditious ways of employing the World's resources so efficiently and omni-considerately as to be able to provide a higher standard of living for all of humanity — higher than has heretofore been experienced by any humans — and on a continually sustainable basis for all generations to come, while enabling all of humanity to enjoy the whole planet Earth without any individual profiting at the expense of another and without interference with one another, while also rediverting the valuable chemistries known as pollution to effective uses elsewhere, conserving the wild resources and antiquities. The World Game discards the Malthusian Doctrine which is the present working assumption of the major states. Malthus held that humanity is multiplying much more rapidly than it can supply resources to support itself, and compounds with Darwin's survival of the fittest, to assume that only the side with the greatest arms can survive. The World Game demonstrates that the Malthusian doctrine is fallacious. If we apply to direct human support all the high technology resources now going into the world's annual 200 billion dollar war preparation, all of humanity can be brought to economic success within one quarter century. This eliminates the fundamental raison d'être of war. The World Game employs design science to produce progressively higher performance per units of invested time, energy, and know-how per each and every component function of the world's resources. The World Game makes it possible for intelligent amateurs to discover within a few weeks of simulated design revolution illustrated on the World Map that the foregoing premises are valid. (Fuller, quoted in *World Game/1971/Document 1*, p. 89) The objective of the World Game is to work out ways of how to make humanity a continuing success at the earliest possible moment — in other words, how to make the world work. (from *World Game/1971/Document 1*, p. 41) Furnishing an area with enough electric power for its industrialization brings to that area the potential to satisfy its bare maximum food requirements. Knowing from the energy scenario that we could count on using two per cent of the total electric power for agricultural uses, we then looked at ways to increase the per capita calorie and protein levels to the bare maximum. . . . A startling fact which became obvious upon looking at food production was that the world produces more than enough to feed its people adequately, but that in transport, storage and processing, 90 per cent of the tonnage of food is lost (how do we identify waste?). If we could bring methods to increase worldwide efficiency, at the rate we increased food production in the past, the world could feed its population for some time to come. (Edwin Schlossberg and Medard Gable, quoted in *World Game/ 1971/Document 1*, p. 45) Enlightened = not enlightened. Learning = learning we're not learning. Breaking rules. No use for value judgments. We are all going in different directions. Importance of no rules. Going to extremes (Yuji Takahashi). Absence of boredom. Anarchy. (John Cage, Introduction to *Themes and Variations*) Agitation halts work and could determine whether the country will proceed and public transport. There are signs that Hanoi on how it may impose martial law at any time and other former leaders be removed. The workers are demanding the restoration of paralyzed port operations and temporary asylum but to return to Vietnam. (from the *Christian Science Monitor*, Aug. 19, '88) Paradox is the technique for seizing the conflicting aspects of any problem. Paradox coalesces or telescopes various facets of a complex process in a single instant. (McLuhan, cited in *Marshall McLuhan: Media in America*, p. 146) We hope that the Government as well as the rebels will bite the bullet, an American diplomat said in his opening address to the conference this afternoon. Officials said there is also a sense of caution as fears of possible anarchy take hold. 29 people were being treated for burns a few minutes after the meeting began. (from *The New York Times*, Aug. 26, '88)

Variable Structure

For some time now, I have been using time-brackets. Sometimes they are fixed and sometimes not. By fixed, I mean they begin and end at particular points in time. When there are not points but spaces of time for both beginnings and endings, the situation is much more flexible. These time-brackets are used in parts, parts for which there is no score, no fixed relationship. (John Cage, April, 1988) It was part, I thought, of a movement in composition away from structure into process. Away from an object having parts, into what you might call weather. Now I see that the time-brackets took us back from weather (which had been reached) to object. They made an earthquake-proof music, so to speak, music the

parts of which can move with respect to each other. It is not entirely structural, but it is at the same time not entirely free of parts. Different composing means are used: A, B, and C. A is a non-repetitive passage within a given range. B is nothing but a single tone, silence around it, repeated any number of times. C is the prescribed use of five tones, a gamut, which either remains (is immobile) or is mobile (changes — *Music for*). If, instead of A, B, and C, there's only A, weather is what happens — process undivided happens — changing in its way without clearly separated parts. (John Cage, April, 1988) What do you have to say about rhythm? Let us agree it is no longer a question of patterns. But patterns could arise and disappear. No need for such agreement. Rhythm is coexistence of durations of any length, durations in succession, and synchronicity. Succession is liveliest when, as in Feldman's work, it is not fixed, but, within a given period of time in situation form, it is presented, entrances being at any point in time at all. (This is this moment quoted from *Silence*.) Synchronicity is liveliest, most unpredictably changing, when the parts are unfixed by a score — no two performances yielding the same resultant durations. (That was thirty-three years ago.) (John Cage, April, 1988) Music the parts of which can move with respect to time-brackets form it is presented away but it is at the same time not entirely weather and disappear but spaces of time most unpredictably changing coexistence of durations of any length by a score no two performances B is nothing but a single tone in parts it is not fixed (John Cage, April, 1988) Here ordinary language resorts to the words 'seems' or 'appears'. It says a_1 seems to be equal to a_2, whereas this appearance has ceased to exist in the case of a_1 and a_5. But it uses the word 'seems' ambiguously. For its meaning depends on what is opposed to this appearance as reality. In one case it is the result of measurement, in another a further appearance. And so the meaning of the word 'seem' is different in these two cases. (Wittgenstein, *Philosophical Remarks*, p. 270) A smooth white surface can reflect things: But what, then, if we made a mistake and that which appeared to be reflected in such a surface were really behind it and seen through it? Would the surface then be white and transparent? (Wittgenstein, *Remarks on Colour*, p. 8) All that we see could also be otherwise. All that we can describe at all could also be otherwise. (Wittgenstein, *Notebooks*, p. 80) "How does it come about that I see the tree standing up straight even if I incline my head to one side, and so the retinal image is that of an obliquely standing tree?" Well, how does it come about that I speak of the tree as standing up straight even in these circumstances? "Well, I am conscious of the inclination of my head and so I supply the requisite correction in the way I take my visual impression." —But doesn't that mean confusing what is primary and what is secondary? Imagine that we know nothing at all of the inner structure of the eye — would this problem altogether disappear? We do not supply any correction here — that explanation is gratuitous. Well — but now that the structure of the eye is known — how does it come about that we act, react, in this way? But must there be a physiological explanation here? Why don't we just leave explaining alone? — But you would never talk like that, if you were examining the behavior of a machine! —Well, who says that a living creature, an animal body, is a machine in this sense? (I have never yet read a comment on the fact that when one shuts one eye and "only sees with one eye" one does not simultaneously see darkness (blackness) with the one that is shut.) (Wittgenstein, *Zettel*, pp. 107–108) Look at yourself when you are writing, and notice how your hand forms the letters without your actually causing it to do so. To be sure, you feel something in your hand, all sorts of tensions and pressures, but that they are necessary to produce these letters is something which you know nothing about. (Wittgenstein, *Remarks on the Philosophy of Psychology*, Vol. II, p. 10) The phenomenon is similar to that of weighing in a balance. (Wittgenstein, *Lectures and Conversations*, p. 32) . . . a mind that is burdened with knowledge cannot possibly understand that which is real, which is not measurable . . . (Krishnamurti, quoted by L.C. Beckett, in *Neti Neti*, p. 35) . . . "inner direction" depends upon a "fixed point of view." A stable, consistent character is one with an unwavering outlook, an almost hypnotized visual stance, as it were. (McLuhan, *Gutenberg Galaxy*, p. 28) Rite words in rote order. (McLuhan, *The Medium is the Massage*, p. 58) The dropout represents a rejection of nineteenth-century technology as manifested in our educational establishments. The teach-in represents a creative effort, switching the educational process from package to discovery. As the audience becomes a participant in the total electric drama, the classroom can become a scene in which the audience performs an enormous amount of work. (McLuhan, *The Medium is the Massage*, p. 101) The manual was necessary to the student, not only so far as it served for his university courses, but also because it would be useful in his future career. . . . Moreover the university required that students present themselves at their courses furnished with books they had made, and if not that at least there be a book shared among every three students. (Istuan Hajnal, *L'Enseignement de l'écriture aux universités médiévales*, cited in McLuhan, *The Gutenberg Galaxy*, p. 96) What was an avant-garde program for the 1920 expatriates is now the teenagers' norm. (McLuhan, *Understanding Media*, p. 120) The movement toward a new pact with South Korea appears to demonstrate tension in Illinois. Late last week, Greek authorities in a response to a letter sent on Monday doubt that the decision makes it 98 percent sure this was a more moderate and realistic course. (from the *Christian Science Monitor*, July 22, '88) Infected with the AIDS virus, forty to fifty thousand troops in Baghdad helped lead the fight for the occupied territories. Previously only arrests came next week. The division will push

ahead with alarming speed for a prison of limits and revolutionary. (from the *Christian Science Monitor*, Aug. 3, '88) And droughts of wheat are to the steepest decline for ending hostilities in Northern Ireland, hostility by Washington. Compensation to the families after he flew after United Nations investigators were killed in the stock piles ever recorded. (from *The New York Times*, Aug. 4, '88) In Argentina the dollar went into effect dominated by tax-free payments to thousands of consumer goods his country will no longer help. The US official argued against a Secretary of State. Payments will begin in about a year in Hanoi and Washington with Pakistan's foreign minister, saying they would not improve. (from the *Christian Science Monitor*, Aug. 5, '88) Sensitive information is at the heart of the fraud and bribery investigation. Both black and white Palestinian representatives in Beirut, however, said the hospital also treats wounded Angolan rebels, saying the earthquake churned up heavy waves. What is happening was terribly overcrowded and there are slim chances of survival. (from *The New York Times*, Aug. 8, '88) A gun battle broke out Friday night where more than three million Afghan refugees live. But the police went on the offensive arresting a spokesman for the United States Embassy. Moscow denies the charge. Everybody is still waiting because of rising evidence and beating many of them as they dragged them away. (from *The New York Times*, Aug. 16, '88) There is some of the same fitness in a man's building his own house that there is in a bird's building its own nest. Who knows but if men constructed their dwellings with their own hands, and provided food for themselves and families simply and honestly enough, the poetic faculty would be universally developed, as birds universally sing when they are so engaged? (Thoreau, *Walden*, p. 36) In my house we were so near that we could not begin to hear, — we could not speak low enough to be heard; as when you throw two stones into calm water so near that they break each other's undulations. If we are merely loquacious and loud talkers, then we can afford to stand very near together, cheek by jowl, and feel each other's breath; but if we speak reservedly and thoughtfully, we want to be farther apart, that all animal heat and moisture may have a chance to evaporate. If we would enjoy the most intimate society with that in each of us which is without, or above, being spoken to, we must not only be silent, but commonly so far apart bodily that we cannot possibly hear each other's voice in any case. (Thoreau, *Walden*, p. 98) I love to see that Nature is so rife with life that myriads can be afforded to be sacrificed and suffered to prey on one another; that tender organizations can be so serenely squashed out of existence like pulp, — tadpoles which herons gobble up, and tortoises and toads run over in the road; and that sometimes it has rained flesh and blood! With the liability to accident, we must see how little account is to be made of it. The impression made on a wise man is that of universal innocence. Poison is not poisonous after all, nor

443

are any wounds fatal. Compassion is a very untenable ground. It must be expeditious. Its pleadings will not bear to be stereotyped. (Thoreau, *Walden*, p. 211) Respect and protect the living systems which make up the gameboard. The Earth is the gameboard. (from "The World Game," [augmented by Cage], World Game Projects, Inc., 1987) GAME THEORY provides a method for the mathematical exploration and study of decision-making in challenging situations. (from "Dymaxion World of Buckminster Fuller," by Robert W. Marks, and "Buckminster Fuller," by John McHale, in *World Game/1971/Document 1*, p. 103) The students, individually and in teams, were out to solve practical world problems, one of which was how to feed the entire world at what the students called a "bare maximum." (from *World Game/1971/Document 1*, p. 41) Shipping food halfway around the globe is inefficient. For example, in 1967, Asia imported and exported the same amount of rice. Ships could be used to transport materials not native to a particular area or the metal from the ships could be used more profitably elsewhere. Part of the electrical power set aside for agriculture could be used to increase efficiencies in short transport to some areas with low farming efficiency. The increased use of fertilizers and farm equipment, in addition to the increase in knowledge of farming brought about by higher communications capabilities, would help bring the needed increase in efficiency necessary to have the entire population at bare maximum in ten years. (Edwin Schlossberg and Medard Gable, quoted in *World Game/1971/Document 1*, p. 45) Meaninglessness as ultimate meaning. Mind can change. To do more rather than less. To sober and quiet the mind thus making it susceptible to divine influences. The means of thinking are exterior to the mind. Art is criminal action. Love = leaving space around loved one. (Cage, Introduction to *Themes and Variations*) The ecumenical movement is synonymous with electric technology. (McLuhan, cited in *Marshall McLuhan: Media in America*, p. 146)

Nonunderstanding

People often ask what music I prefer to hear. I enjoy the absence of music more than any other, or you could say silence. I enjoy whatever ambient sounds there are to hear. What I like is that they aren't saying anything. They just do what it is they are. I listen, no matter in what else I happen to be engaged. Experience. Not knowing what will happen next. (John Cage, April, 1988) I am, of course, a percussion composer. What I wanted to do was to find a way not to know what the beat was even though what I'd write would be measured. Make the measure long (twelve to fifteen beats), only five of which were to be heard. Slow the tempo down to sixty. You can't, in metrical terms (*Ryoanji*), understand what you're hearing any

more than you can when you listen to ambient sound, traffic for instance. I decided to go further in this direction (*Etc, 2/4 Orchs*). Keeping 5 icti, I doubled the number of beats per measure (27–36), at the same time reducing the tempi to such slow speeds that they became chronometric — something for which you couldn't have a feeling except through the ear. (John Cage, April, 1988) We are in the world of Duchamp: sounds lasting, leaving from different points in space, musical sculpture. *Collection of rocks*. When will the sound change? There is no way ever to know. Surrounded by mystery, reality. What is clear'n'concise, Joyce said, can't deal with reality. We are in the dark. We are losing our minds getting Mind. It is as though sounds occur of their own accord. We are no longer supervising. To what lengths do I go? There is no stopping or going. O moon, why are you so willow tree? Many sounds? We can never know, if so the end. A book of instructions, what to do, to take it apart and put it back up again. *Nohopera*. (John Cage, April, 1988) Any it is as though than no music more than any other what i wanted to do was to find a way traffic for instance what i'd write ambient sounds made the what long twelve to fifteen beats joyce said chronometric and put it back up we are losing. (John Cage, April, 1988) Understanding the rule and how to carry it out in practice always only helps us over finite stretches. To determine a real number it must be completely intelligible in itself. That is to say, it must not be essentially undecided whether a part of it could be dispensed with. For in that case it simply isn't clearly given, for there is no extension which would be equivalent to it, and in itself it is indeterminate. Pi' in that case sets out to seek its fortune in infinite space. (Wittgenstein, *Philosophical Remarks*, p. 230) We don't talk about hypothesis, or about high probability. Nor about knowing. What is the criterion of reliability, dependability? Suppose you give a general description as to when you say a proposition has a reasonable weight of probability. When you call it reasonable, is this only to say that for it you have such and such evidence, and for others you haven't? (Wittgenstein, *Lectures and Conversations*, p. 57) Now do I, in the course of my life, make sure I know that here is a hand — my own hand, that is? I know that a sick man is lying here? Nonsense! I am sitting at his bedside, I am looking attentively into his face. — So I don't know, then, that there is a sick man lying here? Neither the question nor the assertion makes sense. Any more than the assertion "I am here", which I might yet use at any moment, if suitable occasion presented itself. — Then is "2 × 2 = 4" nonsense in the same way, and not a proposition of arithmetic, apart from particular occasions? "2 × 2 = 4" is a true proposition of arithmetic — not "on particular occasions" nor "always" — but the spoken or written sentence "2 × 2 = 4" in Chinese might have a different meaning or be out and out nonsense, and from this is seen that it is only in use that the proposition has its sense. And "I know that there's a sick man lying here", used in an unsuitable situation, seems not to be nonsense but rather seems matter-of-course, only because one can fairly easily imagine a situation to fit it, and one thinks that the words "I know that . . ." are always in place where there is no doubt, and hence even where the expression of doubt would be unintelligible. (Wittgenstein, *On Certainty*, p. 3) If "I know etc." is conceived as a grammatical proposition, of course the "I" cannot be important. And it properly means "There is no such thing as a doubt in this case" or "The expression 'I do not know' makes no sense in this case". And of course it follows from this that "I know" makes no sense either. (Wittgenstein, *On Certainty*, p. 10) And in fact it is the grammar of the word time which puzzles us. We are only expressing this puzzlement by asking a slightly misleading question, the question: "What is . . .?" This question is an utterance of unclarity, of mental discomfort, and it is comparable with the question "Why?" as children so often ask it. This too is an expression of a mental discomfort, and doesn't necessarily ask for either a cause or a reason. (Wittgenstein, *Blue & Brown Books*, p. 26) "Why do you demand explanations? If they are given you, you will once more be facing a terminus. They cannot get you any further than you are at present." (Wittgenstein, *Zettel*, p. 58) Why can't a cat be taught to retrieve? Doesn't it understand what one wants? And what constitutes understanding or failure to understand here? (Wittgenstein, *Zettel*, p. 33) While I am looking at an object I cannot imagine it. (Wittgenstein, *Zettel*, p. 109) For here (when I consider colours, for example) there is merely an inability to bring the concepts into some kind of order. We stand there like the ox in front of the newly-painted stall door. (Wittgenstein, *Remarks on Colour*, p. 16) And if I were now to say to him: "I have spent the whole day in fear (here details might be added) and now too I am full of anxiety" — what are we to say about this mixture of report and statement? Well what should we say other than that here we have the use of the word "fear" in front of us? (Wittgenstein, *Remarks on the Philosophy of Psychology*, Vol. II, pp. 30–31) The softest thing on earth outweighs the hardest thing on earth. The non-existent penetrates even there where there is no interstice. (Lao-tzu, quoted by L.C. Beckett, in *Neti Neti*, p. 24) . . . the ground, or usage, changes our experience of anything that is a figure in that situation. (McLuhan, *City as Classroom*, p. 13) . . . and it was this immediate application of everything to life in Italian Renaissance society (like the substitution of a cinema for a history-book in a school) that made the Italian influence so vivid in the rest of Europe. (Wyndham Lewis, *The Lion and the Fox*, as cited in McLuhan, *The Gutenberg Galaxy*, p. 119) . . . poised at the point of transformation . . . (McLuhan, *Understanding Media*, p. 154) The movie form now begins to acquire the non-narrative structure of a Symbolist poem of a century before. (McLuhan, "Art As Anti-Environment," p. 3) It was as if the Greeks felt

that the penalty for one break-through was a general sealing-off of awareness to the total field. (McLuhan, *Understanding Media*, p. 39) The only way we are going to stop the cutbacks would not apply in Rangoon. Some foreign diplomats opened fire on youths in the Arab world and that amounts to a total obsession. What is to be done? (from *The New York Times*, July 23, '88) The assassinated priest was one of the four Cambodian groups for improvement in Chinese-Soviet relations. Losses and waste cannot be apologized effectively. (from the *Christian Science Monitor*, July 26, '88) The suggestion, which was quickly suppressed also commanded an army. A total of nine people were killed and appeared to promise confusing evidence. We will use our influence in Burma to a Cabinet. (from *The New York Times*, July 27, '88) Nicaragua has suspended suppression of riots ending the 13-year-old cease-fire in the eight-year-old Persian Gulf war after thousands of masked students held responsible with the PLO offered Tuesday to grant independence to Namibia. (from the *Wall Street Journal*, Aug. 4, '88) Europe is possible over a nuclear arms reduction of all the best known prisoners, save seven, who seem to have no immediate hope. Clashes in the Burmese capital capitalized on doubts about grave consequences, faces challenges after a week of negotiations. (from *The New York Times*, Aug. 11, '88) Most men, even in this comparatively free country, through mere ignorance and mistake, are so occupied with the factitious cares and superfluously coarse labors of life that its finer fruits cannot be plucked by them. Their fingers, from excessive toil, are too clumsy and tremble too much for that. Actually, the laboring man has not leisure for a true integrity day by day; he cannot afford to sustain the manliest relations to men; his labor would be depreciated in the market. He has no time to be anything but a machine. How can he remember well his ignorance — which his growth requires — who has so often to use his knowledge? (Thoreau, *Walden*, p. 9) With respect to wit, I learned that there was not much difference between the half and the whole. One day, in particular, an inoffensive, simple-minded pauper, whom with others I had often seen used as fencing stuff, standing or sitting on a bushel in the fields to keep cattle and himself from straying, visited me, and expressed a wish to live as I did. He told me, with the utmost simplicity and truth, quite superior, or rather inferior, to anything that is called humility, that he was "deficient in intellect." These were his words. The Lord had made him so, yet he supposed the Lord cared as much for him as for another. "I have always been so," said he, "from my childhood; I never had much mind; I was not like other children; I am weak in the head. It was the Lord's will, I suppose." And there he was to prove the truth of his words. He was a metaphysical puzzle to me. I have rarely met a fellow-man on such promising ground, — it was so simple and sincere and so true all that he said. And, true enough, in proportion as he appeared to humble himself was he exalted. I did not know at first but it was the result of a wise policy. It seemed that from such a basis of truth and frankness as the poor weak-headed pauper had laid, our intercourse might go forward to something better than the intercourse of sages. (Thoreau, *Walden*, p. 105) A saner man would have found himself often enough "in formal opposition" to what are deemed "the most sacred laws of society," through obedience to yet more sacred laws, and so have tested his resolution without going out of his way. It is not for a man to put himself in such an attitude to society, but to maintain himself in whatever attitude he find himself through obedience to the laws of his being, which will never be one of opposition to a just government, if he should chance to meet with such. (Thoreau, *Walden*, p. 214) Respect, protect and foster the diversity of human beings on Earth. (from "The World Game," World Game Projects, Inc., 1987) World Game mode of operation/experience involves foremost the accurate definition of the problem. By evolution/refinement of problem definition the strategy for problem elimination unfolds; when definition is complete, strategy is complete and problem's solution is manifest. The more adequately we state the problems of today, the more apparent will the solution of tomorrow become. To the degree we can define the problems of today we can redefine our perception of the future. The aspects of the future which relate to our problem will afford us a key to unlock as many of the complex interrelationships of the future as we care to deal with, plus synergetically shedding more light on the present. (from "Dymaxion World of Buckminster Fuller," by Robert W. Marks, and "Buckminster Fuller," by John McHale, in *World Game/1971/Document 1*, p. 103) Fuller's World Game is mankind's first practical alternative to politics. . . . It is now possible for anyone anywhere to take positive constructive action in shaping the destiny of our society completely outside the realm of politics as we know it. (from *World Game/1971/Document 1*, p. 41) The efficiency would be somewhere between the U.S.'s (feeding about two people per acre) and Japan's (feeding six people per acre). It would be difficult to raise the world's efficiency to that of Japan's, using her methods, because a tremendous amount of manpower would be drawn into agriculture. (Approximately 40 per cent of Japan's people are engaged in agriculture as opposed to nine per cent in America). There are many new ways to produce food. Examples: using algae (chlorella and others) for food; feeding bacteria plant wastes such as stalks, sawdust, and letting them convert these to food for man; and synthesizing amino acids. However, we didn't employ them in our scenario because we did not want to make a move which would assume changing people's food habits. (Edwin Schlossberg and Medard Gable, quoted in *World Game/1971/Document 1*, p. 45) Utilities, not politics (intelligence; problem solving). Anarchy in a place that works. Not just self- but social-realization. Unemployment (cf. artists). Giving up ownership, substituting use.

Whole society (including, e.g., the mad: they speak the truth). Religious attitude (George Herbert Mead); world consciousness. More with less. (John Cage, Introduction to *Themes and Variations*) The State Department said its antiPakistan campaign broke the Soviet-backed regime that killed eight British soldiers in Burma. A man believed to be a Royal Navy officer refused to resign and said the recent wave of troops shot and wounded on issues of peace and sharing would have forced the evictions in 1987. (from the *Wall Street Journal*, Aug. 23, '88) The effect of extending the central nervous system is not to create a world-wide city of ever-expanding dimensions but rather a global village of ever-contracting size. (McLuhan, cited in *Marshall McLuhan: Media in America*, p. 146) In the electric environment of information, all events are simultaneous. There is no time or space separating events. Information and images bump against each other every day in massive quantities, and the resonance of this interfacing is like the babble of a village or tavern gossip session. The absence of space brings to mind the idea of a village. But actually, at the speed of light, the planet is not much bigger than this room we're in. In terms of time and the speed of the event that are now programmed, they hit each other so fast that even a village is too big a thing to use for a comparison. The acoustic or simultaneous space in which we now live is like a sphere whose center is everywhere and whose margins are nowhere. Acoustic space cannot be cut into pieces, as visual space can. It is both compressed and indivisible. (McLuhan, cited in *Marshall McLuhan: Media in America*, p. 35) The new electric environment of simultaneous and diversified information creates acoustic man. He is surrounded by sound — from behind, from the side, from above. His environment is made up of information in all kinds of simultaneous forms, and he puts on this electrical environment as we put on our clothes, or as the fish puts on water. (McLuhan, cited in *Marshall McLuhan: Media in America*, p. 225)

Contingency

Music resulting from a separation of cause and effect. A conch shell partially filled with water. Time spent tipping it first one way and then another. You may notice shells are very temperamental. Mostly no sounds take place. Silence. Sometimes, on the other hand, it's easy. The shell speaks continuously, a gurgling voice. Amplification's required for it to be heard by an audience at any distance. Shells of differing sizes, three players, an improvised music over which no one has control though each musician's action is necessary. (John Cage, April, 1988) An old flimsy music stand, made of metal, driven upside down across the floor. Ears are tourists. Once again, the musician has no control, no way to know what sound he'll make and when. (John Cage, April, 1988) Music written for percussion but without names for instruments, just numbering them. This brings about a music not in any way anticipated by the composer, though without his writing it, it wouldn't happen. Not looking for other breaks between cause and effect. Just remaining ready. (John Cage, April, 1988) Music written sometimes though without his writing three players without names for instruments though other breaks this brings action shells are very temperamental. (John Cage, April, 1988) What reason have we for calling "E" the sign for a sensation? For "sensation" is a word of our common language, not of one intelligible to me alone. So the use of this word stands in need of a justification which everybody understands. — And it would not help either to say that it need not be a sensation; that when he writes "E", he has something — and that is all that can be said. "Has" and "something" also belong to our common language. —So in the end when one is doing philosophy one gets to the point where one would like just to emit an inarticulate sound. —But such a sound is an expression only as it occurs in a particular language-game, which should now be described. (Wittgenstein, *Philosophical Investigations*, p. 93) The problem of finding different ways of reaching the same result in mathematics may seem analogous to finding different ways of looking into the next room. It might be said that any way of solving the problem will do, so long as it is in accordance with the rules of arithmetic. But the ways will differ according to the system of arithmetic. What one calls mathematical problems may be utterly different. There are the problems one gives a child, e.g., for which it gets an answer according to the rules it has been taught. But there are also those to which the mathematician tries to find an answer which are stated without a method of solution. They are like the problem set by the king in the fairy tale who told the princess to come neither naked nor dressed, and she came wearing fish net. That might have been called not naked and yet not dressed either. He did not really know what he wanted her to do, but when she came thus he was forced to accept it. The problem was of the form, Do something which I shall be inclined to call neither naked nor dressed. It is the same with a mathematical problem. Do something which I shall be inclined to accept as a solution, though I do not know now what it will be like. (Wittgenstein, *Lectures 1932–1935*, pp. 185–186) Don't for heaven's sake, be afraid of talking nonsense! But you must pay attention to your nonsense. (Wittgenstein, *Culture and Value*, p. 56) But couldn't we imagine that someone without any training should see a sum that was set to do, and straightway find himself in the mental state that in the normal course of things is only produced by training and practice? So that he knew he could calculate although he had never calculated. (One might, then, it seems, say: The training would merely be history, and merely as a matter of empirical fact would it be necessary for the production of knowledge.) —But suppose now he is in that state of certainty and he calculates wrong? What is he supposed to say himself? And suppose he then multiplied sometimes right, sometimes again quite wrong. — The training may of course be overlooked as mere history, if he now always calculates right. But that he can calculate he shews, to himself as well as to others only by this, that he calculates correctly. (Wittgenstein, *Foundations of Mathematics*, p. 335) "This body has extension." To this we might reply "Nonsense!" —but are inclined to reply "Of course!" —Why is this? (Wittgenstein, *Philosophical Investigations I*, p. 90) Something unknown is doing we know not what. (Eddington, quoted by L.C. Beckett, in *Neti Neti*, p. 40) Would it be best to come before that time to attend to them? (McLuhan, *Letters*, p. 144) Psychologists have long taught us that much of our hearing takes place through the skin itself. After centuries of being fully clad and of being contained in uniform visual space, the electric age ushers us into a world in which we live and breathe and listen with the entire epidermis. . . . our unified sensibility cavorts amidst a wide range of awareness of materials and colors which makes ours one of the greatest ages of music, poetry, painting, and architecture alike. (McLuhan, *Understanding Media*, p. 122) Man in the electronic age has no possible environment except the globe and no possible occupation except information-gathering. By simply moving information and brushing information against information, any medium whatever creates vast wealth. . . . But this wealth is not money. Money is obsolete because it stores work (and work, as we have seen, is itself obsolete). In a workless, non-specialist society money is useless. What we need is a credit card, which is information. (McLuhan, "The Agenbite of Outwit," p. 3) . . . sink deep or touch not the Cartesian spring. (James Joyce, as quoted in McLuhan, *The Gutenberg Galaxy*, p. 154) The circuited city of the future will not be the huge hunk of concentrated real estate created by the railway. It will take on a totally new meaning under conditions of very rapid movement. It will be an information megalopolis. (McLuhan, *The Medium is the Massage*, p. 72) In the latest, most drastic action, the law-enforcement agencies announced yesterday that we must choose one of two alternatives to obtain a comprehensive settlement. This means that after six days of rioting soldiers opened fire to influence the negotiations against as many prisoners as possible. (from *The New York Times*, July 23, '88) The official radio had been widely tipped to narrow the section of the flow of illegal narcotics into this country. Five years ago about 1500 jobs were out of control who, from the start of the war until now, after six days declined to comment. (from *The New York Times*, July 23, '88) A Soviet spokesman said yesterday the two states broken off in a dispute with the Dutch Embassy. Brazil's new constitution has to do everything to stop them. Officials fear the South African government cannot fulfill an agreement with the U.S. to launch this project.

(from the *Christian Science Monitor*, July 29, '88) Washington said the country experienced more unemployment than the Soviet Union. A Congressional Panel still unaccounted for was freed and expelled. Secret American-sponsored talks from the young, the families, West German efforts to determine what happened. (from *The New York Times*, Aug. 4, '88) Famine, war, violence against children and homelessness have worsened with the apparent collapse of a government plan to form a Palestinian government of internment to carry out their side of the bargain. Advance parties of UN observers will now be put to a stop to bridge the gap. (from the *Christian Science Monitor*, Aug. 10, '88) Diplomats made antigovernment speeches in front of White House aide at a time when they were on a hunger strike the first of two. In another development with the Soviet Union, security forces were said to have relied on them for public libraries, political tensions, and other leaders now in disgrace. (from the *Christian Science Monitor*, Aug. 18, '88) One says to me, "I wonder that you do not lay up money; you love to travel; you might take the cars and go to Fitchburg to-day and see the country." But I am wiser than that. I have learned that the swiftest traveler is he that goes afoot. (Thoreau, *Walden*, p. 40) It is darker in the woods, even in common nights, than most suppose. I frequently had to look up at the opening between the trees above the path in order to learn my route, and where there was no cart-path, to feel with my feet the faint track which I had worn, or steer by the known relation of particular trees which I felt with my hands, passing between two pines for instance, not more than eighteen inches apart, in the midst of the woods, invariably, in the darkest night. Sometimes, after coming home thus late in a dark and muggy night, when my feet felt the path which my eyes could not see, dreaming and absent-minded all the way, until I was aroused by having to raise my hand to lift the latch, I have not been able to recall a single step of my walk, and I have thought that perhaps my body would find its way home if its master should forsake it, as the hand finds its way to the mouth without assistance. (Thoreau, *Walden*, p. 117) I left the woods for as good a reason as I went there. Perhaps it seemed to me that I had several more lives to live, and could not spare any more time for that one. It is remarkable how easily and insensibly we fall into a particular route, and make a beaten track for ourselves. . . . How worn and dusty, then, must be the highways of the world, how deep the ruts of tradition and conformity! I did not wish to take a cabin passage, but rather to go before the mast and on the deck of the world, for there I could best see the moonlight amid the mountains. I do not wish to go below now. (Thoreau, *Walden*, pp. 214–215) Recognize the planet as the context for problem solving, not the continent, nation-state or region; the whole Earth contains the problem, not the locality; problem solving begins with the whole system and moves toward the local system, not vice versa. (from "The

World Game," World Game Projects, Inc., 1987) The facts of experience are set in order and communicated by decelerating the events which are too swift to be differentially comprehended or by accelerating the events where trending is unapprehended because the rate of transformation is too slow to attract attention and thereby permit comprehension of the trend significance. Part of the "problem" consists of making all vital but invisible evolution visible to others. (from "Dymaxion World of Buckminster Fuller," by Robert W. Marks, and "Buckminster Fuller," by John McHale, in *World Game/1971/Document 1*, p. 103) Mr. Fuller thought aloud about his ideas, concepts, inventions, and discoveries. The students did individual research into trends, energy sources, and many other information areas. They were constructing a base on which to develop ideas about the whole earth. We saw films, read extensively, and traveled through the minds of the others in the room. We watched as man successfully stood on another body in space and could see the earth as a spaceship. The students were working to make visible the coordination of that spaceship in order to accelerate the trend toward physical success for all humanity. (Edwin Schlossberg and Medard Gable, quoted in *World Game/1971/Document 1*, p. 42) At present, most of the important variables in farming are not controlled because the system is as yet open. In a closed system such variables as weather effects, insect pests, loss of water and nutrients would be controlled, or the detrimental effects eliminated. One experimental system could feed 500 people per acre — which would mean a population of six billion people could be fed using only 24 thousand square miles of land. (We're now using around 7 million square miles.) This would be approximately the area Japan uses to feed her people today. (Edwin Schlossberg and Medard Gable, quoted in *World Game/1971/Document 1*, p. 45) Music is permanent; only listening is intermittent (Thoreau). Invention. Not things, but minds. Dealing with 1, not 2. To make a garden empty-minded. Music = no music. Inclusive, not exclusive; aperiodic; no vision, etc. (John Cage, Introduction to *Themes and Variations*) Man's right to his own ignorance might be said to be his principal means of private identity. (McLuhan, cited in *Marshall McLuhan: Media in America*, p. 147)

Inconsistency

To avoid the paralyzing effects of experience, to use the mind in four different ways. Artha: the world of success and failure, the concern always not to fail but to win, not to die but to live. (John Cage, April, 1988) Kama: to act in terms of pleasure and pain, giving pleasure, not pain. Sex and art. The beautiful is only what clicks for you. Keep a clicker in your pocket (Wittgenstein) just in case you encounter ugliness that needs transformation — ugliness that after one click you accept as beautiful. Transformation. Sudden change of mind. (John Cage, April, 1988) The third (India) is dharma: good'n'evil, true'n'false, right'n'wrong, in the moral sense, discrimination, following in a general way the Buddhist, the Christian, the Islamic, or the any other outlines of life'n'action. (John Cage, April, 1988) Finally, moksha: liberation, the flower, the smile, the return bearing gifts to the village, freedom from concern, concerns that return before you can say you're free. (John Cage, April, 1988) These various ways of using one's faculties coexist, interpenetrate, producing: I am not sure; I am surprised; how can you say that, you just said this. Whether determinate or indeterminate, conducted or not, purposeless purpose, way, the way. (John Cage, April, 1988) These various ways in the islamic in terms of mind the third (india) is dharma of life'n'action ugliness liberation after moral sense conducted or not you. (John Cage, April, 1988) When man lives in an electric environment, his nature is transformed and his private identity is merged with the corporate whole. He becomes 'Mass Man.' (McLuhan, "The Rise and Fall of Nature," p. 2) You can describe the experience of learning a particular language, but you can't describe the experience of learning to use language because you would then have to be able to think what it was like to have no language at all — i.e. to think what it would be like not to think. (Wittgenstein, *Lectures 1930–32*, p. 85) For it is not the 'thought' (an accompanying mental phenomenon) but its use (something that surrounds it), that distinguishes the logical proposition from the empirical one. (Wittgenstein, *Remarks on Colour*, p. 19) A disposition is thought of as something always there from which behavior follows. It is analogous to the structure of a machine and its behavior. (Wittgenstein, *Lectures 1932–35*, p. 91) When one talks of selves of other people, one thinks of some sort of spatial relation. Let us examine the supposition that each of us has a shilling to see how it differs from the supposition that each of us has a self. (Wittgenstein, *Lectures 1932–35*, p. 61) Does "not seeing a picture IN THIS WAY" mean: seeing it differently? (Wittgenstein, *Remarks on the Philosophy of Psychology*, Vol. II, p. 58) (We don't feel that memories call for an interpretation in the same way as we feel this about dreams.) (Wittgenstein, *Lectures and Conversations*, p. 47) The country that is nowhere is the true home. (attributed to Lieh-tzu, quoted by L.C. Beckett, in *Neti Neti*, p. 58) The decision to use the printed medium in place of the telephone medium is unfortunate in the extreme (communication link for emergencies). (McLuhan, *Understanding Media*, p. 33) With the telegraph, the entire method, both of gathering and of presenting news, was revolutionized. Naturally, the effects on language and on literary style and subject matter were spectacular. (McLuhan, *Understanding Media*, p. 252) Amherst seniors walk out on graduation address by Secretary of Defense Robert McNamara, June, 1966. (McLuhan,

The Medium is the Massage, p. 55) . . . "though he might have been more humble, there's no police like Holmes," . . . (James Joyce, as quoted in McLuhan, *The Mechanical Bride*, p. 107) Our life is an apprenticeship to the truth that around every circle another can be drawn; that there is no end in nature, but every end is a beginning; that there is always another dawn risen on midnoon, and under every deep a lower deep opens. (Emerson, "Circles," in *Selected Essays*, p. 225) He hoped the leak and pump the test firing Thursday is blamed for attacks in the size of the party bureaucracy. A two-part countdown is normal. But he stopped short of saying what constitutional reforms are to be introduced by the parliament gunmen on Feb. 17. (from the *Christian Science Monitor*, Aug. 1, '88) The United Nations encourage workers to present a report on bull fighting to end conflicts in Washington. The Philippines would be between Iran and Iraq angry over the action but pleased by protest over the continued presence of American-sponsored talks. (from *The New York Times*, Aug. 6, '88) Hundreds of demonstrators charged into crowds on horseback and on foot and capsized as it reached the middle of the Ganges, after flash floods and heavy rains, missing and presumed dead. The people are not listening to do more to let the North Sea live. (from *The New York Times*, Aug. 8, '88) I learned from my two years' experience that it would cost incredibly little trouble to obtain one's necessary food, even in this latitude; that a man may use as simple a diet as the animals, and yet retain health and strength. I have made a satisfactory dinner, satisfactory on several accounts, simply off a dish of purslane (Portulaca oleracea) which I gathered in my cornfield, boiled and salted. I give the Latin on account of the savoriness of the trivial name. And pray what more can a reasonable man desire, in peaceful times, in ordinary noons, than a sufficient number of ears of green sweet corn boiled, with the addition of salt? (Thoreau, *Walden*, p. 46) In our most trivial walks, we are constantly, though unconsciously, steering like pilots by certain well-known beacons and headlands, and if we go beyond our usual course we still carry in our minds the bearing of some neighboring cape; and not till we are completely lost, or turned round, — for a man needs only to be turned round once with his eyes shut in this world to be lost, — do we appreciate the vastness and strangeness of nature. Every man has to learn the points of compass again as often as he awakes, whether from sleep or any abstraction. Not till we are lost, in other words not till we have lost the world, do we begin to find ourselves, and realize where we are and the infinite extent of our relations. (Thoreau, *Walden*, p. 118) I learned this, at least, by my experiment: that if one advances confidently in the direction of his dreams, and endeavors to live the life which he has imagined, he will meet with a success unexpected in common hours. He will put some things behind, will pass an invisible boundary; new, universal, and more liberal laws will begin to establish themselves around and within him; or the old laws be expanded, and interpreted in his favor in a more liberal sense, and he will live with the license of a higher order of beings. In proportion as he simplifies his life, the laws of the universe will appear less complex, and solitude will not be solitude, nor poverty poverty, nor weakness weakness. If you have built castles in the air, your work need not be lost; that is where they should be. Now put the foundations under them. (Thoreau, *Walden*, p. 215) Convert weaponry to "livingry"; political dogma, nation-state self-interest at the expense of the rest of the planet, and warfare are obsolete. Any resort to armed conflict immediately disqualifies players; individual interests can be best furthered through global growth; the top "haves" are not pulled down as in all previous revolutions, rather, the whole system, including the bottom have-nots are elevated. (from "The World Game," World Game Projects, Inc., 1987) Availability of enough energy for the healthful internal and external metabolic regenerating and functioning of Spaceship Earth and its human passengers, living and to be living, all accomplished at the highest rate of economy and efficiency . . . (from "Dymaxion World of Buckminster Fuller," by Robert W. Marks, and "Buckminster Fuller," by John McHale, in *World Game/1971/ Document 1*, pp. 103–104) Each day the growth of the students and the growth of World Game was extraordinary. Without fear, without competition, the students worked together to realize World Game as fully as they could. The last three weeks were intense with research and organization on how to display the findings that were being made. The energy and information grew visibly before us. We were working at the frontier and each student was working at his frontier. It is dramatic to see human beings so concerned with the operation and well-being of the earth. Edwin Schlossberg and Medard Gable, quoted in *World Game/1971/Document 1*, p. 42) Given enough electrical power, the external metabolics, the earth could feed as many people as she needed — up to 7.8 trillion, for example, on presently-farmed land using the elsewhere-mentioned experimental system. (Edwin Schlossberg and Medard Gable, quoted in *World Game/1971/ Document 1*, p. 46) Objective within; going in all directions. Demilitarization of language (no government). A music that needs no rehearsal. Feet on the ground. To set all well afloat (Thoreau: Yes and No are lies. The only true answer will set all well afloat.). Art's self-alteration. Impossibility of repeated actions; loss of memory. To reach these two's a goal (Duchamp). (John Cage, Introduction to *Themes and Variations*) A squad of urban guerillas seized a seat on a local government council to broadcast a distress message without firing a shot. Terrorism experts are urging the combatants to call a truce and emancipate about 10,000 people. (from *The New York Times*, Aug. 22, '88) Refugees fleeing tribal massacres were detained. Meanwhile, in the occupied West Bank, 25 people face a series of hurdles. "Nobody won," said some 350 members of a United Nations observer force. In connection with the next large demonstration, in Rangoon, no disciplinary action is warranted. Pentagon leaders said, "Everything is okay." (from the *Christian Science Monitor*, Aug. 22, '88) A cliché is an act of consciousness; total consciousness is the sum of all the clichés of all media or technologies we probe with. (McLuhan, cited in *Marshall McLuhan: Media in America*, p. 147) There is no more past under electric culture — every past is now — and there is no future. It is already here. You cannot any longer speak geographically or ideologically in one simple time or place; we are now dealing with very universal forms of experience. (McLuhan, cited in *Marshall McLuhan: Media in America*, p. 168) That is what pollution comes from: pollution is merely the revelation of a changing situation at very high speeds. We now regard all our institutions as polluted, because we can see that they have many patterns that have nothing to do with the function they are supposed to perform. (McLuhan, cited in *Marshall McLuhan: Media in America*, pp. 171–172) State-run television said ten people including one guerrilla proposed a compromise starting Nov. 1. 1,700 jailed protestors killed civilians in ethnic fighting and the fighting involves police. An interim government suspected of cooperating with the majority acknowledged Israeli authorities. (from the *Wall Street Journal*, Aug. 26, '88)

Performance

Practicality, action is action. The metal ones won't burn, wooden statues of the Buddha, winter fire. Quick o quick, a word of truth. One arm holding the cat, the other the knife. Quick, or I slit the cat's throat. (John Cage, April, 1988) What you have doesn't help, less is more, feathers pulled out, gradual improvement. It needs a long time, but like thunderclap, its own time, no time at all. (John Cage, April, 1988) Punctuation, its removal. The removal of the curtain, constant theatre. Poetry contest. Life is a mirror, it collects dust, problem is removal of the dust. That is not a good poem. What would you write? I can't write. (John Cage, April, 1988) Sixth Patriarch, so tell us what you would say. What mirror, what dust. In the middle of the night. The fifth. Take this robe, this bowl, or whatever these are, my insignia, they are yours. Escape this night, as fast as you can. They'll come after you. (John Cage, April, 1988) They did. They caught up with him. Demanded the robe, the bowl. He offered them without hesitation, placing them on the rock between them, but they were unable even to touch the robe, the bowl, let alone pick them up. (John Cage, April, 1988) There is no dust. If there isn't any dust, why are you always taking baths? (Centuries later.) No reason. My dips're dips, just a dip, no why. No causing of effects. What effects are these? (John Cage, April, 1988) They did they caught up with him less the removal he offered them the fifth take this robe this bowl centuries later no reason one arm insignia they are yours long time what would you write i can't the robe the bowl. (John Cage, April, 1988) If someone said to me that he doubted whether he had a body I should take him to be a half-wit. But I shouldn't know what it would mean to try to convince him that he had one. And if I had said something, and that had removed his doubt, I should not know how or why. (Wittgenstein, *On Certainty*, p. 34) Someone says: "I see a house with green shutters." And you say: "He's not seeing it, he's merely imagining it. He's not even looking; don't you see him staring into space?" —Very loosely, it could also be put this way: "That's not the way it looks when somebody sees something; rather, that's the way it looks when he has an image of something." In this case we're comparing phenomena of seeing with phenomena of imagining. Likewise if we were to observe two members of an unknown tribe using a word as they perform a certain activity — a word which we have come to recognize as an equivalent of our "seeing." And we follow their use of that word upon this occasion, and come to the conclusion that here it must mean "to see with the inner eye." (Similarly, one might also come to the conclusion that the word must here mean to understand.) (Wittgenstein, *Remarks on the Philosophy of Psychology*, Vol. II, p. 25) But — one would like to say — whether joy is a sensation, or what it is, is something one has to notice when one has it! —(And why especially when one has it, and not when one doesn't have it?) Do you also notice the nature of one, when you are eating one apple, and the nature of zero when you are eating none? (Wittgenstein, *Remarks on the Philosophy of Psychology*, Vol. I, p. 143) "The ideal clock would always point to the time 'now.'" This also connects up with the language which describes only my impressions of the present moment. Akin is the primal utterance that is only an inarticulate sound. (Driesch.) The ideal name, which the word "this" is. (Wittgenstein, *Remarks on the Philosophy of Psychology*, Vol. I, p. 132) I would almost like to say: It is true that in the game there isn't any "true" and "false" but then in arithmetic there isn't any "winning" and "losing." (Wittgenstein, *Philosophical Grammar*, p. 293) What I always do seems to be — to emphasize a distinction between the determination of a sense and the employment of a sense. (Wittgenstein, *Remarks on the Foundations of Mathematics*, p. 168) Did I make an experiment, whose result was that whoever begins must always win? Or that we are inclined to play in such a way that this happens? No. —But the result was not what you would have expected! Of course not; but that does not make the game into an experiment. (Wittgenstein, *Foundations of Mathematics*, p. 202) If you find the signpost, you don't now look for further instruction — you walk. (Wittgenstein, *Zettel*, p. 51) As long as thought continues through memory, through desire, through experience, it can never renew itself. (Krishnamurti, quoted by L.C. Beckett, in *Neti Neti*, p. 66) Psychologists define hypnosis as the filling of the field of attention by one sense only. At such a moment "the garden" dies. (McLuhan, *Gutenberg Galaxy*, p. 17) And a story . . . about the missionary to the Eskimos who preached on the fiery torments awaiting the wicked. Afterwards his flock clamoured around him expressing deep interest. "Yes, yes, yes, we know. But you haven't told us how to get there." (McLuhan, *Letters*, p. 125) Twain proceeds to become mysterious and ends by explaining that he and his brother were twins and that they got mixed in the bath one day and so he can never hope to be sure whether it was Bill or himself that died (later). (McLuhan, *Letters*, p. 77) Man can be everywhere at once, whereas the angels are subject to limitations of space and can only be in one space at a time. (McLuhan, "The Rise and Fall of Nature," p. 2) It seems likely that markets and the pricing system, as we have known them, are already obsolescent in relation to the computerized programming and processing of materials and the organization of work. (McLuhan, "The Guaranteed Income," p. 7) A 1978 Supreme Court decision recently removed restrictions on credit card interest rates without seriously jeopardizing the status quo in all other aspects. Equally historic is the impact of the drought that doubled in size to more than 24 percent to buy about four million tons of food. (from *The New York Times*, July 26, '88) A document dealing with the second week of August Palestinian uprising is being pushed into the spotlight. It will take extreme diplomatic skill to arrange refuge response. South Korean legislators yesterday would be automatic it had started. (from the *Christian Science Monitor*, July 28, '88) Iran Air Flight official said timetable for stunt by decline in droughts and violating the Soviet military men still leaving to South Africa, accusing Washington Square of secret for ending hostilities, sharply cutting the world's production of wheat, corn, and other cereal crops and are leading to the steepest. (from *The New York Times*, Aug. 4, '88) The bill would bring the total military budget to the Persian Gulf. Both nations warned against anarchy when combined with right-wing groups that rallied in several cities almost certain to be vetoed by would be the first. (from the *Wall Street Journal*, Aug. 12, '88) What good I do, in the common sense of that word, must be aside from my main path, and for the most part wholly unintended. Men say, practically, Begin where you are and such as you are, without aiming mainly to become of more worth, and with kindness aforethought go about doing good. If I were to preach at all in this strain, I should say rather, Set about being good. (Thoreau, *Walden*, p. 54) Once in a while we sat together on the pond, he at one end of the boat, and I at the other; but not many words passed between us, for he had grown deaf in his later years, but he occasionally hummed a psalm, which harmonized well enough with my philosophy. Our intercourse was thus altogether one of unbroken harmony, far more pleasing to remember than if it had been carried on by speech. (Thoreau, *Walden*, p. 120) I desire to speak somewhere without bounds; like a man in a waking moment, to men in their waking moments; for I am convinced that I cannot exaggerate enough even to lay the foundation of a true expression. Who that has heard a strain of music feared then lest he should speak extravagantly any more forever? In view of the future or possible, we should live quite laxly and undefined in front, our outlines dim and misty on that side; as our shadows reveal an insensible perspiration toward the sun. The volatile truth of our words should continually betray the inadequacy of the residual statement. Their truth is instantly translated; its literal monument alone remains. (Thoreau, *Walden*, p. 215) Maximize human free time, minimize human coerced time. (from "The World Game," World Game Projects, Inc., 1987) Availability of enough food for the healthful functioning and satisfactory metabolic regeneration of all mankind . . . (from "Dymaxion World of Buckminster Fuller," by Robert W. Marks, and "Buckminster Fuller," by John McHale, in *World Game/1971/Document 1*, p. 104) Finding the needs of one man led us to finding the needs for mankind. As we began to deal with man on the collective level we realized the need for establishing a frame of reference, or conceptual tool, to deal with collective mankind's needs. The "bare maximum" was what evolved. Rather than take what was thought to be the bare minimum for mere subsistence levels, we elected to establish levels which would allow man to realize, not his minimum potential, but his maximum potential, anything less than this being, by our definition, sub-human. (Edwin Schlossberg and Medard Gable, quoted in *World Game/1971/Document 1*, p. 42) After working out scenarios for satisfying what we considered the two most vital bare maximums — external electric energy and internal food supply — we evolved into some of the possible synergetic scenarios that would result from the first moves. The establishment of bare maximum levels of the above throughout the world would engender the need for bare maximums in housing, medical attention, income, communications and travel. (Edwin Schlossberg and Medard Gable, quoted in *World Game/1971/Document 1*, p. 46) Complexity of nature; giving up simplicity of soul, vision, etc. Constellation of ideas (five as a minimum). Problems of music (vision) only solved when silence (non-vision) is taken as the basis. Giving unto others what they wish to be given, not what you would wish to be given (alteration of the Golden Rule). Use all solutions; do everything! Inactivity (the camera). Goal is not to have a goal. (John Cage, Introduction to

Themes and Variations) The blast followed a car bombing in the Costa Rican capital. Hungarian coal miners said the move followed was the third straight day of mass protest. Meanwhile, China is the first step toward ending Vietnam's nine year strike warned Israel that relations between the two countries might lead to direct talks between the rebels and the Irish Republican Army. (from the *Christian Science Monitor*, Aug. 25, '88) A federal judge exchanged gunfire with search warrants yesterday to protest who quit in April. Since the attorney general resigned in India the federal government should receive only the retirement benefits they earned to tighten their searches for Israeli troops elsewhere in the Pentagon. (from the *Christian Science Monitor*, July 22, '88) Communication, creativity, and growth occur together or they do not occur at all. New technology creating new basic assumptions at all levels for all enterprises is wholly destructive if new objectives are not orchestrated with the new technological motifs. (McLuhan, cited in *Marshall McLuhan: Media in America*, p. 147) In terms of, say, a computer technology we are heading for cottage economies, where the most important industrial activities can be carried on in any individual little shack anywhere on the globe. That is, the most important designs and the most important activities can be programmed by individuals in the most remote areas. (McLuhan, cited in *Marshall McLuhan: Media in America*, p. 173) Well, I think that we live in post-history in the sense that all pasts that ever were are now present to our consciousness and that all the futures that will be are here now. In that sense we are post-history and timeless. Instant awareness of all the varieties of human expression constitutes the sort of mythic type of consciousness of 'once-upon-a-timeness' which means all time, out of time. It is possible that our new technologies can bypass verbalising. There is nothing inherently impossible in the computer, or that type of technology, extending consciousness itself — as a universal environment. There is a sense in which the surround of information that we now experience electrically is an extension of consciousness itself. What effect this might have on the individual in society is very speculative. But it has happened — it isn't something that's going to happen. Many people simply resort instantly to the occult, to ESP and every form of hidden awareness, in answer to this new surround of electric consciousness. And so we live, in the vulgar sense, in an extremely religious age; and I think we are moving into an age which, in popular notion at least, is probably the most religious that has ever existed. We are already there. (McLuhan, cited in *Marshall McLuhan: Media in America*, pp. 175–176)